Preface

An independent mass media is one of the important foundations of a democratic society. Indeed, the democratic credentials of a nation-state are often sought to be measured against the degree of independence enjoyed by its media professionals. Journalists are considered by many to be society's 'watchdogs'. They are not supposed to be 'lapdogs' of the establishment—some would argue that they should be compared to dogs that attack those who abuse power and authority as well as guide-dogs for the visually challenged or the underprivileged sections of society. They not only provide information of interest and use to the public but also help ensure that those in important and influential positions remain transparent and accountable for their actions. Independent journalism seeks to expose corruption and upholds democratic rights, including the right to free expression. Media ethics is a complex, sticky and often controversial subject. Journalists are bound to uphold certain accepted modes and codes of conduct to ensure the veracity and authenticity of their work. These modes and codes of conduct comprise what are broadly understood as media ethics. While media professionals on occasion claim that certain facts are in the 'public interest' to disclose and need wide dissemination for that purpose, journalists are often accused of sensationalizing information, distorting reality, trivializing events, transgressing individual privacy, and worse: lying, cheating and deceiving.

Media ethics as a topic of discussion and study has received perhaps the greatest attention in the US, where the first journalistic code of ethics was developed in 1923 by the American Society of Newspaper Editors. It was followed by codes of conduct devised by the Society of Professional Journalists/Sigma Delta Chi and the Associated Press Managing Editors. Ethics of journalism gained increased attention during the 1960s and the early 1970s with the growth of investigative journalism. During the war in Vietnam, the media in the US played a significant role in shaping public opinion, thereby accelerating the exit of the American army from an unpopular war. In 1971, the US government tried to stop *The New York Times* from publishing a secret study of the Vietnam War that came to be known as the Pentagon Papers, claiming that their publication would damage national security interests. However, the Supreme Court of the US ruled that since the government could not demonstrate the extent of the damage to national security, the newspapers should be free to publish the information. Subsequently, during their investigation into the Watergate episode, two persistent reporters from *The Washington Post*, Bob Woodward and Carl Bernstein, aided by a senior source in the US government who leaked information to the reporters on condition of anonymity, succeeded in uncovering facts that eventually led to the resignation of President Richard Nixon in 1974.

Even as the role of the media in exposing corruption in high places was acknowledged and hailed in the US and elsewhere, views were often expressed that the media went too far on occasions, crossing the thin and subtle dividing line that distinguishes the appropriateness of the public's right to know and the individual's right to privacy as well as the obligation of the government to protect national security. The media was also criticized for its excessive emphasis on 'bad news'; sentences like 'if it bleeds, it leads' began to be commonly used.

India would not be able to proudly describe itself as the world's largest democracy without the existence of an independent media. The Indian media is unique in many ways. Unlike in the developed countries of the West, in India, all mass media—print, radio, television, cinema, and the internet—have been growing simultaneously and are expected to continue to grow in the foreseeable future.

On the other hand, the Audit Bureau of Circulations of the US reported that in the first half of 2008, the average circulation of the 530 biggest daily newspapers in that country had fallen by 3.6 per cent, while total newspaper revenues from advertising fell from a peak of $48.7 billion in 2000 to $42.2 billion in 2007. It has been estimated that the proportion of American citizens who read at least one newspaper every day has halved from roughly 70 per cent in the early 1970s to around 35 per cent in 2007. Among young adults (below the age of 30), this proportion was a low 16 per cent. In the US, the total circulation of all newspapers has been steadily falling since the late 1980s.

The situation in many other countries of the world, especially in the developing countries, is markedly different. The Approach Paper to the Eleventh Five Year Plan that started on 1 April 2007, put together by the Government of India's Planning Commission pointed out that 'one of the sectors which has consistently outperformed' the rate of growth of gross domestic product in India is the 'entertainment and media services sector'.

In 2008, India was the only country in the world with over three dozen 24-hour television channels that broadcast news and current affairs programmes. There have been instances when these channels have used unethical means to attract the attention of viewers. In the hope of increasing viewership which, in turn, leads to higher flows of advertising revenue, there have been occasions when certain television channels have not authenticated information before broadcasting these as 'facts'. Truth can and does become a casualty in the desperate rush to 'grab eyeballs'. The world over and in India, television reports (as well as newspaper articles) are often 'dumbed down', facts are sensationalized, or used selectively and out of context to add 'spice' and 'colour' to events and developments considered newsworthy. What is considered 'news' is itself periodically changing and in certain instances, undergoing a significant metamorphosis. In the recent past, even if much of the mass media in India has by and large acted in a responsible manner, there have been many instances of television channels and other mass media organizations abusing the tremendous power enjoyed by them while deploying questionable methods and tactics in the hope of gaining easy and quick popularity. A related case study on the controversies surrounding the media coverage of the November 2008 terrorist attacks in the city of Mumbai, often described as India's commercial capital has been included in this book.

About the Book

This book intends informing and educating not only students of journalism but also media practitioners, academicians and the public in general about the ethical issues related to the functioning of media professionals and mass communication organizations in a democracy. The mass media today impacts virtually all aspects of society and intrudes into the lives of virtually each and every citizen. Since the media is playing an increasingly important role in influencing not only the way people dress and speak but also the way they think and act—in other words, moulding public opinion and lifestyles—the significance of media ethics can hardly be under-emphasized.

The book will be useful not only to those who aspire to pursue a career in the media but also to those who are working as journalists and have to frequently confront ethical issues while fulfilling their professional obligations. Journalists are not above the law but they occupy a special position in any democratic society because their functions and roles directly or indirectly impact large numbers of people. Their work has a public dimension even if they are employees of commercially run organizations.

Thus, they are accountable not only to their employers but also to their constituents (readers, listeners, viewers and the public at large).

Teaching Tools and Pedagogy

The teaching strategies or pedagogy of the book highlight the main ethical concerns that journalists and other media professionals should keep in mind. Each chapter discusses important aspects of these ethical concerns. The case studies in the book are used as examples to indicate how news reports can and should become tools for objective journalism. These case studies are also used to demonstrate how news stories/articles/reports can be misleading, biased, unfair, imbalanced or lack credibility. The book includes a number of examples to indicate the different ways in which a news story can be reported; what the merits and demerits of each type of reporting are; and what ethical concerns are raised by each type of reporting. At the end of the chapters, there are review questions to be answered, issues to be discussed and/or debated, and exercises and projects to be completed—all of which are designed to help the readers evaluate their levels of understanding.

Key Features

- It focusses on the day-to-day ethical issues related to the working of the mass media and how to confront these.
- It contains numerous case studies and examples from India and other countries.
- The book provides review questions and exercises to help the readers evaluate their levels ofunderstanding of the issues delineated.
- It includes topical chapters on the media market, sting operations, the new media (or the internet), advertising and public relations.

Chapter Coverage

In its first chapter, Introduction, the book defines and explores the origin of ethics. It then provides an overview of ethical theories of relevance to the media. Thereafter, it outlines the history of media ethics in different parts of the world, including in the US and in India. The chapter then delineates what is to follow in the eleven subsequent chapters. It also includes a brief account on the debate relating to a broadcasting code in India. Appended to the introduction of the book are

- the text of former British Prime Minister Tony Blair's June 2007 speech in which he compared the media to a 'feral beast';
- a note on American radical intellectual Noam Chomsky's views on the political economy of the mass media; and

- the India section of the May 2008 report entitled 'In the Balance: Press Freedom in South Asia (2007-08)' produced by the International Federation of Journalists on behalf of the South Asia Media Solidarity Network.

Central to the profession of journalism are issues such as getting facts 'right', fairness, and 'correctness' of the language used for reporting an event. These issues are dealt with in Chapter 2 of the book on Truth, Fairness, and Objectivity. The chapter highlights why these issues are extremely significant in the context of the multi-cultural, multi-ethnic, heterogeneous, plural, deeply-divided, highly-hierarchical, and strife-ridden character of Indian society and its different segments.

Chapter 3, Sources of Information, delineates the importance of a journalist's decisions on what sources to use while reporting a story. Using a fictitious case study, this chapter lays stress on issues such as getting the 'other side' of a news story to ensure fairness and impartiality. It also explains the need to maintain the confidentiality of a source under certain circumstances. Appended to this chapter are some of the ethical guidelines issued by the Press Council of India (PCI), the regulatory body for the print medium.

Chapter 4, Sensitivity examines how journalists need to act and behave while interacting with individuals, society in general, public officials and the judiciary in particular. This chapter considers issues relating to decency and obscenity (in India and elsewhere), social sensitivities, reporting ethnic conflicts, the role of ideology in reporting, stereotyping on the basis of religion, caste and gender, treatment of children, national interest, and reporting on election campaigns, judicial proceedings and situations of conflict. The relevant guidelines of the PCI have been included. This chapter includes a detailed case study on the manner in which the media covered the November 2008 terrorist attack that took place in Mumbai.

How does one distinguish between invasion of privacy and the right of the public to receive information? Is there any justification for showing television footage of a grief-stricken family or images of mutilated bodies? Conversely, do horrific images of destruction and death help raise a public outcry and thereby, act as a deterrent to the commission of such acts by others in the future? Issues such as these are explored in Chapter 5 of the book, Privacy.

The commercial nature of media organizations can come into conflict with the democratic ideals of objective journalism and social responsibility. Journalists are often called upon to strike a balance between market pressures and public interest. Chapter 6, Media Market examines this and related issues such as the difference between editorial and advertorial content.

The chapter deals with relationships between media owners and advertisers that can, and often does, lead to conflicts of interest that throw up a host of ethical issues. This chapter also provides an overview of the working of the mass media in India. It deals with the specific case of how a large media organization (Bennett Coleman & Company Limited, publishers of *The Times of India* and other publications) has broken down the 'Chinese Wall' between editorial and advertising content and struck private financial arrangements with advertisers, and analyses their consequences. Another case study from the Cyber Media India group is on how the 'trade' press writes about its advertisers and the ethical issues that are involved.

Chapter 7, Media Laws, discusses some of the legislative mechanisms to regulate the media in India. The chapter explains what constitutes libel and the legal implications of invasion of privacy. It also briefly touches upon intellectual property rights (including copyright), contempt of court, the right to information in the Indian context, and analyses PCI guidelines. Annexed to this chapter are extracts from a report of the Law Commission of India on 'trial by media' and guidelines for reporting criminal cases. Issues relating to plagiarism are dealt with in this chapter, including the plagiarism case relating to V.N. Narayanan, former editor of the *Hindustan Times* and the one pertaining to Kaavya Viswanathan.

Chapter 8 of the book, Sting Operations, starts with descriptions and explanations of investigative journalism—the Watergate scandal in the US is used as a case study. Sting operations using hidden cameras captured the attention of the Indian public in 2000 with *Tehelka*'s expose on cricket match-fixing. The same media organization went on to rock India's political and military establishment with another expose known as Operation West End that involved important political personalities. Since then, many media organizations in India have resorted to sting operations, using concealed cameras and recorders, ostensibly to highlight corruption in high places. These operations can, however, go wrong—for instance, after the Live India/Uma Khurana episode (detailed later) a journalist found himself behind bars for having committed a fraud—raising a host of ethical questions about invasion of privacy and what really constitutes public interest. This chapter also discusses the legal aspects of this form of journalism. Appended to this chapter are the ethical principles of journalism provided by the Council of Europe's Parliamentary Assembly.

Chapter 9 discusses ethics of the new media or the internet. The internet is the new medium that not only has to grapple with older ethical issues but also deal with a host of new issues because of the technology deployed by the world wide web and the relative anonymity it provides. In certain senses, the internet is different from other media in that it is a medium of mass communications as well as a medium of personalized communication. The impact of blogging on traditional journalism is looked at. There is also a discussion on Wikipedia, the popular online encyclopaedia.

Not only journalism but other media-related activities, including advertising and public relations (PR), have to constantly confront ethical issues. Advertising and PR practitioners have to deal with, and confront, issues relating to obscenity and stereotyping, over and above information considered unfair, inaccurate, and incomplete. Chapter 10 is on Advertising Ethics. Much more than journalism, advertising is directly motivated by commercial concerns. An advertising company gets a contract to run campaigns to promote a particular product, service or message. Questions arise as to whether it is the advertiser's ethical or moral responsibility to ensure that a product or a service or a message is not inimical or harmful to the interests of specific vulnerable sections of society. Besides having to conform to ethical standards, advertising campaigns (like other media content) should not be derogatory to women, any community or religion. Moreover, when a product is marketed for consumption by children, the advertiser needs to be especially careful about the impact of the messages on impressionable minds. Appended to this chapter is the advertising code of India's public broadcaster Prasar Bharati (including All India Radio and Doordarshan).

Chapter 11 is on the Ethics of Public Relations. In this chapter, various questions are sought to be addressed. One such question could be: Is the distribution of expensive gifts to influential journalists or taking them on 'junkets' an important (or even an essential) aspect of the job of professionals engaged in public relations or corporate communications? PR practitioners too have to adhere to a code of conduct and confront ethical dilemmas relating to truth, fairness and objectivity.

The final chapter of the book is on Media Freedom. This chapter contains the transcript of an interview on the 'exclusionist' Indian media with the 2007 Ramon Magsayasay award-winning Indian journalist Palagummi Sainath; the transcript of another interview with Aidan White, Secretary General of the International Federation of Journalists on various aspects of media ethics; and the text of the K.C. Mammen Mapillai memorial lecture delivered in New Delhi in November 2007 on 'Freedom of the Press in an Age of Violence' by noted journalist Harold Evans, former editor of *The Times* and *The Sunday Times of London.*

PARANJOY GUHA THAKURTA

Acknowledgements

Acknowledgements

When I told some of my more cynical friends that I was working on a book on media ethics, they smirked. Media ethics? That's an oxymoron, a contradiction in terms, they claimed. Others were more encouraging and said a book like this could be useful to young journalists and those aspiring to become media professionals. While this book refers to a number of books on media ethics published in different countries, including the US, many of the examples and case studies used are from India. What became apparent to me as I wrote this book was that the image of journalists had taken quite a battering.

It is not as if journalists were always glorified as crusaders for the truth and as those who exposed corruption in high places. In 1981, Ashwini Sarin, who was then with *The Indian Express* newspaper, broke the law to expose how poor women were being trafficked by actually going ahead and 'purchasing' a woman named Kamala. The story was avidly discussed all over the country and was converted into a play by well-known Marathi writer Vijay Tendulkar and thereafter made into a feature film. In these so-called works of fiction that were inspired by a real-life incident, the journalist concerned was portrayed in rather poor light as an ambitious and hypocritical person. However, until not very long ago, most journalists in popular cinema made in India were depicted as 'good' individuals—persons who fought against the corrupt and for the rights of the downtrodden. That image has changed over the years. A number of films that have been recently produced in the country show journalists as people who act in a stupid and insensitive manner, thrusting microphones in the faces of those who had undergone traumatic experiences—all in search of an 'exclusive' story that would 'sell' well. Media ethics has indeed become too important an issue to be left to journalists and media personnel alone—the topic concerns all of us, irrespective of whether we actively produce content or passively consume it.

This book is in every respect a tribute to the many sincere, dedicated, and, above all, honest journalists and other media professionals who I came into contact with over the last 30 years and longer, during which period I worked as a journalist with a number of media organizations in India and as a teacher with various educational institutions. The list of such people is too long to recount here—many of them are unsung heroes, journalists who treat their profession much less as a means of livelihood than as a public mission despite being described as old-fashioned, if not, downright foolish; people who are not just talented in telling a story but who are consumed by a burning desire to change the world we live in; scribes with a social conscience; individuals who are not ashamed to reveal their bias in favour of the underprivileged; people who think that facts can often be more interesting than fiction; and those who believe they have to continually search for the truth even as they recount it day in and day out for the benefit of others. This book is dedicated to journalists who are not consumed by the cancer of cynicism so endemic to members of this tribe of mass media practitioners at a time when reality shows on television humiliate the gullible and exploit innocent children to gain viewers and advertising revenue.

This book would not have been written but for the tenacity of the Higher Education editorial team at Oxford University Press India in New Delhi, who not only reposed their faith in my ability to complete the manuscript but also stoically stood by me despite my missing many self-imposed deadlines.

I am especially grateful to Samantha R.A. Earle who persevered patiently and laboured hard while doing the background research and in writing the initial drafts of most of the chapters of the book. Kaushiki Sanyal also assisted in the background research and in drafting the first four chapters. Bulan Lahiri assisted in editing portions of the book. Dhananjay Kumar Jha helped with the chores and patiently tolerated my tantrums. Media critic Sevanti Ninan read through the unpublished manuscript and made a number of useful suggestions that were accepted. Brian Dwyer and Nilanjan Gupta helped me compile the case study on the November 2008 terrorist attacks in Mumbai and read through other chapters and sections. Ayaskant Das helped me check the proofs with diligence and care and made suggestions on information to be included. Despite their assistance, I am responsible for all the limitations that remain in the book.

I have learnt a lot from many journalists, editors and media entrepreneurs, some of whom I had the privilege of working under or who headed organizations that employed me (and with whom I often disagreed). Here is a tentative (not exhaustive) check-list: Bhabani Sengupta, M.J. Akbar, Kiron Kasbekar, Aroon Purie, Vinod Mehta, A.K. Bhattacharya, Raghav Behl and Pradeep Gupta. Among my many friends who are journalists I am grateful to Shankar Raghuraman and Rajesh Ramachandran who convinced me that what I was attempting would not be considered completely futile. P. Sainath gave me a most insightful interview on the Indian media for Lok Sabha Television, a transcript of which has been included in the book.

I wish to place on record my deep appreciation to the following individuals for allowing me to reprint gratis various articles in the book written or published by them: Sucheta Dalal, Sukumar Muralidharan (of the International Federation of Journalists), Pradyuman Maheshwari and Prasanto K. Roy (of the Cyber Media group), besides Mammen Mathew and K.S. Sachidananda Murthy (both of the Malayala Manorama group) for permission to reprint Harold Evans' lecture.

On the personal front, I have to express my gratitude to many. My late father Pranab Guha Thakurta (who hardly protested about the fact that I did not pick a career of his choice and instead chose to become a journalist) and my late mother-in-law Shakuntala Bhatnagar did not get to see this publication. My mother Krishna Guha Thakurta and my father-in-law Dr Narendra Kumar Bhatnagar encouraged me to persevere. My wife Jayshree generously and gracefully tolerated my prolonged periods of absence from home. As for my children, Triveni (Triya/Chhoti) and Purnajyoti (Babu), I hope one day they will read what has been written here and forgive me for the time I did not spend with them.

A short while before I completed the manuscript of the book, I learnt about the sudden passing away of a dear friend Indrajit (Funnie) Lahiri, media professional and teacher. There are many other friends, well-wishers, relatives and acquaintances who supported me and but for whose encouragement I would never have been able to complete this manuscript. I hope they will not mind my failing to mention them individually by name.

There are many shades of grey between the black and the white of the printed page. Writing is a lonely activity but, in this case, its outcome is meant for many. Those students, practitioners of journalism, and others who go through this book will be the final arbiters of the quality of the pages that follow.

PARANJOY GUHA THAKURTA

Contents

CHAPTER

1

INTRODUCTION

This introductory chapter first defines and explores the origin of ethics, and then provides an overview of the ethical theories of relevance to the media. A brief history of media ethics in different parts of the world, including the US and India, follows. Thereafter, the debate on a code of conduct for television broadcasters in India is outlined.

The appendices to this chapter provide a flavour of some of the contemporary discussions and debates on different facets of media ethics. In June 2007, former British Prime Minister Tony Blair compared the mass media in his country to a 'feral beast' that tore individual reputations to bits (see Appendix 1.1). The views of the radical American thinker Noam Chomsky on the political economy of the mass media have been included in Appendix 1.2. A section of the May 2008 report entitled 'In the Balance: Press Freedom in South Asia (2007–08)', produced by the International Federation of Journalists on behalf of the South Asia Media Solidarity Network, written by Sukumar Muralidharan, highlights the loss of diversity in the mass media in India despite robust growth (see Appendix 1.3).

This chapter aims at providing a quick overview of some aspects of the current state of play of media ethics in India and the world. The objective of the chapter is to prepare you for a more detailed exposition of issues relating to truth, fairness and objectivity that follow. The book's introduction also seeks to condition you to appreciate concerns relating to sensitivity in reporting and invasion of privacy. Further, it provides a curtain-raiser to issues relating to the conflict between commercial considerations and public interest, the laws that govern the media, the ethics of sting operations using hidden cameras and recorders, the working of the new media or the internet in providing unlimited information and ethical issues concerning advertising and public relations.

DEFINING ETHICS

The word 'ethics' originates from the Greek word *ethos* which means 'character'. The subject of ethics has been discussed and debated by people the world over, particularly by philosophers, for centuries. It is said that some 2500 years ago, Greek philosophers had divided their work into three broad segments: aesthetics or the study of beauty; epistemology or the study of knowledge; and ethics or the study of choices between good and evil, truth and falsehood, virtue and vice. Ethics is a subject that seeks to use rational and systematic principles, values and norms to determine what is good or bad, correct or incorrect, right or wrong, as far as human actions are concerned. Though used interchangeably on occasions, ethics is different from morality as the latter pertains more to conventions and customs that determine or govern behaviour and relatively less to whether the action being judged is good or bad.

WHY MEDIA ETHICS?

Journalism is a social practice. Various media (the plural of medium) of mass communications—print, radio, television, cinema and the internet—reach out to large numbers of people. The word 'mass' usually has a negative class connotation or image—hence, the frequent references to the proverbial unwashed masses, the ignorant, illiterate, uneducated, poor, unruly, irrational and common masses. However, in the context of the phrase 'mass communication', we refer to reaching out to a large, heterogeneous, shapeless, faceless, amorphous, undefined and undifferentiated body of people.

We communicate with ourselves (intra-personal communication) when we meditate, think and write. We communicate with our family members, friends and neighbours (interpersonal communication), within communities, groups and organizations. The most difficult and challenging form of communication is mass communication because it entails communicating with large numbers of people, often from different sections of society and across societies.

The function of the mass media—sourcing, reporting and dissemination of information—is aimed at public. The media revolves around society; it is people who provide the news and it is people to whom the news is reported. Social welfare is the *raison d'être* for the existence of the media. Individuals are complex. Societies are even more complex, especially societies that are highly heterogeneous, plural, variegated and even deeply divided such as Indian society. There is perhaps not a group of professionals who understand this aspect of society better than journalists. They are faced with social nuances at every turn and have to come to terms with these complexities.

In sourcing information while presenting news, journalists have to report on gender crimes; exploitation of the underprivileged; indulgence of the affluent; arrogance of those in positions of power and authority; natural calamities and man-made accidents; communal tensions and riots; conflicts and wars; acts of terrorism—the list is long. While reporting news, explaining facts, analysing information and placing these in their historical, social, economic and political contexts, journalists have to be aware of their audience (readers, listeners and viewers) and accordingly use the language and tone considered appropriate, proper and relevant.

The imperative of the journalist—to use an allusion by German philosopher Emmanuel Kant (1724–1804) whose work is referred to later—is the service of society which, in turn, is founded on an ethical premise. Journalism serves society by providing it with accurate information which is necessary to facilitate reason-based ethical behaviour. Knowledge is an invaluable social commodity and that is reflected in legal provisions such as the right to information, freedom of expression, speech and debate—all of which lead to the freedom of the media. Reason, which is facilitated by information and knowledge, has often been recognized by philosophers such as Kant as the best means for determining ethical action. Ethics is such an important area of concern because it views humans as being inextricable from society and that social interaction should be governed by mutual consideration and respect.

Journalism is concerned with promoting ethically based decision-making and behaviour. Now, given the fact that journalists are themselves constantly interacting with all sections of society at different levels, the fundamental importance of ethical practices in journalistic endeavours cannot be overstated.

THE MEDIA FORM

The mass media has traversed a long distance from the time Johannes Gutenberg invented the printing press in Germany in 1456. At present, the media comprises a huge, diverse and variegated conglomerate of enterprises that exercise considerable influence on not just the way people talk and dress but also the way they think. The origin of the word 'journalism' is in the Latin word *diurnalis* meaning daily and signifying the current and timely reporting of events. But journalism has, over the centuries, been transformed into a far more complex series of endeavours, especially in a day and age where news is read/watched 24 hours, seven days a week.

Historically, the media has enjoyed various degrees or levels of freedom. In the years when print was the dominant medium of mass communication, the press was stringently monitored and regulated by governments (see Box 1.1: Two Pages from the Past). The unparalleled and unprecedented power of the press to reach and influence people was promptly recognized by governments and those in positions of power and authority. Consequently, governments wanted to utilize and harness the awesome power of communication that the press enjoyed. Strict licencing laws existed for publications. Governments and authorities sought to control the press to ensure that they did not publish anything that would be considered vaguely derogatory or derisive to those in power, even if such information was based on verifiable facts.

Box 1.1

Two Pages from the Past

In 1690, Benjamin Harris started a publication, *Publick Occurrences both Foreign and Domestick*, which was not only the first newspaper published in the US, but arguably, the first tabloid of its kind. The short-lived newspaper carried articles on incidents of kidnapping, suicide and fire, stories similar to events covered by many tabloids even today. One particular article, however, turned out to be famous (or notorious, depending on a person's perspective). The article accused the King of France of sleeping with his son's wife. The colonial government in the US shut down Harris's paper after just one issue had been published. This decision was in tune with restrictions imposed on the press earlier in Europe. The British government had banned all newspapers from 1632 to 1641, and for many years thereafter, no publication was allowed to print any information that could even mildly upset the King of England.

The first newspaper to be printed in India, Hickey's *Bengal Gazette* or the *Calcutta General Advertiser*, was started by James Augustus Hickey in 1780. The two-sheet newspaper specialized in writing stories about important individuals of the time, including officials of the East India Company. Hickey even dared to publish what was deemed to be a scurrilous attack on the wife of the first Governor-General of India Warren Hastings that landed the erstwhile 'printer to the Honourable Company' in deep trouble. He was sentenced to jail for four months and fined Rs 500. But Hickey continued to attack Hastings as well as the Chief Justice. He was again sentenced to one year in prison and the fine was increased tenfold. A sum of Rs 5,000 was a lot of money those days and Hickey was driven to penury. Many believe that Hickey took the first tentative steps towards independent journalism in India.

Unlike the authoritarian model of controlling the media (still practised in certain countries), the libertarian model believed that an independent media was an extension of a fundamental human right, the right to free expression. Libertarianism represented the beginnings of a free press, one that operated independent of state control and which emphasized the capacity of the citizenry to make informed and responsible decisions. The libertarian model was influenced by the thinking of the 17th-century English poet John Milton (1608–74). He stressed the importance of free speech as a means to create open, public debates through which, he believed, the truth would inevitably come out. This libertarian model prevailed throughout the 18th and 19th-centuries and it radically changed the function of the press, which attempted to free itself from the shackles of government censorship. Later trends of psychoanalysis presented some challenges to the libertarian model. Where reason had previously been lauded as a sovereign principle of human behaviour, psychoanalysts pointed out that not all human behaviour was rational.

The first proponent of utilitarianism as an ethical principle was Jeremy Bentham (1748–1832), the British jurist, philosopher, social reformer and political radical. He noted that 'nature has placed mankind under the governance of two sovereign masters, pain and pleasure'. Another English philosopher and political economist John Stuart Mill (1806–73), whose book *Utilitarianism* was published in 1863, argued that ethical actions are those that generate the 'greatest good for the greatest number of people'. In this sense, utilitarianism directly refuted the views espoused by Italian political philosopher Niccolo Machiavelli (1469–1527) who, in his treatise *The Prince*, argued that 'the ends justify the means'.

Egalitarianism developed out of the libertarian model in response to the significant transformation of the media in the 20th-century. Egalitarianism focused on social equality and responsibility and two main ethical theories often used to determine media behaviour—consequentialism and deontology (see Box 1.2: Ethical Theories of Relevance to the Media).

The development of broadcast media such as radio, television and internet, has exponentially increased the reach of the mass media and the speed with which news is reported. The vehicles of mass media, the world over, have their eyes and ears open to alert the world about an impending disaster before it strikes. The sheer volume and reach of the mass media has meant that individuals and organizations in positions of power, influence and authority have to function under the constant, scrutinizing glare of the media. It is in this capacity that the media has extended its role to that of intervening in the social process. A free media is often described as the cornerstone of democracy: historically, the press used to be accountable to the government but today those in government (and other bodies that enjoy significant power) are accountable to the media.

Box 1.2

Ethical Theories of Relevance to the Media

There are two main ethical theories which are frequently employed to determine correct media behaviour: consequentialism and deontology.

Consequentialism

The consequentialist theory holds that the ethical value (the goodness or the badness) of an action should be judged on the consequences. Actions themselves lack inherent value, but can be appraised in hindsight by virtue of their consequences. Therefore, all actions should be thoroughly considered in terms of their possible outcomes before being executed. The outcomes of an action can be evaluated from two perspectives: ethical egoism or ethical altruism. Ethical egoism holds that actions whose consequences will benefit the agent of the action can be considered ethical. This perspective does not present a cohesive social model as such actions might harm others. Ethical altruism, on the other hand, holds that actions that benefit others can be considered good. One of the most popular consequentialist theories, utilitarianism, develops on this perspective. The utilitarian approach is applicable to the media as it considers the well-being of society at large and is thus commensurate with the socio-centrism of journalism.

Utilitarianism

As already stated, utilitarianism considers ethical that which is designed to create the greatest good for the greatest number. Mill, who formalized the ideas of Bentham, argued that an action should have positive consequences for as many people as possible. Mohandas Karamchand Gandhi's concept of *sarvodaya*, the welfare of all, resembles the utilitarian theory. However, Gandhi was keen to stress that *sarvodaya* was not utilitarian because he felt that the utilitarian objective of satisfying as many as possible was not a sufficiently ethical model. He asked two important rhetorical questions on the philosophy of utilitarianism. Why should the well-being of the minority be of any less value than that of the majority? Why should the welfare of certain people be sacrificed? There are many arguments against consequentialism and the utilitarian theories of ethics. Notably, is it possible to qualify and quantify levels of 'happiness'? If not, then how is it possible to determine all the potential consequences of an action?

We could make reasonable estimations based on experience but there is a danger of making wrong judgements. Society is always in a state of flux. Attitudes, goals and practices change with passing years and it is, therefore, inadequate to offer only a static understanding of what constitutes happiness. It is possible that the consequences of an action will not reveal themselves for several years after the event. By this time the predicted consequences that would be beneficial could instead be harmful by the time they are manifest, due to changing social standards. Consequentialist theories focus only on the outcome of an action, without regard for the means, that is, how the consequences came about.

The utilitarian approach encourages responsible and thoughtful behaviour. Although it is possible to make mistakes of judgement, it is still advisable to invest time in considering all the possible outcomes of a certain action, to determine (at least roughly) whether the overall good is greater than the negative consequences. This theory is constantly applied in decision-making by journalists, although it is seen most pertinently in decisions to conduct sting operations (a topic dealt with separately in a chapter in this book). 'Sting' implies that certain people will be duped or inconvenienced to ascertain a truth that would be for the greater good of the public. Generally, if the consequence of a sting operation can be reasonably said to benefit society as a whole, it is considered permissible provided it is conducted lawfully. But the situation is not that simple. The very nature of a sting operation may entail breaking the letter of a law, if not its spirit. It needs to be remembered that the 'means' can be 'ends' in themselves: every action will have consequences, not just for the agent but for others as well. The methods of sting operations are always scrutinized in hindsight, sometimes as an attempt to divert attention from a wrongdoing exposed by the sting. Consequentialism should not be taken as a licence to behave with gratuitous disregard for those who represent the 'means'.

Deontology

Deontology focuses on a person's duty (*deon* means duty in Greek) as a means to determine appropriate action. Kant was the most famous deontologist. He felt that it was the intentions behind an action that rendered it ethical or unethical. Kant argued that the only right intention was the intention to act out of duty. This duty is that which can be said to be good in all situations. He believed that there was only one virtue which was good without qualification: goodwill. Actions motivated by goodwill are done out of respect for moral law and out of duty. The real definition of 'duty', however, is a little unclear. Kant's categorical imperative—will to act well out of duty—has three important guidelines.

1. An agent should be motivated by a principle, which he would be happy to see as a universal maxim.
2. Always treat people as an end in themselves and not just a means.
3. Act as if you were a lawmaker in the kingdom of 'ends'.

This is a very pertinent concept for the media: it is the media's duty to serve the public by providing information which is impartial and which promotes knowledge and reason. It is the duty of the judiciary to pronounce judgement over certain questionable acts. Problems can and do occur when the media assumes the right to judge a purported crime.

Journalists have many duties, however, and there is no guarantee that these will always be concordant. For an honest and sincere journalist, the duty to serve the public, the duty to protect sources and the duty of loyalty to the employer can and do sometimes stand on opposite sides of the ethical battleground. There are no easy answers to such dilemmas. It is, therefore, important to be familiar with all aspects of these ethical systems to determine the most appropriate course of action. It, thus, becomes an important duty of the journalist to be aware of the implications of a report before publishing it.

An independent media, in its role as an auditor, has often been described as society's watchdog. Unerring, loyal, vigilant, unforgiving and ready for corrective action—these are supposed to be the qualities of a watchdog. Society needs its watchdog but journalists, as mere mortals, are sometimes prone to doubt and misguided action. At times, the media has let down society and has been subjected to scrutiny and fierce criticism. Several questions related to ethics arise in journalism. They are:

- What happens when a journalist sets her or his sights on destroying the reputation, career, and dignity of an innocent woman or man?
- What happens when the media, voluble and bullying like a mob, levels unsubstantiated and false accusations against an individual or an organization?
- What is the way to ensure journalists act in a sensitive and responsible manner when reporting on the grief-stricken?
- When do journalists trade their conscience and humanity for a sensational story?
- How many journalists take seriously the oft-repeated quote attributed to American writer Finley Peter Dunne (1867–1936) who remarked that the 'job of the newspaper is to comfort the afflicted and afflict the comfortable'?

IS THE MEDIA A 'FERAL BEAST'?

The media, collectively, gets a bad name when journalists lose the trust of those whom they set out to serve. Gandhi, the 'Father of the Indian nation', had warned: '...just as an unchained torrent of water submerges the whole countryside and devastates crops, even so an uncontrolled pen serves but to destroy....' Former British Prime Minister Tony Blair did not cloak the expression of his disillusionment when he famously called the media 'a feral beast' (Appendix 1.1). The comparison to an unruly pack of hungry animals was part of a speech delivered by Blair in June 2007 to highlight the problems of the media in today's world of 'impact' journalism. According to him, the state of the media—in particular its relationship with politics—has reached a point where corrective redress is warranted.

In April 2008, the Russian Parliament urgently passed the first reading of a special law that would empower courts to shut down media houses that published stories considered libellous and/or unsubstantiated. The move came in the wake of a tabloid story alleging that President Vladimir Putin was going to divorce his wife of twenty five years to marry an attractive young gymnast in her twenties. The story was picked up by the media all over the world and widely publicized before it was denied by the publication itself, *Moskovsky Korrespondent*, whose owner then announced that the tabloid would be suspending publication due to financial problems. An embarrassed Putin blamed journalists who, 'with their snotty noses and erotic fantasies, prowl into others' lives'. Russia's lawmakers voted to give courts powers to close a news outlet that 'disseminates deliberately false information damaging individual honour and dignity' of public personalities.

The world over and in India, concerns are frequently expressed that given market pressures, to maximize profit the media is not really as free and independent as it purports to be. Business imperatives of increasing revenue have taken (and continue to take) their toll on editorial freedom and journalistic excellence: the demands of advertisers and the drive to increase circulation figures. At worst, the media is entirely controlled, albeit indirectly, by market pressures and, consequently, the imperative of public service has fallen by the wayside and neo-authoritarianism is the media model of the moment. At best, the media risks compromising its role as society's watchdog, becoming instead a lapdog of advertisers and owners of media organizations.

Instead of providing information that, on occasions, not merely entertains but educates and empowers as well, media products and services have become merely vehicles to bring advertisers closer to consumers. As for the integrity of journalists, the phenomenon of 'embedded' reporters, who travelled with American troops and stayed with them while reporting on the war in Iraq in March 2003, has raised a host of questions about the 'independence' of such reporting. In India, certain journalists have argued that by reflecting the class interests and biases of proprietors and managers of media organizations, the media has ended up becoming one of the most exclusionist institutions in Indian society (see interview with P. Sainath, Chapter 12 on Media Freedom). Even as these issues continue to be avidly debated, the fact is that ethical issues related to the media are as old as the media organizations themselves (see Box 1.3: History of Media Ethics in the US and Europe).

Box 1.3

History of Media Ethics in the US and Europe

Ethical issues have had to be confronted by those working in the mass media ever since the media came into being. An illustrative (not exhaustive) list of notable examples of incidents (Rodman 2001) involving media ethics from the US—except the first one which is from the UK and the last one from Norway—is provided here; some of these instances have been detailed in subsequent chapters in this book.

1719: Daniel Defoe wrote *Robinson Crusoe*, considered by some to be the first novel in the English language, as a work of 'fiction' whereas the book was publicized and sold as a work of 'fact'.

1735: John Peter Zenger, publisher of the *New York Weekly*, was jailed for accusing Royal Governor William Cosby of stealing land at a time when the law of seditious libel made any criticism of the government and its agents illegal, irrespective of whether the allegations were true or not. His lawyer argued that truth was Zenger's defence and a jury held him not guilty of sedition.

1848: The invention of the telegraph in 1844 made possible the formation of the world's first news agency, the Associated Press of New York. Six newspapers printed out of New York, all of which had correspondents in Boston, agreed to cut costs and share one correspondent. The Associated Press (AP) grew to become a nationwide institution and then, an international giant that today remains one of the world's largest news agencies. On the ethical side, the fact that newspapers espousing different political ideologies had to share a correspondent ensured that the correspondent concerned would adhere to the journalistic ideals of objectivity and fairness and would adopt writing styles that separated fact from opinion.

1898: The phrase 'yellow journalism' was coined at a time when newspapers began to be printed in colour and the comics section was put on pages that had yellow borders. During this period, the publications owned by two well-known American media magnates, William Randolph Hearst and Joseph Pulitzer, were intense competitors. Many US historians hold Hearst and Pulitzer responsible for the war between America and Spain in Cuba as their publications exaggerated facts about so-called Spanish atrocities and urged the US government to declare war on Spain.

Two anecdotes about this period are significant:

An artist, Fredrick Remington, wanted to be relieved of his Cuban assignment because it seemed unlikely at one stage that the US would get involved in the war. Hearst is believed to have cabled him: 'Please remain. You furnish the pictures and I'll furnish the war.'

Hearst also told a reporter whose duties he had taken up after the reporter was wounded in a battle: 'I'm sorry you are hurt, but wasn't it a splendid fight? We must beat every paper in the world!'

In 1941, Orson Welles scripted and directed a classic film, *Citizen Kane*, about the rise and fall of a newspaper tycoon, that most believed was a thinly disguised biography of Hearst. On its release, Hearst banned his newspapers from reviewing the film. The film traced the life and career of a man whose career in publishing was first motivated by ideals of public service but who eventually became a ruthless businessman who could go to any length—including organizing a murder—to be the first to report 'news'.

As for the Hungarian-American Pulitzer, he left a large amount of money with Columbia University in New York to institute a series of awards for excellence in print journalism and literature. The Pulitzer prizes, considered to be the most prestigious in the US, have over the years been awarded to prominent personalities that include Ernest Hemingway, Robert Frost, Arthur Miller, Eugene O'Neill, Edward Albee and John Updike.

1901: During the 100-day war when American forces destroyed the Spanish fleet of ships outside Santiago harbour in Cuba, seized Manila in the Philippines and occupied Puerto Rico, the US President was William McKinley (1843–1901) who died after a mentally unstable anarchist shot him. McKinley was President during a time of economic *depression and after his* death, *The Brooklyn Eagle* carried an editorial headlined 'Yellow Journalism and Anarchy' that, in part, read: 'The journalism of anarchy shares responsibility for the attack on President McKinley. It did not mean that he should be shot. It only wished to sell more papers by commenting (on him) and cartooning him as a tyrant reddening his hands in (the) blood of the poor and filling his pockets and those of others with dollars coined out of the sweat and tears and hunger of the helpless strikers, their wan wives and their starving children.'

1906: US President Theodore Roosevelt first used the word 'muckrakers' to describe journalists who, he felt, had ignored his government's achievements while highlighting instances of corruption. He stated in a public speech: 'In John Bunyan's *Pilgrim's Progress*, you may recall the description of the Man with the Muckrake, the man who could look no way but downward, with a muckrake in his hands; who was offered a celestial crown, but who would neither look up nor regard the crown he was offered, but continued to rake to himself the filth of the floor.'

1923: A group of journalists opposed to 'tabloid' journalism that sensationalized facts formed the American Society of Newspaper Editors that adopted an ethical code simply called 'canons of journalism' that the code emphasized responsibility, sincerity, truthfulness, accuracy, impartiality, fair play and decency while upholding the freedom and independence of the press.

1930: A motion picture code for rating movies was put in place by the US film industry to avoid government censorship. The code sought to limit depiction of sex, violence and activities considered disrespectful to the government. Eight years earlier, in 1922, a silent film actor, Fatty Arbuckle, had been accused of murdering a young woman after a drunken party. He was tried three times; the jury delivered hung verdicts twice and after the third trial, Arbuckle was acquitted. This incident had conservative sections of the American society criticizing the film industry as a degenerate place.

1954: American physician Samuel H. Sheppard was convicted of killing his pregnant wife in Cleveland. The trial received extensive publicity prompting the US Supreme Court to call it a 'carnival atmosphere'. Some newspapers were criticized for labelling Sheppard as the only viable suspect and thus creating a bias against him. In 1966, a court exonerated Sheppard of the crime after he had served ten years in prison.

1958: A series of television quiz shows were found to have been rigged by the organizers who provided answers in advance to favoured contestants. Federal laws were passed placing the onus of ensuring fairness on the television networks.

1964: After the famous *New York Times* versus L.B. Sullivan case, it became difficult for public personalities to claim that they had been libelled. A group of religious ministers from Alabama had placed an advertisement in *The New York Times* stating that the local police had unleashed an 'unprecedented wave of terror' against civil rights activists. A police commissioner, Sullivan, sued the ministers and the newspaper saying he had been indirectly libelled though he had not been named. Though the court in Alabama ruled in his favour, Sullivan lost the case in the US Supreme Court where judges ruled that the media should have greater latitude in criticizing public figures as opposed to private persons. The judges said democracy is best served by robust debates about public issues and public personalities could not be separated from issues concerning themselves or the organizations they represented.

1964: While being repeatedly asked to define obscenity, US Supreme Court judge Potter Stewart said in a moment of frustration: 'I can't define it, but I know it when I see it.'

1970: A member of the popular music band, The Beatles, George Harrison was let off lightly by a judge in a case of infringement of copyright. His 1970 hit song *My Sweet Lord* was found to be almost identical to a song released seven years earlier by a band called Chiffons entitled *He's So Fine*. The judge said Harrison had not meant to copy the song knowingly but that the melody had somehow got stuck in his brain without him realizing it!

1971: *The New York Times* and the *Washington Post* published a series of leaked documents called the 'Pentagon Papers' that disclosed that the US government had not been honest about revealing facts relating to the conduct of the war in Vietnam.

1974: The same newspapers reported on the Watergate scandal that led to the resignation of President Richard Nixon.

1980: Janet Cooke's series of articles about a non-existent eight-year-old heroin addict called Jimmy in the *Washington Post* sparked off a frenzied 17-day search in America's capital city at the behest of the then mayor Marion Barry. Though the child was not traced, Cooke received a Pulitzer prize. After an internal enquiry, she confessed that she had fabricated the story. She later claimed that she had actually heard of such a boy but was unable to find him. She then created a story about him to 'get her editors off her back'. She resigned and the *Post* returned her prize.

1989: At least fifteen US airlines censored a sequence from the Oscar-winning film *Rain Man* for in-flight viewing. In the film, an autistic character played by Dustin Hoffman reels off statistics about aviation accidents.

1991: A group of police officers were videotaped assaulting Rodney King, an African American, in Los Angeles. After the officers were acquitted by a local court, rioting broke out in the city. The same videotape was used as evidence to convict the officers by a federal court.

1992: *NBC* showed a truck made by General Motors exploding after a collision at low speed. It was later revealed that the truck had remote-controlled explosive devices attached to it. The company sued the channel and won a settlement. The channel's news head Michael Gartner had to resign.

1995: In what became known as the 'trial of the century', American football player O.J. Simpson was acquitted of the murders of his ex-wife and her friend even as the verdict became the most watched event on American television.

1996: Wal-Mart, the largest retail chain in the US and the world, refused to stock compact discs and cassettes of a music album by Sheryl Crow since in one song in the album, she sang the following words: 'Watch out sister, watch out brother. Watch our children as they kill each other with a gun they bought at Wal-Mart discount stores'. Crow refused to change the lyrics of her song for the retail company and reportedly had to bear with loss of sales.

1998: *CNN* and *Time* reported stories alleging that 'sarin' nerve gas had been used by US forces, in Laos, in a secret operation known as Tailwind, and that American defectors were intentionally killed. After these stories provoked strong denials, an internal investigation, overseen by an attorney, was launched. The investigation found that the allegations about the use of nerve gas and the killing of defectors were not supported by evidence and the television channel and the magazine apologized.

1998: The *Cincinnati Enquirer* ran a front-page apology to Chiquita Brands International, Inc. saying its series of stories questioning the company's business practices were 'untrue' and based on stolen voice mail. The newspaper sacked the lead reporter of the story and agreed to pay more than $10 million to settle any claims against it by the company, even before a lawsuit had been filed against the publication.

1998: The *Boston Globe* writer Patricia Smith, who was a finalist for the Pulitzer prize, had to resign her job after admitting that she had used fake quotations in four of her columns. Stephen Glass, associate editor of *The New Republic,* was also fired after he confessed that he had 'embellished' an article about computer hackers. The magazine later alleged that he had concocted material in 27 out of 41 articles written and published over a period of three years.

1999: Warner Brothers' Television, owners of the *Jenny Jones Show*, was successfully sued by the family of Scott Amedure who was shot dead shortly after he appeared on a recording of the programme that was never broadcast. During the recording, Amedure (who was homosexual) revealed that he had a crush on another participant in the show, Jonathan Schmitz. The anchor, Jenny Jones, had apparently coaxed Amedure to graphically reveal his fantasies about Schmitz. Schmitz, who is not homosexual, seemed to have laughed off the attention given to him during the recording of the show. Three days later, Schmitz went to Amedure's house and killed him.

2003: *The New York Times* journalist Jayson Blair resigned after he was confronted with evidence that he had fabricated quotes and facts in at least 36 published articles, among which was an interview with the parents of Jessica Lynch, who had been a prisoner of war in Iraq. The newspaper's executive editor resigned after he was considered partially culpable for Blair's indiscretions. In response to the scandal, *The New York Times* created the position of a public editor—akin to an ombudsman—whose job is to critique the newspaper's own journalists.

2004: Jack Kelley was considered to be a star reporter of *USA Today* until it was discovered that he had fabricated articles or parts of articles that had been published. It was found that Kelley had been favoured by the newspaper's top two editors who later resigned.

2004: The *Boston Globe* published photographs allegedly showing American soldiers abusing and raping women in Iraq that were found to be fake.

2004: Midway through the live broadcast of a major sporting event on CBS, singer Janet Jackson's breast was exposed by fellow performer Justin Timberlake. Jackson apologized calling it an accident and Timberlake also issued an apology describing the incident as a 'wardrobe malfunction'. The Federal Communications Commission imposed a fine of $550,000 on CBS.

2005: Associated Press reported a story with a photograph of an American soldier who was supposed to have been held hostage in Iraq and whose captors were threatening to kill him unless Iraqi prisoners were released. Within hours, it was found that the agency had been duped into releasing false information and that the photograph of the soldier had been taken during a mock exercise.

2006: Norwegian journalist Bjoern Benkow admitted that he had published fabricated interviews of a number of prominent personalities including Bill Gates, Oprah Winfrey, Margaret Thatcher and Michael Schumacher. Benkow claimed that he had met these personalities at times and places that were different from what he had written. He pleaded that he had concocted the interviews 'out of desperation, to pay the rent, the power, food and to survive'. He added: 'I have no excuses, just explanations.'

MEDIA ETHICS IN INDIA

Journalists do make mistakes and Indian journalists are no exception. In 1999, a distinguished journalist, V.N. Narayanan, editor of the *Hindustan Times*, a leading New Delhi-based English-language newspaper, had to resign after it was exposed that a column he had written had been plagiarized from an article written by Bryan Appleyard of *The Sunday Times* in London.

In 2007, a Delhi schoolteacher (Uma Khurana) was duped by a television journalist (Prakash Singh) who conducted a sting operation on her using a hidden camera and claimed that she was luring her students into commercial sex work (*Hindustan Times*, 31 August 2007; *Daily News & Analysis*, 9 September 2007). The episode highlighted the excesses committed by a small section of the mass media. The incident resulted in the teacher having to spend time behind bars after she was sacked from her job. She was publicly humiliated by an irate mob. Singh was subsequently arrested. It transpired that he had made an unsuccessful attempt to have the story broadcast by a different television channel where he used to work as an intern. Thereafter, he pilfered the tape and moved to a new television channel that aired the story without verifying the tapes. This case is dealt with in greater detail in Chapter 8 that deals with Sting Operations.

Recently, there have been a number of instances of Indian television channels abusing the tremendous power enjoyed by the mass media by deploying questionable methods and tactics to gain popularity. One such instance relates to a young Muslim woman named Gudiya who belonged to a poor family from Meerut district in Uttar Pradesh (*The Hindu*, 3 January 2006; *www.rediff.com*, 23 September 2004). Her first husband, Arif, served in the Indian army and had been sent to fight in Kargil soon after they were married. As his family did not hear from him for five years, it was presumed that he had either been killed or was serving time as a prisoner of war in Pakistan. Gudiya then married a distant relative, Taufeeq. When she was eight months' pregnant with Taufeeq's child, Arif suddenly turned up after he was released from a Pakistani prison. He wanted to return to Gudiya and was willing to accept her unborn child as his own though he was not the child's biological father.

For weeks, television channels broadcast discussions and debates on Gudiya's story. Eventually, Gudiya succumbed to the pressures by various so-called experts whose views were aired on television and decided to 'remarry' her first husband. Her first child was born and she started living with Arif. She soon became pregnant for a second time, but this time her child was stillborn. She fell seriously ill, was hospitalized and then died of septicemia on New Year's day 2006. By then, the media had almost forgotten her.

The month Gudiya died, Gopal Krishan Kashyap, a hawker who used to ply his wares on a hand-cart in Patiala, Punjab, set himself on fire near the city's bus terminal. The incident was witnessed by around 200 people, including policemen, and some 20 television channels filmed his act of self-immolation. The channels broadcast the gory incident that evening. Before committing suicide, Kashyap accused the mayor of the local municipal corporation and an adviser to the state chief minister of reneging on their promise to allot sheds to hawkers in the local marketplace. Kashyap had even written letters to the Prime Minister regarding the issue (*The Tribune*, 25 January 2006; *The Indian Express*, 26 January 2006). Nobody attempted to prevent Kashyap from killing himself. After he died, the cause for which he committed suicide was ignored by the media.

The case studies of Gudiya and Kashyap feature in a documentary for the Public Service Broadcasting Trust (PSBT) entitled *Grabbing Eyeballs: What's Unethical About Television News in India* that was directed by the author of this book and broadcast by Doordarshan in March 2008. In the film, one of the questions raised is whether the intensification of competition has resulted in a lowering of standards. Media watchers argue that instead of improving the quality of programming, competition has resulted in a 'race to the bottom', a race in which television news channels have conveniently forgotten basic ethical norms and principles of journalism, principles of fairness, truthfulness and objectivity.

Kevin Carter, a South African photographer, had won acclaim by being the first to photograph 'necklacing' or the killing of a person by garlanding him with a burning tyre during the apartheid regime in his country. In March 1993, he won a Pulitzer prize for photographing an emaciated Sudanese girl toddler being eyed by a vulture. He waited 20 minutes to take the picture and then chased the vulture away. He was severely criticized for not helping the girl. On July 27, 1994, Carter killed himself by inhaling carbon monoxide from a vehicle. He was 33 years old. His suicide note, in portions, read: 'I am depressed … without …money for child support ... I am haunted by vivid memories of killings and corpses and anger and pain … of starving or wounded children…'

When 14-year-old Aarushi Talwar (*The TOI*, 20 May 2008; *www.rediff.com*, 23 May 2008; *Hindustan Times*, 1 June 2008) and her family's domestic help Hemraj were murdered on 15 May 2008 in a house in Noida, near New Delhi, the manner in which it was covered by the Indian media sparked off another debate on how television channels and newspapers sensationalized crime stories to attract viewers and readers. The media coverage of the murders gained momentum after senior police officials suggested that Aarushi's murder might be linked to an alleged extramarital relationship of her father Rajesh Talwar (a reputed dentist like his wife Nupur Talwar) and that the murdered girl might have had an 'objectionable' relationship with Hemraj. Even as the police officials who made these suggestions were transferred from their positions and criminal investigations handed over to the Central Bureau of Investigation (CBI), some television channels and newspapers gave the story unprecedented coverage, much of it speculative and based on unsubstantiated rumours (see case study at the end of this chapter).

BROADCASTING CODE FOR INDIAN TELEVISION

The Aarushi case and the fraudulent sting operation on Uma Khurana came at a time when a furious debate was raging in India about the merits or otherwise of devising a content code for television channels. These episodes strengthened the hands of those who argued in favour of stringent regulation. While most private television broadcasters acknowledged the need for an independent regulatory body for television channels, there were sharp disagreements on who should devise the content code and how the independence of the proposed regulatory authority should be ensured.

Whereas print has its regulator in the form of the Press Council of India (PCI) and there is a self-regulatory body for advertisers and advertising agencies (Advertising Standards Council of India), television content is regulated through inadequate provisions of the law that govern the operation of cable networks. During a public discussion organized by the PSBT in August 2007, Kiran Karnik (associated with television in India since its early days in the 1970s) jocularly remarked that the bill to set up a broadcast authority—that had undergone 20 revisions over a decade—was more incendiary than the India-US nuclear agreement. Interestingly, his words were virtually echoed by the Union Minister for Information and Broadcasting Priya Ranjan Das Munshi while discussing the bill and the content code with a gathering of television broadcasters. The minister said he would he happy if television broadcasters formulated their own content code.

The July–September 2007 issue of *Vidura*, a journal published by the Press Institute of India, focused on the controversy and the debates surrounding the formulation of a content code and a regulatory body for television news broadcasters in India. In that issue, columnist and media commentator Sevanti Ninan pointed out that there are many countries in the world where regulation is in place for the broadcasting industry, including Canada, the US, the

UK, Denmark, Finland, the Netherlands, Greece, Portugal, Hungary, France, Germany and Pakistan. Broadcasters in these countries do not see this as a violation of their freedom of expression, but merely as a necessary way of maintaining some ethical and professional standards, she contended. In the same issue, Ammu Joseph, a Bangalore-based journalist who has closely tracked the topic, lamented the absence of participation by the public. She was of the view that there can be no media regulation in the public interest without public participation in the formulation of a media policy. In the absence of authentic public debate, policies will continue to be made in the name of the public without the public's informed consent. Educator and media commentator Aloke Thakore expressed the opinion that the broadcast bill was basically a hotchpotch of ideas and intentions, lacking clarity and specificity in its intentions (*Vidura* 2007). Nor was there any effectiveness in the regulatory mechanisms suggested in the bill, he argued, adding that what was needed was a new bill that was more cogent.

Exactly a year earlier, on 3 May 2007, designated as World Press Freedom Day, Union Minister Das Munshi said that while India's media barons and employers were enjoying the 'freedom of the press', they did not allow 'freedom of journalists'. 'How many journalists are protected by the norms and regulations of employment?' he asked, adding that on occasions, journalists in India 'work in most pitiable conditions'.

He further alleged that most journalists were paid by 'vouchers' and did not receive regular salaries and wondered whether such practices reinforced the freedom of the press. The minister lambasted television channels for repeatedly showing Hollywood actor Richard Gere kiss Indian actress Shilpa Shetty at a function to generate awareness about HIV/AIDS. 'One 28-second shot was shown on the channels 28 times, 48 times, 88 times, even 100 times. Is it for commercial purposes…? In a country of one billion people, I don't know how this becomes breaking news,' Das Munshi wondered.

In April 2008, the Ministry of Information & Broadcasting (I&B Ministry) mooted a proposal to set up an electronic media monitoring centre to oversee the content of all television channels and radio stations in India. It was reported (in *The Economic Times*, 19 April 2008) that the centre would have facilities to automatically record the content of 100 channels simultaneously that could be subsequently reviewed. Private broadcasters were unhappy with the proposal on the ground that it could lead to covert forms of censorship by the government, politicians and bureaucrats. If any allegation is levelled against a broadcaster for violation of the content code in the Cable

Television Networks (Regulation) Act of 1995, the broadcaster concerned has to provide footage of the content that was aired to the government. In 2007, the I&B Ministry had temporarily banned two foreign television channels, AXN and FTV (Fashion Television), for allegedly violating the content code in the Act. A programme called the World's Sexiest Commercials on AXN and other content on FTV was found 'offensive'. Both channels assured the government that they would not continue screening content deemed 'offensive'. The ministry has also banned the broadcast of particular advertisements and television channels have had to publicly air statements of apology.

The same month, April 2008, the government proposed to monitor television content, the News Broadcasters Association (NBA) of India came out with a code of ethics and broadcasting standards. The code and regulations, which were vetted by Harish Salve, senior advocate and former Solicitor General of India, were submitted by the NBA to the I&B Ministry. One of the fundamental principles of the code is that journalists from the electronic media should accept and understand that they operate as trustees of the public and should, therefore, make it their mission to seek the truth and to report it fairly with integrity and independence. Professional journalists should stand fully accountable for their actions.

The NBA code says that television news channels recognize that they have a special responsibility in adhering to high standards of journalism since they have the most potent influence on public opinion. The code highlights the importance of maintaining impartiality and objectivity in reporting to ensure neutrality. While reporting on crime, the code calls for safeguards to ensure that crime and violence are not glorified and that acts of violence or intimidation against women and children are not shown. The code says television news channels should ensure that they do not show, without morphing, male or female nudity. The channels should also not telecast explicit images of sexual activity, sexual perversions, acts of sexual violence like rape or molestation, pornography or use sexually suggestive language.

As a rule, channels must not intrude on private lives or personal affairs of individuals, unless there is a clearly established larger and identifiable public interest for such a broadcast, the code adds. On the question of endangering national security, the code states: 'In the use of any terminology or maps that represent India and Indian strategic interests, all news channels will use specific terminology and maps mandated by law and Indian government rules.' Further, the code adds: 'News channels will not broadcast any material that glorifies superstition and occultism in any manner. . . news channels will also issue public disclaimers to ensure that viewers are not misled into believing or emulating such beliefs and activity. Therefore, news channels will not broadcast "as fact" myths about "supernatural" acts, apparitions and ghosts, personal or social deviations or deviant behaviour, and re-creations of the same' (see Box 1.4: Reality or Superstition?)

The code states: 'As a guiding principle, sting and undercover operations should be a last resort of news channels in an attempt to give the viewer comprehensive coverage of an news story. News channels will not allow sex and sleaze as a means to carry out sting operations, the use of narcotics and psychotropic substances or any act of violence, intimidation, or discrimination as a justifiable means in the recording of any sting operation. Sting operations will also abide by the principles of self-regulation... and news channels will ensure that they will be guided ....by an identifiable larger public interest. News channels will, as a ground rule, ensure that sting operations are carried out only as a tool for getting conclusive evidence of wrongdoing or criminality, and that there is no deliberate alteration of visuals, or editing, or interposing done with the raw footage in a way that it also alters or misrepresents the truth or presents only a portion of the truth.'

Box 1.4

Reality or Superstition?

A number of television channels have telecast scenes wherein children are thrown over burning coal or dropped from a height or even stamped on by so-called faith-healers and tantriks. There have been innumerable depictions of mystics curing 'possessed' women and stories of children playing with poisonous cobras that are referred to as 'naag devata' or snake gods. Some channels claim that such reports are to help rid people of superstitious beliefs, while media watchers feel that such depictions only encourage people to believe in them.

On airing of contradictions and providing an opportunity to those aggrieved by a television programme, the NBA code specifies: 'All news channels will, in keeping with the principle of due accuracy and impartiality, ensure that significant mistakes made in the course of any broadcast is acknowledged and corrected on air immediately.' The code points out that all television news channels are now also required to receive consumer feedback on their websites.

The NBA had earlier rejected the government's Broadcast Services Regulation Bill seeking to establish a Broadcast Regulatory Authority of India that would enforce a content code. Privately owned media organizations were wary of the government assuming powers to regulate and monitor their activities. Having proposed a model of self-regulation or a system of 'judgement by peers', the association set up its 'own' regulatory body headed by a jurist and consisting of six nominated members. Such a self-regulatory body has the power to impose fines in favour of, or against, a complainant.

On 22 August 2008, the NBA announced the constitution and establishment of the News Broadcasting Standards (Disputes Redressal) Authority to enforce the NBA's code of ethics and broadcasting standards. The authority became operational from 2 October 2008.

SELF-REGULATION

Many countries have regulatory bodies and laws to govern the behaviour of media and we shall examine their provisions in various chapters of this book. However, rules and regulations have their limitations. Not all situations are alike and frequently occasions arise that require at least a careful interpretation of existing regulations to determine the best course of action. Moreover, regulations and laws, for this very reason, are not exhaustive. Specific circumstances often demand unique considerations. Self-regulation is considered the best means to guarantee appropriate behaviour, for two major reasons. First, self-regulation ensures that the media can continue to operate independently. Second, self-regulation is a voluntary act that is not imposed externally and hence, carries more credibility in the eyes of the public. Self-regulation applies not only to media groups and organizations but also to individual journalists. It is, therefore, of fundamental importance that media practitioners nurture a strong ethical value system throughout their careers.

People are remembered more often for their mistakes than for their good work. As Mark Anthony remarked, while addressing a gathering in Rome, standing in front of Julius Caesar's corpse (in 'William Shakespeare's play): 'The evil that men do lives after them; The good is oft interred with the bones...' Life can indeed be cruel and a journalist's entire professional career and credibility can be permanently ruined by one unethical act, a single instance of indiscretion.

Recently there was a spurt in instances of violent attacks against journalists, writers and media organizations in different parts of India. Here are a few instances.

The financial base of the corporate group that publishes *Eenadu*, the most widely circulated Telugu daily, was targeted by the Andhra Pradesh Chief Minister Y.S. Rajasekhar Reddy (*The Hindu*, 23 December 2006). The newspaper had been particularly critical of Reddy and his government.

In June 2008, in Ahmedabad, Gujarat, a case of sedition was lodged by the police against *The Times of India* (*TOI*) and its employees for questioning the selection of O.P. Mathur as the city's police chief. The Editors Guild of India stated (*TOI*, 3 June 2008): 'The action... smacks of vindictiveness as the newspaper had carried articles criticizing the choice of O.P. Mathur as the police commissioner...Sedition is a charge which was slapped on the Indian media by the colonial rulers during the freedom struggle. Abuse of the sedition provision against the media negates the freedom granted to the citizens by the Constitution.'

In the same month, the Gujarat police unsuccessfully sought to arrest academician Ashis Nandy on the basis of a complaint filed against him by a non-government organization (NGO). The reputed political psychologist had written an opinion article in *The TOI* on 14 January 2008 in which he had criticized Gujarat Chief Minister Narendra Modi of the Bharatiya Janata Party (BJP). He accused Modi of promoting politics of 'hate' and also blamed the 'communalized' middle class for the success of the BJP in the state elections in December 2007. The Supreme Court's intervention prevented Nandy from being arrested.

In Kerala, journalists of the Malayala Manorama group were physically assaulted by supporters of the Communist Party of India (Marxist) in the state (*The Hindu*, 25 June 2008).

In June 2008, in Maharashtra, the residence of Kumar Ketkar, editor of a leading Marathi daily, *Loksatta*, was damaged by a group of 70 people owing allegiance to an organization led by Vinayak Mete (*The Hindu*, 6 June 2008). Mete is a former member of the legislative council of Maharashtra and belongs to the Nationalist Congress Party (NCP), which is a part of the coalition government in the state. This group attacked Ketkar's residence because he had 'hurt their sentiments' by writing an article criticizing the state government's plans to install a 309-feet high statue of Maratha king Chhatrapati Shivaji, a historical figure, one kilometre into the Arabian Sea off the coast of Mumbai at Marine Drive.

In the recent past, there have been innumerable other instances of journalists being attacked and offices of newspapers and television studios being damaged by intolerant groups of people. The media in the country has often been criticized and viciously attacked by some politicians, bureaucrats and police personnel. Former Prime Minister Rajiv Gandhi had tried to introduce a Defamation Bill in 1988 before it was withdrawn after vehement opposition from journalists. During the nineteen month Emergency period in 1975–77, the Union government, headed by Indira Gandhi, had imposed censorship on the press—a decision that was later publicly regretted by the then I&B Minister Vidya Charan Shukla. Many supporters and well-wishers of the former prime minister too felt that this specific move contributed considerably to the electoral defeat of her party in March 1977.

On occasions, journalists believe they have been attacked in an unfair manner. In 1999, during the Kargil war, Barkha Dutt of New Delhi Television was accused of endangering the lives of Indian soldiers by using a satellite phone, an allegation she vehemently denies. These allegations resurfaced in a different form in December 2008 when the Indian Navy chief accused a 'woman reporter of NDTV' of behaving in an unethical manner, a charge that was again denied. Earlier, in 1989, television journalist Nalini Singh was accused of concocting interviews with criminals who were supposed to have rigged elections in Bihar—a charge she too denies.

Television programme producer Sohaib Ilyasi, who directed a popular series titled 'India's Most Wanted' on crime and criminals was himself accused by his mother-in-law of being responsible for the unnatural death of his wife Anju in January 2000—the criminal case was dismissed by a court in August 2005. He was later involved in a controversial sting operation on actor Shakti Kapoor (see Chapter 8 on Sting Operations).

Is there a discernible pattern in the manner in which the media in the country has been attacked by those at the receiving end of its criticism over the years? Or is there something different about some of the more contemporary attacks on journalists? In an editorial, *Business Standard* (1 July 2008) wrote: 'Clearly, something has changed for the worse, not only in that the state appears not just indifferent but, also in an increasing number of cases, complicit; and that the public doesn't care. This should worry the media and persuade it to do some serious soul-searching as to how much it is responsible for the way things are turning out.'

The editorial added that public perception of the media had altered—no longer were journalists seen as belonging to a profession with an element of public service in it. 'Today it is seen more often than not as just another business, and not a very ethical business at that. The fact that several media groups use the public service as a cloak for hiding the pursuit of profit by less than honourable means (like selling news columns for money) has not helped matters, nor have the stories about exaggerated salaries in the media business. The adversarial role that the media played was never universal; but with the advent of TV, and the utter degradation of what is presented as TV news, even that mitigation has ceased to exist.'

The *Business Standard* went on to argue that the 'somewhat special status that the media enjoyed—as the fourth pillar of democracy—has been considerably diluted', that 'ignorant reporting and comment' have taken their toll and that it is now 'up to the media to introspect on its own failures'. The editorial closed with the following sentence: 'But, it is for the country as a whole, and especially for the political system, to ponder on the future of the country and its democratic system if the media comes under repeated attack, and finds that it has no defenders.'

The Indian media, in particular twenty-four hour television channels, came under criticism for the manner in which the November 2008 terrorist attacks in Mumbai were reported. Various sections, including the Indian government, argued that the media acted in a less-than-responsible manner and violated ethical norms while covering the incidents of 26–28 November 2008 thereby re-igniting the debate on regulation of television broadcasts (see case study in Chapter 4 on Sensitivity).

This book, in a small way, attempts to highlight certain ethical issues that concern not just every journalist (in India and elsewhere) but every member of society. To turn an oft-repeated phrase around, media ethics is too important an issue to be left to journalists alone.

This book seeks to address a number of key issues related to ethical journalism in the chapters that follow. These issues include:

- Truthfulness, deception, accuracy
- Objectivity, impartiality, fairness
- Sensitivity, privacy, confidentiality, obscenity
- Legal issues, free speech, libel, intellectual property rights, contempt of court
- Conflict of interest, commercial interests versus social service, journalists versus public relations (PR) professionals

It is often difficult for a journalist to determine the right course of action, especially in an abstract theoretical or philosophical context. Throughout the course of this book we examine major areas of media concern, noting, in particular, ethical dilemmas. Where possible, we suggest appropriate or best courses of action. We notice, time and again, that absolute rules are often not practical and that it is necessary to develop a relative and approximate interpretation of ethical norms and values. We hope that this book will help you understand some ethical issues that are most frequently encountered by media professionals. Ultimately, a conscientious approach to journalism is what is required.

CASE STUDY

Aarushi and the Indian Media

The media furore over the Aarushi–Hemraj murder case has raised the concerns of journalists and legal experts in the country.

On 6 August 2008, the Supreme Court of India sharply criticized the media for acting as if it was a 'super' investigating agency and for tarnishing the reputation of the doctor couple whose daughter Aarushi Talwar had been murdered. During the hearing of a case pertaining to corruption in the judiciary (that was completely unrelated to the murder case), Justice G.S. Singhvi remarked: 'See what happened…irretrievable damage has been done to the couple who lost their only child. This is unthinkable in a democracy.' Sitting on the same bench, fellow judge B.N. Agrawal added: 'We are not concerned with what the media says. They will criticize us also. If some high-profile person is involved in some case, you (the media) will continue the show for the whole day. Media must know that it does not affect judicial minds' (*The Hindu*, 7 August 2008).

Less than a fortnight later, on 18 August, the Supreme Court was even more critical of the media coverage in the Aarushi Talwar case during the hearing of a public interest litigation petition that had been filed specifically on the issue. The court issued a notice to the Government of India on the need for laying down norms and guidelines for the print and electronic media in covering criminal cases in which investigations are pending. A bench of the court comprising justices Altamas Kabir and Markandey Katju issued notices to the Uttar Pradesh government, the Press Council of India, newspapers like *The TOI* and the *Hindustan Times* and television channels, NDTV, Aaj Tak and CNN-IBN.

Justice Kabir said: 'Nobody is trying to gag the media. They must play a responsible role. By investigation, the media must not do anything which will prejudice either the prosecution or the accused. Sometimes the entire focus is lost. A person is found guilty even before the trial takes place. See what happened in this case. Till today what is the evidence against anyone?'

Justice Katju added: 'We will lay down guidelines on media coverage. We are not concerned about media criticizing us. Let the media say anything about us, we are not perturbed. Our shoulders are broad enough and we will ignore it the criticism. We are for media freedom. What we are saying is there is no absolute freedom. See what happened to Dr Talwar, his reputation is tarnished.'

'We want to lay down general guidelines and not target individuals,' the bench stated. It said that the print and electronic media had a powerful influence over the masses. 'The media has to be more responsible. It must not do anything by which investigation could be prejudiced against the accused,' it added while responding to the petition that had been filed by an advocate. The petition had raised the question as to whether the media had the right to report whatever was stated during a briefing by police officers, irrespective of the damage it might cause to the reputation of the accused and the mental agony it could inflict on them (*The Hindu* and *The TOI*, 19 August 2008).

The Supreme Court's observations elicited critical responses from certain journalists. Jacqueline Park, director, Asia Pacific, International Federation of Journalists (IFJ), wrote in an opinion article that the 'attempt by India's higher judiciary to write rules for journalism, in response to concerns about media coverage of the murder of Aarushi Talwar, represents a new threat to the autonomy of India's robust media industry'.

She added: 'There is no place for the judiciary to determine how the media goes about its job of informing the public. However, journalists and editors must take this latest attempt to do so as a warning of the need for them to examine their behaviour and to develop and adopt appropriate professional standards if they are to counter state efforts to regulate independent media. Most media houses in India already have well-considered norms in place covering all journalistic contingencies. However, the declaration by India's Supreme Court on August 18 that it intends to lay down norms for media coverage of ongoing criminal investigations is symptomatic of a wider crisis of standards in India's media: one occasioned by the rampant commercialism that has followed the boom in cable television and the new media. . .

'The media abandoned its first responsibility to truth-telling in favour of crass sensationalism. Where they could potentially have served as a window for the public into the investigation, many media outlets instead chose to reproduce and regurgitate every half-formed explanation put out by the police force...A code of professional conduct that is externally imposed, even if it pertains to ongoing criminal investigations, is not guaranteed to be effective and does not serve the best interests of the public. A credible process of self-regulation of the media, on the basis of internally evolved norms, requires that the autonomy of journalism within the media industry be honoured.'

She said the view of the IFJ was that 'the increasing encroachment of marketing and advertising functions into decisions about media content can be seen as largely—though not wholly—responsible for many of the ethical breaches manifest recently in the Indian media. Referring to the Uma Khurana episode, Park pointed out that the Indian media had earlier 'faced the prospect of judicial interventions in content decisions'.

Commenting on the programme code that is 'supposedly in force', she said that the code 'is a fairly loosely worded text drawn up in 1995 as an annexure to the sole existing law on cable television broadcasting'. She added that the code 'has never been subject to any form of public scrutiny, or won the explicit endorsement of the media industry'.

Aarushi's mother Nupur Talwar moved the National Commission for Protection of Child Rights after reports that a television company (Balaji Telefilms) intended using the teenager's murder as part of a popular serial *Kahani Ghar Ghar Ki* (*Story of Every Household*), portraying it as an instance of 'honour killing' of a fictional character called Tannu. Nupur Talwar alleged that Balaji Telefims intended to commercially gain from her daughter's murder in an unethical manner, an allegation the television company denied in its reply to the notice served on it by the commission. Balaji Telefilms claimed that the storyline of the serial had been created well before Aarushi's murder and had many factual differences. The company also accused television news channels of sensationalizing the murder for commercial gain. Nevertheless, the manner in which some television channels and newspapers handled the Aarushi–Hemraj murder case came in for sharp criticism by many senior journalists and media observers. Here are a few instances.

In an article titled 'Murder in the Media', in *Outlook* (9 June 2008), Shefalee Vasudev, editor, *Marie Claire* (India), opined: 'The media has turned this tragic case into a psychological, legal, detective, sociological, sensationalist, filmi drama. One channel actually has anchors dressed as sleuths; another goes into a tizzy quizzing every available mental health professional from NIMHANS* in Bangalore to VIMHANS** in Delhi. Invite a jury of sociologists, journalists, advocates and SJs (*sab jaantewalas* or know-it-alls) to first hyperventilate, then mourn the death of Indian family values and hey presto, you have a "if it bleeds, it leads" debate.'

Akhila Sivadas, who heads a civil society organization, the Centre for Advocacy and Research, argues (*Gulf Times*, 25 May 2008) that television news channels and daily newspapers had gone overboard catering to 'people's thirst for voyeurism and sensationalism'. She adds that 'Between voyeurism, sensationalism and character assassination and a genuine public scrutiny, we have to draw a line'.

With television reporters waiting almost round the clock near the residence of the Talwars, Sivadas argues that the media scrutiny was not wholly unwelcome but should be tempered with informed judgement and sensitivity. After the CBI cleared Rajesh and Nupur Talwar in the Aarushi–Hemraj murder case, Sivadas wrote (*The Hindu*, 3 August 2008): 'Suddenly, the entire complexion of the debate changed. The shrillness of the drama vanished and the media found itself in the dock. It was a rare moment of introspection for them but not without its share of inconsistencies and the usual justifications. Weren't they acting in the public

---

*NIMHANS : National Institute of Mental Health and Neurosciences

**VIMHANS : Vidyasagar Institute of Mental Health and Neuro-Sciences.

interest, acting as a watchdog and exposing the ineffectiveness or veniality of the enforcement agencies, they asked.

'But this is not the first instance when the media had been overreacting and sensationalizing and floating theories and generally going overboard to keep the flock of their viewers and readers... Quite a few other high-profile cases that had happened in and around Delhi also experienced the same sort of treatment. In many of these cases there was the same high-pitched coverage, the wild theories, the showing of gory details from the scene of the crime; every rule of journalistic restraint was thrown to the wind...'

In the same issue of *The Hindu*, Indira Jaising, a Supreme Court lawyer and civil rights activist, argues that 'the harm done by the press to reputation is irreparable and it needs to adopt preventive measures before the damage is done'. Citing the Aarushi–Hemraj murder case as an example, Jaisingh points out that 'much of what passes off as investigative journalism is nothing but press hand outs'. 'There is an unholy nexus between the police and the press...The police release premature opinions to come out looking good in investigating crime and the press laps it up as an "exclusive" story. Both are happy. The law needs to step in here and hold the police responsible for damaging reputations and prevent them from sharing investigation reports with the press,' she adds.

Shohini Ghosh, who teaches at the AJ Kidwai Mass Communication Research Centre, Jamia Millia Islamia, New Delhi, wrote the following in an editorial page article in the *Hindustan Times* (3 June 2008) wherein she describes in detail a show titled *Crime File* that was telecast on Zee News about the Aarushi–Hemraj murder case: 'Inspired by the dubious versions circulated by the police, the episode unambiguously indicts Rajesh Talwar for killing his daughter and the domestic help. Doubling as mind-reader, anchor Manoj Raghuvanshi painstakingly explains the "motives" behind the crime. Rajesh Talwar was having an affair with his friend Anita Durrani. His daughter is upset and starts confiding in Hemraj and they end up having an affair. On that fateful night, Rajesh Talwar discovers them together and kills them in a fit of temper.'

She points out that as if presenting speculation as fact was not bad enough, the show recreated sequences showing Aarushi and Hemraj coming close to each other. Despite this 'spectacular lack of conscience and journalistic ethics', Ghosh points out that the particular television channel (Zee News) was hardly the only culprit. She writes: 'Almost all television channels have been guilty of jumping the gun without bothering to apologize for wrong conjectures....The public has been equally complicit...The presumption of innocence until proven guilty constitutes the core of the fundamental right to liberty. This cardinal principle of criminal justice has been grossly violated by the media. Even if Rajesh Talwar were to be declared innocent by the courts, it would not be adequate compensation for the stigma, harassment and vilification the family continues to suffer. Apart from demanding privacy and defamation laws, it is important that we insist on the undertrial's right to a fair trial.'

Ghosh refers to another film that was telecast by *Zee News* on the 13 December 2001 attack by terrorists on Parliament House. In the film, the then prime suspect S.A.R. Geelani was shown as the mastermind behind the attack. The opening commentary in Hindi declared: 'Presenting news in a new fashion, Zee TV's film December 13 was shot in 16 days. This is a new chapter in the history of India.' Hyperbole aside, it was claimed that the film was based on a charge sheet prepared by the Delhi Police. Geelani's lawyers later argued that the film levelled fabricated allegations that were not even mentioned in the police charge sheet. None of the charges could be proved and Geelani was acquitted by the Delhi High Court.

Geelani's appeal that the telecast of the film be stopped in order not to prejudice the trial was turned down by the Supreme Court of India on the ground that 'judges by their judicial training and the office they hold are not supposed to be influenced by the broadcast of such films'. Ghosh writes that while 'such an aspiration is noble, it is untenable since judges are human beings like everyone else and not above social or political influences'. She adds that the 'right to fair trial' is guaranteed under Article 14 of the International Covenant on Civil and Political Rights (ICCPR) and points out that it was in the interest of a fair trial that the high court in Mumbai had stayed the release of the film *Black Friday* till the judgement about the 1993 serial bomb blasts in the city had been delivered.

Ghosh writes: 'There seems to be some confusion, even among journalists, about the role that the media ought to play. After all, didn't the media do a splendid job in the Jessica Lall case? Should the media not lobby for justice? Of course it should. But that job is best done by doggedly pursuing stories, reporting facts accurately and making a distinction between editorializing and reporting. It is not for the media to establish guilt or innocence. But it should surely monitor the proceedings to ensure that a fair trial is in process. Unfortunately, in the Aarushi–Hemraj murder case, the media have ended up doing just the reverse.'

Senior journalist Surinder Nihal Singh argues (*The Tribune*, 17 June 2008) that the 'scandalous' manner in which the Aarushi–Hemraj murder case was covered seemed to indicate that certain television channels 'are egging on the government to regulate them'. He writes: 'Why a voluble police force publicly floated diverse theories of who could have committed the murder and his motives is for the authorities to investigate. But for the media, particularly the TV channels, to throw the basic tenets of journalism out of the window and revel in salacious details without even using the word "alleged" is a national shame… With the government hot on the television channels' trail with a view to regulating and controlling them, Indian broadcasters are asking for trouble. Irresponsible and salacious reporting of one murder can only convince viewers that broadcast and television channels need regulation and control, despite the viewer ratings these channels might be banking on.'

Singh argues that while governments the world over try to use 'national interest' and 'right to privacy' to try to control the media, journalists 'must themselves police the right to privacy'. 'But Indian broadcasters will carry little conviction if they display the kind of irresponsible reporting they have indulged in on Aarushi,' he adds. Singh, a former editor of *The Statesman*, writes that the government 'could take the case of the Aarushi murder and frame a set of dos and don'ts on murder stories'. He points out that 'those who have lived through the Emergency of 1975–77 (the nineteen-month period during which Indira Gandhi's government censored the press in India) realize how easy it is for the majority to fall in line. Mercifully, the media (has) learnt a few lessons from those days and will probably not cave in as easily. But vigilance, they say, is the price of freedom and the coverage of the Aarushi murder reminds us how vigilant we need to be.'

Discussion Questions

1. Is the media or the police more responsible for tarnishing the reputation of the late Aarushi Talwar and her parents?
2. Should the Supreme Court lay down guidelines for news reporters?
3. What is the dividing line between 'invasion of privacy' and 'public interest'?

REFERENCES

'Aarushi case: Crucial cell phone links,' The TOI, New Delhi, 20 May 2008; 'Noida murders: Aarushi killed over father's affair,' www.rediff.com, 23 May 2008; 'CBI begins probe in Aarushi's murder case,' Hindustan Times, 1 June 2008.

Chomsky, Noam and Edward S. Herman 2002, *Manufacturing Consent: The Political Economy of the Mass Media*, Pantheon Books, New York, US.

Gudiya dies, The Hindu, Chennai, 3 January 2006; 'Prisoner of woe: Private horror behind Gudiya's public trial,' www.rediff.com, 23 September 2004.

Joseph, Ammu 2007, 'Of Chickens and Eggs', *Vidura*, Volume 44, Issue No. 3, pages 13–15.

Ninan, Sevanti 2007, 'Reining in Broadcasters', *Vidura*, Volume 44, Issue No. 3, pages 10–12.

'Rehri owner sets himself on fire in Patiala,' The Tribune, 25 January 2006; 'Man who self-imolated in Patiala dies,' PTI, quoted in the Indian Express, 26 January 2006.

Retief, Johan 2002, *Media Ethics: An Introduction to Responsible Journalism*, Oxford University Press, Cape Town, South Africa.

Rodman, George 2001, *Making Sense of Media*, Allyn & Bacon, Boston, U.S.

Thakore, Aloke 2007, 'Need for a Regulator', *Vidura*, Volume 44, Issue No. 3, pages 16–17.

'Who is Uma Khurana?' Hindustan Times, New Delhi, 31 August 2007; 'Uma Khurana left sobbing for two days,' Daily News & Analysis, Mumbai, 9 September 2007.

APPENDIX 1.1

Media as a Feral Beast

Here are some excerpts from a speech delivered by former British Prime Minister Tony Blair on 12 June 2007. The full text is available at http://news.bbc.co.uk/1/hi/uk_politics/6744581.stm (accessed on 5 August 2008).

'...A free media is a vital part of a free society. You only need to look at where such a free media is absent to know this truth. But it is also part of freedom to be able to comment on the media. It has a complete right to be free...

My principal reflection is not about "blaming" anyone. It is that the relationship between politics, public life and the media is changing as a result of the changing context of communication in which we all operate; no one is at fault—it is a fact; but it is my view that the effect of this change is seriously adverse to the way public life is conducted; and that we need, at the least, a proper and considered debate about how we manage the future, in which it is in all our interests that the public is properly and accurately informed...

The news schedule is now 24 hours a day, seven days a week. It moves in real time. Papers don't give you up-to-date news. That's already out there. They have to break stories, try to lead the schedules. Or they give a commentary. And it all happens with outstanding speed...

I am going to say something that few people in public life will say, but most know is absolutely true: a vast aspect of our jobs today—outside of the really major decisions, as big as anything else—is coping with the media, its sheer scale, weight and constant hyperactivity....

My point is: it is not the people who have changed; it is the context within which they work. We devote reams of space to debating why there is so much cynicism about politics and public life. In this, the politicians are obliged to go into self-flagellation, admitting it's all our fault. Actually, not to have a proper press operation nowadays is like asking a batsman to face bodyline bowling without pads or headgear...

If you are a backbench MP today, you learn to give a press release first and a good Parliamentary speech second. My case, however, is: there's no point either in blaming the media. We are both handling the changing nature of communication. The sooner we recognize this, the better because we can then debate a sensible way forward. The reality is that as a result of the changing context in which 21st-century communications operates, the media are facing a hugely more intense form of competition than anything they have ever experienced before.

They are not the masters of this change but its victims. The result is a media that increasingly and to a dangerous degree is driven by "impact". Impact is what matters. It is all that can distinguish, can rise above the clamour, can get noticed. Impact gives competitive edge. Of course the accuracy of a story counts. But it is secondary to impact...

Broadsheets today face the same pressures as tabloids; broadcasters increasingly the same pressures as broadsheets. The audience needs to be arrested, held and their emotions engaged. Something that is interesting is less powerful than something that makes you angry or shocked. The consequences of this are acute. First, scandal or controversy beats ordinary reporting hands down.

The fear of missing out means today's media, more than ever before, hunts in a pack. In these modes it is like a feral beast, just tearing people and reputations to bits. But no one dares miss out ... rather than just report news, even if sensational or controversial, the new technique is commentary on the news being as, if not more, important than the news itself...

In turn, this leads to …the confusion of news and commentary. Comment is a perfectly respectable part of journalism. But it is supposed to be separate. Opinion and fact should be clearly divisible…

I do believe this relationship between public life and media is now damaged in a manner that requires repair. The damage saps the country's confidence and self-belief; it undermines its assessment of itself, its institutions; and above all, it reduces our capacity to take the right decisions, in the right spirit for our future. I've made this speech after much hesitation. I know it will be rubbished in certain quarters. But I also know this was needed to be said.'

Questions for discussion

Do you agree with Blair's contention that the media hunts like a pack of feral beasts?

Do you believe that sections of the media deliberately confuse 'news' and 'comment' and blur the distinction that is supposed to exist between 'factual information' and 'opinion'? Comment using the Aarushi Talwar murder as a case study.

APPENDIX 1.2

Noam Chomsky on the Political Economy of the Mass Media

Academic and left-wing political activist Noam Chomsky has articulated the view that the mainstream mass media (especially in the US) constrains dialogue and 'manufactures consent' to help promote the interests of the American government and large corporations. In his book, co-authored with Edward S. Herman, entitled *Manufacturing Consent: The Political Economy of the Mass Media*, first published in 1988, several detailed case studies are provided to highlight how the mainstream media circulates propaganda. According to this propaganda model of the media, democratic societies like the US use subtle, non-violent means of control, unlike totalitarian systems, where physical force can readily be used to coerce journalists as well as the population at large. Chomsky has often been quoted as stating: 'Propaganda is to a democracy what the bludgeon is to a totalitarian state.'

The propaganda model attempts to explain a systemic bias in the media in terms of structural economic causes. It argues that the bias derives from five 'filters' which all published news must pass through and this, in turn, distorts news coverage. The five filters are:

1. **Ownership** Chomsky and Herman argue that as most major media outlets are owned by large corporations, the information provided by them will favour their interests.
2. **Funding** As all media outlets depend heavily on advertising revenue, the authors claim that news, as a product, plays a minor role. The theory states that the other major product that newspapers have are the readers and businesses capitalize on this through their advertisements. Hence, stories that will affect the 'buying mood' of the readers or the interests of advertisers will be marginalized or avoided.
3. **Sourcing** As the media needs to churn out information continuously, it has to depend on government institutions and major businesses that have the required material. The theory argues that the information provided by these sources is generally biased and most media outlets are reluctant to provide information that might harm their corporate interests.
4. **Flak** This filter refers to the various powerful groups that target the media directly or indirectly to manage information their way.

5. **Anti-ideologies** This filter exploits public fear and hatred of groups that pose real or imagined threats. Chomsky and Herman feel that after the collapse of the Soviet Union, anti-communism has been replaced by anti-terrorism and other anathemas.

The propaganda model of the mass media describes how the media forms a 'decentralized and non-conspiratorial but nonetheless very powerful' propaganda system that is able to mobilize a consensus among the elite, frame public debate within elitist perspectives and at the same time, provide an 'appearance of democratic consent'.

Chomsky and Herman tested the propaganda model empirically by picking 'paired examples' or pairs of events that were objectively similar except in relation to certain interests. For example, they argue that when an 'official enemy' commits a crime (like the murder of a religious official), the media investigates the crime very thoroughly and devotes considerable space and time to covering the event. However, if the US government or its ally commits a similar offence, the same media would downplay the story.

Chomsky and Herman argue that since mass media news outlets are now run by large corporations, these are under similar competitive pressures as other corporate bodies. The pressures to run profitable businesses invariably distort the news that is reported and the emphasis given to certain kinds of news and the manner of reporting are simply a consequence of market selection. Thus, companies that favour profits over news quality survive and prosper while media organizations that seek to present a more accurate picture tend to get marginalized. As news organizations depend on governments as major sources of news, organizations that fall out of favour with a government can be subtly 'shut out' and other news outlets given preferential treatment. Since this would result in loss of readership/viewership, and consequently, advertising revenue, news organizations tend to report news using a tone that is favourable to governments and big businesses and give less emphasis to news that is not favourable to government and business, Chomsky and Herman observe in their book. The title of the book (*Manufacturing Consent*) is a catch phrase coined by journalist and political commentator Walter Lippmann in his book *Public Opinion* published in 1922.

Despite the fact that Chomsky is one of the most quoted social scientists—the Arts and Humanities Citation Index of 1992 states that he was the eighth most cited scholar in any time period—he has been marginalized by the mainstream media in the US. CNN presenter Jeff Greenfield, when asked why Chomsky was never on his show, claimed that though he was 'one of the leading intellectuals', he 'can't talk on television' and would 'take five minutes to warm up'. Greenfield said that this need to 'say things between two commercials' was news television's requirement for 'concision'. Chomsky's response was that 'the beauty of (concision) is that you can only repeat conventional thoughts'. Nevertheless, Chomsky's book, *9–11* became a bestseller and, of late, the mainstream media in the US has paid more attention to him.

APPENDIX 1.3

Media in India: Robust Growth and a Loss of Diversity

This is an excerpt from a publication entitled In the Balance: Press Freedom in South Asia (2007–08) *produced by the* International Federation of Journalists *on behalf of the South Asia Media Solidarity Network released on World Press Freedom Day, 3 May 2008. The full report can be accessed on the internet at http://asiapacific.ifj.org/en/pages/in-the-balance-press-freedom-in-*

south-asia-2007-2008-2. The following section was written by the publication's editor Sukumar Muralidharan and used with permission.

'India's media grew robustly over the year under review. Concerns about diversity and choice, however, remained high. . . The greatest malaise of the Indian media may well be a lack of transparency. Even so, it seems that the quantitative growth of the media in India has been accompanied by a qualitative deterioration and a loss of diversity…

According to an estimate made by a leading business lobby, the Federation of Indian Chambers of Commerce and Industry (FICCI), revenues of the media and entertainment industry grew by 17 per cent in 2007, to touch an aggregate figure of Rs 50,000 crore (about US$12.5 billion). This estimate places the revenue from advertising at Rs 19,600 crore, or just over 38 per cent of the total industry turnover…

Big corporate houses, both Indian and multinational, have been increasingly making their presence felt in the media sector. Reliance-Anil Dhirubhai Ambani Group, one of India's largest corporate houses, has expanded its presence in FM and announced plans to enter television broadcasting with perhaps 20 channels…

India's media has grown faster and more visibly than other sectors of a rapidly growing economy. Yet, unlike other sectors, investment rules and norms in the media remain opaque and often subject to abuse.

In February 2008, eight journalists from *NewsX*, a news channel that was then yet to be launched, resigned after a dispute with the ownership of the holding company. The episode involved public mud-slinging and allegations of journalists being wrongfully confined and forced to submit resignation letters…

Since the state government in Andhra Pradesh changed hands in 2004, an investigation was launched into Margadarsi, a financial company under the same ownership as the *Eenadu* media group. Figures uncovered by an independent audit of the finance company suggested a pyramid scheme, and possible difficulties in redeeming all the deposits the company had gathered. India's Supreme Court intervened to mandate a scheme for the company to redeem depositor funds as they fell due…

There are no qualifications required in terms of media competence or adherence to ethical norms in any guise.

Two recent events highlight the uncertain consequences for the Indian media:

- In September 2007, a 24-hour television news channel, *Live India*, was ordered off the air for one month as penalty for airing a fake 'sting' operation implicating a teacher in Delhi in a non-existent prostitution racket. The case obviously warranted prosecution under legal provisions covering the offences of falsification of evidence, extortion and incitement to violence. There was also a strong case for lawful recompense to the teacher, who suffered serious trauma and irreparable damage to her reputation. Yet the regulatory response was to take the channel off the air. No explanation has been offered for either the punishment or its duration.
- In November 2007, a radio jockey on the *Red FM* channel was booked under the law for inciting communal violence between the Nepali Gorkha community and others. Red FM broadcasts to various urban markets in India. However, it is not known to have a signal in Siliguri district in the state of West Bengal, where riots broke out over allegedly disparaging remarks made against the Nepali Gorkha community. The individual concerned now faces prosecution in a West Bengal court. *Red FM* offended against a basic rule of ethical journalism, which is 'to

do no harm'. But the sanctions that the individual faces under relevant provisions of the law dealing with the incitement of violence and creating disharmony among communities seem excessive and illogical.

These two events draw attention to a major lacuna in India's regulatory regime: there are no accepted standards on the exercise of the free speech right in the Indian media. Neither is there a credible regulatory framework in place... This raises troubling questions about how far media freedom can be hostage to inconsistent standards...

Meanwhile, in disposing of a public interest petition arising from the sting operation that wrongly implicated a teacher in a non-existent prostitution racket, the Delhi High Court held on 14 December 2007 that any channel planning to broadcast programs involving a sting should be legally obliged to obtain prior permission from a government-appointed committee. It recommended that the Ministry of Information and Broadcasting should appoint a retired judge of a High Court to chair the committee, which should also comprise two others drawn from the bureaucracy.

The judicial intervention, it must be underlined, came well after the offending channel had been ordered off the air by the Ministry. Yet with all this, the grounds on which the Ministry licenses channels are unclear, since the only eligibility criteria specified deal with patterns of equity ownership and the company's net worth (as already mentioned above). The grounds on which the Ministry cancels permissions are even less clear, since the only explanation offered in most cases is a failure to conform to the "broadcast content code" decreed by the Ministry, which is far from being an agreed document...'

CHAPTER

2

TRUTH, FAIRNESS AND OBJECTIVITY

In this chapter, we first demonstrate the centrality of the issue of truth through the example of the life of Gandhi. Then, we consider certain popular theories of what is 'truth', namely, the correspondence, coherence and consensus theories of truth. The conclusion drawn is that common truths derived from the consensus theory comprise a most practical model for discerning truth, as far as the mass media is concerned. Thereafter, the chapter looks at truthfulness and the importance of reason. Falsehood is then considered together with the problems that deception presents to journalism. After that, the criteria for a 'just lie' are laid down. Subsequently, the requirements of, and challenges to, fairness is explored in the context of the media, followed by the notion of objectivity. A more practical notion in journalism is simulated objectivity and impartiality. In conclusion, the chapter examines the notions of truth, fairness and objectivity in the context of the Indian media, outlines the regulatory role of the PCI in this regard and explores some of the tangible positive and negative influences of the media in India.

The objective of this chapter is to explain the ethical complexities of the notions of truth, fairness and objectivity not only from a philosophical angle but also from a practical point of view that would be of relevance to a working journalist. While it is important to appreciate the difficulties in understanding and applying such abstract notions in journalistic practice, these ethical issues cannot be ignored. This chapter argues in favour of a need for moderated and modified versions of these abstract concepts to provide journalists with a set of usable, practical and realizable principles.

WHAT IS TRUTH?

What indeed is truth? Gandhi struggled with this one question throughout his life. Such was the centrality and significance of truth (*satya*) to Gandhi's ideas that he believed that truth was the ultimate goal of all human beings and that it was embodied in all things. Gandhi believed that there was an absolute truth (God), but that he could not understand it directly. He, therefore, sought to inch his way towards absolute truth by grappling with relative truth. Gandhi 'experimented' with truth; and it is interesting for our purposes to note that this experimentation led him to journalism (he founded and was associated with three publications, none of which had large circulations by current standards but which were widely quoted, politically influential and helped shake the might of the British empire). While Gandhi experimented with truth in deed, Western philosophy has attempted to define this difficult concept through some key theories.

Correspondence Theory

The theory of correspondence holds that our notions of what is true and the truth of things are determined by the extent to which they 'correspond' to the reality of things. This theory, which dates back to ancient Greek philosophers, was summarized by Thomas Acquinas in the 13th century as 'truth is the conformity of the intellect to the things'. In this explanation, however, we can see that the theory presupposes the capacity of the intellect to receive objective reality and accurately represent it through expression. Herein lies the fundamental problem with the correspondence theory: what it does not factor in is that all information about the objective world which we receive is interpreted and understood in the light of the rest of our experiences. Therefore, the truth cannot be said to be an absolute representation of reality. Furthermore, as Emmanuel Kant contended, we can only check whether our knowledge of the object agrees with our understanding of the object. This is called 'circular reasoning', which, Kant argued, was in no way sufficient for determining truth. If these are the problems with the accurate interpretation of an objective reality, there are also factors that prevent the absolute accuracy of representation. For example, different languages do not necessarily translate into one another exactly. The Hindu concept of *dharma*, for example, does not have an exact, comprehensive equivalent in English.

Coherence Theory

The coherence theory holds that the truth of something can be determined by the extent to which it 'coheres' with our individual values and world views. Unlike the correspondence theory, the coherence theory does not accept the condition of absolute truth. For example, in the case of reports that statues of Ganesha, the elephant God, were drinking milk or that sea water in Mumbai had turned sweet, people with religious convictions would perceive it as a supernatural occurrence as it coheres with their individual views. A scientist, on the other hand, may believe that it has a rational, and probably provable, cause that is not immediately discernible, as this coheres with her/his particular world view. Here the world views of the religious person and the scientist are, respectively, belief and fact based. A third person, the philosopher Benedictus (or Baruch) Spinoza for example, might interpret such a report as having the capacity to be both true and untrue—depending on the perceiver—but not himself believing the report to be either true or untrue.

The coherence theory, thus, accepts that there are potentially many different and even contradictory truths that are relative and subjective. Gandhi's understanding of (relative) truth fits in with the coherence theory. He suggested that truth is 'being true to ourselves and to the inner light which is our conscience'.

However, there are inherent difficulties with the coherence theory. Although it might satisfy individual definitions of truth it cannot provide a sufficient explanation of general truths. It is, as poet John Donne wrote in the 17th century, 'no man is an island...every man is a piece of the continent, a part of the main'. Donne illustrated the fact that even if society is made up of individuals, these individuals can never be abstracted from society. By this reasoning, 'social norms' carry more weight than individual ones. Furthermore, his theory also falls into the trap of circular reasoning: how could one demonstrate in court, for example, that one was telling the truth, as was concordant with one's own beliefs? And if this could be demonstrated, what value would it have?

Consensus Theory

Consensus gentium, Latin for 'agreement among the people', is an ancient method of determining truth. It holds that something which can be 'affirmed by other people' can be said to be true. Strict consensus theorists require that there must be total consensus about something to render it true. Others, realizing that this would be impossible to measure, moderate the requirements. The problems with the consensus theory are numerous:

- How many people must be surveyed?
- What percentage must agree?
- If ten people interviewed agree, is it sufficient ground for claiming the truth? What if another ten people interviewed all disagree?
- Is a majority opinion sufficient for consensus?
- What if none of the required number of interviewees (once this is determined) agrees with one another and everyone has a different opinion?
- Would what is being tested become true because there was a consensus of 'non-consensus'?
- And if this is the case, what exactly is deemed true? Or would it mean that what is tested has no inherent truth?

Another problem is that for the consensus theory to work, by its own definition, everyone would have to approve of this method. To establish the truth, we must check whether or not everyone agrees and then check whether everyone agrees and this process can continue *ad infinitum.*

There are also extraneous factors which affect the way in which society discerns what truth is. The most important factor is change: change of social values and physical changes in the environment. The certainty of change means that ideas of truth have to be constantly revised. For example, Charles Darwin's theory of evolution undermined the version of the week-long creation of the universe in the Book of Genesis.

Can you think of other examples where the message of an old story, myth or theory should be reconsidered in view of modern scientific or technological developments?

Despite its problems, under the premise of the consensus theory, it is possible to establish some common truths. These may be scientific discoveries, which are proven and generally accepted, or might be, for example, the contention that kindness is accepted as a good quality or attribute and maliciousness as a bad one. These are not substantiated by hard proof but that these are generally and widely accepted renders them truthful by this definition. However, while statements like 'kindness is good' may be logically contended and some individuals may not accept it as an actual truth, it may be understood as true in that it is socially applicable. For example, a journalist may report that 'a person performed an act of kindness for a critically-ill child by donating her/his kidney'. Most people would agree that this was indeed a kind act. Even if some disagree with the notion of organ donation, they might accept that the deed was kind in the generally accepted sense of the word.

TRUTHFULNESS

The different definitions of truth fundamentally grapple with the dichotomy between objectivity and subjectivity. That there are so many different interpretations of truth demonstrates that truth has 'myriad shades and hues' (Bugeja 2008), which, in turn, suggests that truth is not absolute, but is relative and has subjective interpretations.

A more useful notion in journalism, perhaps, is the ethic of 'truthfulness', that is, to present truthfully all information intended for the public. Here the notion of common truths, as demonstrated above, is the most useful method by which journalists can gauge truth, while disseminating information meant for the public.

Truthfulness as a journalistic ethic can be divided into two parts:

1. Determining the veracity of the information that may be reported.
2. The accuracy and honesty with which sourced information is reported.

We shall consider the requirements of sourcing and the need for accuracy and honesty in reporting in Chapter 3 on Sources of Information.

Mind Your Language

As we saw with the correspondence theory, language can often be a barrier to accuracy. This is due to several reasons: for example, limited vocabulary, inexact translation and subjective interpretation. These factors not only challenge accuracy in reporting, but might also result in intended meanings being misconstrued. This would be a likely scenario if we subscribe to the coherence theory of truth.

Language allows humans, as social beings, to label objects which have been identified so that they can be repeatedly recognized and identified by society. However, language presents its own problems and this is one reason why truth must be understood as relative. A good example of language falling short of conveying an absolute truth is in the case of colour. Consider the colour blue: blue, like many other colours, comes in a variety of shades; navy, royal, sky, turquoise and so on. If the generic term 'blue' is used, there is a risk of overlooking potentially significant detail. However, if a more specific word 'turquoise' is used, there could be a greater risk of misinterpretation. Turquoise could be a shade of green for a particular person. The consensus theory of truth would suggest that it is advisable, therefore, to use the simplest language possible both when reporting and when obtaining information to minimize the risk of misinterpretation.

To maintain accuracy, precise language must be used to differentiate opinion or comment from factual reporting. It is important to convey truthfully either comment or fact and ensure that comment is not misconstrued as solid fact. Opinion and fact represent different forms of truth: fact can be determined through the consensus model suggested above, whereas opinion falls into the coherence model. As already emphasized, truths determined under the coherence theory lack general social applicability. Thus, it is necessary to choose words carefully when presenting opinion.

?

Outline the different theories of truth.

Which theory of truthfulness is more relevent for journalists?

What are some pitfalls that language commonly presents?

Words, carelessly chosen, can cause real harm, both to those about whom they pertain to and to the journalist and media organization that disseminates information or comment. Defamation or false claims that are likely to damage a person's reputation or professional endeavours, either spoken (slander) or written (libel), is illegal. This aspect is dealt with in greater detail in Chapter 7 on Media Law. At this point, however, it is worth noting that false claims need not be intentional lies, but can also be errors of fact or of language. So, as a safeguard from potential legal action, it is advisable to choose language which is precise and well considered.

Falsehood

Falsehood haunts the conscience of the professional journalist. The chief form of falsehood faced by journalists is deception. Deception is not a clear-cut issue and is sometimes even a journalistic necessity. The consensus theory used to determine truth can also be used to determine falsehood. Hence, falsehood would be deemed as that which is commonly considered untrue.

Deception can be either active or passive. Active deception includes, for example, lying or purposefully misleading. Passive deception, on the other hand, includes not telling the whole truth—omitting information to create a false or misleading impression or neglecting to correct misinformation or disinformation. It is usually accepted that there are different levels of deception and that not all acts of deception are equally grave. Failing to correct misinformation is arguably less unethical than generating misinformation or disinforming with the intention to mislead or create a false impression. The 'white lie' is the best example of a form of deception which is generally accepted. If you plan a surprise birthday party for a friend and delay his arrival home using some pretence or the other, the deception has been made ostensibly for the other person's benefit. A food critic, for example, acts like an average customer in a restaurant he is assessing. This is a form of passive deception, done to ensure that the food provided and the service experienced is not biased, in order to be able to write a fair review (Retief 2002). The ethical difficulties of deception arise when the potential harm caused is more significant than the benefits enjoyed. This aspect of deception is discussed in Chapter 8 on Sting Operations—an area that involves ethical dilemmas inherent in deception.

Explain different kinds of perception and deception.

What is the difference between misinformation and disinformation?

What are the main ethical objections to presenting fiction as fact?

For journalists, unethical deception cannot reasonably be said to be furthering their objective of serving the public. As we identified earlier, for journalists, serving the public involves disseminating information which then facilitates reason-based ethical decision-making by the people. False information might prevent ethically sound decisions. Deception, such as outright lying, is a temptation in journalism because it saves time in sourcing stories; fictitious stories can be made more 'juicy', can arrest the attention of an audience, and even win acclaim for the journalist (see Box 2.1: *The New York Times* Scandal).

Box 2.1

The New York Times *Scandal*

Here is an edited version of an article by Sucheta Dalal (used with permission from the author) about deception in journalism on her website www.suchetadalal.com (accessed on 5 August 2008).

It is undoubtedly one of the most respected newspapers in the world, and was recently basking in its sweep of the Pulitzer awards. But a couple of weeks ago, *The New York Times*' famous motto—'All the news that's fit to print'—was called into question by its staffer Jayson Blair, who was sacked after several years of serial fabrication of his news reports. Blair's sacking caused as big a media scandal as the discovery that *The Washington Post* writer Janet Cooke had fabricated a human interest story about an eight-year-old drug addict, which won her a Pulitzer in 1981. To its credit, *The New York Times* made a clean breast of the scandal to its readers in a 7,000-word account of Jayson's lies and fabrications. But what is worrying journalists, and is the subject of much discussion, is why Blair was never caught and checked despite innumerable denials and indicators of his mischief.

The question that the media and the readers are asking is: where are the checks and balances? *The New York Times* conducted an investigation into Blair's reports and discovered problems with 36 out of 73 reports filed by Blair (over a period of) eight months. According to *The New York Times*, Blair committed 'widespread fabrication and plagiarism' in articles about the Washington Beltway sniper and the rescue of Army Private Jessica Lynch in Iraq. In April 2002, *The New York Times* did not heed the concerns expressed by its Metro editor Jonathan Landman who had urged (the newspaper's editors) to 'stop Jayson from writing for the *Times*'.

Janet Cooke, too, was apparently a habitual fabricator. She had fibbed about her credentials to land *The Washington Post* job. She had claimed to have graduated from Vassar college, that she attended Sorbonne in Paris, and spoke four languages—all untrue. Ironically, Cooke, who is now 42, has just started an effort to clear her name by appearing on a couple of television shows.

Ethical deception is a contentious area. If an act of deception can be reasonably said to further the public good, it is sometimes deemed ethical. This form of reasoning uses 'consequentialist' ethics: all actions should be judged on the end result and that the end justifies the means. We shall consider this argument and the related utilitarian argument in detail in Chapter 8 on Sting Operations. At this stage, we shall merely consider the criteria for a 'just lie' as formulated in a seminar held by the Poynter Institute for Media Studies in the US (Retief 2002).

Profundity Information sought through deceptive means must be of profound importance to the public, or it must prevent an individual or group from profound harm.

No choice All other straightforward means of ascertaining the information have been attempted, but proven unfruitful.

Disclosure The means, nature and reason for the deception must be disclosed to the public alongside the information.

Commitment Those involved in the deception must approach it with propriety, causing inconvenience or deceiving only where necessary, seeing the endeavour through until the end and producing a comprehensive report at the end which is of discernible value to the public.

Consideration Deception should only be practised after those involved have carefully weighed the following:

- Consequences (short and long term) of the deception on those being deceived
- Legal implications
- Editorial mission in relation to the act of deception
- Reasons or motivation for their actions
- Impact on journalistic credibility
- Consistency of their reasoning and their action

Here it is important to remember the acronym CLERIC.

FAIRNESS

Fairness is an important journalistic ethic and is expected of all journalists. Below are some guidelines which, if followed, can help promote fairness in reporting (Retief 2002):

Language The choice of language should be carefully considered. Words can have more than one meaning, and meanings can change in different contexts. Language is the means by which we can represent information or ideas.

Context This is of utmost importance for ensuring that the information reported will be properly construed. Neglecting to relate the context of an event is a form of deception as it will mislead an audience, and this is unfair because the citizenry deserve to be accurately informed.

The* Rashomon *Effect This is named after a Japanese film, directed by the internationally renowned Akira Kurosawa in 1951, which explores the differing accounts of people involved in the same event. Everybody interprets things differently, in accordance with their own perspective (refer to the coherence theory of truth). Therefore, it is possible that two eyewitnesses may offer significantly varying accounts of the same event. It would be unfair to give one side of the story greater coverage as that would suggest partiality.

Balance Realizing that the truth is not black and white, a reporter should try to address as many aspects of a story as possible. This will help establish the common truth and also provide a more comprehensive and, therefore, a more valuable context.

The British Broadcasting Corporation (BBC) stresses the importance of fairness in its Producers' Guidelines of 1996. 'BBC programmes should be based on fairness... Programmes, therefore, must have clearly defined objectives which are made known to all contributors so that they can be aware of what they are contributing to, and what will be required of them. It is of equal importance to treat an audience fairly: by broadcasting accurate and tasteful material...'

Despite these rigorous guidelines about fairness, in 2007, the BBC got into serious trouble with Ofcom or the Office of Communications (the independent regulator and competition authority for the communications industries of the UK, with responsibilities across television, radio, telecommunications and wireless communications services) on more than one occasion for failing to uphold these standards. An advertisement for a documentary on the Queen of England was edited in such a way that it portrayed the Queen leaving a photo shoot in indignation after being asked to remove her crown (www.abc.net.au, 12 July 2007). After official complaints, it was made public that the BBC had intentionally distorted the event. The intention would have been to increase interest in the programme, but at the cost of making a mockery of the Queen in the eyes of the public. It also came to light that several programmes, featuring phone-in competitions, had been rigged and entries accepted after the competitions had closed. In one case, a member of the production crew had even posed as a winner. These instances seriously questioned the integrity and credibility of the BBC in the eyes of the public.

Challenges to Fairness

Being fair, however, is not a simple matter. Although, all citizens are awarded equal rights in the eyes of the law, social equality is far from reality —certainly in a country like India. In society, it usually turns out that freedom (in all its various forms) is most readily enjoyed by some while it is an unattainable luxury for others. As media organizations are being increasingly driven by market forces, fair and independent journalism becomes difficult. We consider the implications of market pressures in depth in Chapter 6 on Media Market and also in Chapters 10 and 11 on the ethics of Public Relations and Advertising.

There is another problem in determining the exact requirements of fairness. Does fairness mean equality and therefore require that everybody should be treated equally and as equals? Does this mean, however, that differently abled people should not be given any special provisions? Usually, fairness and equality mean giving everyone equal opportunities. For journalists, the issue of fairness arises while selecting a story, addressing sources, seeking a variety of sources and in presenting a report that is fair to both those reported about and those for whom the report is intended.

Another challenge to fairness is that different people have different requirements at different points in time: what is fair to the public at large might not be fair to the subjects of a news story; what is fair to a subject of a story might not be satisfactory for the public; and what is fair to stakeholders (investors and advertisers) might not be fair to editors or journalists. There are many aspects of fairness in journalism because there are so many different groups involved in media activities. John Parry, editor of *News Tribune* of Rome (Georgia, US), has advised his staff to 'forget fair'. He feels that because fairness is almost impossible to achieve, it is not worth pursuing a fool's errand. Parry demonstrates the stalemate of seeking fairness by a real-life example. Two men forced a woman, working a night-shift in a convenience store in Rome, to hand over the cash from the till and then raped her. A news report on the incident carried the name and location of the convenience store but did not mention the victim's name. A store representative complained that it was unfair to disclose the details of the store because the identity of the victim could then be inferred. Parry concludes that, by these limitations, 'the only way the story could have been written to satisfy this complainant, was "A woman was raped last night someplace here…".' (Retief 2002).

Do you agree with John Parry? Can you think of any other way of giving information that would not jeopardize the rape victim's wish to remain anonymous?

Parry's argument could be seen as a reactionary conclusion. We could justify the complainant's accusation of unfairness as the newspaper, apparently being committed to the protection of the victim's identity, nonetheless, provided sufficient information for the victim's identity to be inferred.

Thus, maintaining a fair balance has its problems. What the journalist needs to ask are the following kinds of questions. Am I being fair to the right person or the right section of people? Am I being fair to the underprivileged or the marginalized? The manner in which journalists choose to highlight certain facts in a story and omit certain other facts could determine their bias. In such cases, journalists should be able to justify their bias as being in the bigger interest of the public.

The 'other side' of the story should be considered for several reasons: it will contribute to a comprehensive context; it is unfair or discriminatory to favour one side of the story either through more coverage, or through subjective representation of one side. The media cannot be the judge of issues such as whether or not a crime has been committed, whether or not the judiciary will pronounce judgement and whether or not specific individuals are innocent until proven guilty. The media is not always meant to act like a moral police force.

However, journalists cannot treat all sides of all stories equally and fairly. In a case of genocide through terrorist activity, motivated by religious belief, it may be necessary to present the point of view of the terrorists. A certain amount of understanding of the motivations of the terrorists might have real, discernible value to the public. However, excessive preoccupation with the terrorists' perspective may not be considered desirable as far as the general public is concerned.

Another problem with trying to achieve balance in a crime story is the risk of 'normalizing' the crime (Mindich 1998). If the perspectives of perpetrators of crimes are presented in a news report, there is a danger that their motivations might seem almost reasonable and even justifiable. Thus, the more familiar we become with the motivations behind the crimes the more likely we could become accustomed to it. Hence, the crime becomes 'normalized'.

OBJECTIVITY

'Objectivity' is not the same as being 'objective'. Being objective requires a person 'to see the world as it really is' by shedding the shackles of subjective interpretation. It is, of course, not possible for average mortals to view the world except through their own eyes and perspectives. Earlier in this chapter, the example of colours was mentioned to demonstrate the different perceptions of different people. Most of the time, people verify information about the world by means of consensus. This is to help establish common understandings to facilitate harmony in society—but this is not a substitute or a remedy for the fact that everyone ultimately experiences the world through their own subjective perspective.

If being objective in its purest sense is not possible, then we can at least 'simulate' objectivity (see Box 2.2: The ABC of quality journalese). This objectivity might be a relative version of objectivity—or an 'accepted level' of objectivity, given that pure objectivity is theoretically unattainable. We can attempt to arrive at this relative objectivity by approaching an issue with reason, leaving aside our own personal likes and dislikes. In other words, this moderated form of objectivity might be understood as impartiality. Impartiality means to remain unbiased, to leave aside personal (highly subjective) feelings or opinions. No journalist can be expected to be completely impartial as everybody has particular preferences. But, the responsibility of being impartial requires that personal preferences be kept absent to the extent possible in journalistic endeavours.

The BBC, for instance, asks for 'due impartiality' from its journalistic staff. That the BBC qualifies this ethic shows that determining a moderate degree of impartiality has the most practical value. In this context, 'due' is understood as 'adequate or appropriate to the nature of the subject and the type of programme, (Producers' Guidelines, 1996).

Box 2.2

The ABC of Quality Journalese

The following principles should be followed as closely as possible while sourcing and reporting to create a quality of journalism that fits in with general social standards (of simulated objectivity)

Accuracy
Balance
Context

Simulating Objectivity

An objective report can be presented if fairness and accuracy are weighted according to their relative importance. The more comprehensive the account, the less subjective it will be. However, not being subjective is not the same as achieving objectivity. Reporting a variety of sources will still be subjective as everybody's versions or ideas are equally subjective. However, if objectivity is presenting the unequivocal truth of a matter, it can be achieved by applying the 'consensus' model of truth. In Chapter 3 on Sources of Information, a fictional case study is provided to elaborate on this aspect of reporting.

TRUTH, FAIRNESS AND OBJECTIVITY IN THE INDIAN MEDIA SCENARIO

In a speech delivered on 16 November 2006 Justice G.N. Ray, chairman, PCI, elaborated on what he felt were some of the basic tenets of quality journalism. He said: 'By objectivity, I mean that reporting of facts should be free from any distortion or exaggeration. Very often facts are distorted to suit a particular form of opinion or sometimes the facts are blown out of proportion. There should be distinct separation between news and views. The reporter must avoid conflicts of interest and the competing points of view should be balanced and fairly characterized. Reporting stories should be free from the reporter's personal, economic or political interests. A reporter has to pay attention to accurate attribution of statements made by individuals and other news media. Pictures, sound and quotations must not be presented in a misleading context and simulation, re-enactments, alterations and artistic imaginings must be labelled as such and plagiarism must be strongly stigmatized.

'Reporting the truth is not libel and in the normal course of an assignment, a reporter is free to go about gathering facts and details, conducting interviews, doing research, background checks, taking photos, taping, recording of sound, etc. He has to, however, keep in mind the principle of limitation of harm, which means that there is a need for giving proper weight to the negative consequences of full disclosure, creating a practical and ethical dilemma.'

Press and media councils have been formed around the world to protect and ensure that the basic tenets of journalistic ethics and morality and public welfare are upheld. As a regulatory body for the print medium, the PCI serves a dual constitutional purpose. First, it protects the freedom of the press and independence of the newspapers and news agencies not only from government authorities but also from other external and internal interests and forces. Second, the existence of such a mechanism prevents legal restrictions being placed on the press by the government. The PCI also discharges its advisory jurisdiction by giving opinions to the government and other bodies on various questions related to the working of the mass media. It has the power to decide on complaints made by individuals and public authorities against print media organizations and media personnel. The PCI, however, has no jurisdiction over the non-print mass media including radio and television.

In India, to promote fair journalism, some news organizations (like the publishers of *The Hindu*) have adopted the system of appointing an internal ombudsman. Such an editorial ombudsman is an independent (usually senior) person who ascertains whether the grievances of readers, listeners and viewers are genuine and, if required, need redressing. An ombudsman is not merely meant to take an impartial view of complaints made by the constituents of a media organization; on occasion, ombudsmen have the power and authority to initiate corrective action, including the imposition of penalties on errant employees or contributors to media houses. This is one way in which media organizations keep themselves honest and accountable to the public. This type of self-regulation is an effort to mediate conflicts stemming from internal and external pressures and to maintain accountability to the public for news reported.

In India, the existence of the mass media has had both positive and negative effects as far as truth, fairness and objectivity are concerned, as demonstrated by the following examples.

The media played a positive role in the criminal cases related to the unnatural deaths of Jessica Lall, Priyadarshini Mattoo, Nitish Katara, Satyendra Dubey and Shanmughan Manjunath, to name only five instances. All these individuals were murdered—the last two were considered 'whistle-blowers' who exposed corruption in high places—and the wide coverage given to the investigations of the crimes by the mass media assisted greatly in the administration and delivery of justice. In the cases of Lall, Mattoo and Katara, those held responsible for their murders were influential people—two were sons of prominent politicians while the other was the son of a senior police officer. The following are brief accounts of some cases.

Nitish Katara, a young business executive, was murdered in February 2002 by Vikas Yadav, son of politician D.P. Yadav, against whom several criminal cases had been instituted. Nitish had fallen in love with Vikas's sister Bharti and his murder was considered an 'honour killing' since the Yadav family did not approve of their relationship. In May 2008, Vikas and his cousin Vishal were found guilty of Nitish's murder by a trial court and sentenced to life imprisonment. It was alleged that during the trial, threats and monetary allurements were used to influence witnesses including certain persons who were close to Nitish and Bharti who went back on their original testimonies before the police. Many believe that the intense media scrutiny of the case helped bring about convictions for the accused on the strength of the evidence that existed.

Priyadarshini Mattoo was a twenty-five-year-old law student when she was found raped and murdered at her residence in New Delhi in January 1996. More than a decade later, in October 2006, the Delhi High Court held Santosh Kumar Singh, son of a senior police officer of the rank of inspector general, guilty on counts of both rape and murder and he was sentenced to death. In 1999, a trial court had acquitted him of the charges. The reversal of the verdict is often held as an example of how widespread reportage by the media not only helped accelerate the trial but also ensured that the criminal justice system worked against the son of an influential individual—that the law was really above every person. Santosh Singh appealed to the Supreme Court in February 2007 against the death sentence and his lawyers are expected to argue, among other things, that excessive media coverage and a 'trial by media' influenced the verdict against him.

Jessica Lall was a New Delhi-based model who was shot dead in April 1999 at a party where she was a barmaid. A number of witnesses stated that her killer was Manu Sharma, son of Venod Sharma, a politician from Haryana who was also a minister in the state government. The trial that ensued dragged on for seven years and at different points in time, the police as well as the lower judiciary were accused of conducting the proceedings for prosecution in a deliberately shoddy manner. After intense media attention, the Delhi High Court expedited the trial, held Manu Sharma guilty and sentenced him to life imprisonment in December 2006.

The media in India has also extensively highlighted recent instances of the murders of two 'whistle-blowers' who fought against corruption. One was Satyendra Kumar Dubey, project director, National Highways Authority of India, who was killed in November 2003 near Gaya, Bihar, for opposing corrupt contractors. He had even written to the then Prime Minister Atal Bihari Vajpayee in this connection to check financial irregularities in road construction. The other was Shanmughan Manjunath, a marketing engineer for Indian Oil Corporation, who was murdered in November 2005 for sealing a petrol pump at Lakhimpur Kheri, Uttar Pradesh, after he found it selling adulterated fuel. After considerable media attention on these two murders, the government contemplated a new law to protect 'whistle-blowers' who sought to expose corruption in the organizations they worked for. Such a law is, however, yet to be enacted.

Though the media's role is often positive, this is not always the case. An instance of the negative effect of the mass media was the public attack (by lawyers, among others) on Moninder Singh Pandher, one of the prime accused in the Nithari serial killings, while he was in police custody. (Nithari is a locality in the outskirts of Delhi.) This incident was perceived as an example of vigilantism, an instance of members of the public taking the law in their own hands. For weeks before the incident, television channels had repeatedly broadcast scenes of the Nithari crimes, of the relatives of the distraught victims crying and visuals of members of the public attacking the property of the suspects in the crimes. Media watchers felt that these emotive images had sufficient potential to induce rage and hatred in members of the public, including lawyers, who assaulted Pandher inside the premises of a court.

Delhi teacher Uma Khurana had to suffer public indignation when her clothes were torn off her body in front of television cameras, ostensibly by irate members of the public, after a television channel (*Live India*) conducted a fraudulent 'sting' operation on her and alleged that she had enticed her students into commercial sex work. She was also removed from her job. The journalist who conducted the so-called sting operation (Prakash Singh) was subsequently arrested when it was found that he and his accomplice had distorted the report. Details of this case have been given in Chapter 8 on Sting Operations.

Gobind Thukral states (*The Tribune*, 14 April 2002) that the coverage of the 2002 communal riots in Gujarat by the print and the electronic media attracted considerable attention. The issue became so important that the Editors Guild of India rushed a team of senior journalists to make an on-the-spot assessment and suggest corrective measures. While the team found certain local Gujarati-language newspapers partly responsible for sowing the seeds of discord between the majority Hindus and the minority Muslims and thereby helping the communal virus to spread, it had good words for the national press and major television networks.

Thukral points out, 'With television presenting instant powerful images, the role of the media has assumed greater significance. News is shown as it happens. But the media can colour the events by using them or by not using them at all. By being selective, it often misinforms and acts as a propaganda tool. What gives the media a complex dimension is the daily exposure of multiple items in juxtaposition. Nevertheless, the media remains a major source of information, particularly in a violent situation. How did the local press present the riots to the readers? Has the print media in any way aggravated the relentless tensions through inflammatory or communal reportage? These questions bother all right thinking people...

The most horrific acts of violence were repeatedly sensationalized with the use of a few devices. For example, large bold letters were used as headlines particularly when referring to gruesome acts like the burning alive of people. Photographs of burnt, mangled bodies were a common feature on the front page or the last page which usually carries local news. Most colour photos have the colour of red for blood accentuated in a gory, visual fashion. Alternatively, photographs of militant, *trishul*–wielding *karsevaks* were splashed across the front page. Both kinds of photographs serve to instill fear or terror and to provoke intense passions and mutual hostility between the two communities...

Similarly, the reports of *Gujarat Samachar* (Vadodara) did not give the sources of information in its reports. For instance, the front-page report on 6 March 2002 was apparently based on a conversation the reporter had with the Railway Police Force personnel. The way these reports have been presented is questionable. This is the day when the top story on the last page is about how gradually the situation is returning to normalcy. A report on March 16 describes incidents in Machchhipith as if Muslims were the culprits. The report "Private firing on *Rambhakts*" described the whole incident as pre-planned. Nowhere has it mentioned if the *Ram Dhun* procession was taken out with the police permission and what were the conditions laid out by the police for taking out such a procession. The role played by the mob in the procession was not mentioned. In a Sunday supplement, an article by Bhalchandra Jani justified the demand for Ram Janmabhoomi temple...'

The above examples highlight the need for sections of the mass media in India to be scrutinized periodically, even though the world's largest democracy needs a free and independent 'fourth estate' for strengthening its institutions. If the mass media cannot uphold the tenets of truth, fairness and objectivity, then it has failed in its task to be the eyes and ears of the public.

SUMMARY

In this chapter, we have explored different theories of the concept of 'truth'. We have suggested that the notion of common truths and truthfulness is arguably the most practical of the ethical guidelines for practicing journalists. We should understand the importance of truth and its facets, accuracy and honesty, in the context of the working of the mass media. We should be aware of the problems associated with falsehood and deception in journalism and understand the criteria necessary to justify deception. It is possible for journalists to achieve fairness in spite of some of the challenges to fairness.

We have also considered objectivity in this chapter and found that it is often not a practical concept in its purest sense. It has, therefore, been suggested that the notion of 'simulated objectivity' be understood to be achieved. Finally, we should understand some of the positive and negative aspects of the Indian media considered in this chapter. Overall, we should be familiar with the difficulties in understanding and applying abstract notions such as truth, fairness and objectivity in journalistic practice and understand the need for moderated and modified versions of these concepts to provide journalism with usable, practical and realizable principles.

REVIEW QUESTIONS

1. What do you understand by the correspondence, coherence and consensus theories of truth?
2. What do you understand by common truths and do you think it is an appropriate method for determining journalistic principles?
3. Why is knowledge necessary for ethical social behaviour?
4. What are the major forms of deception in journalism and why are they practised?
5. What is an unethical lie?
6. What are the criteria for a 'just lie'?
7. What qualities constitute fairness in journalism?
8. What are the main challenges to fairness?
9. What are the benefits and problems of presenting the 'other side' of the story?
10. What is simulated objectivity?

11. What is the ABC of quality journalism?
12. Enumerate some of the positive and negative aspects of the working of the Indian media.

DEBATE

1. Objectivity is a myth and it therefore cannot reasonably be demanded of journalists.
2. Everybody should be treated absolutely equally all the time.

CASE STUDY

Tehelka's Rahul Gandhi Interview

In September 2005, *Tehelka* weekly published an interview of Rahul Gandhi with its senior writer, Vijay Simha, describing the story as Rahul Gandhi's 'first major interview'. The introduction to the interview read: 'I could have been PM at the age of 25 if I wanted to. But I decided I wouldn't do things in that fashion. I wouldn't go around yelling at my seniors.' The story triggered a major political controversy and raised several questions about the nature of journalistic ethics.

In the course of the interview, Rahul had reportedly remarked that there was no trace of governance in a centrally ruled, poll-bound state, Uttar Pradesh. This created a political storm and questions were raised whether the Congress president agreed with her son, since the party heading the state government (Samajwadi Party) had been supporting the Congress.

The Congress sought to end the controversy on the remarks attributed to Rahul, saying that the write-up projected as an interview contained several misrepresentations and that it arose from a casual conversation. A party spokesman said, 'Rahul would like to categorically state and reiterate that in this "so-called interview" he never said that he could have been prime minister at the young age of 25. This and numerous other things have been incorrectly reported and are being refuted outright.' The statement also described as a pity that other parties were politicizing the issue.

The weekly initially stood by its reporter and the story, stating that the interview had been formal. The media storm and the political controversy became too big and it issued a second statement apologizing for any misunderstanding caused. It termed the issue as a clear case of misunderstanding and said any errors in it are inadvertent and regretted, superseding its dismissal of the party's claim that no interview took place. It also criticized the attempts made by other political parties to stir up a controversy and put out an edited version of the interview on its website, dropping the contentious part about 'I could have been PM at the age of 25 if I wanted to...' It also changed the headline to: 'If I am to be a complete politician, I think I must lose a couple of elections. I can't be a good politician if I don't lose elections. I am not afraid of losing. That is part of life.'

Many journalists criticized both the party and the weekly for the controversy. The senior writer in question, Simha, maintains that it was a formal interview and that Rahul Gandhi had made those statements. And as he had not been allowed to record the interview, he had written the story from memory and random notes and did not have proof of the authenticity of the interview.

Here are some ethical questions that plagued Simha during the incident, which have been specially written by him for this book:

1. **Should I have told Rahul Gandhi that I would return to my office in New Delhi and send across a formal request for an interview with him?**

   We bonded from the time we started talking and an hour passed by without our noticing. I think it would have been a bad idea to call the conversation off. If I had returned to office and made a request for a formal interview with him, the chances were high that the request would have been politely declined.

2. **Should I have agreed to his request not to record the conversation?**

   Tricky. My instincts as a reporter told me to go ahead and record it anyway. I had the skills to do so covertly. But, my conscience told me not to. He had placed his faith and trust in me and asked me not to record the conversation.

3. **Should I have gone ahead and recorded the hour-long conversation secretly?**

   At no stage did the thought enter my mind. I believe I should not have recorded the conversation covertly and I did not.

4. **Should I have relied on my notes and my memory in an unexpected situation that was potentially a defining period in my professional life?**

   Logically, I should not have. But I had to make a decision in a second or two. I chose to rely on my notes and my memory.

5. **Should I have called the interview off and risked the possibility that I would meet him again, later, perhaps with a photographer to record the event?**

   The thought did not cross my mind.

6. **I asked him thirty-plus questions over an hour-long chat. Did they constitute a casual conversation or a formal interview?**

   Our conversation was not a casual one, by any standards.

7. **At the end of our conversation, he had turned to me and said that he had done it because it would 'help' the weekly. Should I have taken his words as evidence that he had agreed to the interview being published?**

   I interpreted his words as an approval or a clearance to publish the interview. His concluding remarks to me were among the first things I reported when I spoke to the editor-in-chief of the weekly.

8. **Should the weekly have issued the second statement under pressure, after initially standing by the story?**

   No. The ethics of journalism demand that an editor stand by his reporters under any circumstances, especially if the facts are correct. The justification given by the editor-in-chief to the staffers was that he couldn't fight every battle. He mentioned that there were grey areas, and that he had to take a decision under severe pressure. He also mentioned that the government had still not disposed of cases filed against the organization publishing the weekly by the previous government.

9. **Should the weekly have edited the web version of the interview, which is therefore at variance with the printed version?**

   No. The ethics of journalism demand that the same version be available to all readers. Also, altering content under pressure is contrary to the ethics of journalism. Should such a step be inevitable, a disclaimer should have been made available with the altered content stating that some portions of the text had been edited or modified.

10. **Should the weekly have sent the interview to Rahul Gandhi for confirmation before printing?**

    Yes. This would've sorted everything out. In India, this is often not done, but in other countries there is a practice to confirm all quotes before they are published. If I had sent across the content before it was printed, he may not have agreed to its publication, or he may have modified some of the content, or he may not have done so. In any of these situations, there would not have been a controversy on the authenticity of the interview.

REFERENCES

'BBC sorry for misrepresenting Queen,' www.abc.net.au, 12 July 2007.

Bugeja, Michael 2008, *Living Ethics*, Oxford University Press, New York, US.

Hirst, Martin and Roger Patching 2007, *Journalism Ethics: Arguments & Cases*, Oxford University Press, South Melbourne, Australia.

Mindich, David T.Z. ,1998, *Just the Facts: How "Objectivity" Came to Define American Journalism*, New York University Press, New York, U.S.

Retief, Johan 2002, *Media Ethics: An Introduction to Responsible Journalism,* Oxford University Press, Cape Town, South Africa.

Richards, Ian 2006, *Exploring Journalism Ethics: Quagmires and Quandaries,* Anmol Publications Pvt Ltd, New Delhi, India.

Thukral, Gobind 2002, 'Reporting Gujarat: How Objective was Media Coverage?' *The Tribune.*

CHAPTER

3

SOURCES OF INFORMATION

This chapter first looks at the development of the codes of media ethics and considers some of the main duties and responsibilities of journalists. The key ethical issues are examined in a practical context. Thereafter, particular requirements of sensitivity and how the media should act in specific contexts are examined. The objective of this chapter is to explain to journalists how they should deal with sourcing of information in different reporting situations, including situations in which the feelings and sensibilities of particular individuals or organizations could be adversely affected, sometimes inadvertently.

A democracy is successful when public opinion is shaped in an informed manner. The proliferation of newspapers, radio and television has made it possible for more people to become relatively well informed about issues and events in the society. In fact, the mass media can serve as a vital link between the people and those in power and authority at various levels to ensure responsive governance. However, the media's role in shaping public opinion depends on its credibility and acceptability.

There is growing concern about the credibility of the media. A Gallup poll, conducted in December 2000 in the US, asked the following question: 'In general, do you think news organizations get the facts straight, or do you think that their stories are often inaccurate?' Only 32 per cent of the respondents believed that the media get their facts right and 65 per cent thought that the media was often not accurate (Retief 2002). The same question, asked two years earlier, yielded more encouraging results, suggesting that the people's faith in the media had declined.

HISTORICAL CONTEXT

The need to distinguish between fact and fiction has for long been identified as an important ethical issue. Daniel Defoe's *Robinson Crusoe*, published in the early 18th century, considered to be among the first novels written in the English language, tells the story about a man marooned on a deserted island. Defoe wrote the novel after he was inspired by a story recounted to him by the captain of a ship. The author did not hide the fact that Crusoe's story was largely a figment of his imagination although his publisher marketed the book as a work of 'fact'. For publishers today, taking such liberties could prove disastrous.

Since the 1940s, the US, Canada and countries in Western Europe have emphasized the social responsibility shouldered by the media. In 1942, Henry Luce, founder of *Time* magazine, asked his former classmate from the University of Yale, Robert Hutchins, to head a panel at a time when there was growing concern in the US that irresponsible journalism might lead to government intervention. The seminal report of the Hutchins Commission entitled *A Free and Responsible Press* argued that the media should act like a public trust—that is, owned by the people. In this way, the media may serve democracy. The report asked the press to improve itself in the name of morality, democracy and self-preservation.

In India, the right to freedom of expression is provided in Article 19 of the Constitution and freedom of the press is inferred from the same, as there is no explicit mention of freedom of the media in the Constitution. Freedom of the media can be understood as the right to source and report news and other information which can be reasonably said to be in the public interest. As we shall see in Chapter 7 on Media Laws, no rights are absolute, and each right is subject to conditions. Similarly, the media is restricted in its right to source and report, both through legal and self-regulatory provisions.

The mass media has a vital role to play in the implementation of the fundamental objectives in the Indian Constitution, namely, democracy, secularism, national unity and integrity, and the rule of law. The underlying purpose of the media is to assist in the process of resolving social, political, economic and other problems by presenting all the evidence and opinions to enable the public to arrive at conclusions or even take decisions. To fulfil this important role in a democracy, the media needs to be free and independent from the control of government bodies, corporates, advertisers and political parties. It's the media's duty to keep the government and other powerful sections of the society from abusing their discretionary powers. India's first Prime Minister, Jawaharlal Nehru, had declared: 'I would rather have a completely free press with all the dangers involved in the wrong use of that freedom, than a suppressed or regulated press'.

DUTY AND INFLUENCE

Gandhi said: 'The newspaper press is a great power, but just as an unchained torrent of water submerges the whole countryside and devastates crops, even so an uncontrolled pen serves but to destroy. If the control is from without, it proves more poisonous than want of control. It can be profitable only when exercised from within.'

Gandhi's apprehensions about an unregulated media are based on the influence it possesses. There is wide acceptability of the idea that the media is responsible to its constituents (readers, listeners and viewers), that is, to citizens at large. As professionals, journalists are supposed to embody the roles of watchdogs and educators. To fulfil these roles, journalists need to:

- ensure accuracy while reporting a story
- remain free from bias as far as possible
- resist censorship and marginalization of public interest
- include minority and dissenting viewpoints

The mass media exercises power and influence in three crucial ways. First, it has the freedom to decide what to report and how to report it. Second, the very existence of the media implies that centres of power, like the government, are being watched and monitored and will be held accountable to the people. Third, in presenting conflicting opinions, the media creates a forum of open debate and discussion that assists individuals to make up their minds, resolve issues and arrive at conclusions on issues of social importance.

Journalists and other media personnel are obliged to act in accordance with the law and are assigned responsibilities that are derived from the law (not to be libellous, not to defame or plagiarize and so on) and with the policies of their news organizations. Contracted responsibilities or individual responsibility to the news organizations are explicitly and formally defined. However, the responsibilities of a journalist to her/his constituents, readers or audience are less explicit and the onus lies with individual journalists to inform the public accurately. There are certain standards of journalism that are universally recognized and these help journalists regulate their professional conduct. These include:

- Fairness
- Accuracy and truthfulness
- Objectivity
- Sobriety
- Decency
- Confidentiality

PRESS COUNCIL OF INDIA AND CODES OF CONDUCT

The PCI was established to preserve the freedom of the press and to maintain and improve the standards of newspapers and news agencies in India. The PCI helps newspapers and news agencies maintain their independence while having a general code of conduct for journalists. The aim of the code is to ensure high professional standards and foster a sense of the rights and responsibilities of journalists as well as ordinary citizens. The PCI has, over the years, framed a code of ethics for journalists and governs their conduct.

CASE STUDY

Let us consider an example to explain different facets of the code of conduct.

A Blueline bus in New Delhi has accidentally killed a five-year-old child called Monu playing on the streets. The child's parents live in a nearby slum and work as labourers on construction sites. While the driver of the bus has absconded, a mob of local people beat the conductor unconscious. He has been admitted to a hospital. The mob then burns down the bus.

Different reports of the above incident are considered to highlight the different prescriptions of the code of conduct.

Accuracy

One of the key requirements of any news report in the mass media is accuracy. This means that the information should be presented in a correct context and without distortion, exaggeration, material omissions or excessive summarization. Following are the reasons why inaccurate reporting must be avoided at all costs.

(a) It can cause irreparable personal harm to the person or persons featuring in the news report.

(b) It can prevent the general public from making informed decisions (from investing in securities to voting for a particular candidate).

(c) It could adversely affect the journalist concerned and her or his media organization's integrity as well as credibility.

Box 3.1

Blueline Mows Down Seven-year-old Monu

(ABC Agency) NEW DELHI: Delhi's dreaded Blueline bus claimed one more life on Wednesday, taking the number of accidental deaths by Blueline buses to 40. The police have identified the deceased as Monu (7). While the bus driver in the fatal accident managed to escape, the conductor was beaten unconscious by a local mob.

According to the police, the victim, 7-year-old Monu Singh, lived in the nearby slum with his parents and other siblings. Around 1:15 p.m. on Wednesday, while Monu's mother was waiting for a bus, Monu managed to free himself from his mother's lap and ran on to the street. He was hit by a Blueline bus, route number 355, plying between Anand Parbat and Noida. The driver, identified as Bunty, fled from the spot. However, the conductor of the bus, Lucky, was beaten by an irate mob. He was taken to the hospital after a passer-by informed the police about the accident.

Monu was one among three siblings. His elder sister Puja (12) and younger brother Sonu (4) were at home.

While condoling with the parents, Delhi's Chief Minister Smt. Sheila Dikshit expressed concern over the rising death toll from road accidents.

Box 3.1 is an example of inaccurate reporting. The reporter got the child's age wrong and also reported inaccurately about Monu's mother waiting at the bus stop. She was actually at a construction site. His sister Puja was in charge of her siblings.

Avoiding error

Every journalist needs to check facts carefully. When there are reasons to doubt the accuracy of a piece of information, it should be verified. If verification is not possible, this should be mentioned in the report. Inaccurate reporting must be corrected promptly (with an apology if required) and with appropriate prominence. The public has a right to expect quality work from journalists; the people have a right to be served by honest journalists. While the media has the right to comment and criticize, it must avoid the expression of comment and conjecture as fact and falsification by distortion, selection or misrepresentation. A comment should be an honest expression of opinion, without malice or dishonest motives and should be made after a fair and balanced account of all available facts.

The PCI states: 'The press shall eschew publication of inaccurate, baseless, graceless, misleading or distorted material. All sides of the core issue or subject should be reported. Unjustified rumours and surmises should not be set forth as facts.'

It adds: 'On receipt of a report or article of public interest and benefit containing imputations or comments against a citizen, the editor should check with due care and attention its factual accuracy—apart from other authentic sources—with the person or the organization concerned to elicit her/his or its version, comments or reaction and publish the same with due amendments in the report where necessary. In the event of lack or absence of response, a footnote to that effect should be appended to the report.'

Truthfulness

News must be reported truthfully and all the relevant information should be obtained in an honest and straightforward manner. There may be certain circumstances which necessitate covert action to obtain information in public interest, and this will be explored in a later chapter. Truthfulness is the 'spirit of sincerity and transparency'. All media personnel need to collect and disseminate information truthfully to the best of their knowledge and ability. When there are lapses in truthfulness, the repercussions outlined in the section on Accuracy may ensue.

Box 3.2

Blueline Kills Seven-year-old Monu

XYZ Sharma NEW DELHI: Delhi's killer Blueline bus claimed one more life on Wednesday, taking the number of accidental deaths by Blueline buses to 40. The police have identified the deceased as Monu (7). While the bus driver in the fatal accident managed to escape, the conductor was beaten unconscious by a local mob.

According to the police, the victim, 7-year-old Monu Singh, lived in the nearby slum with his parents and other siblings. Around 1:15 p.m. on Wednesday, while Monu's mother was waiting for a bus, Monu managed to free himself from his mother's lap and ran into the street. He was hit by a Blueline bus, route number 355, plying between Anand Parbat and Noida. The driver, identified as Bunty, fled from the spot. However, the conductor of the bus, Lucky, was beaten by an irate mob. He was taken to the hospital after a passer-by informed the police about the accident.

Monu was one among three siblings. His elder sister Puja (12) and younger brother Sonu (4) were at home.

While condoling with the parents, Delhi's Chief Minister Smt. Sheila Dikshit expressed concern over the rising death toll from road accidents.

The report in Box 3.2 is almost a copy of the previous report (by ABC Agency) which means that this reporter (XYZ Sharma) is guilty of plagiarism. Instead of verifying the facts, the reporter merely rehashed an article put out by a news agency under her or his name without giving the original source of information due credit.

Maintaining truthfulness

To avoid plagiarism and to protect the spirit of sincerity and transparency, every piece of information should be attributed to its source. Furthermore, it is imperative for journalists to obtain permission from an individual or corporation to use their material. In the event of misrepresentation or error, the publication should immediately publish a correction with due prominence and offer an apology where necessary (see Appendix).

Fairness

To be fair, a report must be balanced and free from bias or undue emphasis or omission of relevant information. The desire and right of the media's constituents to be presented with a balanced argument should be heeded. Furthermore, the journalist's influence in shaping public opinion and her/his responsibility therein must be kept in mind.

Box 3.3

Blueline Responsible for Death of Five-year-old Monu

DEF Agency NEW DELHI: Delhi's killer Blueline bus claimed one more life on Wednesday, taking the number of accidental deaths by Blueline buses to 40. The police have identified the deceased as Monu (5). While the bus driver, in the fatal accident, managed to escape, the conductor was beaten unconscious by a local mob. He was later taken to the hospital by the police. The mob also burnt down the bus.

According to the police, the victim, 5-year-old Monu Singh, lived in the nearby slum with his parents and other siblings. Around 1:15 p.m. on Wednesday, while playing on the street, Monu was hit by a Blueline bus, route number 355, plying between Anand Parbat and Noida. The driver, identified as Bunty, fled from the spot. However, the conductor of the bus, Lucky, was beaten by an irate mob. He was taken to the hospital after a passer-by informed the police about the accident.

At the time of the accident, Monu was under no supervision. He was frequently left on his own by his parents. While condoling with the parents, Delhi's Chief Minister Smt. Sheila Dikshit expressed concern over the rising death toll from road accidents.

The report in Box 3.3 only gives one side of the picture. It portrays Monu's parents as irresponsible, without stressing the fact that they are construction labourers who do not have the option of supervising their children at all times since the construction site has no crèches.

Ensuring fairness

News should be published with due regard to its context and significance. Each journalist should strive to seek a balance as far as possible by presenting relevant viewpoints on matters of importance. If this is not possible within a single news report, programme or bulletin, it should be done through subsequent reports within a reasonable period. An individual should be given a reasonable opportunity to respond to criticism. Attempts must be made to obtain the 'other' sides of the story, and when, despite strenuous efforts, this is not possible the journalist concerned should explicitly state this in the report. For example, it can be reported that five telephone calls made to a particular person's number were unanswered, that e-mail messages were not replied to, or that a certain individual chose not to answer questions or comment on a particular issue. In short, it should be apparent to the constituents that attempts were made to balance a story with all points of view even if such attempts were unsuccessful.

Impartiality

To maintain impartiality, a journalist must present material in a way that shows she/he has no vested interest in any aspect of the subject. There should be no biases in her/his report. Given that humans are subjective by nature, it is perhaps impossible to achieve real objectivity. However, even if objectivity and impartiality are not possible for journalists as individuals, they still have a responsibility to ensure that their work is impartial given the circumstances under which they function.

Box 3.4

Blueline Responsible for Death of Five-year-old Monu

UVW Gupta NEW DELHI: Delhi's killer Blueline bus claimed one more life on Wednesday, taking the number of accidental deaths by Blueline buses to 40. The police have identified the deceased as Monu (5). While the bus driver in the fatal accident managed to escape, the conductor was beaten unconscious by a local mob. He was later taken to the hospital by the police. The mob also burnt down the bus.

According to the police, the victim, 5-year-old Monu Singh, lived in the nearby slum with his parents and other siblings. Around 1:15 p.m. on Wednesday, while playing on the street, Monu was hit by a Blueline bus, route number 355, plying between Anand Parbat and Noida. The driver, identified as Bunty, fled from the spot. However, the conductor of the bus, Lucky, was beaten by an irate mob. He was taken to the hospital after a passer-by informed the police about the accident. Monu's parents are poor construction workers. They blame the criminal apathy of the transport authorities for their son's death. According to many reports, most of the drivers who ply the Bluelines are without valid licences or any kind of training.

While condoling with the parents, Delhi's Chief Minister Smt. Sheila Dikshit expressed concern over the rising death toll from road accidents.

The report in Box 3.4 has violated the code of impartiality. The reporter has not verified from the transport authorities whether the Blueline bus drivers are actually without valid licences and whether they are untrained. The reporter has also not tried to find out what steps, if any, the transport authorities are taking to minimize the number of accidents.

Remaining impartial

The PCI advises that any information that contradicts aspects of a published report should also be published. This includes contradictory evidence and comment. A newspaper should publish all replies or rejoinders given on matters of public interest to enable readers to judge their value.

There should be a clear distinction between opinion and fact. When opinion is presented as fact it misleads the readers and also transgresses the ethics of accuracy and truthfulness. Furthermore, when opinion is treated as fact and the journalist's partiality is apparent, it will serve to undermine his professional credibility.

To maintain impartiality, adjectives should be avoided except where required. The above reporter (UVW Gupta) has written of the criminal apathy of the transport authorities without clearly indicating as to whether these observations were made by Monu's parents as there are no quotation marks.

Journalists should be free of any obligation to news sources and interested groups, including political parties. Even the appearance of any sort of obligation should be avoided, especially by political and financial journalists. A journalist should report news without regard to her/his personal interest or viewpoint and without favour to a newspaper's advertisers (see Appendix 3.1).

Confidentiality

In most circumstances, it is preferable to cite the sources of information in a report. This imparts authenticity to the report. However, if a promise of confidentiality has been made between a journalist and a source, the identity of that source should be withheld. A newspaper should protect its sources, as there are circumstances under which the exposure of a source might result in danger to the journalist and/or the source. However, in exceptional situations, it may be permissible to break a promise of confidentiality.

Box 3.5

Blueline Responsible for Death of Five-year-old Monu

NEW DELHI: Delhi's killer Blueline bus claimed one more life on Wednesday, taking the number of accidental deaths by Blueline buses to 40. The police have identified the deceased as Monu (5). While the bus driver in the fatal accident managed to escape, the conductor was beaten unconscious by a local mob. He was later taken to hospital by the police. The mob also burnt down the bus.

According to the police, the victim, 5-year-old Monu Singh, lived in the nearby slum with his parents and other siblings. Around 1:15 p.m. on Wednesday, while playing on the street Monu was hit by a Blueline bus, route number 355, plying between Anand Parbat and Noida. The driver, identified as Bunty, fled from the spot. However, the conductor of the bus, Lucky, was beaten by an irate mob. He was taken to the hospital after a passer-by informed the police about the accident.

Monu's parents are poor construction workers. They blame the criminal apathy of the transport authorities for their son's death. According to many reports, most of the drivers who ply the Bluelines are without valid licences or any kind of training. Mr Virendra Singh, one of the licensing officers in the Delhi transport department, stated that the bus driver's licence was false since there was no record of such a licence.

While condoling with the parents, Delhi's Chief Minister Smt. Sheila Dikshit expressed concern over the rising death toll from road accidents.

Assume that in the report in Box 3.5, Mr Virendra Singh had asked for confidentiality while revealing the information about the driver's false licence. In such an instance, the reporter did not respect Mr Singh's request to maintain confidentiality/anonymity.

Keeping confidentiality

In such cases, instead of naming the source, the reporter can describe her/him as a 'reliable source', or 'an informed official who spoke on condition of anonymity', or as a 'knowledgeable person who spoke off the record'. In order to protect their sources, journalists should distinguish between personal and professional conversations. They should be clear while interviewing sources and soliciting information as to whether a conversation is 'on the record' or 'off the record'. Anonymous sources can rob a report of its authenticity. It is therefore best to use them only as a last resort and when there is no other means of getting the information.

If a source has misled the reporter after speaking on condition of anonymity, confidentiality can be withdrawn at the editor's discretion in exceptional circumstances. However, in such cases, the reporter usually ends up looking foolish. Thus, it is advisable, wherever possible, to double-check or verify information that has been obtained in confidence. The PCI advises that a newspaper should not reveal the identity of innocent relatives or associates of the subject of a report if it results in incrimination by association (see Appendix).

Sobriety and Decency

It is important for journalists not to unduly sensationalize news reports to attract the attention of readers, listeners or viewers. Journalists should ensure that they do not violate ethical norms to attract their audience. An example of a sensational news headline for the above report would be: 'Blueline Buses on Killing Spree, Rock Capital'.

The report given in Box 3.6 is an example of fair and ethical journalism.

Box 3.6

Blueline Responsible for Death of Five-year-old Monu

NEW DELHI: Delhi's killer Blueline bus claimed one more life on Wednesday, taking the number of accidental deaths by Blueline buses to 40. The police have identified the deceased as Monu (5). While the bus driver in the fatal accident managed to escape, the conductor was beaten unconscious by a local mob. He was later taken to the hospital by the police. The mob also burnt down the bus.

According to the police, the victim, 5-year-old Monu Singh, lived in the nearby slum with his parents and other siblings. Around 1:15 p.m. on Wednesday, while playing on the street Monu was hit by a Blueline bus, route number 355, plying between Anand Parbat and Noida. The driver, identified as Bunty, fled from the spot. However, the conductor of the bus, Lucky, was beaten by an irate mob. He was taken to the hospital after a passer-by informed the police about the accident.

Monu's parents are poor construction workers and have to leave their children at home unsupervised. Though Monu and his siblings are enrolled in the nearby municipal school, they don't attend school as they have no classes. The parents blame the criminal apathy of the transport authorities for their son's death. According to many reports, most of the drivers who ply the Bluelines are without valid licences or any kind of training. One of the licencing officers in the Delhi transport department, on condition of confidentiality, stated that the bus driver's licence was false since there was no record of such a licence.

While Mr A.K Saxena, head of the Department of Transport, declined to comment on the licence issue, he stated that measures were being taken to stringently verify each licence. The government was also planning to set up training modules on road safety for drivers, he added.

While condoling with the parents, Delhi's Chief Minister Smt. Sheila Dikshit expressed concern over the rising death toll. Mr P. Chauhan, the Minister of Transport, added that the child's parents would be paid adequate compensation and steps would be taken to catch the absconding driver.

SUMMARY

In this chapter, we have looked at the importance of presenting a credible report. We have learnt how to present the information accurately and objectively. Responsible journalists need to protect sources who want to remain anonymous. It is vital to understand the sensibilities of the people concerned while reporting on a situation. While gathering information for reports, journalists need to verify the authenticity of the information and present the story as it is without embellishing the facts.

REVIEW QUESTIONS

1. How can the media influence society in a democracy?
2. What is meant by accurate reporting?
3. Why and how should inaccuracy be avoided in a news report?
4. How can truthfulness in reporting be maintained?
5. What constitutes a fair report in which impartiality is maintained?
6. How important is confidentiality in reporting?

EXERCISE

Choose an article from a newspaper and write a brief appraisal of it. Is it fair, balanced, impartial and so on? As a reader, can you identify information which is not given in the report that could significantly enhance your understanding of what is being reported?

REFERENCES

Retief, Johan 2002, Media Ethics: *An Introduction to Responsible Journalism*, Oxford University Press, Cape Town, South Africa.

APPENDIX 3.1

PCI Guidelines

The following are some guidelines issued by the PCI on sensitive issues like communal disturbances, plagiarism, correction or apology for error and the importance of maintaining confidentiality.

Be careful while reporting communal disturbances

(i) The state government should take upon themselves the responsibility of keeping a close watch on the communal writings that might spark off tension, destruction and death, and bring them to the notice of the council.

(ii) The government may have occasion to take action against erring papers or editors. But it must do so within the bounds of law. If newsmen are arrested, or search-and-seizure operations become necessary, it would be (a) healthy convention if such developments could be reported to the Press Council within 24 to 48 hours followed by a detailed note within a week.

(iii) Under no circumstances must the authorities resort to vindictive measures like cut in advertisements, cancellation of accreditation, cut in newsprint quota and other facilities.

(iv) Provocative and sensational headlines should be avoided by the press.

(v) Headings must reflect and justify the matter printed under them.

(vi) Figures of casualties given in headlines should preferably be on the lower side in case of doubt about their exactness and where the numbers reported by various sources differ widely.

(vii) Headings containing allegations made in statements should either identify the person/body making the allegation or, at least, should carry quotation marks.

(viii) News reports should be devoid of comments and value judgement.

(ix) Presentation of news should not be motivated or guided by partisan feelings, nor should it appear to be so.

(x) Language employed in writing the news should be temperate and such as may foster feelings or amity among communities and groups.

(xi) Corrections should be promptly published with due prominence and regrets expressed in serious cases.

(xii) It will help a great deal if in-service training is given to journalists for inculcation of all these principles.

Avoid plagiarism

The PCI states: 'Using or passing off the writings or ideas of another as one's own, without crediting the source, is an offense against the ethics of journalism'. It also states that: 'The practice of lifting news from other newspapers, publishing them subsequently as their own, ill-comports the high standards of journalism. To remove its unethicality, the "lifting" newspaper must duly acknowledge the source of the report. The position of features articles is different from "news". Feature articles shall not be lifted without permission and proper acknowledgement. The press shall not reproduce in any form offending portions or excerpts from a proscribed book.'

Apologize for errors

The PCI states: 'When any factual error or mistake is detected or confirmed, the newspaper should publish the correction promptly with due prominence and with apology or expression of regrets in a case of serious lapse...The newspaper should promptly and with due prominence, publish either in full or with due editing, free of cost, at the instance of the person affected or feeling aggrieved or concerned by the impugned publication, a contradiction/reply/ clarification or rejoinder sent to the editor in the form of a letter or note. If the editor doubts the truth or factual accuracy of the contradiction/reply/ clarification or rejoinder, she/he shall be at liberty to add separately at the end a brief editorial comment doubting its veracity, but only when this doubt is reasonably founded on unimpeachable documentary or other evidential material in her/ his possession. This is a concession which has to be availed of sparingly with due discretion and caution in appropriate cases.

'However, where the reply/contradiction or rejoinder is being published in compliance with the discretion of the Press Council of India, it is permissible to append a brief editorial note to that effect. Right of rejoinder cannot be claimed through the medium of press conference, as publication of news of a conference is within the discretionary powers of an editor.

'Freedom of the press involves the readers' right to know all sides of an issue of public interest. An editor, therefore, shall not refuse to publish the reply or rejoinder merely on the ground that in his opinion the story published in the newspaper was true. That is an issue to be left to the judgement of the readers. It also does not behove an editor to show contempt towards a reader.'

The council adds: 'An editor who decides to open her/his columns for letters on a controversial subject, is not obliged to publish all the letters received in regard to that subject. She/He is entitled to select and publish only some of them either in entirety or the gist thereof. However, in exercising this discretion, she/he must make an honest endeavour to ensure that what is published is not one-sided but represents a fair balance between the views for and against with respect to the principal issue in controversy.....In the event of rejoinder upon rejoinder being sent by two parties on a controversial subject, the editor has the discretion to decide at which stage to close the continuing column.'

(In the case of television, particularly when news is 'breaking', a story that is factually incorrect or one which is partially true may be broadcast. Once it becomes evident that the facts that were broadcast are incorrect or partially correct, it becomes the duty of the channel and its anchors or reporters to accept their errors, apologize as soon as possible and broadcast the corrected facts.)

On relations with a foreign country and its representatives, the PCI states: 'The media shall make every possible effort to build bridges of cooperation, friendly relations and better understanding between India and foreign states. At the same time, it is the duty of a newspaper to expose any misuse or undue advantage of the diplomatic immunities.'

Importance of maintaining confidentiality

The PCI states: 'If information is received from a confidential source, the confidence should be respected. The journalist cannot be compelled by the Press Council to disclose such source; but it shall not be regarded as a breach of journalistic ethics if the source is voluntarily disclosed in proceedings before the council by the journalist who considers it necessary to repel effectively a charge against her/him. This rule, requiring a newspaper not to publish matters disclosed to it in confidence, is not applicable where: (a) consent of the source is subsequently obtained; or (b) the editor clarified by way of an appropriate footnote that since the publication of certain matters were in the public interest, the information in question was being published although it had been made "off the record".'

CHAPTER 4

SENSITIVITY

In this chapter, we examine some areas of journalism which are of a sensitive nature and thus, must be approached with care, respect and understanding. Such areas include invasion of privacy, handling traumatic situations, the scope of the media's influence on social conduct, obscenity and decency, media influence on religious groups, the media's social responsibilities, national interest, media and the judiciary, electoral campaigning, and the media in situations of conflict. Many of these issues can be contentious and have been dealt with quite comprehensively in media regulatory codes. The appendices to this chapter include the relevant guidelines of the PCI.

This chapter will enable you to understand why certain subjects and situations have to be handled sensitively and why the dignity and respect of individuals have to be maintained while reporting on them or while obtaining information from them.

EDITORIAL CONTENT AND INTEGRITY

Every news organization in a democracy needs to maintain its editorial independence. In an ideal world, it should be free from obligation to any individual/group and should be committed to the right of the public to know the truth. Each piece of information should be evaluated solely on its merit and no advertising, commercial, political, or personal considerations should influence editorial decisions. Journalists should not accept any gifts or privileges that might compromise their integrity. Any such offer should be disclosed to the editor and/or the management of the media organization where the journalist is employed. A journalist has the right to be associated with any lawful organization and to participate in its activities. However, these rights should not compromise the editorial integrity of a newspaper. Employees of certain media organizations may, in specific instances, be allowed to accept outside assignments and commissions, part-time employment or freelance work for other publications with the consent of the editor or the management of the organization concerned (see Appendix 4.1).

Journalists need to pay special attention to avoid situations where there could be conflict of interests. An example of conflict of interest might be a situation in which a particular journalist unearths a story about corruption in a company which is also the biggest advertiser for the newspaper she/he works for. To maintain editorial independence, the newspaper should publish the story without being influenced by a potential loss of business income. However, in many situations, pressures exerted by major advertisers do influence editorial content (see Chapter 6 on Media Market).

INVASION OF PRIVACY

Most codes of conduct for the media insist that journalists should exercise care and consideration while reporting or commenting on the private lives and concerns of individuals. However, it is admitted that in mitigating circumstances of public interest, the right to privacy may be overridden. This inevitably raises a complex debate about the nature of privacy and public interest (which will be examined in Chapter 5 on Privacy and Chapter 7 on Media Laws).

Trauma and Violence

Journalists should not intrude on private grief and distress unless justified by overriding considerations of public interest. While information is the primary objective, it should not be at the cost of causing undue pain to victims and their families. While covering incidents of death and disease, journalists working for the electronic medium should take care not to broadcast extreme close-up visuals to maintain the dignity of the dead. Traumatized people should be interviewed with due care and sensitivity. The PCI cautions against glorification of violence as it eschews the ethical goals of accuracy and objectivity.

In what ways does the glorification of trauma and violence transgress the ethics of accuracy and objectivity?

INFLUENCE

In considering issues of sensitivity, it is important to keep in mind the scope and the power of influence that the media exerts over its audiences. There are certain situations when information should be withheld if there is a chance that its dissemination will have a negative influence on its subjects (see Box 4.1: The 'Werther Effect'). For instance, while covering communal riots, the media must ensure cautious, restrained and responsible reporting so that the reportage does not further incite violence. By mobilizing public opinion against a communal carnage, news organizations can play a positive role in cooling passions and promoting amity.

Box 4.1
The 'Werther Effect'

In the twelve months between early 2007 and early 2008, there were more than 17 suicides of young people (aged between 16 and 26) in the small former mining town of Bridgend, Wales in the UK. The first seven suicides are considered to be a 'cluster' as all the victims knew each other, each died by hanging, none had clear motivations for suicide, and none left notes. The suicides mystified the locals and the authorities. The most prevalent suggestion was that they were copycat suicides.

The phenomenon of copycat suicide has been called the 'Werther Effect' by David Phillips, an academic who studied the phenomenon in the 1970s. The effect is called so after a spate of similar suicides occurred following the publication of Goethe's *The Sorrows of Young Werther* in 1774. Young men killed themselves in the manner of the novel's hero. Phillips noted in previous studies that during the two months following a front-page suicide story, the number of suicides in the area increased by an average of 58.

It appears that the influence of the media—be it books, newspapers or the internet—on its audience is neither just speculative nor new. The local newspaper of Bridgend bore this in mind when it decided not to publish stories of subsequent suicides that appeared to be part of the cluster. The editor made the decision to withhold information (which would be of interest to the public) for the sake of public interest and well-being. In this instance, the editorial judgements are to be commended for the decisive, timely action taken; the making of a difficult decision; and for not being influenced by the 'saleability' of the unreported stories.

Source: Adapted from *The Hindu Business* Line, 13 August 2006.

Do media organizations have the right to judge what the public should and should not know?

Is it justifiable to overlook the outcome of not censoring sensitive material?

How can media organizations censor news that is sensitive in nature without compromising the right of the public to know the truth?

WHAT IS OBSCENITY?

The law relating to obscenity is laid down in Section 292 of the Indian Penal Code (IPC) of Act 36 of 1969 (see Appendix 4.2). It considers material obscene 'if it is lascivious or appeals to the prurient interest or if its effect, or (where it comprises two or more distinct items) the effects of any one of its items, is, if taken as a whole, such as to tend to deprave and corrupt persons who are likely, having regard to all relevant circumstances, to read, see or hear the matter contained or embodied in it'.

This section was amended in 1969 to prevent circulation and trafficking of obscene literature. It was specifically designed to restrict communication of certain types of materials based on their content. However, as the amendment did not offer a definition of obscenity, this section has come under attack for being too vague to qualify as a penal provision. This unacceptably large 'grey area', which is also found in the laws restricting sexual material, is not due to a lack of capacity or effort on the part of the drafters or the legislators. Rather, there appears to be an explicit desire to include inherently nebulous concepts, within these laws, to enable application whenever public concern is raised in relation to material considered obscene.

The obscenity legislation and jurisprudence, prior to the enactment of Act 36 of 1969, were concerned with prohibiting 'immoral influences' of obscene publications and safeguarding the individual in whose hands such material could fall. However, to impose a certain standard of public and sexual morality, solely because it reflects the conventions of a given community, is inimical to the enjoyment of individual freedoms, which form the basis of the Indian Constitution.

The concept of obscenity is different in each country depending on the standards of contemporary society. The precise meaning of 'obscene' is, however, decidedly ambiguous. It has been defined as something that is offensive to modesty or decency, or expressing or suggesting unchaste or lustful ideas or being impure, indecent or lewd.

As times change, so do social standards. What might have been considered taboo fifty years ago might be accepted as the norm today. The issue of homosexuality is a good example of a highly contentious subject: gradually homosexuality is being accepted by society, although there are still many examples of homophobic discrimination. As times change (albeit gradually), there is a need to change attitudes and language about a corresponding subject. The word 'queer' that was used to describe homosexual people is now considered inappropriate and offensive given its obvious derogatory connotations.

Judging Obscenity and Decency

In December 2006, the Supreme Court of India rejected a plea to prevent newspapers from publishing obscene photographs and articles, arguing that such a ban would violate the right to freedom of speech and expression. 'An imposition of a blanket ban on the publication of certain photographs and news items, etc. will lead to a situation where the newspaper will be publishing material which caters only to children and adolescents and the adults will be deprived of reading their share of their entertainment which can be permissible under the normal norms of decency in any society,' said a bench comprising judges A.R. Lakshmanan and Tarun Chatterjee. The bench said that any steps to impose a blanket ban on publishing of such photographs would also amount to prejudging the matter. The petitioner, Ajay Goswami, an advocate, drew the apex court's attention to the publication of what he claimed were obscene photographs, articles on pornography and sex education in two leading newspapers of the capital, *The TOI* and The *Hindustan Times.*

A very thin line divides the obscene from the decent, as far as newspapers, magazines, books, radio stations, television channels, films and the web are concerned. A most contentious issue pertains to balancing the need to protect society, to uphold freedom of expression and to preserve a free flow of information and ideas on the one hand, against the potential harm that may be caused by the publication of obscene material, on the other. The laws covering obscenity are dealt with in the IPC of 1860 and are a legacy of the British colonial rule. Though the Indian Constitution guarantees freedom of expression, Article 19(2) makes it clear that the State may impose 'reasonable restriction' in the interest of public decency and morality. The Indian government is, thus, well within its rights to ban, in the public interest, publication or broadcast of any material it considers obscene.

?

Can you think of patterns of behaviour in Indian society that have become more acceptable today than they were, say, ten years ago?

List a few words or terms which are no longer considered 'politically correct' in India?

DEFINITIONS OF OBSCENITY OUTSIDE INDIA

The following section discusses the definition of obscenity as given in the laws of various countries.

United States

In the US, the Pennsylvania Consolidated Statutes in Section 5903 define any material or performance as obscene, if:

- the average person applying contemporary community standards would find that the subject matter taken as a whole appeals to the prurient interest
- the subject matter depicts or describes in a patently offensive way, sexual conduct of a type described in this section
- the subject matter, taken as a whole, lacks serious literary, artistic, political, educational or scientific value

As in India, social standards of what is considered obscene have changed over time in other countries as well. In 1929, Edgar Rice Burroughs's celebrated novel *Tarzan* was removed from the shelves of public libraries in the US because the title character lived with a woman, Jane, to whom he was not legally married, thereby outraging the accepted moral values of the time.

The administrators of law in the US have been no less perturbed about a suitable definition of obscenity than their counterparts in India. In 1964, as the challenge to define what is obscene continued, Justice Potter Stewart of the US Supreme Court expressed his frustration at the difficulties of defining obscenity when he stated: 'I can't define it but I know it when I see it.'

The late author Norman Mailer, a pacifist, stated that obscenity was not a naked woman but a military general who displays a row of medals on his chest to tell the world how many people he has been responsible for killing.

Box 4.2

Wardrobe Malfunctions—Janet Jackson and Carol Gracias

On 1 February 2004, singer Janet Jackson's breast was exposed on television during the live broadcast of a Super Bowl game. The episode was later described as a 'wardrobe malfunction' and resulted in the issue of a $555,000 fine by the Federal Communications Commission (FCC) on CBS, the channel that broadcast the programme. CBS said that it would not allow Jackson to appear on the channel in future.

The wardrobe malfunction was widely considered indecent exposure and a record-breaking 200,000 citizens complained to the FCC about it. The incident drew criticism as the Super Bowl is generally considered a family-oriented event. What was contentious was not so much the fact that Jackson's breast was revealed but that it occurred during a live telecast and that too at a time when children would be expected to be watching the programme.

On 1 December 2006, during the Lakme India Fashion Week, model Carol Gracias found her halter-neck dress slipping to her waist and was exposed topless in front of video cameras. She said that it was the most embarrassing moment of her life. Though Gracias's wardrobe malfunction was not broadcast live, some television channels obtained the video clip of the event and broadcast it repeatedly after blurring the image of her chest. When another wardrobe malfunction took place involving a different model, the old footage of Gracias was telecast again by some channels.

Source: Adapted from 'Wardrobe Malfunction has Minister Patil's Knickers in a twist, *Indian Express*, 4 April 2006; 'Janet Jackson's wardrobe malfunction fine overturned,' *The Guardian*, U.K., 22 July 2008.

Canada

One of the most progressive and liberal judgements on obscenity was in the *Regina* versus *Butler* case by the Supreme Court of Canada. Some of the issues discussed in the judgement are given below:

The Canadian Criminal Code defines obscene material as: '...any publication, a dominant characteristic of which is the undue exploitation of sex, or of sex and any one or more of the following subjects, namely, crime, horror, cruelty and violence...' The Supreme Court of Canada interpreted the meaning of 'undue exploitation', holding that the dominant test is a community standard one. 'However, it is the standard of tolerance, not taste that is relevant. What matters is not what Canadians think is right for themselves to see but what the community would not tolerate others being exposed to on the basis of the degree of harm that may flow from such exposure.

'The portrayal of sex coupled with violence will almost always constitute the undue exploitation of sex. Explicit sex that is degrading or dehumanizing may be undue if the risk of harm is substantial. Finally, explicit sex that is not violent and neither degrading nor dehumanizing is generally tolerated in our society and will not qualify as undue exploitation of sex unless it employs children in its production.

'In order for the work or material to qualify as "obscene" the exploitation of sex must only be its dominant characteristic, but such exploitation must be "undue".' The courts formulated a workable test to determine if the exploitation of sex is 'undue', based on the 'community standard of tolerance'. The court stated that the community standard test must necessarily respond to changing mores and further held that the State could not restrict expression simply because it was distasteful or did not accord with dominant conceptions of what was appropriate.

South Africa

In South Africa, legislators have detailed a list of prohibited material. Schedule 1 of the amended 1996 Films and Publications Act defines the XX classification of prohibited publications as material which contains a real or simulated visual presentation of:

- child pornography
- explicit violent sexual conduct
- bestiality
- explicit sexual activity which degrades a person and which constitutes incitement to cause harm

Japan

The Supreme Court of Japan ruled that material could be judged 'obscene' under Article 175 of the Constitution if 'it aroused and stimulated sexual desire, offended a common sense of modesty or shame, and violated proper concepts of sexual morality'.

Britain

In Britain, the law governing obscene publications is found principally in the Obscene Publication Act of 1959. It states that an article is obscene if its effect, or (where the articles comprise two or more distinct items) the effect of any one of its items is, if taken as a whole, intended '...to deprave and corrupt persons who are likely, having regard to all relevant circumstances, to read, see or hear the matter contained or embodied in it'. This statute was objected to by Lord Wilberforce of the House of Lords in 1972, who posited that the statute offers no definition of depravity and corruption, and does not identify whether the concern is that the impugned material may cause people to commit wicked acts, or whether the mischief is simply that erotic desires may be aroused.

Namibia

In 1998, the Namibia High Court, in a landmark judgement, held that Section 2(1) of the Indecent and Obscene Photographic Matter Act of 1967 was unconstitutional as it was formulated in an overly broad manner which was not intended, or carefully designed, to prohibit possession of sexually explicit material as is proscribed under the Namibian Constitution. The court held that 'although expression may under certain circumstances be restricted under the Namibian Constitution, the provisions should be interpreted restrictively to ensure that the exceptions are not unnecessarily used to suppress the right to the freedom of expression guaranteed in Article 21'.

Obscenity and What is Harmful

Obscenity laws should avoid using vague and subjective terms, such as 'indecent' and 'harmful to public morals', without clarifying what these terms mean. Obscenity restrictions must be aimed at preventing 'real' harm and not just at preventing 'offense to public sensibilities'. Harm could mean that it predisposes persons to act in an anti-social manner, for example, possible emulation of physical or mental torture of women by men. It is imperative to distinguish between 'offensive' material and material that is actually harmful. A 'community standard of tolerance' test should be taken into consideration. Community standards must be contemporary as times change and ideas keep changing. A community standard should be a standard of the community as a whole and not of a small section of a community.

Do you see a common thread in the laws to check obscenity in the countries mentioned above?

What are the difficulties of assimilating the views and requirements of a multiracial, multicultural society?

OBSCENITY AND BLASPHEMY IN THE INDIAN CONTEXT

India has resorted to banning books, paintings, films, theatrical performances and television channels on grounds of obscenity and the need to maintain public decency. The I&B Ministry banned Sony's satellite channel AXN for two months in January 2007 for airing 'indecent content' in the form of a programme on the world's sexiest advertisements (see Box 4.3: Channels Rapped over the Knuckles). Taslima Nasreen's book, *Lajja*, was banned after a furore over its contents which were said to hurt Muslim sentiments. Earlier, in 1989, India was among the first countries to ban the sale of Salman Rushdie's *Satanic Verses*, after Iran's Ayatullah Ruhollah Khomeini issued a *fatwa* (directive) ordering Muslims to kill Rushdie.

While there is no disputing the fact that some regulatory guidelines for the media are necessary, an independent media should not be strangled. A credible media in India, the second most populous country in the world, has the power to influence the collective consciousness of over one billion people. Newspapers, television, radio and the internet are all powerful tools that can be used by the government and private media organizations to shape or mobilize public opinion in one direction or the other.

Box 4.3

Channels Rapped over the Knuckles

On 14 August 2008, three television channels—MTV, IBN-7 and Headlines Today—were issued show cause notices by the I&B Ministry for allegedly violating the government's programme code. MTV was issued a notice for 'denigration' of women in its reality show *Splitsvilla*. The programme depicted twenty girls seeking the attention of two boys, who act as judges, to become a video jockey (VJ). Acting on the basis of a complaint received, the ministry was of the view that the programme was in 'bad taste' and denigrated women by 'objectifying' the girls. IBN-7 offended the I&B Ministry by claiming in a report that deities of two Hindu Gods had appeared in the form of a ball of fire in a village near Kuala Lumpur in Malaysia. The story allegedly encouraged superstition. Headlines Today had aired a programme on the bikini completing 62 years that was considered 'objectionable' and 'indecent'.

Many media watchers in India feel that there should be strict regulations that restrict the flow of information. However, most media organizations resist the imposition of such regulations on the ground that it would restrict the freedom of expression. For commercial considerations, sections of the media focus more on issues that concern only the elite while the poor and underprivileged are mostly ignored. Journalists need to have a social responsibility to the citizens of their country and an independent media, being one of the main pillars of a democracy, needs to give importance to all sections of society.

Social and Religious Groups

The media should avoid discriminatory or derogatory references to people's caste, race, religion, sex, physical or mental disability, illness or age. The media should not refer to these aspects of an individual in a prejudicial or pejorative context, except where such information is relevant or adds significantly to people's understanding of the person concerned. The media needs to strike a balance between informing the public and withholding information that might instigate violence.

Given the historical inequalities in India with regard to caste and the ease with which communal tensions can develop, the PCI has laid down strict guidelines about any kind of references to caste, religion or community. It states: 'In general, the caste identification of a person or a particular class should be avoided, particularly when in the context it conveys a sense or attributes a conduct or practice derogatory to that caste. Newspapers are advised against the use of the word "scheduled caste" or "Harijan" against which. . . objections have been raised. Perhaps a more politically correct term is "Dalit".' Individuals should not be described by their caste or community unless this is strictly relevant to the story.

In what circumstances would it be appropriate to describe somebody's caste or ethnic community?

The media should not publish/broadcast any works of fiction which distort or portray religious characters in an adverse light, or which transgress the norms of literary taste or offend religious sensibilities. As the media is the bearer of the social right to free speech, it should not exploit the names of prophets, seers or deities for commercial purposes. Global events in recent times have shown that the right to free speech is both contentious and elusive in its definition.

The cartoons/caricatures of the Prophet Muhammad published by Danish newspaper *Jyllads-Posten* in September 2005 were intended to encourage a debate on censorship in Islam. However, many Muslims around the world reacted vehemently against the publication since they believe that there should be no visual representation of the Prophet. There were violent protests against the publication resulting in over a hundred deaths in different countries.What the Danish cartoonists considered an exercise in the right to free speech, the Islamic world considered an indubitable mockery of their religion and culture. The debate caused a rift around the world: the cartoons were circulated on the internet, newspapers in certain countries republished the cartoons in the spirit of 'freedom of expression' while in other countries, Danish products were boycotted. Importantly, most of the mainstream media in the world did not republish the cartoons.

Special attention should be given to the verification of material relating to communal or religious conflict before publication or broadcast. The media has a responsibility to protect the public from violence or communal discord by ensuring that sensationalist or provocative headlines are not used. Furthermore, reportage of criminal activity should avoid evoking feelings of disillusionment and cynicism towards the law. The media also has the responsibility to bring to its viewers, readers or listeners, small success stories that go unnoticed and give due coverage to unsung heroes of society (see Appendix 4.1).

Should the names of members of communities involved in violent acts be revealed while reporting communal riots?

Can the rules be different for print and visual media?

SOCIAL RESPONSIBILITY

There are three main social sections which warrant separate consideration and ethical guidelines: individuals, society in general and governing bodies.

Individuals

The PCI observes that there are no grounds which justify the publication of derogatory, scurrilous or defamatory material about an individual where there is no public interest involved. The media should not base its comments about the fresh actions of an individual on that person's previous behaviour if it has no relevance to the present situation. In the event that public interest necessitates past misdemeanours be divulged, the media should enquire with the authorities concerned about any likely legal implications or repercussions. It is unethical to publish defamatory comments about a deceased person, unless warranted by public interest, on the ground that the deceased cannot have the opportunity to defend herself/himself.

The media coverage of the Aarushi–Hemraj murder case is illustrative in this context. The comments of senior police officials describing the 14-year-old murdered girl as 'characterless' and remarks that she was found in an 'objectionable but not compromising position' were widely quoted in the media (*The Indian Express*, 28 May 2008). At one stage, Union Minister for Women and Child Development Renuka Chowdhury even called for the suspension of the Inspector General of Police, Meerut (Uttar Pradesh), Gurdarshan Singh, for his reported remarks. The relevant question worth debating is whether reporters should be reproducing and publicizing remarks that could clearly be construed as defamatory even when these are made by government officials (in this instance, a senior police officer) responsible for conducting criminal investigations.

If a dead person cannot defend herself/himself against defamation, nor can she/he be offended by defamation, should the issue of journalistic sensitivity be extended to the deceased?

The media has a duty and right to serve public interest by drawing attention to the acts and activities of persons of questionable character, but responsible journalism should observe due restraint and caution while expressing opinions or drawing conclusions about such individuals. The cardinal principle is that the role of the media is to disseminate information to facilitate and enable readers to draw their own conclusions. The media is not endowed with the right to judge. If an impugned publication or broadcast is manifestly injurious to the reputation of the complainant, it is the responsibility of the media to demonstrate that the comments were true or to establish that they merited comment in the public interest.

Society in General

The term 'social responsibility', in this context, pertains to the presentation of information by the media on issues related to violence, obscenity, pornography, indecency, religion and sex. For example, in the case of television, as it is an audio-visual medium, care should be taken to discern the suitability of the material for the viewers. Material of a sensitive nature should be censored if it might be considered inappropriate in any of the following ways:

- harmful to children
- offensive to public sensibilities or to religious convictions
- disruptive of relations between sections of the population
- disruptive to the safety of the state or the public order

The PCI cautions against defamatory writing. It states: 'A newspaper should not publish anything which is manifestly defamatory or libellous against any individual organization unless after due care and checking, it has sufficient reason to believe that it is true and its publication will be for public good.'

The PCI also warns against the publication of photographs which might be considered lewd, vulgar or pornographic. If it is clear that a photograph is intended to arouse feelings of sexual excitement, it should not be published. However, if a photograph is intended to be educative or informative in the fields of science or art, for example, then its publication is permissible.

Another issue pertains to the depiction of corpses—victims of violence, accidents and disasters (natural or man-made). Even when disclaimers like 'visuals you are about to see could be disturbing' are put out, the depiction of blood, body parts and the dead should be avoided to the extent possible.

In July 2004, after more than 80 children between the ages of eight and ten were burnt to death in a fire that devastated a school in Kumbakonam, Tamil Nadu, some local television channels were accused of insensitivity when they repeatedly aired visuals of charred bodies of children.

Box 4.4
Treatment of Children in the Media

The media sometimes portrays children as vulnerable and easy victims and this results in over-censorship, thus undermining their right to information as a group of society. Kavita Ratna of Concerned for Working Children, an NGO in Bengaluru, has pointed out how existing media codes highlight the following:

- emphasis has been laid mainly on the impact of harmful content in the media on children
- right to confidentiality is the only right that has been stressed
- no reference to children's participation in the media has been made
- IFJ (International Federation of Journalists) guidelines for journalists reporting on children only talk of children's opinions appearing in the media
- children are seen as 'victims'
- children are seen as 'vulnerable' and in constant need of 'protection'
- right to information has not been covered
- right to dignified representation: other facets, apart from sexualized representation, that the existing codes/ guidelines mention have not been highlighted
- right to protection from misrepresentation has not been covered
- right to protection from stereotyping has not been covered. The introduction to the IFJ guidelines does recognize this but does not spell it out clearly in the guidelines

According to Ratna, some common traits of the Indian media's treatment of children are:

- children's right to participation is violated
- children's issues are never newsworthy unless they offer scope for sensationalism
- children's rights as 'users' and their right to information are violated
- children are stereotyped as victims, vulnerable, innocent, charming or spoilt
- there is lack of children's programming in the media
- children are rarely portrayed as protagonists
- children's opinions do not appear in the media
- children are 'commodified', treated as objects
- all children do not have equal access to the media
- the media displays insensitivity while dealing with children
- children's contexts are negated
- children's consent is rarely sought before interviewing or photographing them
- children are made to stage or say things that are not part of their reality or history
- children's right to privacy and confidentiality is violated
- children's right to dignified representation is violated

There are a few guidelines and codes of conduct for the media that refer to children and seek to regulate their coverage in the media. However, as Ratna has pointed out (see Box 4.4: Treatment of Children in the Media), these are rather limited in scope. Significantly, none of the codes highlight the right of children to be 'producers' of media in society. The Convention on the Rights of the Child (CRC), adopted in 1989 by the United Nations, clearly spells out the rights to which children everywhere are entitled. Several of the CRC's key articles deal with the media and children and contain the following four basic principles.

- The best interests of the child should be a primary consideration.
- Opinions of children should be heard and valued.
- Child development, not just survival, should be ensured.
- Each child should be able to enjoy her/his rights without discrimination.

Imagine you are a child in today's world of multifarious media. What sort of issues might concern you? How can the media deal with these concerns to appeal to you? How do you think you can be adequately and suitably represented in the media?

National Interest

For the PCI, national interest is paramount. It states: 'Newspapers shall, as a matter of self-regulation, exercise due restraint and caution in presenting any news, comment or information which is likely to jeopardize, endanger, or harm the paramount interests of the State and society, or the rights of individuals with respect to which reasonable restrictions may be imposed by law on the right to freedom of speech and expression under clause (2) of Article 19 of the Constitution of India. The publication of an incorrect map of India is a serious offence, which may compromise the territorial integrity of the country. Any erroneous cartographic depictions must be immediately and prominently retracted with expression of regret.' Indian government authorities regularly rubber-stamp foreign publications stating that the country's international borders have been incorrectly depicted.

Governing bodies and officials

It is not permissible for the government, local authorities or institutions with governmental power to maintain a legal suit for damages against the media for publishing material about the conduct of their official duties, unless they can demonstrate that the material was published with wilful disregard for the truth. Any information concerning offences committed by public officials should be published with the intention of helping to prevent the concealment of offences (see Appendix 4.1).

REPORTING ON THE JUDICIARY

A newspaper has the right to report judicial proceedings, unless the court sits in camera or specifically directs the media not to report on certain proceedings or parts thereof. However, the press/electronic media must not publish/broadcast anything that might obstruct, impede or prejudice the proceedings. The media should not report the progress of a trial in the style of a running commentary or debate, nor should it report or comment on the personal character of the accused.

While the media may, in the public interest, reasonably criticize a judicial act or a court judgement, it should not cast scurrilous aspersions, or impute improper motives, or allege personal bias on the part of the judge. The media should not scandalize the court or the judiciary as a whole, or make allegations of lack of ability or integrity against a judge (see Box 4.5: *MiD Day* and the Former Chief Justice of India).

The media, as a matter of caution, should avoid making unfair and unwarranted criticism which implies that a judge has been partial in the course of fulfilling her/his judicial functions, even if such criticism does not strictly amount to criminal contempt of court.

Box 4.5

Mid Day *and the Former Chief Justice of India*

In 2007, there was a major controversy when *Mid Day* newspaper published a series of articles questioning the integrity of former Chief Justice of India Yogesh Kumar Sabharwal. Among various allegations, it was claimed that the business interests of the former chief justice's sons may have been promoted on account of a series of judgements made by benches of the Supreme Court of India (headed by him) pertaining to the 'sealing' of properties in New Delhi by the municipal authorities. The judge's sons were also accused of using his official address for their business. A bench of the Delhi High Court sought to send a group of Mid Day employees to jail and that resulted in a huge hue and cry in the media. The journalists, who were accused of 'contempt of court' and of tarnishing the reputation of the judiciary, argued that not a single fact in their reports had been contradicted or denied and that these facts were based on official records. Truth, according to them, was their best defence.

Source: Adapted from 'Articles against ex-CJI: Mid Day editor, cartoonist found guilty', www.rediff.com, 11 September 2007.

ELECTORAL CAMPAIGNING

General elections are an important feature of a democracy and it is imperative that the media disseminates fair and objective reports of the campaigns. Freedom of the media, to a large extent, depends on journalists' sense of responsibility and impartiality. It is necessary for the media to adhere to the principle of fair and objective reporting of election campaigns. The PCI has formulated the following guidelines to be observed by the media during elections.

- It will be the duty of the press to give objective reports about elections and candidates. The newspapers are not expected to indulge in unhealthy election campaigns, exaggerated reports about any candidate/party or incident during the elections. In practice, two or three closely contesting candidates attract all the media attention. While reporting on the actual campaign, a newspaper may not leave out any important point raised by a candidate and make an attack on her/his opponent.
- Election campaigns along communal or caste lines are banned under the election rules. Hence, the press should eschew reports which tend to promote feelings of enmity or hatred between people on the ground of religion, race, caste, community or language.
- The press should refrain from publishing false or critical statements in regard to the personal character and conduct of any candidate or in relation to the candidature or withdrawal of any candidate or her/his candidature, to prejudice the prospects of that candidate in the elections. The press shall not publish unverified allegations against any candidate/party.
- The press shall not accept any kind of inducement, financial or otherwise, to project a candidate/party. It shall not accept hospitality or other facilities offered to them by or on behalf of any candidate/party.
- The press is not expected to indulge in canvassing of a particular candidate/party. If it does, it shall allow the right of reply to the other candidate/party.
- The press shall not accept/publish any advertisement at the cost of (the) public exchequer regarding achievements of a party/government in power (during the period the model code of conduct of the Election Commission is in force).
- The press shall observe all the directions/orders/instructions of the Election Commission/returning officers or the chief electoral officer issued from time to time.

CONFLICT

Covering war and conflict situations can pose its problems for the media even as reports on such situations could be of considerable public interest.

For such reports, great sensitivity needs to be employed and objectivity maintained to the greatest extent possible. Robert Karl Manoff has formulated a list of twenty-four objectives of media coverage of conflict and what they might achieve. These objectives demonstrate the areas that require special sensitivity and care (Retief 2002).

1. Promote and help enforce national or international norms regarding human rights, the conduct of war, the treatment of minorities, or other issues.
2. Relay negotiating signals between parties that have no formal communication.
3. Focus the attention of the international community on a conflict, so as to bring pressure on the parties to resolve it or on the international community to intervene.
4. Establish the transparency of the parties in conflict.
5. Engage in confidence-building measures.
6. Support international peacekeeping operations in countries with conflict situations and in countries contributing military contingents.
7. Educate parties and communities involved in conflict and thereby change the information environments of disputes, which is critical to the conflict resolution process.
8. Identify the underlying interests of each party to a conflict for the other.
9. Prevent the circulation of incendiary rumours and counteract them when they surface.
10. Identify the core values of disputants, which are often critical to helping them understand their own priorities and those of their opposite numbers.
11. Identify and explain the underlying material and psychological needs of parties to a conflict, clarifying the structural issues that are perceived to be at stake.
12. Frame the issues involved in conflict in such a way that they become more susceptible to management.
13. Identify resources that may be available to help resolve conflicts or to mobilize outside assistance in doing so.
14. Establish networks to circulate information concerning conflict prevention and management activities that have succeeded elsewhere.
15. Publicize what should be public and privatize what is best left private in any negotiating process, although the definitions in each case are likely to be highly contested and should not be taken for granted.
16. De-objectify and re-humanize conflicting parties towards one another, and avoid stereotyping.
17. Provide an outlet for the emotions of the parties, the expression of which may be therapeutic.

18. Bring international pressure to bear on media organizations that promote xenophobia, racism or other forms of social hatred.
19. Encourage a balance of power among unequal parties where appropriate, or, where the claims of parties are not equally just, strengthen the hand of the party with the more compelling moral claim.
20. Enable the parties to formulate and articulate proposed solutions by serving as a non-antagonistic interlocutor.
21. Provide early warning of impending conflicts.
22. Help the negotiating parties maintain credibility with their own constituents.
23. Participate in the process of healing, reconciliation and social reconstruction following conflicts.
24. Signal the importance of accords that end conflicts by historicizing them as important public occasions in order to embed the resolution process in shared social memories.

The British Broadcasting Corporation, with 2,000-odd journalists reporting events across the world, has officially stated: 'It is incumbent on us as an organization to report conflicts while maintaining the safety of our journalists and their technical and production teams and the local people they work with on the ground to assist them. . . They should report what they see and find out whilst staying neutral and building an understanding of the roots of a conflict. It is our job to conduct rigorous journalistic investigation into situations, not to judge or give opinion on what we find. Our audiences trust us not to take sides. We must put those situations we report on into context and present views from all.'

Two experienced reporters, Mike Nicholson and lan Stuttard, have produced a film, *Shooting the Messenger*, that highlights how journalists have been deliberately targeted and killed in conflict zones from Sri Lanka to Zimbabwe and West Asia. From the beginning of 2007 till the middle of 2008, over 100 journalists had been killed in lraq and the Middle East alone.

Rita Payne of the Commonwealth Journalists Association, said during a meeting of the Action For UN Renewal at the House of Lords, London, UK: 'It is suggested that media coverage after. . . in war has a major role to play in bringing peace and reconstruction. . . According to critics, media reports war in a one-dimensional way. . . the present way of reporting war leaves out the most important part of the story; how to conflict might be transcended. . . Journalists and editors can only hope that responsible reporting and rigorous analysis will point to ways in which a conflict cab be resolved peacefully. . .'

SUMMARY

We have looked at some of the sensitive issues and situations which the media faces regularly and why journalists need to approach these subjects carefully while reporting on them. The exercises and the quiz at the end of this chapter will help sensitize you to some of the social and ethical issues. A firm understanding of these issues is paramount for professionalism in the media and many of them will be revisited in subsequent chapters.

REVIEW QUESTIONS

1. What constitutes privacy?
2. Why could it be important to refrain from mentioning the caste or community of an individual?
3. What is meant by incrimination by association?
4. What do you understand by obscenity and what kind of material is deemed obscene?
5. Under what circumstances could the depiction of nudity be acceptable?
6. What kind of information could be censored on television and not in the print medium?
7. What are the highlights of the PCI guidelines for the media during electoral campaigning?
8. What are the ways in which children are commonly treated in the media?
9. List some of the objectives suggested by Robert Karl Manoff that should be considered while reporting conflict situations.

DEBATE

The identities of convicted and released paedophiles should be exposed by the media in the public interest and for the sake of safety.

REFERENCES

'Renuka slams UP cops for statements in Aarushi murder', *The Indian Express*, 28 May 2008.

Retief, Johan 2002, *Media Ethics: An Introduction to Responsible Journalism*, Oxford University Press, Cape Town, South Africa.

CASE STUDY

Terrorism and Journalism

On 26 November 2008, when a group of ten terrorists attacked people at several well-known locations in Mumbai, the Indian media in general and 24-hour television news channels in particular were immediately confronted with unprecedented challenges. These attacks by terrorists in Mumbai, the capital city of Maharashtra in western India, often described as the country's commercial and entertainment capital, were unique for several reasons: these were not only aimed at locations where ordinary people gather such as the Chhatrapati Shivaji Terminus (CST) railway station but also targeted places where the affluent, including foreign tourists and businesspersons, live and frequent—notably the Taj and the Oberoi Trident hotels. Over and above these locations, the attacks by a group of young men armed with grenades and automatic weapons took place in a popular restaurant (Leopold Café), the Cama Hospital and at Nariman House where orthodox Jews live. The onslaught continued for two and a half days, roughly 60 hours, till 29 November 2008. Government agencies stated that at least 173 people were killed and 308 injured in the attacks.

The news media, especially television channels covering the event 'live', had an abundance of eyeball-gripping material as millions of viewers all over India and the world were glued to their television sets. In this highly-charged atmosphere, certain journalists on particular occasions acted in a manner that was less than sensitive or ethical. Facts were presented sporadically, out of context and sometimes, incorrectly. Rumour and speculation were sought to be passed off as facts. This was, to an extent, also a consequence of government authorities not deputing official spokespersons to brief the media that was ravenously hungry for every bit of 'new' information that would come. In the process, the veracity of information that came from different sources was not cross-checked. It was argued that, on occasions, journalists may well have compromised the security of those who had been held as hostages in the hotels and buildings. Further, the media could also have passed on information that helped the terrorists, their minders and supporters. Even as the television coverage of the events was avidly watched, subsequently there was considerable public criticism of the manner in which media personnel behaved while attempting to fulfil their professional responsibilities as providers of unbiased information and responsible comment.

Though it would be unfair and inaccurate to lump the entire media fraternity into one category, there were undoubtedly some who acted in a way that was questionable and would be considered unethical. At the Taj and the Oberoi Trident hotels, television cameras depicted just how close the reporters were allowed to come to the buildings for almost the entire duration of 60 hours that the hotels were occupied by the terrorists. The absence of major restrictions on the movements of journalists and television camerapersons was used by reporters to their advantage so come as close as they possibly could to the hotels that were set on fire as well as other places where the terrorists were holding hostages. Some hostages wrote messages like 'Please Save Us!' in shaving cream on the glass window panes of their hotel rooms to alert possible rescuers —these images were repeatedly shown on television channels although, even at that time, it was suspected that the terrorists were using satellite phones. This meant that the terrorists were obtaining crucial information through television broadcasts, including information about the exact locations of hostages. It transpired that after several television channels reported that there were hostages taking shelter in the 'Chambers' restaurant inside the Taj hotel, the terrorists went to that specific location and opened fire, randomly killing those present.

The crucial question is that if there was any indication that what was being reported could result in more deaths, would media personnel have allowed such information to be broadcast? A charitable view would be that journalists acted in a naïve manner and were simply unaware of the consequences of their actions. A less charitable opinion would be that in their rush for being the 'first with the news' in order to obtain higher viewership ratings, journalists put out any and every bit of information that they felt could attract audiences without cross-checking for the authenticity of the information.

One television channel, India TV, claimed it had its own reporter stationed inside the Taj hotel for three days who apparently knew where the hostages had taken cover, but did not disclose the information. The same channel stirred a controversy when it decided to broadcast interviews with two terrorists who were inside Nariman House and the Taj hotel and who used mobile phones of hostages. Prakash Tiwari, Mumbai bureau chief of India TV, claimed the interview was to help Indian authorities gather information. However, many felt the channel should not have aired the purported conversations with the terrorists.

A 'perception survey' published in the December 2008 issue of the monthly magazine *Impact* done by the research firm, IMRS, that was conducted among advertising, marketing and media professionals stated that 72 per cent of the respondents spoken to believed that interviewing a terrorist glorifies him/her. However, among the media professionals that were interviewed, 56 per cent disagreed with this view.

While responding to questions asked by Barkha Dutt, Group Editor, English News, New Delhi Television (NDTV) who doubled up as the channel's field reporter in Mumbai during the terrorist attacks, a hostage who had just escaped from inside the Taj hotel accidentally revealed the location of his wife who was still hiding inside the hotel building. Questions were raised as to whether interviews of freed hostages should have broadcast at all. It was contended that it was highly insensitive of reporters to interview a person who had been face-to-face with death minutes earlier and ask them how they were feeling? At one point in the coverage, television channel CNN-IBN's camerapersons outside the Taj hotel focused on a group of journalists who were involved in a scuffle–it transpired that a group of some 20 journalists were scrambling to speak to a person who had just been able to come out free after having been held hostage. To return to the *Impact*-IMRS survey, 57 per cent of the respondents interviewed believed that journalists were insensitive when asking questions of victims and their victims' families. Only 44 per cent of media professionals, however, felt their peers had acted in a way that was insensitive.

There were accounts of reporters harassing victims for sound-bytes when they were inside ambulances on their way to hospital. Whereas Barkha Dutt was singled out by media critics like *The Times of India's* Pronoti Datta for the persistent manner in which she interviewed those who had been able to escape from the terrorists and also for allegedly breaching security barriers, Dutt defended herself stating: 'At every point, relatives of those trapped inside the hotels, spoke to us because they wanted to speak—either to express pain, grief, anger or just to feel part of a wider community at a time, when they had no one else to talk to'. (http://timesofindia.indiatimes.com/Mumbai)

Television in a situation of terror, she claimed, is a medium through which victims can convey their emotion. B.G. Verghese, columnist and a former editor of the *Hindustan Times* and *The Indian Express*, disagreed with Dutt's view, and wrote: 'Some things are not done—rushing to get bytes from just rescued hostages, for instance'. (http://www.livemint.com) Many journalists who were on the scene, like Dutt, defended themselves against the accusation that they had chosen to disclose too much information. They claimed that it was the fault of government officials present who did nothing to restrain the media by placing physical barriers on the movements of journalists and photographers. At the same time, there were indeed certain camerapersons who did not exactly behave with dignity as they scrambled to photograph corpses being carried away.

Here are excerpts from what Dutt wrote while responding to criticism against the media on the NDTV website (http://www.ndtv.com):

'Sixty hours of live television at the best of times is impossibly difficult. But when it involves an ongoing and precarious terrorist operation and a potential danger to the lives of hundreds of people, it throws up challenges of the kind that none of us have ever dealt with before…As India debates where to go from here…I notice there is a different sort of civil war brewing; one that places us in the media on the other side of the enemy line….Please do note that at all times, the media respected the security cordon…

'If, as is now being suggested, the assessment is that the media was allowed too close to the operations, here is what we say: we would have been happy to stand at a distance much further away from the encounter sites, had anyone, anyone at all, asked us to move. In the 72 hours that we stood on reporting duty, not once were we asked to move further away. We often delayed live telecasting of images that we thought were sensitive so as to not compromise the ongoing operation. Not once, were we asked by anyone in authority, to switch our cameras off, or withhold images. When we did so, it was entirely our own assessment that perhaps it was safest to do so. Across the world, and as happened in the US after 9/11, there are daily, centralized briefings by officials to avoid any inadvertent confusion that media coverage may throw up. Not so in Mumbai. There was no central point of contact or information for journalists who were often left to their own devices to hunt down news that they felt had to be conveyed to their country. No do's and don'ts were provided by officials. While we understand that this situation was new for everyone involved, and so the government could not have been expected to have a full plan for media coverage, surely the same latitude should be shown to us? The NSG (National Security Guards) chief even thanked the media for our consistent co-operation. Later the NSG commandos personally thanked me for showcasing their need for a dedicated aircraft—which they shockingly did not have and which they have now been given after NDTV's special report was aired…

'Why did we interview waiting relatives who staked out at the hotels as they waited for news on their families and friends? Quite simply, because they "wanted" to talk. Allegations that I or any of my colleagues across the industry shoved a microphone in the faces of any waiting relative are untrue in the extreme. Television, for many of these people, became a medium to express pain, grief, anger and hope…. Capturing suffering on live television is a delicate issue that needs the utmost sensitivity. We believed we showed that sensitivity, by not thrusting microphones in people's faces, by respecting privacy if people asked for identities or images to be withheld, by never showing a ghoulish close-up of a body, and by respecting the limits set by the people themselves. Those limits were different for different people and had to be adapted to subjectively. But every interview of a relative that was aired on any of my shows was done so with the full consent and participation of the people speaking... to say that we had no business talking to families is an entirely naive and misplaced criticism.

'Could we have been more aware of the suffering and tragedy of those killed in the first few hours at the CST railway station and not got singularly focused on the two hotels? On this one point, I would concede that perhaps, this was a balance we lost and needed to redress earlier on during the coverage. But, mostly our attention was on the hotels, because they were the sites of the live encounters, and not because of some deliberate socio-economic prejudice. Still, when many emails poured in on how important it was to correct this imbalance, most of us, stood up, took notice, and tried to make amends for an unwitting lack of balance in air time…'

In an extremely competitive environment, how realistic is to expect media personnel to exercise 'due restraint' and 'self-regulation'? Expressing his frustration with irresponsible reporting, Chief Justice of India K.G. Balakrishnan said: 'One of the ill-effects of unrestrained coverage is that of provoking anger amongst the masses. Furthermore, the trauma resulting from the terrorist attacks may be used as a justification for undue curtailment of individual rights and liberties.' (www.thehindu.com)

'The tone of (the media's) coverage reconfirmed one's worst fears that the media's content assessment mechanism may be flawed and its perspective limited by the narrowly defined concerns of its practitioners,' wrote A.K. Bhattacharya in

Business Standard (3 December 2008). Bhattacharya seemed to suggest that the journalists who used exaggerated language did so because they believed it was accurate. During the 60-hour episode, some reporters tried to reflect the sense of frustration they believed citizens were feeling and this became evident from the tone of the language used. Jingoistic phrases like 'liberating Mumbai' were used. On 27 November 2008, the headlines of some of the prominent newspapers read as follows:

Daily News & Analysis: 'Mumbai Under Siege'
The Times of India: 'War on Mumbai'
Mumbai Mirror: 'Night of Terror'
The Economic Times: 'Bloody Hell'

The BBC was accused of jingoism for referring to the attackers as 'gunmen' or 'militants' instead of 'terrorists'. The distinction is a slight but important one–labelling them merely as 'gunmen' makes the hideous act seem commonplace apart from blurring out the diabolical and mercenary motives of the attackers. When London was attacked in July 2005, the gunmen were described throughout as 'terrorists'. Senior Indian journalist M.J. Akbar said he dissociated himself from the BBC because of the distinction that was sought to be drawn between 'attackers' and 'terrorists'. (www.rediff.com)

In an article in *The Telegraph* published on 4 December 2008, columnist Mukul Kesavan justified the language used by journalists in reporting the Mumbai siege by saying that 'journalists felt the need to anticipate and echo a public revulsion.' The 'need to anticipate' is not the duty of the media and, in fact, may have led to many pitfalls during the standoff. It misleads viewers towards unnecessary panic while heightening the sense of importance of the story. Chetan Chauhan in an article in the *Hindustan Times* wrote that, 'a senior (Information and Broadcasting) ministry official admitted that the coverage was done in a responsible manner by the national media, except a few aberrations'. (http://www.hindustantimes.com)

Journalists are required to remain calm and speak in a dispassionate, unemotional tone in conflict situations. While the media is also meant to act as an outlet for public emotion, journalists and editors are required to regulate the outlet in order to ensure that the information provided is credible so that their audiences have confidence in them When commended for his channel's reporter's 'sober' handling of the Mumbai attacks, Editor-in-Chief of the Times NOW television channel, Arnab Goswami, said: 'Our reporters are always told: "you are not the story". We avoid postcard journalism'. (www.timesofindia.indiatimes.com)

Bhattacharya noted that the November 2008 Mumbai attacks in which less than 200 people were killed, received much more media attention than the July 2006 bombings in crowded commuter trains in same city that resulted in the deaths of 209 people and injuries to some 700 more. The reason for this, Bhattacharya argues, is on account of the terrorists in the 2006 bombings remaining 'nameless and faceless' and also because the terror attacks lasted only 11 minutes–unlike the long drawn-out series of encounters in November 2008. Many television channels acknowledged later that in the rush to cover the events 'live', unverified information was put out as 'facts'. Given the rush of developments, it was not surprising that facts were interpreted in different ways. For instance, a reporter for Times NOW, while talking about the arrival of an ambulance was not sure if the vehicle was meant for the hostages or the terrorists or whether it signified the end of the stand-off (which it was not). Similarly, the CNN-IBN television channel aired the footage of a man holding a white flag on the roof of Nariman House (that was under siege) but was unsure whether it meant a sign of surrender or a plea for help. Television channels like CNN-IBN and BBC used information put up on blogging sites like Twitter to get updates—even if the sources of information were unknown. Journalists conceded that use of unverified information (in the name of citizen's journalism) was unethical. But there was considerable pressure on them to fill up time slots over a 60- hour period while the terrorist attacks were on. In the process, other important news developments were ignored altogether. For example, the death of former Prime Minister of India Vishwanath Pratap Singh in this period was almost completely ignored by certain television channels.

Two months before the Mumbai attacks, terrorists had bombed several areas in the national capital, New Delhi, and even then, many felt that media coverage had been unduly hyped. The Delhi Union of Journalists (DUJ) compiled a report in November 2008 ('Delhi Blasts: A Look at Encounter Coverage') of the manner in which the bomb blasts in Delhi had been covered by the media that had pointed out many of the mistakes that the media later repeated during the Mumbai terrorist attacks. Journalists were accused of speaking in excited and exaggerated tones. Though the only confirmed facts a day after the Delhi blasts were the identities of the three killed and one arrested, unconfirmed information was sought to be presented as hard facts by Indian newspapers. There were five different times given for when the shootout began, eight different accounts of its duration and five different figures (ranging from five to 50) of the number of policemen who were supposed to be present at the sites where the bomb blasts took place. 'The media is not equipped to investigate and uncover the truth in severely complicated cases', the DUJ report argued, adding: 'Accuracy in reporting facts is the first responsibility of the media. Where facts are disputed, the discrepancies should be pointed out and the sources questioned. Presenting several versions of incidents and using multiple sources of information is an inalienable part of credible reporting'.

Yet it would be incorrect to hold journalists solely responsible for inaccurate reporting. During the November 2008 terrorist attacks n Mumbai, government officials released contradictory bits of information and these were published or broadcast without further corroboration. On 27 November 2008, the Director General of Police (DGP) of Maharashtra A.N. Roy said: 'All people in the Taj hotel have been rescued. There is no hostage-like situation there right now'. This information turned out to be factually incorrect. After it was announced that there were no hostages left in the Oberoi Trident, NDTV decided to broadcast a live interview with an army officer who said there were more than 100 hostages still left inside the hotel. Perhaps one of the most dramatic and memorable images of the Mumbai attacks were the ones that depicted NSG commandos being lowered on to the roof of Nariman House from helicopters—these images were broadcast live and could well have revealed crucial information to the terrorists.

Who is to blame when information released by a government source is incorrect? At a discussion organized at the Press Club of India, New Delhi, by the Forum for Media Professionals on 12 December 2008, CNN-IBN's Editor-in-Chief Rajdeep Sardesai raised this question. He said he had been given information by a government source early on while the Mumbai attacks were on that there were 25 terrorists involved–it later transpired that the number was ten. Should information of this kind be double-checked before being broadcast? Does it matter if the information emanates from a source in the government? Sardesai was criticised for reporting rumours to the effect that there had been more firings inside the Chhatrapati Shivaji Terminus on the morning of 28 November 2008—he apologised on air when it was confirmed that there had been no such incident. Government authorities claimed at one stage that the terrorists could have come from Malaysia—subsequently it was found that the documents on the basis of which this claim had been made actually belonged to a hotel guest from Malaysia.

The problem, according to senior journalist Saeed Naqvi, who participated in the discussion that took place at the Press Club of India, was that there was no centralised source of information from the government to brief media personnel that led to contradictory bits of information being broadcast or published. Joe Leahy of *The Financial Times* of London was among those who defended the role of the media during the Mumbai attacks in keeping the public informed of developments as they unfolded. 'They were able to keep Mumbai citizens far better informed of the state of play on the ground than their own government, perhaps saving lives by keeping people at home', he said. (http://www.ft.com) As a matter of fact, many television viewers were troubled by what they were not seeing when the Deputy Commissioner of Police in Mumbai ordered a blackout of live television coverage for a few hours.

On the most persistent criticisms of the media coverage of the Mumbai attacks was its class bias. The Taj and the Oberoi Trident hotels are places which only the affluent can afford. The media was focused on what was happening in these hotels and less concerned about the events at the CST where ordinary people were killed. 'The media always revolves around the power centres, and hence is usually pro-elite...That is why the Taj Palace hotel, which is frequented by the creamy layer of the society and foreigners, remained at centre stage...I do not know the name of even a single person who died at CST or VT (Victoria Terminus),' said sociologist Prabha Dayal. (http://www.hardnewsmedia.com)

Journalist-writer in the Tamil language Gnani Sankaran asked the question 'Hotel Taj: Icon of whose India?' in response to stories printed in newspapers like The *Hindustan Times* and *The Times of India* recalling fond memories of the hotel or recapping its history. (http://openspace.org.in) Writing in The *New Indian Express* (6 December 2008) Mohan Ramamoorthy wondered where all the Mumbai-kars were in the reporting, who could argue that the Taj is only the icon of the elite and most have never been inside it. (http://www.expressbuzz.com). Writing in *The Times of London* (29 November 2008), Booker prize winning novelist and author of *The White Tiger*, Aravind Adiga, likened the Taj hotel to a town hall at the centre of the town that few had access to. (http://www.timesonline.co.uk)

In his article entitled 'Terrorised by TV' (*The Times of India*, 5 December 2008) Anil Dharker wrote that 60 hours after 26/11 began he first heard the term 'TV terrorism'. He said there many who felt that television channels had in their coverage of the terrorist attacks, unleashed their own brand of terrorism. He said the coverage was elitist and television channels became the unwitting tools of terrorists by giving vital information to them. He said competition among the channels had been unhealthy and wondered why during a national calamity, there was so much emphasis on airing 'exclusives'. 'Why were the anchors so loud and hysterical? Why couldn't they be more restrained?' Dharker asked, adding that 'there were quite a number of television journalists who were balanced, moderate and tried to be dispassionate'. He felt it was time for television networks to introspect.

Other commentators added that the live television coverage tended to be simplistic—good versus bad, heroes versus villains, India versus Pakistan and so on. Certain television journalists also acted in a manner that was downright stupid (asking a hostage 'Were you scared?'), often invasive and insensitive towards the family members of the victims (for instance, the way in which Shantanu Saikia, husband of journalist Sabina Sehgal Saikia who was killed, was asked questions), emotionally loaded (with frequent use of terms like 'dastardly' and 'heinous') and theatrical.

Jayati Ghosh, writing in *The Asian Age* on 2 December 2008, wondered: 'Who will hold up a mirror to the media?' She wrote: 'The prolonged nature of the operations in all three locations suggests that… media hyperactivity certainly could not have helped the brave men who risked their lives in a very dangerous, complex operation against deadly enemies…On several occasions, jostling and confusion among the crowd of assembled journalists created such confusion that the police had to be called in to control them. And because of the continuous presence of cameras, we were treated to the sorry spectacle of complete lack of sensitivity of the TV journalists when the traumatised survivors came out. Even when they begged for restraint and respect, microphones were shoved into their tired faces by the melee of journalists. Those who had lost family members in a terrible personal tragedy were not spared media scrutiny as the cameras panned in on their tears and watched their agony'.

Ghosh raised a number of questions: 'Is it that we as a society are now so degraded that even something as ghastly, tragic and horrifying as these incidents of terror and their awful personal aftermath for the victims can be treated like a television reality show? Or is it a sign of media gone crazy, an explosion of competitive journalism that is so obsessed with sensationalism that it has lost sight of humanity? It is common in such situations to call for introspection but even that is not enough if there is no subsequent change in behaviour. We have had to suffer the main presenters, especially on the English language channels, hold forth pompously and at length on the need to change polity, society and the nature of governance. "Enough is enough!" they announced, and said that citizens would not tolerate it any more. Unfortunately, none of them recognized any problems with the media's behaviour, or acknowledged that there was any need to change. Is it possible for society to now hold up a mirror for the media?'

In the week following the attacks, chief of the Indian Navy Admiral Sureesh Mehta, was outspoken in his criticism of the media at a public media conference describing it a 'disabling instrument'. Information divulged by the media, he claimed, compromised rescue efforts and may have cost lives. Referring to reports that Union Defence Minister A.K. Antony had pulled him up for the Navy's alleged lapses in not being able to prohibit the entry of the terrorists into Mumbai by the sea route despite specific intelligence inputs of an impending attack, Admiral Mehta said: 'You have put my reputation in the dock. I think the press has a responsibility'. At one point, he even told reporters that 'I would have chopped your heads off' for 'breach of privilege'.

Opening up what sections of the media described as a 'can of dead worms', Admiral Mehta held the television news channel NDTV responsible for the deaths of three soldiers during the 1999 Kargil conflict on account of what he claimed was a result of over-zealous coverage. He said that during the Kargil conflict, a 'Colonel was dismissed after he fired an artillery round on requests by an NDTV reporter that resulted in retaliatory fire which killed three jawans'. Without naming her, Admiral Mehta was apparently referring to NDTV's group editor Barkha Dutt. In turn, Dutt retorted that the Navy chief's tirades were 'nothing but ill-informed rumour-mongering' and argued that official records do not testify to such a dismissal.

This is what Barkha Dutt wrote on the NDTV website: 'We have only the greatest respect and admiration for our armed forces, and throughout the coverage repeatedly underlined how they are our greatest heroes. But we were taken aback to hear the Navy Chief, branding us as a "disabling force", for reporting on an ongoing operation. If that is the case, why were his own officers briefing us on camera, being in the middle of an ongoing operation and that too when they only had a few rushed moments at the site of encounters? Even before the encounter was over at either the

Taj or the Oberoi, his marine commandos held a hastily called press conference that was telecast live, with their permission, across channels. If we were indeed the obstacle, or the "disabling force" why did they have time for us in the middle of an operation? While shooting the messenger is convenient, the government also needs to introspect and determine whether it has an information dissemination system in place that is geared for such crises. Blanking out channels—as was done for a few hours—may not be the ideal solution. It only leads to more rumour mongering, panic and falsehoods spreading in already uncertain situation.

'Should there be an emergency code of 'dos' and 'don'ts' for the coverage of such crises? We in the media would welcome a framework for sensitive events and are happy to contribute to its construction. But it is important to understand that in the absence of any instructions on site and in the absence of any such framework we broke 'no' rules....we have an official acknowledgement of that, including from the then Army Chief, V.P. Malik. I would urge Admiral Mehta to read General V.P. Malik's book on Kargil for further clarity. General Malik was the Army Chief during the operations and puts to rest any such controversy in his book. In a formal letter, NDTV has also asked for an immediate retraction from the Navy and officially complained that the comments amount to defamation. Several writers have already pointed out how the Navy Chief has got his facts wrong. (*DNA, The Indian Express*, Vir Sanghvi in the *Hindustan Times*, Sankarshan Thakur in *The Telegraph*). This, incidentally, was the same press conference where the Admiral threatened literally to "chop the heads off" of two other reporters who aired his interview ahead of schedule.

'I believe that criticism is what helps us evolve and reinvent ourselves. But when malice and rumour are regarded as feedback, there can be no constructive dialogue. Viewing preferences are highly subjective and always deeply personal choices, and the most fitting rejection of someone who doesn't appeal to your aesthetics of intelligence, is simply to flick the channel and watch someone else. The viewer, to that extent, is king. But, when, comments begin targeting character, morality and integrity of individuals and the commentary becomes more about the individual, than the issue, then frankly, the anger is just destructive and little else. More than anything else, it is tragic that at this time, we are expressing ourselves in this fashion. Surely, India has bigger lessons to learn and larger points to mull over, than to expend energy over which television journalist tops the charts or falls to the bottom. The viewer has his own way, of settling such matters. And the last word belongs to him.'

The terrorist attack in Mumbai was akin to a '*jihadi fundraiser*', Prem Panicker argued in an article published on the rediff.com website on 2 December 2008. Panicker wrote that the attacks were as much about fund raising for the *jihadi* cause as it was about maintaining the 'drumbeat of terror'. He quoted Namrata Goswami, Associate Fellow at the Institute for Defence Studies and Analyses, New Delhi, saying: 'The attack was a corporate performance. Three days of terror, beamed live to living rooms across the country and transmitted around the world. There's a lot of money in it. An attack of this kind usually sees a spike in sponsorships and donations from abroad.'

As expected, viewership ratings for many television news channels were very high during the 26–28 November 2008 terrorist attacks in Mumbai. According to TAM Media Research—TAM is an acronym for Television Audience Measurement—Hindi language news channels saw a 153 per cent increase in the time viewers spent watching on 27 November 2008 (Thursday). English news channels too saw a 24 per cent increase in the time that was spent in watching television compared to the previous four Thursdays. For instance, the Hindi news channel Aaj Tak saw its Gross Rating Point (GRP) rise from 28.8 per cent to 36.8 per cent on 27 November 2008 against an average GRP of 6.3 per cent recorded in the four previous Thursdays. The 'exchange4media' website described the coverage of the Mumbai terrorist attacks coverage as 'the single most viewed telecast of the year'. Because of the duration of the crisis and the absence of authenticated information, the difference in the ratings between the channels turned out to be minimal. This was ironical in the sense that television channels that reported in an ethical and sober manner (and did not exaggerate or sensationalise) may have fared better in terms of viewership than those that exaggerated or sensationalised the reportage. (http://www.exchange4media.com)

Shortly after the attacks that began on 26 November 2008, the Information and Broadcasting (I&B) Ministry of the government of India began discussions to establish a committee that would formulate guidelines for the coverage of 'emergencies' like terror strikes, riots and natural disasters. The Ministry sent out a request to 42 broadcasters that run 200 news channels to practice 'restraint' and advised that 'gory scenes should not be shown'. The advisory was unanimously rejected by news broadcasters.

In December 2008, a committee formed by the News Broadcasters Association (NBA)—a self-regulatory body of television news broadcasters in India—under the chairmanship of retired Chief Justice of India Justice J.S. Verma issued a set of six guidelines, including a 'rule' that stated there should be no live contact with militants or hostages, no mention of security operation details and no images of people killed. Government officials, including those in security agencies, were not convinced that the media would be able to regulate itself adequately and refrain from overstepping these rules or guidelines during a crisis situation.

Thereafter, the I&B Ministry proposed the following amendments to the Cable Television Network Rules, 1995:

1. District magistrates and sub-divisional magistrates, besides commissioners of police, will have the power to block live transmission by any channel and confiscate transmission equipment.
2. Visuals and footage will be provided through a nodal agency in any such situation deemed 'nationally important'.

3. Officers will have the power to decide whether repeat telecast of a footage is necessary (and thereby in the national interest) or not.
4. They will also decide if any information is unauthenticated and should, therefore, be blocked.
5. Decisions regarding the nature of phone-in of reporters and victims or their interviews and if these disturb public order, will also rest with these officers. They will also decide if such phone-ins and interviews are against national interest.

Alarmed at the government's move to place such curbs and restrictions, the editors of several leading television news channels wrote a letter to Prime Minister Dr Manmohan Singh urging him not to impose these 'draconian' measures and that these would be nothing less than a 'historical blunder'. The letter stated, 'We are aware that our right to keep a vigil also brings with it a responsibility to function according to the highest standards of ethics and national interest. If instruments of the state begin to regulate us, the damage to democracy and all stakeholders in democracy would be irreparable'.

In a meeting with senior editors of several leading media organizations in New Delhi on 14 January 2009, Prime Minister Singh put to rest all speculation about the proposed amendments to the Cable Television Networks Rules, 1995. He said that there would be no changes to the rules without 'the widest possible consultation with all the stakeholders and eliciting their different points of view on the proposed changes'.

In the book *Ethical Issues: Journalism and Media* (edited by Andrew Belsey and Ruth Chadwick, Routledge, 1992, London and New York), contributor Paul Gilbert in the chapter entitled 'The Oxygen of Publicity: Terrorism and Reporting Restrictions' recounts the observation made in 1985 by the then British Prime Minister Margaret Thatcher who said 'Terrorism thrives on the oxygen of publicity' in the context of attacks from supporters of the Irish Republican Army (IRA) that had wanted to 'liberate' Northern Ireland from British control. She contended that in a war, civil liberties may have to be suspended.

In any counter-terrorist or military operation secrecy is of the essence, Gilbert points out, adding that this is generally achieved by two means: by controlling the flow of information available only to the government and by censorship. The extent to which either of these measures can be justified during a war or a counter-terrorist operation is debatable. 'But since both methods are in question, this debate turns on the balance between State secrecy and the public's alleged right to know, rather than on that between enforced secrecy and freedom of expression. Whatever the extent of the public's right to know, it is evident that it is often in the interests of people in a war zone, to know enough about it to take effective precautions,' Gilbert has written.

Journalists and politicians share a love-hate relationship. Each needs the other and each frequently criticises the other. The last few words in this section go to a rather controversial statement reportedly made by the President of Pakistan Asif Ali

Zardari on January 15, 2009, in Islamabad while addressing a delegation of some 40 businessmen from the North West Frontier Province. He is supposed to have remarked on the occasion that 'journalists are bigger terrorists than terrorists themselves'. Since no media persons were present when Zardari made his remarks, his statement was widely reported in many newspapers and televison channels on the basis of accounts given by those who were present. Five days later, the Information Minister in the government of Pakistan sought to play down the President's remarks saying he was not against all journalists. One of the businessperson present on the occasion replied that he was willing to testify in court that President Zardari indeed said what he was reported as saying.

Discussion Questions

1. Do you think that the media coverage of the Mumbai attacks was class biased?
2. Do you think Barkha Dutt's criticism of the comments made by Admiral Sureesh Mehta is justified or not?
3. Do you think government officials should regulate media coverage of emergency situations like a terrorist attack?

References for the Case Study

http://timesofindia.indiatimes.com/Mumbai/Blow-by-blow_breaking_news_breaks_viewer_patience/articleshow/3785897.cms

http://www.livemint.com/2008/12/04003806/Indian-Pakistani-media-trade.html

http://www.ndtv.com/convergence/ndtv showcolumns.aspx?id= COLEN 20080075194

www.thehindu.com/2008/12/14/stories/2008121456480100.htm

www.rediff.com/news/2008/dec/14mumterror-mj-akbar-slams-bbc-for-biased-coverage-of-mumbai-terror-attack.htm

http://www.hindustantimes.com/StoryPage Fullcoverage StoryPage.aspx? section Name=IndiaSectionPage&id=5c7befa5-27d9-499e-bcb28425d8f699ba Mumbaiunderattack_Special&&Headline=I%26amp%3 bB+may+ take+action+ against+TV+channels

www.timesofindia.indiatimes.com/Mumbai/Blow-by-blow_breaking_news_breaks_viewer_patience/articleshow/3785897.cms

http://www.ft.com/cms/s/0/72a3f44a-c21d-11dd-a350-000077b07658.html

http://www.hardnewsmedia.com/2008/12/2454

http://openspace.org.in/node/808

http://www.expressbuzz.com/edition/story.aspx?Title= The+channel +box+ carnage &artid= bGVFbYMd Cnk=&SectionID=f4OberbKin4=& MainSectionID =f4OberbKin4=&SEO=&Section Name=cxWvYpmNp4fBHAeKn 3LcnQ==

http://www.timesonline.co.uk/tol/comment/columnists/guest_contributors/article5254236.ece

http://www.exchange4media.com/e4m/news/fullstory.asp?section_id=6&news_id=33335&tag=28287

APPENDIX 4.1

Journalistic Ethics

The PCI states: 'While newspapers are entitled to ensure, improve or strengthen their financial viability by all legitimate means, the press shall not engage in crass commercialism or unseemly cut-throat commercial competition with their rivals in a manner repugnant to high professional standards and good taste. Predatory price wars/ trade competition among newspapers, laced with tones disparaging the products of each other, initiated and carried on in print, assume the colour of an unfair "trade" practice, repugnant to journalistic ethics. The question as to when it assumes such an unethical character...depends on the circumstances of each case.'

Guilt by Association

The PCI states: '...newspapers should eschew suggestive guilt by association. They should not name or identify the family or relatives or associates of a person convicted or accused of a crime, when they are totally innocent and a reference to them is not relevant to the matter reported.'

Though this suggestion is valid, the question that arises is what the media should do if a person is held guilty by association by an official authority (see Box 4.6).

Box 4.6

Haneef and the Australian Media

In July 2007, following the Glasgow bombings, Indian physician Mohammed Haneef was detained in Brisbane by Australian authorities on allegations of aiding and abetting terrorism. Haneef's cousins had been accused of masterminding the failed bombings by UK authorities. Haneef's visa was cancelled amidst political controversy and considerable media attention. He was detained for a long period without any charges. Eventually, all allegations against him were withdrawn and he returned to India.

Respecting Communal and Religious Sentiments

The PCI states: 'News, views or comments relating to communal or religious disputes/ clashes shall be published after proper verification of facts and presented with due caution and restraint in a manner which is conducive to the creation of an atmosphere congenial to communal harmony, amity and peace. Sensational, provocative and alarming headlines are to be avoided. Acts of communal violence or vandalism shall be reported in a manner as may not undermine the people's confidence in the law and order machinery of the state. Giving community wise figures of the victims of communal riot, or writing about the incident in a style which is likely to inflame passions, aggravate the tension, or accentuate the strained relations between the communities/ religious groups concerned, or which has a potential to exacerbate the trouble, shall be avoided...In general and particularly in the context of communal disputes or clashes

- provocative and sensational headlines are to be avoided
- headings must reflect and justify the matter printed under them
- headings containing allegations made in statements should either identify the body or the source making it or at least carry quotation marks'

Reporting Official Information

The PCI states: 'So far as the government, local authority and other organs/institutions exercising governmental power are concerned, they cannot maintain a suit for damages for acts and conduct relevant to the discharge of their official duties unless the official establishes that the publication was made with reckless disregard for the truth. However, the judiciary which is protected by the power to punish for contempt of court and the Parliament and legislatures, protected as their privileges are by Articles 105 and 194 respectively, of the Constitution of India, represent exception to this rule.....Publication of news or comments/information on public officials conducting investigations should not have a tendency to help the commission of offenses or to impede the prevention or detection of offenses or prosecution of the guilty. The investigative agency is also under a corresponding obligation not to leak out or disclose such information or indulge in disinformation... The Official Secrets Act, 1923, or any other similar enactment or provision having the force of law, equally bind the press or media though there is no law empowering the state or its officials to prohibit, or to impose a prior restraint upon the press/media.'

APPENDIX 4.2

What is Obscene?

Section 292 of the IPC relating to obscenity reads as follows.

'Sale, etc., of obscene books, etc.: [(1)] for the purposes of sub-section (2), (a) book, pamphlet, paper, writing, drawing, painting, representation, figure or any other object, shall be deemed to be obscene, if it is lascivious or appeals to the prurient interest or if its effect, or (where it comprises two or more distinct items) the effects of any one of its items, is, if taken as a whole, such as to tend to deprave and corrupt persons who are likely, having regard to all relevant circumstances, to read, see or hear the matter contained or embodied in it.]

[(2) Whoever sells, lets to hire, distributes, publicly exhibits or in any manner puts into circulation or for purposes of sale, hire, distribution public exhibition of circulation, makes produces, or has in

(a) possession any obscene book, pamphlet, paper, drawing, painting, representation or figure or any other obscene objects whatsoever, or

(b) imports, exports or conveys any obscene objects for any of the purposes, aforesaid, on knowing or having reason to believe that such objects will be sold, let to hire, distributed or publicly exhibited or in any manner put into circulation, or

(c) takes part in or receives profit from any business in the course of which he knows or has reasons to believe that such an object are for any of the purposes aforesaid, made produced, purchased, kept, imported, exported, convey, publicly exhibited, or in any manner put into circulation, or

(d) advertises or makes known by any means whatsoever that any person is engaged or is ready to engage in any act which is an offense under this section, or that any such obscene object can be procured from or through any person, or

(e) offers or attempts to do any act which is an offense under this section, shall be punished [on first conviction with imprisonment of either description for a term which may extend to two years, and with fine which may extend to two thousand rupees, and, in the event of a second or subsequent conviction, with imprisonment of either description for a term which may extend to five years, and also with fine which may extend to five thousand rupees.]

[Exception…(to) this section does not extend to:

(a) any book, pamphlet, paper, writing, drawing, painting, representation of figure

  (i) the publication of which is proved to be justified as being for the public good on the ground that such book, pamphlet, paper, writing, drawing, painting, representation or figure is in the interest of science, literature, art or learning or other objects of general concern, or

  (ii) which is kept or used bona fide for religious purpose

(b) any representation sculptured, engraved, painted or otherwise represented on or in

  (i) any ancient monument within the meaning of the Ancient Monuments and Archaeological Sites and Remains Act,1958 (24 of 58), or

  (ii) any temple, or any car used for the conveyance of idols, or kept or used for any religious purpose.]

Section 292 of Act 8 of 1952 was amended by Act 36 of 1969. The objects and reasons laid down by the Parliament for the amendment states that:

Under the present Section 292 and Section 293 of the Indian Penal Code, there is a danger of publication meant for public good or for bona fide purpose of science, literature, art or any other branch of learning being declared as obscene literature as there is no specific provision in the Act for exempting them from operations of those sections. The amendment to the Act removes that lacuna so as to bring the law into conformity with modern practice in other civilized countries.

APPENDIX 4.3

AIDS and the Media

The Press Council of India under the mandate of Section 13(2)(b) of the Press Council Act, 1978 has built up a set of guidelines to facilitate the functioning of the Media. Of these, the guidelines on coverage of HIV/AIDS related matter was drawn up in the year 1993.

A writ petition no. CMP 52/2008 was filed by National Network of Positive People before Honourable Court of Juvenile, Thiruvananthapuram objecting to an incident relating to visuals screened by the media of two children Bensy and Benson and the subsequent false reporting of the demise of Bensy, a child with HIV/AIDS. The Hon'ble Court observed that the Press Council of India should give appropriate direction to the Media while reporting HIV/AIDS by them. In pursuance of this matter the Council approached the representatives of UNAIDS and activists in the field to update the guidelines on HIV/AIDS reporting as the matter has undergone sea change since 1993. The core group held two workshops on 18 September 2008 and 10 October 2008 to discuss and debate on the guidelines formulated and proposed that these guidelines should be translated into as many languages as possible for the benefit of the journalists at various levels. These guidelines are equally relevant to print as well as electronic media.

Be Objective, Factual and Sensitive

Journalists must ensure that their story is objective, factual and sensitive, more so when they are reporting on HIV and AIDS. They should seek truth and report it in a balanced manner. Journalists should hold all decision makers accountable, from government to the pharmaceutical industry and advocacy groups. They should be engaged with, but not captive to, any interest group.

This means highlighting positive stories where appropriate, without underplaying the fact that HIV and AIDS is a serious issue. Omitting key information because it does not fit into the story is a breach of faith. The story must give both sides of the picture. Telling the whole story also means giving it a human face. The voices of people with HIV and AIDS must be heard more strongly and they must include the vulnerable and marginalised people.

The focus should be on facts. Distortion of facts in any manner to make the story salacious and therefore 'more saleable' is unacceptable. Censorship of relevant information too is unethical.

Accuracy is critical since important personal and policy decisions may be influenced by media reports. In the context of HIV and AIDS, journalists need to be very careful about the scientific and medical details as well as statistics. With the combination of drugs and treatment regimens available known as antiretroviral therapy (ART), people infected with HIV can live for many years before showing any signs of illness. ART is a combination of drugs that reduces the amount of HIV in the body (viral load) by interfering with its replication. ART does not completely destroy the virus or cure the disease. With reduced virus in the body, the immune system can become stronger and fight infection more effectively, resulting in decreased morbidity for the patient. ART has been shown to benefit both adults and children living with HIV and AIDS.

Reporting on HIV and AIDS is complex and sorting through the epidemiological data can be challenging. Whether using data to support a story or reporting on the data itself, the specific data chosen and how they are used, will play a large role in determining what kind of story is told. In addition, the data is often so complex that there is a risk of misinterpretation. For example, some reporters may use 'incidence' and prevalence' interchangeably even though they represent two different ways of measuring the epidemic. Experts/ epidemiologists should be consulted.

Ensure Accurate Language and Terminology

When reporting on HIV and AIDS, language is extremely important. Journalists should be particularly careful to get scientific and statistical information right. They must integrate this with correct terminology. For instance, it is essential to know and make clear the difference between HIV and AIDS. Being a syndrome or a collection of symptoms, AIDS cannot itself be transmitted, nor is there an AIDS virus, nor an AIDS carrier. Similarly, a person either does or does not have AIDS. Since there are no degrees of AIDS, the expression 'full-blown AIDS' is meaningless.

With effective treatments now available, HIV infection does not necessarily lead to AIDS. It is important to reflect this in reportage. Since HIV is not synonymous with AIDS, 'HIV/AIDS' as a term is no longer considered accurate.

With AIDS not being a singular disease but a syndrome defined by a variety of diseases and cancers, a person does not 'die of AIDS'. It would instead be accurate to report that he or she died of an HIV-related illness.

Terminology used must be appropriate and non-stigmatising. The media must cross check changes in terminology and language. Terms like 'scourge' to describe the infection have been discarded. Other terms like AIDS carrier, prostitute, drug addict, AIDS patient/victim/sufferer also lead to stigma and should not be used.

Debunk Myths Related to Prevention of HIV and Miracle Cures

The press should take care not to promote myths related to prevention and transmission of HIV or to claims that advertise protection from the infection. Nor should it give any credence to traditional cures that have no scientific verification. False hopes are raised by reporting claims around cures. Researchers have been working hard for decades yet there is no known cure for HIV or AIDS although the infection is treatable with a positive impact on the quality of life. The media should include telephone numbers of HIV and AIDS helplines/counselling services.

Advertisements related to HIV, STIs, skin diseases, tuberculosis and other opportunistic infections can be potentially misleading and should be carefully checked.

Make Photographs, Illustrations and Cartoons Positive

Visuals have an immediate impact on audiences and are important to highlight stories. But the use of photographs in HIV and AIDS stories raises a lot of ethical issues. Care should be taken to ensure that photographs do not breach the confidentiality or privacy of infected people and their families.

Avoid photos that promote stereotypes related to HIV and AIDS and those that victimize the infected. Care should be taken to ensure that captions to photographs are factually correct and do not increase stigma.

Illustrations and cartoons also should avoid any negative implications.

For Visual Media

The visual media must deal sensitively and ethically with the identities of those who have HIV and AIDS as well as their families and associates. Care must be taken during interviews, off-the-record conversations, while taking photographs and recording their stories so that identity is kept confidential. Some pointers for the same are as follows:

- Keep the camera away from focussing directly on the face of person/case study. Instead, shoot hands, feet or back of the head.
- Shoot in silhouette, keeping the camera behind the subject.
- Since voice can also be an identifying factor, ask questions softly so that the replies are soft. In most cases, superimposition of subtitles should be used so that the audio does not need to be upped too much.
- Do not show pictures of the family. These too can lead to identification of the person.
- Try to keep the location of the shoot ambiguous, for instance, avoid naming the village.
- Establish the concerned person's journey through a third party's voice whenever possible.

- An interview should be a one-to-one chat that allows the person to speak. Ensure questions are not deeply personal or accusatory. They should not put the person on the defensive.
- Hidden cameras should never be used.
- Try to show people living with HIV in a positive light by portraying them as individuals instead of 'victims'.
- Wherever possible, obtain written consent.

Consent Form

I, ________________Son/ Daughter of ________________, am a responsible adult / Parent/legal guardian of ______________ Aged______________ years, agree that you________________ (name of interviewer/photographer) and your photographer/cameraman have my permission to record my statement/interview and take my photograph for print/audio visual media, on HIV and AIDS related issues.

I understand that my statement/interview will not be distorted or misused in any way wherever it is used. The photographer will also ensure that photographs do not breach my confidentiality or that of my family.

You will also ensure that statement/interview taken of ______________ (name of interviewee), who is a minor, does not reveal his/her identity in any way.

It has also been explained to me in my language (______________) that there could be a potential fallout of my statement that could include stigma and discrimination directed towards me, my family members, relatives and friends.

ADDRESS: ____

Phone: ____

DATE: ____

SIGNATURE: ____

Even with permission, it may be best not to disclose the infected person's identity. The repercussions and pressures of being revealed on TV particularly can be terrible, especially for the family. The stigma gets heightened. In many cases permission to shoot openly is given without understanding the power of the visual media.

The person may feel safe appearing on TV in Delhi, away from his/her community, not realizing the possibility that his/her family is watching the story in a village/ town far away.

For News Desk Including Sub-editors and Newsroom Staff

Special attention must be paid by the news desk and newsroom staff to ensure that the eye-catching headlines reflect the issue accurately and that the story is balanced and free of damaging stereotypes.

Uphold Confidentiality and Obtain Informed Consent

Journalists should not disclose the identity of the person infected with HIV unless they have specific permission to do so. Whenever possible, they should get written consent. If written consent is not possible, informed consent must be obtained. This means ensuring that people living with HIV and AIDS (PLHIVs) are aware of the implications of their identification.

The moral and professional responsibility of the story should be that of the journalist. Therefore, the journalist must exercise caution and use his/her judgment on how PLHIVs are to be portrayed. To minimize damaging repercussions it would be best to avoid identification even when written consent is obtained. This can be done by changing names and locations in the story.

Avoid Discrimination

Journalists should avoid references to caste, gender or sexual orientation when reporting HIV and AIDS. Such references entrench existing prejudices against sexual minorities, certain communities or groups already targetted, be they men who have sex with men (MSM), injecting drug users (IDUs), sex workers or migrants.

Sexual minorities include people who are lesbian, gay, bisexual and transgender (LGBT) and covers men, women and all those who do not identify either as men or women (that is, transgender). Among the transgender are *hijras*. *Hijras* are essentially biological born males who do not identify as men and prefer to identify as women.

It is important to understand that MSMs may never identify as homosexual. Therefore, the word MSM is used to denote behaviour only. So it is appropriate to say Oscar Wilde was a gay man and not Oscar was gay.

Sexual minorities are sometimes derisively referred to by terms which reinforce stereotypes about the community. Instead, it would be more appropriate to use terms like sexual minorities, gay man or lesbian. It is not necessary to call them that either as long as one does not stigmatise them.

While infomation about modes of transmission are important, instead of making value judgements the reports should try to focus on how the infection affects people, their work, their families and the gaps in policy and implementation of HIV programmes. Focussing needlessly on how a person was infected reinforces an attitude that seeks to blame those with HIV or AIDS for being infected.

Care should be taken to ensure that a particular region's language, cultural norms and traditional practices are understood and accurately reported.

Ensure Gender Sensitive reporting

The media must guard against gender stereotyping. It must not stigmatize HIV positive women. For instance, portraying sex workers and bar girls as being responsible for spreading the infection is common. Instead, stories should explore how the infection makes women particularly vulnerable to different forms of exploitation. Stories must focus on how it is possible to live a productive and reasonably normal life with HIV, about the inherent strength that enables women to shoulder challenges and about the ethical and legal rights of sex workers.

Stories should also focus on the new technology and medication available for prevention of infection from mother to child and the fact that infected women can have children who may be free of the infection.

An example of gender sensitive reportage is the use of PPTCT (Prevention of Parent to Child Transmission) instead of PMTCT (Prevention of Mother to Child Transmission). This way the report does not hold the mother solely responsible for passing the infection.

Ensure Sensitivity on Child-Related Stories

The identity of children infected and affected by HIV should not be revealed. Nor should their photographs be shown. This include orphans and children living in orphanages, juvenile homes, etc.

International and national laws specifically prohibit publication of any information or photograph that may lead to the identification of these children and violate their rights.

In India, the Juvenile Justice (Care and Protection of Children) Act, 2000 lays down that no report in any newspaper, magazine or visual media regarding a juvenile in need of care and protection shall disclose the name, address, school or any other particulars that lead to their identification. It also prohibits the publication of any photograph related to the child.

Journalists must also be sensitive to the fact that a child may or may not be aware of her/his HIV status. This fact must be ascertained before the journalist gets into the process of enquiry. This is of prime importance as some questions can be perceived as intrusive or insensitive and can leave a lasting impression on the child.

Keeping that in mind, it is nevertheless important for children to participate in matters that concern them. However, their identities must be protected while sharing their views/stories.

The fact that paediatric doses of ART medication are now available must be widely disseminated.

Ensure Balanced and Responsible Coverage

News organizations (NGOs) should take the initiative to lessen the impact of a 'negative' story such as suicide due to HIV-related illness by carrying statements from positive people who have faced the challenge successfully or by giving helpline numbers.

Care should be taken that stories on infected individuals are not sensationalized. The stories should avoid falling into the trap of projecting infected persons as either 'victims' or 'culprits'.

When reporting on specific professional groups such as uniformed services, health professionals, etc. care should be taken to obtain data from authorized sources. Inaccurate reports will have an adverse impact on their morale and will also increase stigma. Such reports will also create an impression of lack of confidentiality that will hinder voluntary testing.

Ensure Regular Training on HIV and AIDS for Media

Journalists must keep abreast of the changing realities of this fast-evolving infection. News organizations across the country must actively encourage training workshops and modules on the issue. Journalists should also keep themselves updated on court judgements related to the issue.

HIV is no longer just a health issue. Instead of concentrating on health reporters alone, people at all levels of the news organization should be trained and sensitised on the various dimensions, especially terminology of HIV and AIDS. The infection impacts on the country's development, economics, business and politics. Surveys have shown that with training and sensitization, media reportage on HIV and AIDS, particularly in high-prevalence states, has been relatively more balanced and accurate.

Adopt Existing Stylebook or Guidelines on HIV and AIDS Reportage

News organizations should adopt and widely disseminate existing standardized guidelines and terminology on reporting on HIV and AIDS. This will encourage responsible coverage of the issue.

AIDS and the Media—Do's and Don'ts

Do's

- Media must inform and educate the people, not alarm or scare them

- Be objective, factual and sensitive
- Keep abreast with changing realities of fast-evolving infection
- Use appropriate language and terminology that is non-stigmatising
- Ensure headlines are accurate and balanced
- Be responsible; give all sides of the picture, using voices of people living with HIV and AIDS (PLHIVs)
- Dispel misconceptions about prevention and transmission
- Debunk myths about miracle cures and unscientific claims of protection from infection
- Highlight positive stories without underplaying seriousness of the issue
- Uphold confidentiality of infected people, their families and associates
- Ensure photographs do not breach their confidentiality
- Ensure photo captions are accurate
- Ensure gender sensitive reporting and avoid stereotyping
- Obtain data from authorized sources as inaccurate reports have adverse impact on morale and increase stigma
- Journalists are responsible for ensuring interviewees understand repercussions of revelations/identification
- Ensure informed consent, in written form wherever possible
- Balance coverage of a negative story like HIV-related suicide or incidence of discrimination by including contacts of helplines/counselling centres
- Broaden reportage to examine impact of infection on economic, business, political and development issues
- When in doubt contact the local network of positive people or state AIDS control society or existing terminology guidelines for clarification
- Ensure questions are not deeply personal or accusatory
- Show PLHIVs in a positive light by portraying them as individuals instead of 'victims'

Don'ts

- Don't sensationalise the story
- Don't make value judgements that seek to blame PLHIVs
- Don't use terms like 'scourge' to describe the infection or describe a PLHIV as AIDS carrier, prostitute, drug addict, AIDS patient/ victim/sufferer
- Don't focus needlessly on how a PLHIV was infected
- Don't identify children infected and affected by HIV and AIDS by name or through a photograph even with consent
- Don't use hidden cameras
- Avoid alarmist reports and images of the sick and dying that convey a sense of gloom, helplessness and isolation
- Don't use skull, crossbones, snakes or such visuals as graphics
- Avoid references to caste, gender or sexual orientation
- Don't reinforce stereotypes about sexual minorites including those who are lesbian, gay, bisexual or transgender (LGBT)
- Don't portray infected persons as victims, culprits or objects of pity
- Don't promote misleading advertisements related to HIV, STIs, skin diseases, tuberculosis and other opportunistic infections
- Don't breach the confidentiality of those opting for voluntary testing

CHAPTER

5

PRIVACY

The concept of privacy has a deep bearing on media ethics. Though it is generally agreed that every individual has the right to privacy, the issue of whether this right can be transgressed, and under what circumstances, is a topic of considerable contention and debate. In this chapter, we shall first look at the development of privacy rights and then consider the provisions of the law for the right to privacy in India. We shall identify the various facets of privacy as laid down in the PCI's guidelines. Thereafter, the nature of public interest as an excuse for transgressing privacy rights is explored. An understanding of the ethical dimension of the right to privacy at this stage will enable the comprehension of some issues addressed in Chapters 7 and 8 on Media Laws and Sting Operations.

This chapter aims at providing an overview of privacy laws and differentiates between the individual's right to privacy and what is in the public interest. It explains the circumstances under which public interest can override an individual's right to privacy.

A BRIEF HISTORY OF PRIVACY LAW AND PROPERTY RIGHTS

Privacy has been described as the 'right of a person to be left alone' in successive judgements by courts of law in the US and elsewhere. In 1928, in the *Olmstead* versus *US* case (Olmstead versus US (1928) 277 US 438), the Supreme Court of the US reviewed whether or not the use of wire-tapped private telephone conversations, obtained by federal government agents without judicial approval and subsequently used as evidence, constituted a violation of the defendant's rights provided by the Fourth and Fifth Amendments to the American Constitution. In a close five–four decision, the court held that the rights of the defendant had not been violated but this decision was later reversed in 1967 in another judgement of the court in the *Katz* versus *US* case. In a 1952 case (*Public Utilities Commission* versus *Pollack* (1952) 343 US 451), Justice William O. Douglas opined: 'The right to be left alone is indeed the beginning of all freedom.' This case involved an attempt to impose audio messages on an audience in a public streetcar. Douglas argued that a 'streetcar audience is a captive audience...there as a matter of necessity and not by choice…One who enters any public place sacrifices some of his privacy. My protest is against the invasion of his privacy over and beyond the risks of travel.'

A seminal article on privacy law in the US and its roots in common law entitled 'The Right to Privacy' was written by Samuel Warren and Louis D. Brandeis and originally published in the *Harvard Law Review* in December 1890. The article argued (Retief 2002) that following the recognition of the legal value of thoughts, sensations and ideas, it was only a question of time before the right 'to be left alone' was recognized. The authors explained how the protection from actual bodily injury was extended to the protection from the cause of the fear of such injury. Thus the action of battery grew from that of assault.

Qualified protection became available against noises and odours, against dust and smoke, and excessive vibration. Analogous to the expansion of the concept of life was the inclusion of intangibles like trade secrets and trademarks, in the concept of property. Attempting to examine whether the existing law had space for protection against the invasion of privacy, the article concluded that resemblance to defamation was merely superficial; the latter involved a radically different class of effects.

Published material can have a tendency to injure the claimant by subjecting her/him to the hatred, ridicule or contempt of fellow people—conditions which an invasion of privacy need not necessarily satisfy. On the other hand, Warren and Brandeis attempt to explain how common law rights to artistic or intellectual property are but extensions of the right to privacy. The common law decrees the individual's right to determine the extent to which his thoughts and ideas are communicated to others. This right is independent of the mode of expression chosen, and also of the value of the particular sentiment, thought or idea (Aju 2008).

The belief that the concept of property, in its narrow sense, included unpublished manuscripts which merited protection, led courts of law to refuse, in several cases, injunctions against the publication of private letters, on the grounds that 'letters not possessing the attributes of literary compositions are not property entitled to protection'; and that it was 'evident the plaintiff could not have considered the letters as of any value whatever as literary productions, for a letter cannot be considered of value to the author which he never would consent to have published'.

However, these decisions were not followed and now the protection afforded by the common law to the author of any writing is entirely independent of its pecuniary value, its intrinsic merits, or of any intention to publish the work, and, of course, also wholly independent of the thought or sentiment expressed. This leads us to the conclusion that the protection afforded to thoughts, sentiments and emotions, expressed through artistic media, is an instance of the enforcement of the more general right of the individual to be left alone. This is a principle, not of private property, but of inviolate personality. The conclusion of Warren and Brandeis was that the existing law provided a principle which could be invoked to 'protect the privacy of the individual from invasion either by the too enterprising press, the photographer, or the possessor of any other modern device for recording or reproducing scenes or sounds'.

The ambit of the right, however, differs in various legal systems, depending on common law or judicial pronouncements on constitutionally enumerated rights, or fragmented legislation. The American courts have moved the right to privacy from the realm of private law into constitutional law, recognizing it as an issue of legitimate public interest for the restriction of expression. In the *Breard* versus *City of Alexandria* case of 1951, it was observed that however valuable freedom might be, it could not be used to defeat the corresponding or competing rights of other persons, which are of equal value *(Breard* versus *City of Alexandria* (1951) 341 US 622). The proposition that the State may legitimately curtail the publication of news which intrudes on the privacy of individuals, if it is devoid of public interest, is now law in the US. Canada has gone to the extent of enacting the Privacy Act of 1968 which decrees that in the absence of 'public interest', an invasion of privacy would be actionable in damages without proof of damage and irrespective of any trespass having been committed by the defendant.

PRIVACY LAW IN INDIA

In India, the right of privacy is recognized in both common law and constitutional law. Article 19(1)(a) of the Constitution of India guarantees the fundamental right to freedom of speech and expression. In accordance with Article 19(2), this right can be restricted by law only in the 'interests of the sovereignty and integrity of India, the security of the State, friendly relations with Foreign States, public order, decency or morality or in relation to contempt of court, defamation or incitement to an offence'. The Supreme Court of India has concluded that the fundamental right to privacy ensues from the right to life (Article 21 of the Constitution).

In 1964, in the *Kharak Singh* versus *State of Uttar Pradesh* case, the Supreme Court held that the right to privacy was an 'essential ingredient of personal liberty' which is 'a right to be free from restrictions or encroachments'. In the Kharak Singh case, the court said that nothing is more deleterious to a man's physical happiness and health than a calculated interference with his privacy. In 1975, in the *Govind* versus *State of Madhya Pradesh* case, the Supreme Court expounded the law on this subject thus: 'Privacy-dignity claims deserve to be examined with care and to be denied only when an important countervailing interest is shown to be superior.'

Surveillance

In the Kharak Singh case, the Supreme Court undermined the regulation which authorized domiciliary visits as being unconstitutional, but upheld the other provisions of surveillance under that regulation. At that time, the court did not recognize the right to privacy. Its view was based on the conclusion that the infringement of a fundamental right must be both 'direct' as well as 'tangible' and that the freedom guaranteed under Article 19(1)(a) was not infringed by a watch being kept over the movements of a suspect. But in the *Govind* versus *State of Madhya Pradesh* case, also a surveillance case, the Supreme Court, while upholding the regulation on authorized domiciliary visits by security personnel, also held that depending on the character and antecedents of the person and the limitation under which surveillance is made, domiciliary visits would not always be an unreasonable restriction on the individual's right of privacy. Hence, a citizen's right to privacy must be subject to restriction on the basis of compelling public interest.

What kind of information might be of compelling public interest? What are some of the considerations in discerning public interest?

An encroachment upon privacy is shielded only if the offender is the state rather than a private entity. If the offender is a private individual, damages can be claimed for intrusion of privacy only in tort. In the

R. Rajagopal versus *State of Tamil Nadu* case (1994) (6 SCC (Supreme Court Cases) 632), the Supreme Court held that the right to privacy is a right to be left alone. No one can publish material pertaining to another without her/his consent, regardless of whether the material is truthful or otherwise, laudatory or critical. Doing so would violate that person's right to privacy and would be liable in an action for damages.

PCI GUIDELINES ON PRIVACY AND PUBLIC INTEREST

The PCI has laid down certain guidelines regarding the right to privacy: 'The press shall not intrude or invade the privacy of an individual, unless outweighed by genuine overriding public interest, not being a prurient or morbid curiosity…however, …once a matter becomes a matter of public record, the right to privacy no longer subsists and it becomes a legitimate subject for comment by the press and the media, among others.' The guidelines explain that 'things concerning a person's home, family, religion, health, sexuality, personal life and private affairs are covered by the concept of privacy excepting where any of these impinges upon the public or public interest'.

What is Public and What is Private?

The PCI distinguishes between private and public citizens, stating that: '...the degree of privacy differs from person to person and from situation to situation. The public person who functions under public gaze as an emissary/representative of the public cannot expect to be afforded the same degree of privacy as a private person. His acts and conduct as are of public interest ("public interest" being distinct and separate from "of interest to public") even if conducted in private may be brought to public knowledge through the medium of the press. The press has, however, a corresponding duty to ensure that the information about such acts and conduct of public interest of the public person is obtained through fair means, is properly verified and then reported accurately. For obtaining information in respect to acts conducted away from public gaze, the press is not expected to use surveillance devices. For obtaining information about private talks and discussion, while the press is expected not to badger the public persons, the public persons are also expected to bring openness in their functioning and cooperate with the press in its duty of informing the public about the acts of their representatives.

'Interviews/articles or arguments/comments pertaining to public persons which border on events that are supposed to be public knowledge, if reported correctly, cannot be termed as intrusion into private life. There is a very thin dividing line between public and private life and public persons should not be too thick-skinned when it comes to comments or criticism of their actions or views by journalists. The mass media are allowed certain latitude in criticizing persons who are in seats of power because their conduct constitutes public interest, provided their criticism is not merely motivated to gratify private spite of opponents/rivals of a particular public figure.'

Under Indian law, the extent to which a person can claim a right to privacy is dependent on her/his public status. A person who welcomes media interest in her/his life will not be able to claim a right to privacy as easily as a 'private individual'. However, in the absence of any 'public issue', the publication of material that invades the privacy of any individual can invite an action for damages.

In the UK, a section of the British press wanted to write about whether or not the prime minister's infant son had been given a controversial vaccination (see Box 5.1: Media Attention on Blair's 19-month-old son). Ironically, after Blair demitted office, his wife Cherie Blair published a 'tell-all' autobiography entitled *Speaking for Myself* that some claimed had violated the privacy of some of her past acquaintances, including her former boyfriends/lovers.

Box 5.1

Media Attention on Blair's 19-month-old Son

In 2001, the then British Prime Minister Tony Blair was outraged by the attempts of certain newspapers to elicit information from his wife's family about whether his son Leo had been given the controversial measles, mumps and rubella (MMR) vaccination. At that time, serious health warnings had been raised about the safety of the vaccine. Blair called it 'horrible and unjustified' that his son was being subjected to media intrusion when he was only nineteen months old.

Source: Adapted from 'Blair condems media intrusion over MMR job', *The Independent*, 24 December 2001.

When individuals 'sell' or 'exchange' their privacy for commercial gain, the dividing line between what is 'private' and what is in the 'public' domain gets blurred. Many celebrities now sell the photo rights to their weddings and newborns to tabloids. For example, British actress Elizabeth Hurley and her husband of Indian origin Arun Nayar sold the photo rights to their wedding in India to *Hello!* magazine.

Do you think that Tony Blair was right in wanting to withhold this information about his infant son? In what ways would the newspapers in question have justified their seeking to publish this information?

Vulnerable Victims

The PCI states: 'While reporting crime involving rape, abduction or kidnap of women/females (sic) or sexual assault on children, or raising doubts and questions touching the chastity, personal character and privacy of women, the names, photographs of the victims or other particulars leading to their identity shall not be published.... Minor children and infants who are the offspring of sexual abuse or "forcible marriage" or illicit sexual union shall not be identified or photographed.'

Why is it important to protect the identity of women and children who are victims of crime?

Recording Conversations

On recording interviews and phone conversations, the PCI states: 'The press shall not tape-record anyone's conversation without that person's knowledge or consent, except where the recording is necessary to protect the journalist in a legal action, or for other compelling good reason....The press shall, prior to publication, delete offensive epithets used by a person whose statements are being reported.'

Photography

On photography, the PCI stipulates that 'intrusion through photography into moments of personal grief shall be avoided. However, photography of victims of accidents or natural calamity may be in the larger public interest.' But, photographing public figures in an intrusive, unjustified manner should be avoided. There are instances of public figures obtaining damages from publications that printed their photographs against their wishes (see Box 5.2: Sienna Successfully Sues *The Sun*). Exceptions to these general principles are dealt with in Chapter 8 on Sting Operations.

Box 5.2

***Sienna Successfully Sues* The Sun**

British actress Sienna Miller successfully sued News Group, a subsidiary of News International, in December 2007, for publishing nude photographs of her taken against her will and published in British tabloids *The Sun* and *The News of the World*. News Group and Xposure Photo Agency were forced to pay £37,000 in damages to the actress. The newspapers agreed not to reprint the photographs and to destroy any copies of the pictures that were in their possession. The amount is believed to be the biggest payout in a case of invasion of privacy in the UK.

Source: Adapted from 'Sienna Miller sues paparazzi for harassment', *The Guardian*, UK, 31 October 2008.

?

Can you think of a scenario where the private life of a public person should be protected?

PRIVACY AND PUBLIC INTEREST

Different media, and different channels within the same medium, require different treatment in terms of opportunities or practices that might prompt accusations of intrusion of privacy. One of the key problems in deciding the media's rights to intrude on an individual's right to privacy is the insufficient recognition that has been given in balancing these competing rights. The terms 'public interest' and 'privacy' present distinct difficulties in usage and meaning. Questions of taste and decency must be balanced against public interest. On occasions, the media's social role has been overlooked when controversies have risen. What authority do people give the media to represent their interests? What is expected of the media by audiences?

Though concepts such as 'privacy' and 'public interest' lack precise definitions they do not lack substance. Their value, however, is determined by contextual circumstances. In discerning whether privacy has been breached, or public interest served, people will take into account the medium involved, the treatment and methods used to acquire information, the circumstances of the situation, and the manner and nature of the acts. It is necessary, therefore, to justify any intrusion of privacy as well as the method of intrusion.

Whether privacy can be intruded upon, and by what methods, appears to be governed by widely held norms of what can be considered 'deserving' circumstances. When an act threatens an individual's or people's psychological or physical well-being, the perpetrator's claim to the right to privacy is weakened and the severity of the threat determines the manner of that intrusion. In certain instances, the intrusion of privacy by the publication of photographs, for example, has a semblance of public retribution, in that the individual is paraded on physical display (Morrison and Michael 2007).

In the confusion between privacy and public interest, the media at times oversteps its rights. The media is sometimes guilty of sensationalizing a story to satisfy what is believed to be in the interest of the public. Gandhi said: 'One of the objects of a newspaper is to understand the popular feeling and give expressions to it, another is to arouse among the people certain desirable sentiments and the third is the fearlessness to expose popular defects.'

Do you agree with these three objectives? What do you think Gandhi meant by the phrase 'desirable sentiments'? What problems, if any, are there in expressing 'popular feeling', and in arousing 'desirable sentiments'?

Some journalists are often unapologetic about looking into the intimate details of the lives of public figures, claiming that privacy needs can be violated in the 'public' or even the 'national' interest. However, when journalists come under public scrutiny they cite privacy or confidentiality as an excuse not to reveal anything. Such a position could damage the credibility of the journalist concerned or the media organization to which she/he belongs.

Privacy laws are a double-edged weapon which often prevent the full facts of a case from coming out. Senior journalist and editor-in-chief of *The Tribune*, H.K. Dua has said that the Indian press has generally been conservative about reporting the private lives of national leaders, which '... seems to be an outcome of the freedom struggle when many leaders were treated with reverence'. But he also points out the lapses which have occurred because the Indian press chose not to pry into the lives of politicians. He feels that if the Indian press had reported on Muhammad Ali Jinnah's deteriorating health much before 1947, the decision to partition the subcontinent might not have been taken.

The right to information is often set against official regulation and management of information—or 'regimes of truth'. 'Public interest', an amorphous yet important feature of democratic society, is juxtaposed against the 'right to privacy'. 'Human interest' is set against the exploitation of grief. A working definition of 'public interest' is crucial for setting limits to permissible investigation and recognizing unacceptable levels of intrusion. Where the boundaries are laid, and who constructs them, lies at the heart of self-regulation and media accountability debates. Journalists need to strike a careful balance between unwarranted intrusion and reporting the news as they find it. They must neither exploit grief and suffering nor sanitize the news, excluding the viewer from the information and its implications. The reporting of disasters and the observation of tragedy can never be a detached business. Yet, some form of detachment is important if the story told is not to be overburdened with the emotion of the moment, or stripped of context and, therefore, meaning. Detachment is an important requisite of objectivity. Media representatives are news managers, if not news manufacturers. The investigative journalist, then, is pushed inevitably into the heart of the story, searching people's truths. And here lies the apparent dichotomy

—public interest demanding personal intrusion. Some, however, would argue that reporting need never entail intrusion. We shall address in depth the ethical contentions inherent in investigative journalism in Chapter 8 on Sting Operations.

Can you think of some of the duties inherent in the role of the media and news managers?

Think of an incident of public disaster or trauma, and write a short article about it. What information is important to report and what can/should be withheld? Compose some questions that you would ask a victim or witness by which you can extract information without being insensitive.

EXAMPLES OF INTRUSIONS BY THE MEDIA IN INDIA

When reporters of a website www.tehelka.com masqueraded as arms dealers and secretly filmed their 'transactions' on the sale of a fictitious product to the Indian government's Ministry of Defence in 2001, their act was defended widely as one that was in the larger public interest as it exposed corruption in a key organ of the government entrusted with the country's security. In its expose, www.tehelka.com used sex workers as the price for 'fixing' its fictitious deal with Indian army officials and claimed that it had to do so to win the officials' confidence. The website argued that the sex workers were 'arranged' by a politician who acted as a middleman between the undercover reporters and the army officials (*The Hindu*, 7 December 2004; *The TOI*, 15 March 2005).

On 20 February 2005, sadhus (or ascetics) of the Swaminarayan sect in Gujarat were shown exploiting childless married women devotees. A television channel, India TV, broadcast the story that was obtained using hidden cameras since neither the sadhus nor the women were willing to publicly admit to such relationships. Some sadhus were arrested later.

Another story was broadcast by the same channel a week later on 27 February 2005 when the results of the state assembly elections in Bihar, Jharkhand and Haryana were awaited. India TV aired a story that showed three politicians from Bihar in a hotel room with sex workers allegedly provided by members of a mafia in return for favours. Though the channel named the politicians, they edited out the 'unsuitable' portions.

The I&B Ministry described the programme as obscene and offensive and sought an explanation from the channel for airing it. Acting under the Cable Regulation Act and the 'uplinking guidelines' for news channels, the ministry threatened to revoke the channel's licence if it failed to give a convincing answer to its notice. Rule 6 of the Cable Television Network Rules, 1994, prohibits showing any programme in the cable service which is offensive to good taste or decency; contains anything obscene, defamatory, false or suggestive innuendos and half-truths; and is not suitable for unrestricted public viewing.

India TV denied that the programme was vulgar or indecent and claimed that it took absolute care to ensure that it did not hurt public sentiment: not only were objectionable visuals covered up, but the audiotrack of the episode, shown for less than one and a half minutes, was also muted. India TV's editor-in-chief Rajat Sharma also denied that the channel encroached on the privacy of politicians. Rather, the objective, he said, was to bring to light their hypocrisy and the way in which they had misused public money, which, according to him, are relevant issues for an electorate. Underlying Sharma's view is the belief that public figures cannot use privacy as a cloak for activities that are either illegal or worthy of blame, activities in which the media has a justifiable interest in reporting.

The same channel broadcast a third controversial story using hidden cameras that was telecast on 13 and 17 March 2005. The story aimed at exposing the phenomenon of the 'casting couch' (a euphemism for aspiring actors finding roles in film or television in return for sexual favours) in the film industry in Mumbai. It featured its reporter, Ruchi, who approached actor Shakti Kapoor and television host Aman Verma and sought their help to secure roles in movies. Ruchi invited Kapoor to a hotel room, where a spy camera caught him seeking sexual favours from her in return for his help in arranging meetings with some film producers. In the programme, Kapoor also cast aspersions on some popular film stars. After the exposé, Kapoor apologized to those stars and alleged that the reporter persisted in inviting him to the hotel room and that the channel had deliberately edited out her overtures to him.

When Ruchi met Verma, he invited her to his home in Mumbai. The channel aired the relevant parts of their conversation, caught on the spy camera, which it claimed revealed the existence of the casting couch in the Mumbai film industry. Verma, like Kapoor, protested against the clandestine filming and filed a criminal complaint against India TV alleging that it wanted to 'blackmail and extort money' from him.

Did the channel violate privacy laws? Sohaib Ilyasi, the anchor of the programme, said that it was absolutely fair. 'Had Shakti been with his girlfriend we would not have filmed him, but he was not,' he said. Asked whether the television channel was justified in inviting him to a hotel room and then exposing him the way it did, Rajat Sharma said: 'Shakti would not make such overtures to a stranger if invited to Shivaji Park [a public park in Mumbai]. It was obvious that it could be done only in a closed room. We did not claim absolute freedom: we did not enter someone's bedroom uninvited, and we did not talk about the extramarital relations of the person being exposed. The focus was clearly on certain favours being done in lieu of sex' (Venkatesan, *Frontline*, 23 April 2005).

Can you think of an ethical framework which would account for the differences in the case relating to politicians and that relating to the 'casting couch'?

In September 2004, the Gudiya controversy raised the issue of right to privacy in the public domain. The manner in which a TV channel held a mock panchayat in its studios to decide the fate of Gudiya's marriage seemed to cross the thin line between a citizen's right to information and the invasion of her/his privacy.

In June 2005, another event which was apparently sensationalized by the media was the Imrana Bibi rape case. Imrana Bibi of Chhartawal village in Muzaffarnagar district, Uttar Pradesh, was raped by her father-in-law. She raised an alarm. The village *panchayat* (council) decreed that she was no longer 'pure' for the husband and must, therefore, marry her father-in-law. It also decreed that the marriage stood annulled and her five children would remain the responsibility of her husband. Issues concerning the status of Muslim women and Islamic injunctions became the subject of media debates and drawing room discussions (as these had during the Gudiya episode). Various political parties tried to capitalize on Imrana's tragedy by demanding a uniform civil code.

SUMMARY

In this chapter, we have seen how we should approach with propriety, issues relating to public and private figures, recording conversations and photography as stipulated by the PCI. The right to privacy is complicated: rights and clauses depend upon a variety of circumstances. This is why it is important to understand the basic ethical ideas and concepts relating to privacy. We should also be aware of some of the circumstances under which privacy rights might be transgressed.

REVIEW QUESTIONS

1. What do you understand by the right to privacy?
2. What constitutes 'private affairs'?
3. What do you understand by 'public interest'?
4. Explain the differences between the right to privacy of a private citizen and a 'public' individual.
5. Privacy and public interest are dependent on certain circumstances. What are some of these circumstances?
6. List the arguments for and against the methods deployed by India TV in its 'casting couch' exposé.

DEBATE

1. If you transgress your rights as a public citizen, you forfeit all your rights to privacy.
2. Full exposure of criminal activity will always benefit society.

REFERENCES

Aju, John 2008, 'Will the Operation Lose its Sting?', at http://news.indlaw.com/guest/columns/default.asp?aju2 (accessed on 5 August 2008).

Morrison, David E. and Michael Svennevig 2002, 'The Public Interest, the Media and Privacy', at http://www.bbc.co.uk/guidelines/editorialguidelines/assets/research/pubint.pdf (accessed on 5 August 2008).

Morrison, David E. and Michael Svennevig 2007, 'The Defence of Public Interest and the Intrusion of Privacy', Sage Journals Online at http://jou.sagepub.com/cgi/content/abstract/8/1/44 (accessed on 5 August 2008).

Retief, Johan 2002, *Media Ethics: An Introduction to Responsible Journalism*, Oxford University Press, Cape Town, South Africa.

'Tehelka: CBI registers 5 cases', *The Hindu*, New Delhi, 7 December 2004; 'Full video will further embarrass Shakti', *The TOI*, Mumbai, 15 March 2005.

Venkatesan, V. 2005, 'Public Interest vs Privacy', *Frontline.*

http://www.legalserviceindia.com/articles/pri_r.htm (accessed on 5 August 2008).

6SCC (Supreme Court Cases) 632, at http:/www.fxi.org.za/pages/publications/Medialaw/india.htm.(accessed on 29 November 2008).

CHAPTER

6

MEDIA MARKET

This chapter looks at the commercial nature of media organizations and how it impacts the democratic ideals of objective journalism. Thereafter, there is a brief overview of media regulation around the world and in India. The differences between editorial and 'advertorial' content are then explored as these represent a central issue in the schismatic interests of market-oriented journalism versus objective journalism. Sometimes, the media's need to satisfy the requirements of the market compromises the quality and value of journalism. Given the role played by the media consumer (reader/listener/viewer) in this process, a complete overhaul of market-driven media would be a difficult, if not an impossible, task.

This chapter also provides an overview of the Indian 'mediascape'–print, radio, television and the internet–and discusses the contentious practices of 'paid editorial content' and 'private treaties' that compromise editorial integrity and the journalistic goal of providing objective and impartial news.

DEMOCRACY AND MARKET

The debates about media ethics revolves around the media's role in the maintenance of a democratic society. A healthy democracy requires, among other things, the participation of informed citizens, and one of the roles of the media is to enhance the level of public participation by providing information and analyses on a range of political, economic, social and other issues. Although the media plays an essential role in the formation of public opinion and personal choices, most media organizations are commercial enterprises which seek readers/viewers/listeners, advertising revenue, favourable regulatory decisions and other advantages. The conflict between the media's social and commercial obligations sometimes results in a compromise on media ethics.

The media industry has become increasingly difficult to regulate due to several reasons: technological developments, the globalization of media conglomerates, and the trend of certain suppliers and creators of news and entertainment (PR practitioners, advertisers, etc.) getting closely involved with the working of media organizations. The extent to which the media can influence public opinion is reason enough for subjecting the business activities of media organizations to critical scrutiny.

The concepts of democracy and the market are both built on the principle of individual choice, but the principles governing the evaluation of choice in these two cases differ fundamentally. There is a danger of those who have accumulated wealth in the market using it to exert influence in the decisions that govern democratic principles. Accordingly, defining and policing the boundaries between the market and democracy is a perennial problem in modern liberal societies. Media institutions face particular dilemmas because they represent a key element of an effective democracy while being, for the most part, commercial entities seeking to maximize profits. Commercial activities and market interests of media institutions can distort the role they play in the formation of public opinion and consequently in upholding democracy. For commercial reasons, if the media favours those in positions of power and authority, it might influence the decisions made by these people.

A widespread problem is the attempt to influence public debate through the purchase of advertising space and the purchase of (favourable) editorial comment. Although most editors try to erect a firewall between journalists and buyers of advertising space, the firewall has many convenient access doors. Those seeking legal or ethical regulation of the media often meet with flat denials of the existence of such a problem. They may be asked to prove that media corporations have misused their capacity to influence public opinion by favouring particular candidates, supporting certain policies or by following a single line of argument. Such actions are difficult to prove because they will not, by nature, be transparent or open.

Most journalists are employees of companies or organizations whose primary aim is to maximize profits and returns to shareholders. The ethical dilemmas they face begin with the inherent conflict between their roles as journalists and their employers' objective to maximize profit. In its crudest form, this ethical compromise is manifest in the quest for higher ratings and circulation on the part of some organizations that can lead to excessive zeal among journalists. In jostling for higher ratings or circulation, the journalist brings into question the ethics of sensitivity.

The media faces a huge dilemma regarding its *raison d'être.* On the one hand, in a democratic society, the media is meant to be egalitarian in its commitment to the dissemination of information for the benefit of the public. On the other hand, the commercial and corporate nature of most media institutions means that they also operate with very different motivations. Thus, the media has dual purposes that do not complement each other.

Richards (2006) has observed the same conflict of interests in business ethics between stockholders and stakeholders. Although this is more an aspect of business ethics, it has relevance in the case of corporate media as well. The interests of stockholders are clear: revenue. Stakeholders are a more diverse group and their needs are more complicated. For example, the stakeholders of a newspaper can include its advertisers, employees, readers and other journalists.

INDUSTRIAL JOURNALISM

The market pressures which underpin a media institution lead to what has been called 'industrial journalism'. The hallmark of industrial journalism, according to Andrew Belsey (Richards 2006), is to promote the production of information which the public is interested in, rather than information that is in the public interest. Let us analyse this interesting distinction.

Let us assume that Belsey considers information in the public interest as information that serves to protect and promote the welfare of the public. What then is information that the public is interested in? Belsey is perhaps referring to entertainment as opposed to news. If this is the case, questions are raised over the appropriateness of the media assuming that the public is not interested in what is supposed to be in its interest. This could be construed as another form of authoritarianism. Certainly there is a difference between entertainment and news. The media is motivated to sell 'news' that its marketing departments have assessed as popular and saleable. In such a scenario, the 'news' that is published/broadcast is to mollify advertisers.

John O'Neil points out that the market 'inhibits the dissemination of information and diverse opinions required of a democratic society' (Richards 2006). Though this difference has been documented, Belsey concludes that there is no solution to this paradox.

It seems that the paradox cannot be resolved so long as the dual motivations of the media are juxtaposed. It is not possible to juggle and balance such differing and often conflicting interests. However, attempts to achieve a balance have been made by media regulatory bodies around the world. But, in a liberal democracy, only few institutional restraints or regulations can be placed on the media, leaving the market as the final arbiter. In matters that vitally involve the public interest, where there is a risk of social disorder or offence to decency and good taste, decisions are left to the prudence and the sense of social responsibility of media practitioners themselves.

It could also be argued that to maintain the uneasy balance between information as commerce and information as a basic human entitlement, the focus should be more on ensuring diversity of information than on the pursuit of profit. Commerce may not be antithetical to the right to information if the public is provided sufficient information from diversified sources.

EDITORIAL AND ADVERTORIAL

In newspapers, editorials are generally printed in a clearly demarcated space and are almost invariably distinguished as editorials or articles and essays expressing an opinion that is separate from factual news reportage. Editorials often address current events or public controversies. When covering controversial topics such as election issues, some opinion-page editors will run debates or 'duelling' editorials to present opposing sides of an issue. Many magazines or periodicals also feature editorials, often written by the publication's editors or publishers. An editorial in a newspaper or magazine normally expresses the opinion of the editor, the editorial board or the publisher. An 'op-ed' article (abbreviated from 'opposite-editorial' which refers to the tradition of its placement in the page opposite the editorial page) is similar in form and content to an editorial, but represents the opinion of an individual contributor, who is sometimes, but not always, affiliated with or aligned to the broad views of the publication.

An advertorial, on the other hand, is an advertisement written in the form of an editorial, and presented in a printed publication—usually designed to look like an independent news story. The term 'advertorial' is a combination of 'advertisement' and 'editorial'. Advertorials differ in appearance from regular advertisements, although in both instances the advertiser or marketer must pay a fee to the media company for content placement. Media organizations normally do not exercise control over both advertisements and advertorials unless their content is considered inappropriate. Many publications differentiate advertorials from editorial content by disclaimers, subtle or not so subtle. Instead of the word 'advertisement', terms such as 'special promotional feature' or 'sponsored article' may be used. Newspapers and magazines may assign staff writers or freelancers to write advertorials, usually without a byline or credit.

An advertorial is an attempt to add editorial authenticity to the advertiser's claim. Advertorials can now be spotted in many newspapers, supplements and magazines. Some Indian periodicals (such as *India Today*, *Outlook* and *The Week*) regularly include advertorials that are sometimes lengthy. However, some advertorials are designed to look like proper news features and their identities as advertisements are not fully or obviously disclosed. In such cases, the reader is not aware of the difference. This is an abuse of an individual's right to information (which includes information about authorship and intentions), and in not providing comprehensive information, the media organization concerned falls short of its duty to serve the public interest.

The blurring of lines between editorial content and advertisements takes several forms. An advertorial comprises text or other content, which occupies purchased space, and masquerades as editorial content. The television equivalent of an advertorial is an 'infomercial', which is an extended advertisement but is produced and designed to resemble regular programming. Many travel and tourism programmes/articles, providing uncritical information, are sponsored by hotels, tour operators or tourism authorities (on occasions, these are hardly different from advertisements). Similarly, automobile manufacturers and restaurants also sponsor television shows and/or printed supplements.

Advertorials usually follow the journalistic feature format. When addressing a political theme, the journalistic feature writer must convince the reader of her/his objectivity, while at the same time following a personal journalistic horizon. While reading a newspaper or a magazine, a reader trusts the journalist's sense of news and values to evaluate what is newsworthy and what is not. Ideally, the reader believes that a journalist strives to present facts as they are, without excessive embellishment and without being susceptible to any inducements. Thus, when the media sells news space, which belongs to objective factual information and viewpoints of experts, it is a breach of the public's trust.

How can 'advertorial' content mislead gullible members of the public? Analyse with examples.

MEETING ADVERTISERS' NEEDS

The rising influence of advertising has spelt significant changes for the Indian media, in terms of both format and content. Advertisers are interested in the content of the media as long as it is complementary to their own advertising campaigns. Understandably, as advertisers spend a lot of money to avail themselves of the benefits of media reach and influence, they do not want their campaigns to be negated by content which is contrary to their aims. On the other hand, because advertisers provide the bulk of their revenue, some media organizations are often more than willing to comply with their demands. Thus, topics of specific interest to the upwardly mobile classes tend to dominate sections of the media.

Mahajan (2004), a journalist, suggests that new media products, such as supplements, special sections and pull-outs, have been created in response to the increasing demands of advertisers. These supplements often feature 'lifestyle' stories, focusing on cars, beauty products, home furnishings, tourism and restaurants. Niche interest supplements like the *Education Times* (*TOI*), *Ascent* (*TOI*), *HT Careers* (*Hindustan Times*), and subsidiary publications like the *Outlook Traveller* and *India Today Travel Plus* allow advertisers to directly target specific interest groups.

We shall consider in greater detail the various motivations and techniques employed by PR practitioners and advertising agencies to make use of the media in subsequent chapters.

MEDIA REGULATIONS AROUND THE WORLD

Ammu Joseph (2005) has considered some of the attempts that have been made around the world by civil society to help regulate market pressures on the media.

US

The Federal Communication Commission (FCC) in 2003 slackened the regulatory rules of media ownership, which led to massive public opposition

—nearly 3 million people wrote to members of the US Congress complaining about the relaxation of rules on grounds that media consolidation was perceived to have negative effects on family and community life. Attempts to relax restrictions on media ownership were overturned by a court ruling in 2004.

Canada

The Friends of Canadian Broadcasting, a non-profit, independent organization, financed by members of public to act as a media watchdog, helped ensure that funding for the Canadian Broadcasting Corporation from the federal budget was used to diversify regional programming.

Britain

Voice of the Listener and Viewer (VLV) initiated a campaign in 2005 to facilitate the participation of citizens in decision-making about the future of broadcasting in Britain, with particular focus on the BBC. It was hoped that the campaign would 'raise awareness of the vital role that broadcasting plays in British life and democracy, and of the threats to the quality of radio and television that now exist'.

Germany

German residents pay licence fees for public service broadcasting, which supplements the broadcaster's advertising revenues. The Deutsche Kulturrat, a cultural organization, appealed against a political decision not to increase licencing fees. The importance of sufficient funding for public service broadcasting was emphasized at a conference organized by the Initiativkreis, a group which represents the interests of listeners and viewers in that country.

AN OVERVIEW OF THE INDIAN MEDIA SCENARIO

The entertainment and media industries are among the fastest growing segments of the Indian economy. However, media reach to the lower socio-economic classes is low. Attempts to remedy this situation are unlikely to yield significant results, given the sheer numbers in the lower socio-economic groups. According to a 2006 report by PricewaterhouseCoopers and FICCI, the annual turnover of the entertainment and media industry in India is over Rs 35,000 crores and is expected to grow at a compounded annual growth rate of 19 per cent over the next five years.

The Approach Paper to the Eleventh Five Year Plan that started on 1 April 2007 pointed out that 'one of the sectors which has consistently outperformed' the rate of growth of gross domestic product in India is the 'entertainment and media services sector'. This sector is expected to grow at a compounded annual growth rate of 19 per cent till the year 2010 and beyond, or more than twice the growth rate of the economy. The paper has put out estimates of the growth rates of different media over the five-year period. The fastest yearly growth would be recorded by television (42 per cent), followed by print (31 per cent), films (19 per cent), advertising (3 per cent), music and live entertainment (2 per cent) and radio (1 per cent).

The Planning Commission document points out that the media is one sector where 'demand grows faster than income'. It adds that 'the "convergence" of different media, along with technological breakthroughs, provide scope for (a) growth rate even higher than what has been currently predicted'.

Print

Compared to many developing countries, the Indian press is relatively unfettered. In 2001, India had 45,974 newspapers, including 5,364 daily newspapers published in over 100 languages. There are several major publishing groups in India, the more prominent among them being the *TOI* group, the Indian Express group, the Hindustan Times group, the Hindu group, the Anandabazar Patrika group, the Eenadu group, the Malayala Manorama group, the Mathrubhumi group, the Kerala Kaumudi group, the Sahara group, the Sun group, the Bhaskar group and Dainik Jagran group. There are more than 40 domestic news agencies, largest among them being the Press Trust of India (PTI) and the United News of India (UNI). Some like The Times of India group and the Indian Express group have their own news agencies.

There are currently close to 60,000 publications of various kinds registered with the Registrar of Newspapers of India (RNI) (www.rni.oc.in), which functions under the I&B Ministry. Currently, 1,900-odd 'large' daily newspapers are published in the country—42 per cent in Hindi, 8 per cent in English and the rest in dozens of other languages and dialects. The total annual advertising revenue earned by all newspapers together in India totalled around US $1 billion in 2006. Until the early 1990s, the RNI's main tasks were to register names of publications and to allocate, what was then scarce, imported paper ('newsprint' grade) at subsidized rates. As the imports of newsprint gradually deregulated from the mid-1990s, the RNI's role and importance diminished.

The Indian press includes a mind-boggling variety of publications, ranging from neighbourhood freesheets, to school magazines, to newspapers like the *TOI*, which claims to be the most widely circulated English-language daily in the world. While the *TOI* sold around 2 million copies per day in 2006, a number of non-English Indian dailies individually sold more copies every day in 2006. Leading non-English daily newspapers in India include the two largest Hindi dailies, *Dainik Jagran* and *Dainik Bhaskar*, the *Malayala Manorama* in Malayalam, the *Daily Thanthi* in Tamil, the *Ananda Bazar Patrika (ABP)* in Bengali and *Eenadu* in Telugu. Not only do many of these newspapers print multiple editions from different locations, at least one, the *Manorama*, also prints an edition outside India in West Asia. The *ABP* is not only the most circulated Bangla-language newspaper, but also has the distinction of being India's most read single-edition newspaper printed out of Kolkata (see Appendix 6.1).

No city in the world publishes as many newspapers as does New Delhi (www.indianews.in), with more than a dozen English dailies alone. Delhi's two largest English dailies, *The TOI* and the *Hindustan Times* (*HT*), account for roughly three-fourths of the total circulation of all English newspapers printed in the city. Why then do so many other newspapers exist in the capital, when quite a few evidently lose money? This may have something to do not just with individual or organizational egos, but also with the fact that many newspaper organizations are sitting on expensive land that had been given to them decades ago by the government on long leases. In comparison to the revenue earned from printing publications, many of these newspapers make a significant return by simply renting out their premises. Magsaysay award winner and senior journalist P. Sainath states that in cities like New Delhi and Mumbai, the fourth estate has become 'real estate'! See interview with Sainath in Chapter 12 on Media Freedom.

Despite its size and diversity, much of the Indian press is controlled by a few families. When five decades ago Nehru talked of the 'jute and steel press', he was referring to a few families in particular: the Jain family (then part of the Sahu Jain group), which controls Bennett, Coleman & Company Limited (BCCL), *The TOI*'s publisher and former jute millers; the late Ramnath Goenka, who used to head the Indian Express group and who had made an aborted attempt in the late 1960s to control the Indian Iron and Steel Company; and the Tata group which has substantial interests in the steel industry and which used to be a part-owner of the company that publishes *The Statesman.* What Nehru meant was that the news business was often an ancillary or a side business for proprietors, who would use their newspapers to lobby for their key or main business interests. Things have changed substantially since then (www.atimes.com, 18 May 2004).

At present, most of the families that control India's largest media conglomerates (the majority having moved beyond print to radio, television and the internet) focus on media as their main activity. This transformation was led by the rapid expansion of the mass media in India and the money involved in the business. Some of the important family-dominated media organizations in India are the Chennai-based Hindu group (controlled by the Kasturi family), the Living Media/India Today/Aaj Tak group (the Poorie family), the ABP group (Sarkars), the BCCL/TOI group (Jains), Dainik Jagran (Guptas) and Dainik Bhaskar (Agarwals). A notable exception is the Malayala Manorama group—the most widely circulated newspaper chain in Kerala—whose key business interests include not just news. The group also controls MRF (formerly Madras Rubber Factory), a major automotive tyres venture.

As these large media organizations expand, they are increasingly challenging one another's market hegemonies (www.cmsindia.org). The battle for market share between the two largest English dailies in India, *HT* and *The TOI* is quite apparent, especially in the capital. After *HT* successfully conducted its initial public offering of shares, it took on *The TOI* on the latter's home turf, Mumbai. With the launch of *Daily News* & *Analysis* (*DNA*), in October 2005, *Time* magazine described India as the world's 'last great newspaper market'.

While publications have become big business for these family-controlled conglomerates, the growing commercialization of the press has brought with it constraints typical of market-driven journalism. These go beyond the influence exercised by large advertisers on editorial content, although that is still a crucial issue. Advertising revenue accounts for 75 per cent to over 90 per cent of the gross revenues of large media groups, thereby ensuring that subscribers' payment has no relation to the cost of production.

Unlike certain developed countries, the circulation of newspapers and magazines is on the rise in India. The print medium is certain to continue to grow in the foreseeable future with the growth in literacy. The circulation numbers boasted by existing newspapers today are despite the fact that roughly one out of three Indians is illiterate.

Radio

In striking contrast to the press, radio was a monopoly of the government-owned All India Radio (AIR) until the end of the 20th century. As an organization, AIR is unique in more ways than one. It is the only radio broadcaster that produces programmes in roughly 100 languages and dialects, reflecting India's cultural and linguistic diversity.

In the 1990s, radio broadcasting was gradually opened to private players with the government allowing them to set up FM (frequency modulation) radio stations. The official policy in this regard underwent a major change when the I&B Ministry did away with the licensing system and opted for a revenue-sharing system—as in the case of the telecommunications industry in the late 1990s. Till July 2008, India was the only democracy in the world where 'news and current affairs' programmes on radio remained a monopoly of the government although private FM radio stations are using subtle methods to bring 'news' content into 'entertainment' programmes.

Interestingly, the then head of the government-owned broadcaster Prasar Bharati (of which AIR is a part), K.S. Sarma, stated in 2006 that his organization was not opposed to privately owned companies airing news and current affairs programmes on radio. Till as late as 2006, Nepal, India's smaller and economically less developed neighbouring country, had around 50 FM radio stations, nearly twice the number in India. By the end of 2007, the number of FM radio stations in India had almost quadrupled and was twice the number in Nepal.

Television

The Indian government has been far more 'liberal' in allowing private enterprises and foreign capital in television broadcasting compared to other mass media. Till early 1991, the government-owned Doordarshan (a part of Prasar Bharati) enjoyed a monopoly over television broadcasting. This monopoly got rapidly eroded within a few years.

India's first experiment with television broadcasting had begun in September 1959 and for the first 17 years, it spread haltingly and transmission was mainly in black and white. Many intellectuals and policy-makers in the country frowned upon television, looking on at it as a luxury Indians could do without. Sales of television sets, as reflected by licences issued to buyers, were less than 700,000 until 1977. In 1975, satellites were used in India for the first time to broadcast television programmes anywhere in the world during the Satellite Instructional Television Experiment (SITE) that was the outcome of a joint venture between the US National Aeronautical and Space Administration (NASA) and the Indian Space Research Organization (ISRO). The programmes that were broadcast as part of SITE were meant for rural audiences. Colour television came relatively late to India, in the early 1980s, in the wake of the debate on whether the government should at all be spending taxpayers' money on building an infrastructure for television in the country.

During the mid-1980s, Doordarshan expanded faster than any television network in the world—from covering around 30 per cent of India's geographical area in late 1983 to covering roughly 70 per cent by early 1986. Between 1983 and 1985, one low power transmitter was inaugurated by Doordarshan each week while 18 production centres came up in different state capitals. This phenomenal expansion was largely motivated by the country's ruling establishment (Indira Gandhi was then prime minister) to exercise tight control over the electronic media. In the late 1980s, two television serials on Doordarshan, the *Ramayana* and the *Mahabharata*, attracted the biggest television audiences anywhere in the world—a record that is yet to be broken.

Though Prasar Bharati was formally granted autonomy in 1996, its two main wings, Doordarshan and AIR remain, to a great extent, an important propaganda tool for those in power. The issue of financial independence of Doordarshan (without which genuine autonomy is believed to be impossible) has been debated and discussed from time to time. A proposal to levy a 'licence fee' on owners of television sets—along the lines of the UK model to fund the BBC—has been mooted but has invariably met with staunch opposition.

Although in the mid-and late 1980s Doordarshan experienced a brief stint with freedom—with programmes like *Janvani* and *Newsline* taking positions that were not just critical but even antagonistic of politicians and bureaucrats in power—it has by and large remained subservient to the ruling regime. This resulted in an unusual phenomenon in 1988–89: news and current affairs programmes (like *Newstrack* and *Eyewitness*) that were critical of the government were marketed on videotape as Doordarshan refused to air these programmes.

From the early 1990s, satellite technology dramatically changed the television scenario in India. STAR (Satellite Television Asia Region) started beaming to India in 1991 and Zee News, the first privately owned television news channel in the country, began in 1994. India's skies were invaded by a host of channels. Till 2005, India was the only country in the world where the number of television sets with cable and satellite connections exceeded the number of telephone lines. There were approximately 100 million television sets in the country at that time and roughly 60 million television sets had cable connections. Compared to this, the same year,

India had only around 46 million fixed telephone lines, 54 million mobile phones and less than 20 million personal computers.

The number of television sets with cable and satellite connections increased significantly between 1995 and 2005. At the end of 2007, there were roughly 120 million television sets in India, of which roughly 80 million had cable or satellite connections. By then, the total number of mobile phones in the country had touched the 200 million mark while the number of landlines had fallen marginally to around 40 million.

India is also the only country in the world where for the equivalent of between US $4 and $6 a month a subscriber can receive anywhere between 30 and over 100 television channels. The remarkable fact is that cable television arrived in India only in 1991. At the end of 2007, the I&B Ministry had officially allowed nearly 200 private satellite channels to be uplinked from India and more than 70 channels had been allowed to downlink. India was the only country in the world with close to 40 twenty-four hour news and current affairs television channels at the end of 2007 with more waiting to enter this already crowded market. More recently, with the entry of direct-to-home or (DTH) broadcasting, the television scene in India is expected to evolve further in terms of quality and number of channels.

INDIA'S 'MEDIASCAPE'

As the above overview of the Indian 'mediascape' indicates, the mass media in the world's second most populous country is truly unique. 'Mediascape' is a term believed to have been first used in 1990, by an academic of Indian origin, Arjun Appadurai, to describe the way that visual imagery impacts the world and to describe and situate the role of electronic and print media in 'global cultural flows'.

The National Readership Survey (NRS) 2006, with a sample size of over 2,80,000 estimated that the reach of the print medium increased from 216 million to 222 million between 2005 and 2006. Comparatively, the reach of satellite television grew phenomenally from 207 million individuals to 230 million in this period.

According to the NRS, between 2005 and 2006, the reach of radio jumped from 23 per cent to 27 per cent. Much of this increase was driven by the listenership of FM radio jumping by 55 per cent in the same period. As for the internet, the number of users who logged in every week increased from 7.2 million to 9.4 million—the growth was far more pronounced in urban India.

The Planning Commission's Approach Paper to the Eleventh Five Year Plan pointed out that in 2006, only 75 per cent of the male population and 54 per cent of the female population in the country were literate. The Indian government hopes to lower the drop-out rate in primary schools from around 52 per cent at present (the highest in Asia) to around 20 per cent by 2012, by which year the literacy level would have gone up to 85 per cent. Even if these targets are not met, it is clear that the print medium in India will continue to grow as for a neoliterate the ability to read a publication is a major source of empowerment.

At the end of 2007, there was more than one television set for every ten Indians and two mobile phones for every ten citizens and less than three personal computers for every 100 Indians. These statistics clearly indicate the long distance that has to be traversed before the internet, as a medium of mass communication as well as personalized communication, makes a significant and discernible impact on Indian society. Though the expansion of the 'old' media has gone beyond urban areas and is fast spreading across the length and breadth of rural India, the growth of the 'new' media has become dependent on the penetration of technology and the development of the telecommunications infrastructure.

Mobile technology, touted to be the next revolution in communication, is gaining ground in India. India's telecom sector has expanded at an incredibly rapid pace in recent years. There were barely two phones for every 10,000 Indians when the country became politically independent in 1947. Fifty years later, in 1997, three years after the telecommunications sector had been opened up to private enterprises, this proportion was less than two out of 100. By the end of 2007, there were two phones for every ten Indians. The number of fixed and wireless telephone connections in the country doubled between the middle of 2004 and mid-2006 to exceed 150 million. This number, as already stated, touched the 200 million mark at the end of 2007. On an average, 5 million new mobile phone connections were added each month in 2006 and India is currently enjoying the lowest call rates anywhere in the world (against one of the highest till 1997). The spread of telecom facilities in the country has, however, been rather uneven.

At the end of 2007, while there were 70 phones for every 100 residents of cities like Delhi and Mumbai (the proportion was even higher in Chennai), the teledensity levels in states like Bihar, Jharkhand, Chhattisgarh, Assam and Orissa stood at between 3 per cent and 4 per cent. The whole of rural India too had barely six to seven telephones for every 100 individuals. In the 600,000-plus villages in the country, all but 25,000-odd villages had at least one phone (at the end of 2007). Of these, between a quarter to one-third of the phones were out of order. However, these numbers are changing rapidly. The government claims that there would not only be an electricity connection in each village by 2009 and a telephone line by November 2007, it is aiming for broadband connectivity in each village by 2011–12.

IDEOLOGICAL CLASSIFICATION OF THE INDIAN MEDIA

During the Cold War, much of the Indian media positioned itself somewhere between emphasizing liberal forms of journalism and development journalism. From the early 1990s, as processes of deregulation and economic liberalization started, India started welcoming private foreign capital and the government initiated market-friendly policies. While the entry of foreign capital was disallowed in most of the media till 2002, the changing character of the Indian economy made some observers feel that the country's media embraced the present form of a post-privatization model. Some considered this to be the fifth media perspective within the larger ambit of development journalism and described it as the 'guardians of transparency model of media'. The other four media perspectives are: modernization/nation-building model; media as government partner; empowerment of masses/participatory model; and watchdog model. However, many disagreed with this kind of characterization of the Indian media and found this paradigm directly correlated to the liberal media model.

The theoretical basis for the post-privatization media model came from international organizations like the neoliberal International Monetary Fund (IMF) and the World Bank as well as organizations that were part of the United Nations such as the United Nations Development Programme (UNDP). The UNDP's 'revised strategies of development' philosophies were replete with phrases like 'good governance', 'linking good governance with economic growth' and a 'participatory, transparent, and accountable state'. Given the impetus to improve transparency for the sake of good governance and human development, the IMF, the World Bank and the UNDP displayed new interest in building journalists' capacities to ensure that governments communicated openly with citizens. This approach argued that any restriction of free speech undermined good governance and economic development.

BRINGING DOWN THE CHINESE WALL

In the 1980s, after Sameer Jain became the executive head of BCCL, publishers of *The TOI*, the rules of the Indian media began to change. Besides initiating cut-throat cover-price competition, marketing was used creatively to make BCCL the most profitable media group in the country. It currently earns more profit than the rest of the media companies in the country put together though as a corporate conglomerate, the STAR group has in recent years recorded a higher annual turnover. In the process, many believe a stiff price has been paid, by sacrificing good journalistic practices and ethical norms (*Himal*, August 2006).

This transformation is crucial considering the history of the Indian press. A number of Indian newspapers that are now into their second century of publication were integral to the country's freedom movement. For Gandhi, Nehru and many others, newspapers were the only means of spreading their messages to large numbers of people. During the 1950s and 1960s, a few publications had well-deserved reputations for taking on the establishment and exposing acts of corruption.

It was only during the Emergency in the mid-1970s that the subcontinent saw its press severely censored. Most newspapers in India today, however, deploy more subtle forms of censorship—those driven by the market, or by those in power who can bribe journalists with lavish international junkets.

At the same time, media houses have become less censorious about what they portray as newsworthy. The media phenomenon that has perhaps caused the most outrage in recent times has been BCCL's 2003 decision to start a 'paid content' service called Medianet, which, for a price, openly offers to send journalists to cover product launches or celebrity-related events. When competing newspapers pointed out the blatant violation of journalistic ethics implicit in such a practice, BCCL's bosses argued that such 'advertorials' were not appearing in the *TOI* itself, but only in the city-specific colour supplements that highlight society trivia rather than hard news. BCCL's argument was that as PR firms were already 'bribing' journalists to ensure the coverage of their clients, there was nothing wrong in eliminating the intermediary—the PR agency (*TOI* and *Business Standard*).

Besides Medianet, BCCL devised another 'innovative' marketing and PR strategy. In 2005, ten companies, including India-based Videocon and Kinetic Motors, allotted unknown amounts of equity shares to BCCL as part of a deal to enable these firms to receive discounts for advertising in BCCL-owned media ventures. The number of companies that became part of the 'private treaties' scheme of BCCL went up considerably thereafter. Even as this scheme was apparently aimed at undermining competition to the *TOI*, a number of the newspaper's competitors as well as television channels like CNBC started similar schemes.

The 'private treaties' scheme, pioneered in the Indian media by BCCL (www.hardnewsmedia.com, December 2005), involves giving advertising space to private corporate entities/advertisers in exchange for equity investment—the company officially denies that it also provides favourable editorial coverage to its 'private treaty' clients and/or blacks out adverse comments against its clients. This business, hailed as 'innovative' and 'ingenious', taps into the importance of brand identity in marketing. Private treaties have also been credited with finally bridging the gulf between the corporate sector as a whole and media enterprises by creating a common objective. The success of the scheme has reportedly turned BCCL into one of the largest private equity investors in India. At the end of 2007, the media company boasted of investments in 140 companies in aviation, media, retail and entertainment, among other sectors, valued at an estimated Rs 1,500 crore. According to an interview given by a senior BCCL representative (S. Sivakumar) to a website (medianama.com) in July 2008, BCCL had between 175 and 200 'private treaty' clients, with an average 'deal' size of between Rs 15 crore and Rs 20 crore, implying an aggregate investment that could vary between Rs 2,625 crore and Rs 4,000 crore.

Private treaty schemes have been subject to strident criticism. Journalist Sucheta Dalal states (*'News for Sale', Money LIFE,* 2 January 2008) that an editor of a publication allegedly mentioned in an e-mail that journalists in his newspaper were being obliged to provide favourable editorial coverage to companies that had entered into private treaties with the publication. He was reportedly concerned that the Chinese Wall between editorial and advertorial content had been corroded by market pressures. Kundan R. Vyas, chief editor of the Janmabhoomi group of newspapers and a member of the PCI, cast aspersions on this practice of entering into private treaties and described these as 'most unethical'. He noted that while the media organization concerned was keeping its promises to its clients, it had forsaken its promise to provide the public unbiased and objective journalism.

BCCL was not the only media organization that went in for private treaties. The Network 18 group (formerly the Television Eighteen group), a diversified media conglomerate, headed by Raghav Bahl, owns a number of television channels (including CNBC India and CNN-IBN) and websites. The group has entered into a private equity acquisition programme through an investment associate called Capital 18. A senior company representative told *Business*

World magazine (24 March 2008) that the formula followed was that 70 per cent of the investment was in the form of cash or equity while the balance was traded against subsidized advertising airtime. Bahl defended private treaties in an interview to the magazine saying it was a 'legitimate business investment strategy' and 'does not involve any trading for editorial content'.

Speaking to Gurbir Singh of *BusinessWorld*, Bahl said: 'Unlike the *Times*, we (at Network 18) have a few tens of crores (of rupees) in investments in just four or five companies.' Bahl added: 'We do not compromise editorial. If you want to compromise content, you don't need the torchlight of a private treaty to do it. It need not show on your books (of account) either. We do have a policy on private treaties, but what is wrong with a business plan that monetizes our media reach? What difference does it make if we pay for a stake in a company in cash or kind? It is true that the companies we invest in get access. It is also true they may try and influence us, but that is the occupational hazard every journalist faces.'

What are the main arguments for and against the use of private treaties in the media?

CLOUT OF THE ADVERTISER

In June 1982, *Sunday* magazine (now defunct) published by the ABP group ran a cover story entitled 'The Bubble that Will Burst' that was critical about the Ambani-family controlled Reliance group of companies. Soon afterwards, the group withdrew all advertising support to the entire ABP group including the *ABP* the largest circulated newspaper in eastern India. Subsequently, the Reliance group mended its fences with the ABP group and resumed advertising in the latter's publications. What became apparent through this episode is that the ABP group needed Reliance less than the latter needed the former. If the corporate group 'needed' the newspaper because it reached out to large numbers of consumers in eastern India, the ABP group was relatively less dependent on Reliance because it was one among many advertisers who contributed to the newspaper's revenues.

By 1986, another newspaper chain, The Indian Express group had started a campaign (www.afaqs.com, 30 July 2008) against the Reliance group's alleged acts of commission and omission. The newspaper's journalists (led by Arun Shourie, who went on to become an MP and S. Gurumurthy, a Chennai-based chartered accountant) published a series of articles (most of them prominently displayed on the front page) exposing how the government of the day had favoured the business interests of the Reliance group. Even as the newspaper campaign was at its peak, there were occasions when it published advertisements of the Reliance group of companies on its front page simultaneously with articles that exposed the so-called nexus between Reliance and the then governments. Unlike what had happened with the ABP group in 1982, the media managers of the Reliance group preferred to appear magnanimous.

However, very often, media companies kowtow to the pressures of advertisers and the latter are able to exert their influence on editorial content. In an interview broadcast on Lok Sabha TV, Harold Evans, former editor of *The Times* and *The Sunday Times*, said that the decline in the importance of the 'classified' section in newspapers (where individuals and small firms would advertise) had increased the relative influence of large advertisers on editorial content. In the Indian context, media analyst Vanita Kohli noted: 'It is routine for advertisers to pull out entire campaigns if there is even mildly objective reportage on them. It happens not necessarily to critical stories, but ones which analyse the financial performance of the company and report market perceptions of its weaknesses' (Kohli 2003).

In a world where media organizations are crucially dependent on revenue from advertisers to survive, it is not at all surprising that care is taken to avoid aggravating this integral source of funding. This leads us to readership and reaching out to constituents (listeners and viewers). Would the constituents of a media company be ready to pay a higher price to ensure the integrity and independence of the company? It is unrealistic to expect that market pressures would not exert influence on the management of media products and services. However, the question raised is whether a newspaper like the *TOI* has an ethical duty to publish details of private treaties so that its readers are aware that the content might be advertorially inclined.

An oft-repeated question in the ongoing debate on this aspect of media ethics is why newspapers selling editorial space remain popular. It is not that difficult to find the odd complaint in the 'Letters to the Editor' column of newspapers about the so-called 'deterioration' of news content and the increasing 'commercialization' of the news media. But there is no strong reaction from readers as a whole to this phenomenon. There are a number of reasons for this.

- As reading newspapers is a habit, many do not find it easy to switch from one to another; the reader therefore continues to put up with whatever a chosen newspaper offers.

- The reader is perhaps unaware that the newspaper/magazine is selling editorial space.
- As T.N. Ninan, editor of *Business Standard*, points out: '. . . readers choose a newspaper for several attributes, of which editorial integrity may be just one. A paper may have the most comprehensive classified advertisements, useful when you want to rent a flat or sell a car . . . Then a paper may have the best TV review columns. It may offer a free plastic chair in return for a three-month subscription (as some Hindi newspapers do). Or simply, everyone in the neighbourhood reads it. And so on' (Kohli 2003).

SUMMARY

In this chapter, we have seen how media companies are dependent on the market and advertising. We have looked at the commercialization and the 'commodification' of the media. There is an acute need for a rise in the awareness levels of media consumers.

Few would disagree that a media shackled by government regulations is unhealthy for democracy. As advertisement revenues account for a disproportionate share of media earnings and given the commercial interests of owners of media organizations, would the coverage of news change?

REVIEW QUESTIONS

1. What are the ways in which market-driven mass media compromises the integrity of objective journalism?
2. What are some of the tools for regulation of the media employed across the world?
3. What is understood as the 'fifth perspective' in ideologically classifying the media?
4. What is the purpose of an editorial and what is the purpose of an advertorial?
5. In what ways does the media meet advertisers' needs?
6. How is India's experience with television unique?

DEBATE

1. The media in a capitalist society can be neither 'free' nor 'objective'.
2. It is the responsibility of the audience to distinguish news from advertorial content and to understand the market-conscious motivations of the media.
3. Advertising has desensitized consumers and hence, there is no point worrying about its effects.
4. Are private treaties 'ingenious' or 'indigestible'?

REFERENCES

'Demoting news and readers,' www.hardnewsmedia.com (December 2005).

'Dirty laundry at the Times of India,' www.atimes.com (18 May 2004).

Joseph, Ammu 2005, The Media, the Market, the Message, at http://www.indiatogether.org/(accessed on 5 August 2008).

Kohli, Vanita 2003, *The Indian Media Business*, Sage Publications, New Delhi.

Mahajan, Deepti 2004, Advertorials: Blurring the Dividing Line, at http://www.indiatogether.org/ (accessed on 5 August 2008).

PricewaterhouseCoopers, 2006, The Indian Entertainment and Media Industry: Unravelling the Potential, at http:// www. pwc. com/extweb/pwcpublications. nsf/docid/BE7E56C3FF8E90 A6CA257185006A3275/$file/Frames.pdf (accessed on 5 August 2008).

Richards, Ian 2006, *Exploring Journalism Ethics: Quagmires and Quandaries*, Anmol Publications, New Delhi, India.

'The News Business Part III: The dumb blonde is here to stay,' by Vanita Kohli-Khandekar, www.afaqs.com (30 July 2008).

www.cmsindia.org,

www.indianews.in/delhinewspapers.htm

www.rni.oc.in

APPENDIX 6.1

Manipulating Newspaper Readership Figures?

In April 2008, the Media Research Users' Council (MRUC) released data for the first round of the Indian Readership Survey (IRS) 2008 pertaining to the previous calendar year. The data indicated that the highest readership of any Indian language daily newspaper was commanded by the *Dainik Jagran with* its 30-odd editions topping the charts again with a total readership of 56.6 million. *Dainik Bhaskar* followed with a total readership of 31.9 million. Among dailies in the Hindi language, the most widely spoken language in India, in third position was *Amar Ujala* with a readership of 29.6 million; followed by *Hindustan* with a readership of 25.2 million, *Rajasthan Patrika* with 13.7 million, *Punjab Kesari* with 11.1 million, *Aaj* with 7.4 million, *Navbharat Times* and *Navbharat* both had a total readership of 5.2 million while *Prabhat Khabar* stood at the tenth position with a readership of 5 million.

The IRS is a biannual readership survey that is used by newspapers and magazines to assess their relative competitiveness and also to set advertising rates. In turn, the data is also used by buyers of advertising space to decide on their media plans.

Interestingly, the IRS data for 2007 indicated a marginal decline in the readership of six of the top ten publications in the country. Ranked fourth was *Malayala Manorama*, the only non-Hindi daily in the top ten publications. Among the top twenty dailies were Tamil daily *Dinakaran* and the Bengali daily *ABP* at the twentieth position. The *TOI* was the only English-language daily newspaper in the top 20.

As the world's largest circulated English daily, the *TOI* had a total readership of 13.6 million for all its editions put together, according to the IRS data. Among English dailies, *The TOI* was followed by *HT* with a readership of 6.3 million followed by *The Hindu* with 5.6 million. *The Economic Times* and *The New Indian Express* were at the fourth position, each with a total readership of 2 million. Then came *MiD Day* with a readership of 1.8 million, *Mumbai Mirror* with 1.6 million and *DNA* with 1.3 million.

The IRS 2008 indicated that leading non-English dailies maintained their position although some witnessed a marginal drop in readership. For instance, the total readership of *ABP* dropped from 15.8 million to 15.6 million from the figure given in the IRS 2007. *Malayala Manorama* also saw a drop in readership from 12.9 million to 12.7 million in this period. According to the IRS 2008, the leading daily newspaper in Gujarati was the *Gujarat Samachar* with a readership of 8.8 million. *Lokmat* was the leading Marathi daily—its total readership dropped slightly from of 20.7 million to 20.6 million. *Vijay Karnataka* was the most widely read Kannada daily with a readership of 9.6 million against 9.9 million in the IRS 2007, *Daily Thanthi* in Tamil had a readership of 20.6 million (down from 20.9 million), while *Eenadu*, the leading Telugu-language daily, had a readership of 14.7 million, the survey added.

In a statement, the MRUC stated that it had delayed the release of the 2008 data due to additional and repeat fieldwork: 'Hansa Research Group Pvt. Ltd that undertakes the fieldwork for IRS had reported to MRUC that some publications were trying to influence the results in some markets as a result of which fieldwork was being redone.' The council went on to state that certain issues had cropped up in Rajasthan, 'where the research agency's quality control process found evidence of an attempt to manipulate and influence research findings'.

In an e-mail published by *Mint* newspaper (21 April 2008), MRUC's general manager Sabina Solomon wrote: 'We are currently investigating the issue...It is true that interviewers were being influenced and, as a result, we have scrapped the fieldwork done till now as well as withdrawn the field staff. The move by MRUC is to sensitize all parties involved that acts like these affect the entire industry irrespective of the parties involved. In a way everyone pays a price—the publications, the advertisers and their agencies as well as the research agency—since the data if suppressed or fieldwork not done will impact the quality of research having a cascading effect.'

She added that the council has put in mechanisms that would create a code of conduct to which all constituencies would agree to abide by. There would be a standing committee to investigate issues related to publication interference in the research process, whether identified through the quality control process of the research agency or through complaints raised by the members. The standing committee would be empowered to appoint an external agency to investigate such issues if required, the *Mint* reported.

APPENDIX 6.2

News for Sale

The following are excerpts from an article written by Sucheta Dalal on 'private treaties' in MoneyLIFE. *The full text of the article is available on http:/www.suchetadalal.com/articles/display/569/2686.article (accessed on 5 August 2008). In her article, she alleges that 'journalists are being designated as "champions" for private treaty clients to tailor editorial coverage to enhance the value of the companies and* TOI's *investment'.*

'If you are an investor who depends on India's largest-selling economic newspaper for unbiased news, then you must know and understand the concept of "private treaties" (PT). Since *The Times of India* (*TOI*) far outsells every other English newspaper and *The Economic Times* is by far the market leader in the economic news category, the concept is of universal interest... Although PTs sound like agreements between two sovereign nations, they are, in fact, pacts between the Times of India group and approximately 100-odd companies, under which *TOI* buys shares of small and fast-growing companies. The list is expanding rapidly.

'In an article for *India-Seminar* on "The changing Indian media scene", T.N. Ninan, editor of *Business Standard*, described PTs as "basically the transfer of shares in return for advertising". He said, Bennett, Coleman & Company Limited, which owns the Times of India group of publications, "invests in usually mid-rung companies that are keen to jump into the big league but are perhaps without the big bucks to spend on marketing. The share purchase money is immediately taken back against the promise of guaranteed advertising in Bennett publications—to build the investee company's brand(s). Part of the deal is even said to be editorial coverage, though this remains unconfirmed." Ninan goes on to say, "If true, by definition, this will have to be positive coverage" because "the brands have to be built up, so that the shares bought by Bennett gain in value and can be sold." Well, reports of guaranteed editorial coverage are no longer "unconfirmed", as Ninan put it...

'These are www.privatetreaties.com and times private treaties.com. In the past two years, *TOI* has invested over (the rupee equivalent of) $500 million in 114-odd companies in diverse businesses. It is a private equity firm.

'*TOI* claims that when these companies are mentioned editorially, its investment in them is mentioned...

'Typically, the Times group buys a 5 per cent-10 per cent in mid-sized companies that are planning to go public or looking for private equity. The investment can vary from Rs 10 crore to Rs 100 crore. The company agrees to invest an equal amount in advertising in Times publications over a three-to-five-year period at a steep discount to the normal advertising rates...

'This unique "win-win" situation indeed works wonderfully well in a monster bull run. While companies and the publishing group are the real winners, the investors are losing nothing at the moment. But remember this is a two-year-old concept and the implications of tearing down every shred of the wall between editorial, advertising and PR will be evident only when things look less sunny for the markets and the economy.'

APPENDIX 6.3
Selling News or Buying Silence?

The following are excerpts from another article by Sucheta Dalal that appeared on rediff.com. The full text is available on http://www.rediff.com/money/2003/mar/05dalal.htm (accessed on 5 August 2008).

'The newspaper world has been cast into turmoil over the last few weeks. First, there was the furore, within media circles, over the Times of India group deploying "paid content"—or what in plain words means—selling news. The group has a division called Medianet (http://medianet.indiatimes. com), complete with a rate card for the sale of news...

'The reader has no clue that the adulatory report is nothing but a paid advertisement masquerading as objective reportage or opinion. Even while the debate over the ethics of a newspaper "selling news" was hotting up into a regular war of words between two of the country's top-selling English dailies, journalism was dealt another stunning blow.

'Last week, the Mumbai police arrested Rishi Chopra of *The Economic Times* along with an accomplice (a former journalist with another business daily) in an alleged extortion attempt...

'A little before Chopra's arrest, Ravi Dhariwal, an executive director of Bennett, Coleman & Company Ltd, which owns *The Times of India* and *The Economic Times*, 'had pointed out in a signed article on the edit page of *The Economic Times* that— "all those shouting from the roof-tops admonishing sponsored stories have also turned a blind eye to the fact that some stories get into their newspapers, after veiled deals between public relations agencies and large sections of the media."

'This may be true. Indeed, some *TOI* journalists believe that blatant "planting" of news and photographs by journalists acting in cahoots with PR agencies had triggered off the Medianet initiative.

'Dhariwal's article labels Medianet an attempt to "bring about more transparency and disclosure to the entertainment and lifestyle supplements" of the group. But Rishi Chopra's arrest would suggest the problem is not restricted to the entertainment and lifestyle segments.

'Chopra was a business journalist that too connected to the research bureau. Also, he is the third *ET* scribe under a cloud for shady links with speculators in the last two years. . .

'Let us look at the issue from another perspective. *TOI* is the world's largest selling English language newspaper and sells more copies per day than *The New York Times or USA Today*.

'It has also been at the forefront of breaching the "walls" that separate advertising, management and editorial in a newspaper organization. The group has frequently shuffled senior employees on either side of the "wall"...

'The Times group claims each of its paid news items carries the words "Medianet promotions" at the bottom. But without proper disclosure to the reader about what the word Medianet implies, the disclosure is meaningless.

'In the absence of such clarity, the reader ought to be outraged at the attempt to pass off paid news as the real thing. But readers either don't care, or newspapers are so habit-forming that they refuse to dump the product despite their irritation. . .

'When the reader is not discerning, his/her loyalty can always be bought through low "invitation pricing" of the publications or cross promotions, titillating photographs and stage-managed events. . .'

APPENDIX 6.4

Media Ethics and the Trade Press

The following are case studies from CyberMedia. Established in 1982, CyberMedia is India's first and largest speciality media house with a range of 15 publications, besides other media products and services. Prasanto K. Roy, president and chief editor of the ICT (Information and Communications Technology) publishing division at CyberMedia, including Dataquest, PCQuest *and other publications, wrote this section especially for this book.*

The trade press is in a somewhat different and difficult situation with respect to media ethics. Readers expect our editorials to be impartial, unprejudiced, critical where warranted, and unaffected by advertising considerations, as they do for any other type of media. Yet the trade press has to very frequently write about its advertisers and their products. We would write about IBM or HP and their business performance or products, and they could be our biggest advertisers. We have done surveys of Indian states and their e-readiness, and state governments are major advertisers.

This may occasionally be true for general or news media, and more frequently true for the business press, but the overlap is very high for the trade press. By contrast, for many genres of publications, advertisements and subject matter are completely distinct. For instance, film magazines—consumer magazines covering cinema—write about film stars and movies, while their advertisers are FMCG, apparel, and so on.

Managing the Conflict

There are (apparently) easy ways out, not necessarily at variance with acceptable ethics. Writing 'softer' editorials about large advertisers clearly falls below the line. But it is easier to play safe and leave out critical stories or reviews. For instance, if you review ten products, or do a survey of twenty Indian states, you can simply leave out the bottom performers instead of writing about them. This is not quite a violation of media ethics: one could take the view that 'we are simply featuring the toppers, or recommending the best products…there is no need to feature the bottom performers'. And this is something we (in the CyberMedia group) simply do not do.

For over the past quarter century that our media group has been around, every incident that has tested the ad—edit Chinese wall has strengthened the realization that long-term survival and growth of a publication depends on its credibility. The reader has to trust the editorial content provided, especially in the technology trade press, where recommendations are made: on which products to buy or technologies to adopt. If there is an important product or technology out there, and it performs below par, it is our duty to our readers to publish. In the process, we constantly face advertisers (from vendors to state governments) blacklisting us, withdrawing advertising, issuing threats, sending legal notices, and occasionally, going ahead and suing.

Advertising Pressures

In some of our magazines, we do comparative product reviews, and there are winners and losers, and most are advertisers. Sometimes, the top vendors—our largest advertisers—lose out in the review listings. And yes, the losers sometimes pull out advertising and more, but that has not affected our neutrality and our recommendations.

Dataquest and IDC (which is engaged in market research) conduct an annual survey of state governments and their e-governance initiatives. In an issue of *Dataquest*, three of the largest, most influential states (and among our top advertisers) fared poorly. There was considerable pressure to withdraw or change the rankings or publish 'clarifications'. *Dataquest* stuck to its guns, convinced that the survey was a fair reflection of citizens' views of state initiatives. Finally, two of the states withdrew advertising support for our annual e-governance conference and for our publications.

A big challenge around ethics for the trade press is 'issue-specific' advertising. Let us say we intend bringing out a special issue on laptops or on printers. This is announced in advance and there is a spurt in advertising from vendors in these product categories. Our sales department would also specifically approach such vendors for advertising support. Two broad questions arise.

One, can you link coverage with advertising? If a vendor advertises, should it expect editorial coverage? Our stance is: vendors cannot be promised editorial coverage. If, however, the salesperson is aware of vendors (including advertisers) who should feature in the story, he or she is welcome to inform the editorial team and the latter will decide, based on merit, whether or not they should be featured. (It often happens—at least once a month—that a focus story actually leaves out a major advertiser.)

The bigger question is: what happens when there is a major advertiser in a particular issue in which a story is sharply critical of its products?

Product Review

A 2007 issue of *PCQuest* featured an annual 'shootout'—a comparative review of computer servers, done in our test lab. A top advertiser had booked major advertising for its servers in that issue. It so happened that its servers did not fare well in that 'shootout'. The advertiser would have looked silly with its advertisements for its 'great' products, next to an editorial saying that it had reached the bottom of the list.

We followed our rulebook that said: 'Editorial is untouchable'. We informed the advertiser that its products had fared badly in the review and whether it would like to withdraw its advertisements? It withdrew. We lost that advertising. But we did gain confidence and the appreciation of the vendor.

Ideally, we should inform vendors even when their products have done particularly well, and suggest that they withdraw advertising from that issue. Just in case a reader wonders if there is a connection between the advertising and the product topping. Unfortunately, revenue pressures do not allow us to do exactly what we want, when it is more about reader perception than a breach of ethics or of our rulebook. What we do ensure, however, is that information about positive editorial content (for example, a product topping a review) is not available to either the in-house advertising salesperson or the external advertiser.

We also ensure that sponsorships for award events exclude companies that are in the awardee list or in the running. For instance, a 'vendor awards' event would exclude all information technology (IT) vendors from sponsorship or any other association with the event.

These are not the only ways in which the waters of ethics for the trade press are tested.

The Junket

'Junkets' are tours (inside or outside the country) organized by vendors for journalists. These are often held at an 'exotic' location, say, a popular holiday resort. Expenses incurred on travel, food, drinks and lodging are paid for by the vendor. We accept these invitations, but when publishing a report, we have a policy of disclosing, along with the journalist's byline to the news report or article, the fact that the author was hosted by the vendor or company concerned. We also have a policy of declining gifts or cash 'for expenses' that are often given on such junkets.

We do convey and reinforce to our journalists and authors that their reports need to be objective, but I do believe that you cannot completely do away with the softening effect of being hosted on a foreign trip by a vendor: the resulting reports could well be 'critical'. Very few publishing houses go all the way and refuse 'junkets' or insist on paying for airfare and all expenses if their reporters need to cover an event.

Overall, stories in the trade press do tend to be 'softer'. Stand-alone stories are rarely harshly critical, and investigative stories or 'sting operations' are very rare. We do have some investigative stories, though, in our regional IT newspapers. Interestingly, it is not our biggest advertisers who exert pressures to influence editorial content. In fact, many of them are mature multinationals with their own code of conduct and ethics. It is often the smaller vendors or advertisers that exert pressures. Sometimes, publications can be subjected to harassment through a simple defamation suit in some remote district court.

The Lawsuit

In March 2003, we carried a news report in our *DQWeek Madras* newspaper on a dealer in Tuticorin, Tamil Nadu, who owed a lot of money to Chennai dealers and about how his cheques were bouncing. The dealer objected to the story. We were sure of it and stuck to our guns. The dealer sued, naming the author, publisher and editor. For five years, the author of the report together with the editor and the publisher made over thirty trips to Tuticorin, several times under a threat that 'non-bailable warrants' would be issued against them if they did not appear in court. However, court hearings were adjourned several times and through most of these hearings, the dealer himself did not make an appearance! We refused to budge or publish a retraction. Finally, five years later, in 2008, the dealer withdrew the case. We spent over Rs 500,000 by way of legal fees and expenses. This does not exclude the opportunity cost of the time spent by the author, editor and publisher.

Too often, I have seen our competitors in the trade press take the easy way out: with integrated ad–edit deals, special coverage for advertisers, getting editorial 'approved' by vendors, and a lot more that we consider against our ethics. These work for a while. However, over time, the publication's credibility drops and with it, the readership, and thus the publication's ability to draw in advertising. The good thing is that, over time, most advertisers realize the value of a publication's credibility, and most fall in line with the demands of objective, often critical, reporting, the occasional poor review, a crash in rankings in a 'best employer' survey and the other 'side-effects' of dealing with a trade publication conforming to ethics and principles.

CHAPTER

7

MEDIA LAWS

This chapter begins by analysing the media's right to free speech and expression in the two largest democracies of the world, India and the US. It goes on to explore the limitations of this crucial right and instances when the law overrides the freedom of expression that news organizations enjoy in a democratic society. A detailed overview of libel, intrusion of privacy, violation of intellectual property rights, obscenity and contempt of court follows. Some aspects of the Right to Information Act in India are also presented. The application of some existing laws is examined through case studies and questions are raised about the ethical implications of these laws. The chapter also highlights the key provisions of the Right to Information Act, the circumstances under which information can be withheld, and the protection afforded by the Act.

MEDIA AND DEMOCRACY

The growth of an independent and free mass media in societies has contributed significantly to the development of democratic institutions and laws. Campbell (2002) suggests that 'cultural and social struggles over free speech and the freedom of the press have defined the nature of American society'. This is not in the least reflected in the concerns of the First Amendment of the American Constitution's Bill of Rights (1791) which reads: 'The US Congress shall make no law respecting an establishment of religion, or prohibiting the free exercise thereof; or abridging the freedom of speech, or of the press; or of the right of the people peaceably to assemble, and to petition the government for a redress of grievances.'

There has been some confusion over whether the issues dealt with in the First Amendment have supremacy and override the issues addressed in the other nine amendments to the US Constitution, or whether its position at the top of the list is arbitrary and the numbering of the list does not denote hierarchy but is simply for convenient distinction. However, it is not difficult to argue that the primacy of the First Amendment does, in fact, mean supremacy. A.C. Grayling (2007), in an article for www.guardian.co.uk, has enumerated the many reasons why the right to free speech underpins all other civil liberties. Without free speech we would not be able to articulate and debate our civil rights; we cannot defend our rights against any violations; we cannot enjoy broad and diverse education; we cannot document history and learn from it; we would not be able to enjoy literature, art, music or dance; and, above all, there would not be a free and independent mass media. Grayling's comprehensive argument is plausible, but not exhaustive.

Can you think of a few more arguments in favour of the supremacy of the right to freedom of speech and expression?

Areopagitica and the Puritan Settlers in America

The argument over free speech was hotly debated among the founders of America. The incipient culture and society of the US was like a tabula rasa or blank slate, which meant that it was free to develop rules either in accordance with or contrary to the established laws of imperialist Britain. The first publishers in Britain enjoyed little freedom as they belonged to an era of authoritarianism. They were controlled by the government through rigorous licensing which in effect prohibited the publication of anything remotely unfavourable to the government.

Poet and author of *Paradise Lost*, John Milton is widely credited with offering the most eminent counter-argument to authoritarianism, and for being a key protagonist for free speech. In 1644, Milton wrote a pamphlet entitled *Areopagitica* in which he argued that the laws governing the licencing of the press should be slackened to enable free and open speech and debate. His apparently libertarian views were based on his belief that truth is a dimension of God and that, therefore, truth would ultimately prevail in its battle against falsehood. *Areopagitica* was a seminal work and is still cited often in free speech arguments. However, Milton was conspicuously concerned with promoting a specific theological interest. He was a puritan and his views in *Areopagitica* were set in the context of the civil war in England at that time. Dissatisfied with the state of the church in England, many puritans had settled in America, bringing with them their puritanical ideology and philosophy.

The Constitution of India was drawn up in 1950. It made provisions under Article 19 honouring the inherent right of every citizen of India to freedom of speech and expression. Interestingly, freedom of the press is not mentioned per se, but is understood to be covered by the provisions of Article 19. The Constitution also outlines reasonable circumstances in which the rights of Article 19 might be restricted (see Box 7.1: Freedom of Speech and Expression in the Indian Constitution). Laws for the press in India have existed since the end of the 18th century. Authoritarian restrictions and licensing of the press were then propounded in a document called *Press Regulations.* The press, for more than a century, was an important feature of colonialism, aiding the imperialistic drive of European nations.

Box 7.1

Freedom of Speech and Expression in the Indian Constitution

According to Article 19 of the Constitution of India, all citizens of the country shall have the right:

(a) to freedom of speech and expression. The State is not prevented from making new laws restricting this right in the interest of the sovereignty and integrity of India, security of the State and friendly relations with foreign States, public order, morality and decency, defamation or incitement to an offence

(b) to assemble peaceably and without arms. The State is not prevented from making new laws restricting this right in the interest of the sovereignty and integrity of India, or in the interest of maintenance of public order

(c) to form associations or unions. The State is not prevented from making new laws restricting this right in the interest of the sovereignty and integrity of India, public order or morality.

? **What are the main differences between the provisions for the right to freedom of speech in the Constitution of India and the First Amendment to the American Constitution?**

FREE SPEECH AND THE LAW

The wording of the First Amendment would lead us to think that the various forms of freedom of expression are innate and absolute rights. Indeed, the very premise of Grayling's article is that 'liberty is indivisible'. This means that all civil rights must be awarded, respected and realized as a whole. This, in turn, implies that liberty—the right to rights—is absolute.

However, if the right to freedom of speech and expression was absolute, there would be no opportunity for people to defend themselves against written or spoken defamation. The opportunity to defend yourself, then, coheres with the right to freedom of expression, but is contrary to the idea that rights are absolute. That rights are relative and context sensitive is seen again and again in the various conflict of interests inherent in media law. For example, what is wanton libel to one person might be a fair comment and an exercise of the right to free speech and expression to another. These issues are considered in depth later in the chapter. For now, what is important to indicate is that the law is not clear-cut, that rights cannot be absolute. There are cases when the rights of one person may impinge on the rights of another.

It is important to realize that although free speech boasts a strong argument for supremacy over other rights in theory, it is not always the case in reality. In the case of *Near* versus *Minnesota* (1931), which saw a state government try to prevent the publication of 'malicious, scandalous or defamatory' material capable of causing public nuisance, the court decreed, among other things, that the 'liberty of the press is not an absolute right, and the state may punish its abuse'. As all forms of the mass media have been involved in lawsuits, it is important for media practitioners to be aware of the law and its restrictions. It should be noted that there is a difference between law and ethics (Retief 2002), which means, in practical terms, that even if one has a clear ethical stance, it is not necessarily consistent with the law. Laws are not the cornerstone of democracy—it is the moral respect for the law that provides the foundation for democratic culture (Retief 2002).

Though laws are constantly revised in the light of shortcomings and new socio-environmental considerations, it is nonetheless important to nurture a healthy understanding and respect for existing laws as these are designed to promote and uphold democratic values. In fact, it can even be suggested that democracy and its incumbent values provide the foundations for the law. Viewed in this light, the ideology and thinking behind the law would be easier to recognize and this will, in turn, help develop an informed understanding of the laws which govern professional conduct for those in the media.

There are certain key areas of the law which pertain to the media. In most cases there are also established, recognized and well-tested defences against certain claims. These areas are libel, privacy, intellectual property rights and contempt of court. These are discussed in detail in the following sections.

LIBEL

Libel is the written or broadcast form of defamation of a person, business or product. This is different from slander which is spoken or oral defamation. To defame someone is to make false claims about a person in a way that damages her/his reputation or to expose a person to public contempt or hatred which could be injurious to her/his professional activities. Libel is considered more serious than slander because:

- in written/broadcast form, defamation is enduring, fixed and recorded
- defamation by slander can be excused as impassioned and therefore, uttered without proper consideration
- defamation by slander is fleeting and therefore unlikely to cause subsequent harm in the future

A case of libel is determined by different criteria depending on whether the complainant is a private individual or a public figure. For a private person, a libel case must be substantiated by proof that the statement was false, caused actual damage and that the accused was negligent in publishing or broadcasting the defamatory report. A public figure has to provide additional evidence that the defamatory material was published or broadcast in the spirit of actual malice. Malice is generally understood as being predominantly motivated by a desire to injure. Where a defamatory statement is made without sincere belief in its sentiments, it can usually be taken as evidence of malice (see Box 7.2: Actual Malice Rule).

If a statement is defamatory to a general unidentified group of society, it is not considered libellous. This is because its general nature is unlikely to cause harm to individuals unlike in a statement which specifically refers to individuals. However, statements which constitute hate speech intended to incite violence or offence are not constitutionally protected by the right to free speech.

In most countries, a case of libel must be filed within one year of publication or broadcast of the alleged defamatory information or comment.

> **Box 7.2**
>
> ***Actual Malice Rule***
>
> The actual malice rule is sometimes known as the 'Times' rule, after the famous *New York Times* versus *L.B. Sullivan* case in the US in 1964. A senior police official, L.B. Sullivan, in Montgomery, Alabama, filed a libel suit against *The New York Times* for publishing an advertisement which made certain allegations about the law enforcement strategies employed to control civil rights demonstrations. Sullivan felt that he had been indirectly defamed by the advertisement. The Circuit Court of Montgomery upheld his claims and awarded him $500,000 in damages. The case was appealed against and reheard in the Supreme Court, which overturned the verdict on the grounds that actual malice with 'reckless disregard' for the truth must be proved, but was not done by *The New York Times*. The Supreme Court stipulated further that the media must be given more leeway in criticizing public officials and that *The New York Times* was, in this case, constitutionally protected under the First Amendment.

Later, the actual malice rule came to pertain to public figures as well as public officials. One subtlety of this rule is that at times a distinction needs to be made between the public and private lives of a public figure. However, it is exceedingly difficult to prove actual malice and in this sense the law seems to have been determined with the intention of protecting the media from excessive censorship. But, because libel suits can be costly even if the case is won, many media companies try to avoid libel altogether through self-censorship.

Besides the expense, what other reasons might deter the media from risking libel? What are the dangers and benefits of self-censorship of the media?

Defences against Libel

Truth

The best defence against libel is truth. If a statement's veracity can be proved with evidence, then there is no case for libel. Proving a statement's veracity means that the defendant does not have to prove that the statement was published in the public interest or that it was not intended maliciously.

If a statement is devoid of truth, but can be shown as a quote rather than the words of the writer or broadcaster, it may not be libel. However, there are unanswered questions here. Does slander become libel when it is reported? In repeating slander verbatim, can the reporter be held accountable for someone else's opinion? To avoid a case of libel, media organizations can clarify that the defamatory statement is someone else's opinion and is not endorsed or supported by them.

If a statement is devoid of truth, the publisher/broadcaster should endeavour to show that she/he believed it to be true after steps had been taken to verify the information and that she/he is, therefore, not culpable for negligence.

If a statement is found to be untrue after it is published, the publisher should try to prove that all possible steps had been taken to verify the information prior to publication and, therefore, the publisher is not guilty of libel through negligence (see Box 7.3: The Bogoshi Case in South Africa).

Hence, the best way to guard against libel is to be reasonably convinced of the truthfulness of a statement after the utmost care has been taken to prove the same. If there is any scope for reasonable doubt of the veracity of the information, it is best not to publish it.

Do you feel that slander becomes libel when it is reported? What defences are there for quoting slander?

Box 7.3

The Bogoshi Case in South Africa

In September 1998, the Supreme Court of Appeal in South Africa 'liberated the media from the shackles' (Retief 2002) which severely limited and over-censored the press in libel cases. Morele Bogoshi, a lawyer, sued the *City Press* newspaper for libellous material it had published in a series of articles. The articles accused Bogoshi of several counts of fraud. The defence claimed that it had not been negligent, that it did not intend to defame and was constitutionally protected by the right to free speech. Prior to the trial, the media in South Africa had been subject to a 'strict liability' rule, which meant that in libel cases the media's only defence was to prove a statement's truth. This precluded the media from using lack of negligence and intent to defame as a defence. However, in the Bogoshi case, Judge Joos Hefer said that the 'strict liability' rule was 'clearly wrong'.

The Bogoshi case resulted in legitimizing the absence of fault as a defence against libel. In other words, what was accepted as valid was the claim of the media that it was neither negligent nor that it intended to cause harm through defamation. The ruling in this case also allowed for 'innocent ignorance' and pardonable levels of human error.

What do you think is meant by pardoning ignorance and human error? What might be the problems of this line of defence?

What should be a pardonable level of human error in libel cases? Discuss with hypothetical or real examples.

Qualified privilege

Public officials may enjoy or be granted privilege to speak freely in their official capacities without danger of slander. The media is granted qualified privilege to accurately report the speeches of officials exercising their privilege (say, in Parliament) without being accused of libel. In the case of part-time officials, both the privilege and the qualified privilege extend only to speeches made in official capacity. This privilege is provided in Article 361A of the Constitution of India. It stipulates that a person will not be liable to prosecution for reporting the proceedings of Parliament or legislative assemblies, as long as the report is substantially true and devoid of malice.

Fair comment

The right to fair comment and criticism recognizes that opinions which may be derogatory or defamatory can be published or broadcast without being libellous. In such circumstances, it is necessary to make clear that a statement is an opinion rather than a fact. To this end, care must be taken over the language chosen to express an opinion. For example, to say that a famous actress looked like a prostitute is an expression of opinion whereas to say that the actress is a prostitute is not clearly an expression of opinion and (if untrue) would be libellous. Comedy and satire are protected against libel, as are reviews of books, films, plays, restaurants and so on. Fair comment and criticism are usually awarded constitutional protection in democracies (see Box 7.4: Libel-Proof Plaintiff).

Libel cases are often time-consuming and costly even when charges are successfully defended (see Box 7.5: *Patom* and the KSSP). Writers on media law frequently observe two recurring features of libel:

Box 7.4

'Libel-Proof Plaintiff'

Donnie Brasco, a 1997 film, based on a real-life incident, starring Al Pacino and Johnny Depp, portrayed the murders of three mafia leaders by mobster John Cerasani. But, Cerasani was cleared of the murder charges and later claimed that the film libelled him. The judge, however, did not uphold the claim suggesting that the many misdemeanours for which he had been previously convicted (including racketeering, drug-dealing and robbery) effectively disqualified him from libel. The reasoning was that since his reputation had already been repeatedly blackened by his own doing, he could not be further defamed. The judge described him as a 'libel-proof plaintiff'.

(i) Juries usually side with the individual (at least when the individual concerned is a private figure) and display what has been described as a 'disposition to punish' (Rodman 2001) by awarding 'outsize' compensations.

(ii) The high costs involved in libel cases have a 'chilling effect' on the media. Organizations are reluctant to probe into contentious issues fearing libel, which results in perceived restrictions of the Constitutional right to free speech; the 'dumbing-down' of news stories to 'safe' subjects; undermining the democratic principle of public debate and thereby, the public's right to knowledge.

Do you think that it is fair to impose a limitation on someone's reputation? If you were deemed 'libel-proof' what arguments would you offer in your defence?

Box 7.5

***Patom* and the KSSP**

The Kerala Sasthra Sahitya Parishad (KSSP), a left-wing non-government organization, launched a case of libel against political journal *Patom* for publishing defamatory comments about it in an article in May 2004. *Patom* had accused the KSSP of anti-nationalism and engaging in activities with foreign agencies. The article, covering 20 pages of the journal, described high-profile leaders of the KSSP, and had including Dr M.P. Parameswaran, Dr B. Ekbal and Dr T.M. Thomas Isaac, as 'imperialist stooges, foreign agents and spies'. The article claimed that the KSSP was providing information like maps and charts to foreign agents in exchange for money. The complainants claimed that the article was intended to undermine the image of the KSSP, and had caused it public humiliation and damaged its professional activities by creating an internal schism and prompting several members to discontinue their alliance with the KSSP.

A court in Kerala held that the article was defamatory in that its language was 'excessive and volatile' and had damaged the reputations of otherwise respected KSSP leaders. The court, however, took into account the character of *Patom's* editor, Professor M.N. Vijayan, who was known as a 'leading light' of Kerala society and a reputed left-wing intellectual. The court recognized the article as a 'corrective effort' and reasoned that on the basis of the article, no one would think the KSSP was guilty of espionage. The case led to wide media interest in the state. While speaking on the key aspects of the judgement at a media conference a few days after it was delivered, Prof. Vijayan suffered a fatal heart attack in front of media cameras. His last words defended the decisions of *Patom*. He said: 'We are accused of using foul language, but it was Bernard Shaw who said "if you want to catch attention you need to use strong language..."

Source: Adapted from 'A defamation Verdict from Kerala', www.thehoot.org, 13 October 2007.

PRIVACY

Privacy is understood as the right to be left alone. Campbell (2002) has made this useful distinction: 'Where libel is concerned with protecting a person's public life, privacy protects a person's life outside the public domain, her/his feelings and peace of mind. Privacy cases can be contentious and often involve a conflict of issues. The media, in pursuit of information (ostensibly) relevant to a story, and (ostensibly) in the public interest, are in danger of infringing on a person's basic right to be left alone.' Theoreticians have argued that all instances of invasion of privacy are ultimately guilty of causing the same effect: depriving an individual of her/his right to control how she/he is perceived by other people. This implies that as soon as the private is transformed into the public, the subject loses autonomy of image. It is because of the contentiousness of privacy cases that they tend to be very high profile and frequently involve big names: celebrities and huge media corporations. The right to privacy involves three main areas, intrusion, private facts and appropriation.

Intrusion

Intrusion can be divided into two forms, active and passive. Active intrusion is the trespassing on a person's property or private space out of the public domain. This form is physical and could include climbing trees or fences to

Box 7.6

Media Intrusion

In 2000, actress Jennifer Aniston sued *Celebrity Skin* magazine for publishing nude photographs of her that were taken while she was sunbathing in her garden. It was claimed that the photographer had climbed a neighbour's fence to take the photos.

Manu Sharma led a reclusive life following his acquittal by a lower court in the Jessica Lall murder case. A team of reporters and camera crew from CNN-IBN, pretending to be activists of the National Students' Union of India, convinced Sharma to grant them a meeting at his office in Chandigarh. The channel broadcast images of Sharma's office alongside images of a candlelight vigil held for Jessica Lal and Sharma leaving court. In the course of the meeting, Sharma realized the identity of the impostors and demanded that they be removed from the premises. This is an example of an invasion of privacy on several counts; access was not properly authorized; the footage gathered by the crew was banal and of no relevance to the case, nor could it claim to be of public interest. The footage seemed to insinuate Sharma's guilt in the Jessica Lall case (Sharma was subsequently arrested and jailed after he was held guilty of Jessica Lall's murder).

Source: Adapted from 'Jennifer Aniston Topless Photo Lawsuit gone', www.hollywood.com, 21 February 2007.

Imagine you are a reporter desperate to get a glimpse of an elusive figure like Manu Sharma. Consider what your motivations are and the extent to which they could be considered legitimate. If you can identify some bona fide reasons for seeking access to Sharma, in what ways could you acquire the material you desired in an appropriate and legal manner? If your attempts were unsuccessful, what would you do?

afford a view of the victim, or it might involve disguising one's identity and deceitfully earning access into a private space. In short, physical intrusion refers to any unauthorized access (see Box 7.6: Media Intrusion).

Passive intrusion refers to the use of technology to intrude on a person's private life. The use of telephotolenses on cameras, telescopes, binoculars, spy cameras and concealed microphones or amplifiers all run the risk of infringing on someone's privacy rights if used in a concealed and unauthorized manner. Another important aspect of passive intrusion relates to invading the privacy of a deceased person (see Box 7.7: Princess Diana's Death) like in the case of Aarushi Talwar whose reputation was questioned on the basis of certain insinuations made by senior police officers.

Box 7.7

Princess Diana's Death

The deaths of Princess Diana and her friend Dodi Al Fayed have been embroiled in controversy for more than a decade since they died in a car accident in Paris. Initial speculation by the media suggested that the paparazzi had pursued the couple which ultimately led to the accident that killed them. The paparazzi were held responsible for causing the accident. Nine members of the French paparazzi were arrested and later cleared of all charges. The driver of the car, who also died in the crash, was blamed for the accident for driving while drunk and speeding. However, three members of the paparazzi were convicted in 2006 for breaching France's privacy laws. They were ordered to pay a symbolic fine of one euro each. Many photographs that were taken at the scene of the crash—depicting the princess trapped in the wreckage but still conscious—have been banned from publication by French courts.

In 2004, Diana's family argued that the footage of Diana speaking candidly on film (her BBC interview with Martin Bashir), which attracted much interest and speculation after her death, should be protected under privacy laws. The plea was unprecedented as privacy laws do not include protection after death. However, the media argued that this particular footage did not infringe privacy rights as the Princess knew that she was being filmed and did not stipulate a wish for confidentiality. Further-more, as the law did not recognize a dead person's reputation, the right to privacy could not legally be extended in Diana's case. Dodi's father, Mohammed Al Fayed, had alleged that the deaths of his son and Diana were the result of a conspiracy. This has fuelled media interest with journalists offering controversial, speculative conspiracy theories that have kept the accident topical more than a decade after it took place.

Source: Adapted from 'Diana jury shown paparazzi death photos', www.telegraph.co.uk., 12 October 2007.

Should there be a law protecting the privacy of the dead? Can you think of reasons why privacy rights of the dead should be honoured? Or do you believe privacy laws after death are obsolete?

Why do you think the French court issued a symbolic, nominal fine on the convicted paparazzi in the Diana case?

Does the existence of the paparazzi mock privacy protection laws?

Private Facts

Private facts refer to information of a personal, sensitive or embarrassing nature whose publication is deemed gratuitous and unrelated or unnecessary to a story about an individual (see Box 7.8: Sipple's Sexuality). This aspect is covered in Section 8 (j) of India's Right to Information Act, 2005.

In some cases, where private facts are reported, truth is not necessarily a valid defence and the best defence would be newsworthiness. This is not always easy to prove and it involves drawing a clear distinction between the interest of the public and in the public interest.

Box 7.8

Sipple's Sexuality

In 1975, Oliver Sipple saved the life of President Gerald Ford in an assassination attempt. Interest in Sipple in the aftermath of the incident led the media to report pieces of information about him. Sipple's homosexuality was among the details that were reported. Sipple objected to the publication of his sexual orientation because he did not want his parents to be exposed to the information. He claimed that his privacy had been violated—that the information had been published gratuitously and without his consent. However, when the case went to court, the judge ruled that his privacy had not been violated because he was an active member of the San Francisco gay community, which was understood as demonstrating that the issue of his sexuality was already, and voluntarily, in the public domain.

Source: Adapted from 'Caught in Fate's Trajectory, Along with Gerald Ford', *Washington Post*, 31 December 2006.

Can you think of any subtleties about the nature of privacy that this case has raised? In your opinion, whose argument holds more weight, Sipple's or that of the judge?

Appropriation

Appropriation means using somebody's name or physical image without permission. It is not permissible to use somebody's face or name to endorse a product or a particular interest, without that person's consent. However, privacy rights through appropriation are usually considered violated when the violation is for commercial purposes. Thus, appropriation for private financial or professional gain is illegal while appropriation for educative, scientific or artistic purposes is more likely to be conceded as legitimate.

INTELLECTUAL PROPERTY RIGHTS

Copyright laws award an author of a piece of work the right to reproduce it and control its distribution. India's Copyright Act, 1957, lists the kinds of work that are eligible for copyright protection. These are original literary, dramatic, musical and artistic works, cinematographic films and sound recordings. A work's copyright protection is finite. In the US, the duration of copyright laws has been changed substantially on many occasions and this has led to some confusion. Usually copyright on a certain work is governed by the laws at the time the work is produced. Once the copyright has expired the work falls into the public domain. In India, the duration of copyright for published work lasts until sixty years after the author's death. The duration of copyright for unpublished work is not specified. If a work is published posthumously, it is under copyright for sixty years from the date of publication.

Under the Copyright Act, it is illegal to reproduce a work, store it electronically in any medium, to issue copies not already in circulation, to perform or screen in public (a film or a play), to facilitate the selling or hiring of copies, to abridge and/or to translate. However, translation rights can be obtained from the Copyright Board in India seven years after the publication of a work. The copyright laws in different countries are not adequate as far as infringement across borders is concerned. For example, if an article or essay authored in the US is reproduced in India and accessed via the internet, it is not clear which country's copyright laws would be applicable. Also see Appendix 7.3 and 7.4.

Intellectual property is meant to be automatically copyrighted and can enjoy the privileges therein by virtue of its existence. It is also important to note that copyright includes all sorts of subsidiary works as well. This means that letters and electronic mail messages, notes, sketches or any kind of work in progress are also copyright protected.

The author of the novel *Catcher in the Rye*, J.D. Salinger, successfully sued a biographer for using some of his private letters without his consent. Franz Kafka instructed that all his unpublished work and manuscripts be burnt after his death as he did not want any of it published. However, Max Brodd, Kafka's close friend, decided to ignore his friend's wishes, recognizing the literary merit of his work. If Kafka's wishes had been carried out, some of his most important and acclaimed works such as *The Trial* and *The Castle* would never have been published.

Can Brodd be accused of copyright infringement in spirit if not in law?
What reasons can be cited as evidence of copyright infringement?
Do you think that a judge ruling today would sympathize with Brodd's decisions?

Should there be more stringent copyright laws for unpublished work?

First Sale Doctrine

The first sale doctrine means that once a work has been sold, the purchaser has the right thereafter to sell or distribute that particular copy. It does not allow the right to reproduce the work.

Fair Dealing

The fair dealing rule is the Indian equivalent of the American 'fair use' rule. It appears in the Copyright Act of 1957 under Article 52 which outlines acts of copying which do not breach copyright. It was formulated to allow a degree of latitude in the use of copyrighted material, for the sake of upholding 'free culture'. Free culture is understood as providing the liberty to access material to facilitate public debate, historical references and cross-cultural references.

Fair dealing means the following:

- any work can be reproduced if the material is used for non-profit-making activities of cultural value, such as education, art, science or if the material is used in a newspaper or any other medium of mass communication for the sake of reporting current affairs or in the public interest
- if the material is used for commercial gain, however, it is not generally protected by the fair use rule
- the nature and content of the material will determine the extent to which it can be fairly used

- the quantity of material used will determine whether its use is deemed fair. Generally, up to 200 words of text, but not more than 5 per cent of the full text of a published work, can be fairly used. Similarly, a few lines of a song or a short excerpt from a film or television programme running into, say, less than half a minute, may be reproduced in a 'fair' manner
- the use of material should not damage its saleability

However, there are certain aspects of technology which undermine and run contrary to established norms and laws pertaining to copyrights. These aspects of technology also undermine the principles of free culture. This area of contention has been comprehensively argued by Lawrence Lessig (2004) in his book *Free Culture.* Lessig considers how, as a reaction to the scope and uncontrolled nature of the internet, certain technological features have been introduced to prevent the violation of copyright laws. Where the law pertains to conventional media, he argues, it is 'code' which ultimately controls the internet.

Lessig uses the example of his Adobe eBook Reader. This programme allows a user to read e-books purchased on the internet. For each book, the programme has formulated a series of permissions which determine the extent of use the reader has. It covers issues like whether the book may be printed, how frequently it can be read and whether the text may be copied. There are a few examples of such books which, though in the public domain, have very limited permissions granted by the programme. Lessig points out that these permissions are not necessarily concurrent with the law, nor are they permissions which may be transgressed: the programme is designed in such a way as 'to deny the ability to transgress its permissions'. For example, if you are permitted to print ten pages and try to print a eleventh page, the programme's controls for printing will not respond. This is what Lessig calls 'code'. He is concerned that code has a greater reach than the law and that it does not factor in the norms of fair use.

The best way to guard against infringement of copyright is to ask for permission from the copyright holder before use. This applies to extensive use of text, letters, photographs, art work, lyrics, poems and tables, regardless of whether the work is published or not.

Framing

Framing is the practice of copying text or content from one website to use on another site. If the lifted content is then presented in the frame or borders of the second website, in a way that is intended to look like an original part of that site, it is an infringement of copyright. Framing is more reprehensible if it is done for commercial gain. If its practice can be proved to be in the public good, it will probably be deemed a lesser offence. The best way to draw attention to material of significance from another website is to offer a link to that site.

Obscenity

In the chapter 4 on Sensitivity, the nature of obscenity was explored in detail. Let us now briefly relook at some of the salient points which have a special relevance as far as the law is concerned. First, it must be realized that although free speech and a free media legally afford considerable scope for unrestricted expression, obscenity is not constitutionally protected by these rights. This brings us back to the problem of defining what exactly constitutes obscenity.

- Obscenity is often understood as material which offends the sensibility of the 'average' person, using 'contemporary standards' as a benchmark. However, that leaves open to interpretation who the average person is and what contemporary standards are. The recognition of contemporary standards, however, does allow for changing values over time. For example, James Joyce's acclaimed novel *Ulysses* was initially banned in the US because it was deemed obscene. Copies of a magazine which published a series of excerpts from the book were burned and the magazine fined. This public outcry deterred British and American publishers from accepting the novel for publication.
- In the US, the Comstock Act of 1873 banned all material which included reference to sex education, abortion and birth control, claiming all such issues indecent. Today, however, the idea of censoring information about birth control and sex education is counter-intuitive and would be considered ludicrous.
- Material which is intended to evoke feelings of prurient lust is usually considered obscene. However, if graphic material can be proved to have educative, scientific or cultural value, it is not deemed obscene.
- Accepting that different eras will have different social standards, it is also the case that different places and societies, although contemporaneous, will have differing cultural values. It is likely, therefore, that different places will have their own laws pertaining to obscenity, and this should be carefully considered and researched when using the media (like the internet) to disseminate information.
- In discerning whether the material is appropriate or obscene, it must be considered as a whole and not in part. A holistic approach protects works

of literary, artistic or social value from being censored for containing small amounts of imprudent language or depiction in an otherwise seminal work.

CONTEMPT OF COURT

Criminal contempt of court includes publication of material which interferes with or undermines the process of a trial, scandalizes, or debases the authority of the court (Contempt of Court Act, 1971, Section 2, Clause C ff). The media should be particularly careful while reporting crime. Such stories are considered 'hot news' for the media since these stories would be of public interest as well as be in interest of the public. This can lead to a temptation by the media to provide extensive coverage to crime stories and also to speculate about who is responsible for the crime and offer editorial comment. There is a danger in such cases of the media interfering with the proper course of justice. The phrase 'trial by the media' is often used by those critical of the media's style of reporting criminal cases. Reporting on a criminal case that is sub judice may be construed as contempt of court and an attempt to influence the course of justice. The Law Commission of India, in its 200th report submitted in August 2008, has examined this issue in great detail and recommended a number of amendments to the Contempt of Court Act (extracts from this report are provided in Appendix 7.1).

The Madeleine McCann case has attracted considerable media attention all over the world—the parents of a missing girl first sought media attention to trace her and then ended up suing a publication for libel. The parents successfully won a libel case against a Portuguese paper that had accused them of murder, which they argued was untrue, distracted the work of the investigation and caused them severe humiliation and stress (see Box 7.9: Media Interference in the Madeleine McCann Case).

When the media publishes evidence or speculates about a case which is in the process of judicial hearing, it runs the risk of contempt of court if it is considered an attempt to influence the course of justice. However, the media is free to publish material about a case once it has been closed in court. The media should regulate the nature of its speculation on a criminal case that is under adjudication (see Appendix 7.2).

Box 7.9

Media Interference in the Madeleine McCann Case

In June 2007, a four-year-old British girl, Madeleine McCann, went missing from the holiday apartment her parents had rented in Portugal. Her parents used the media as a means to help find their daughter. However, despite the media hype and her parents' efforts, Madeleine has still not been found. The media coverage of the case aroused widespread sympathy and public interest.

As time passed with little or no new developments in determining Madeleine's whereabouts, the media began to run stories speculating about the involvement of her parents in her disappearance. DNA samples of Madeleine had been found in the car which her parents had hired twenty-five days after her disappearance. This was taken as reason enough to insinuate that her parents could have had a hand in her disappearance. The media speculated that the DNA samples recovered suggested that the car had been used to convey and dispose of her dead body. There were no questions raised as to how her parents could have concealed her body for at least twenty-five days given the substantial presence of the police and the media at the location from where she disappeared. The McCanns filed a libel case against a Portuguese publication and won. Following this, in March 2008, four British newspapers ran front-page apologies to Madeleine McCann's parents.

Source: Adapted from 'Parents hope sacking of Madeleine McCann police chief is turning point in probe, www.timesonline.co.uk, 3 October 2007.

Consider the advantages and disadvantages of the wide media coverage given to the disappearance of Madeleine McCann. What evidence is there in this case to support a libel suit? Consider the rights of privacy that might reasonably apply to the McCann family.

Criminal contempt of court includes the publication of any material which undermines the authority of the court. The media is permitted to offer bona fide criticism of a judicial act, provided that it is not defamatory. Criticism which suggests improper motivations of the judiciary is not acceptable. However, there is certainly a fine line between freedom of expression and contempt of court.

Shield Law

Shield law is designed to protect the confidentiality of a journalist's sources. There are certain circumstances in which the anonymity of a source should be upheld to protect that person's safety. If a person offers information about the working of a group engaged in secret and sensitive activities or even organized crime, that person may demand confidentiality fearing persecution by those implicated. However, if there is a compelling need for a source to testify in court or if further information has to be revealed about the source —for example, to verify its authority—the court can demand that the identity of the source be revealed (see Box 7.10: Leaks in High Places and Contempt of Court, and Box 7.11: A Close Shave).

Box 7.10

Leaks in High Places and Contempt of Court

Joseph Wilson, an American career diplomat and ambassador, was asked by the Central Intelligence Agency (CIA) to conduct a mission in Niger to examine claims that Iraq was negotiating the purchase of uranium from Niger. As uranium is used in nuclear weapons it was feared that Iraq intended to acquire uranium to develop weapons of mass destruction (WMDs). Wilson did not find any evidence for the claims. In 2003, after the war in Iraq had begun, Wilson, published an article in *The New York Times* in which he suggested that President George Bush had misrepresented intelligence reports which would have otherwise undermined the cited reason for the US going to war with Iraq.

After this article was published, on 14 July 2003 political commentator Robert Novak published an article in which he claimed that two senior administration officials had told him that Wilson had been assigned the Niger mission because his wife, Valerie Plame, who was a CIA undercover agent associated with the proliferation of WMDs, had arranged it.

Two days later, David Corn, the Washington editor of *The Nation*, a political weekly, wrote an article which quoted Wilson as saying that by identifying his wife, her whole career as a secret agent had been compromised. The CIA then requested a federal investigation into the leak of the identity of one of its secret agents. Attorney Patrick Fitzgerald was appointed to head the investigation and he convened a grand jury.

The names of several high-ranking officials in the Bush administration came out including those of Richard Armitage, Karl Rove and Lewis 'Scooter' Libby. Armitage was revealed as Novak's primary source. He cooperated fully with the investigation and was not penalized, although he resigned from his post in 2004. Armitage admitted that he had revealed the name of Valerie Plame in an interview with Novak, but claimed that he did not know that she was an undercover agent as he had seen her name on a memorandum with the position of 'analyst' with the CIA.

Rove was the official to whom Novak appealed for confirmation of Plame's identity. Rove claimed that he had come to know this from Libby and from other journalists. Moreover, Rove said that he had not provided information about Plame, but merely told Novak that he had heard about her role as a secret agent of the CIA. Libby came to know of Plame's identity through Vice-President Dick Cheney. However, Libby's statements during the investigation were confusing and contradictory: at one point he claimed that he first learned of Plame's identity from reporters. Libby was convicted on four counts of perjury and obstructing the course of justice by making false claims. He was sentenced to 30 months' imprisonment and fined $250,000. President Bush later commuted his sentence.

Several journalists who had knowledge of Plame's identity were called to cooperate in the investigation by revealing their sources.

Source: Adapted from 'Profile : Joseph Wilson', www.bbc.co.uk, 20 October 2005.

Among them, Matthew Cooper and Judith Miller were both in possession of information about Plame's association with the CIA. Cooper had written an article about the association in October. Miller, on the other hand, had not published anything about Plame. Both journalists were prepared to conceal the identity of their sources, respecting the supremacy of their right to confidentiality. Both faced prison sentences for not revealing their sources, which amounted to contempt of court. Miller spent three months in prison for the offence but defended her decision saying: 'If journalists cannot be trusted to keep confidences, then journalists cannot function and there cannot be a free press.' The evening before Cooper's sentencing, he received a call from his source's lawyer freeing him of his obligation of confidence. Cooper revealed that his source was Karl Rove.

Though nobody was convicted for leaking confidential information, several people were convicted for obstructing the course of justice in a case which was eventually dropped. Several people involved in the investigation claimed that they were not aware of Plame's undercover status in the CIA.

Box 7.11
A Close Shave

In 2007, a case of espionage in India brought several journalists into the heart of judicial proceedings despite their involvement being indirect. An employee of Videsh Sanchar Nigam Limited (VSNL), a telecommunications company, provided confidential information electronically to an employee of Reliance Communications, a rival firm. This information was leaked to the press. The court requested that the journalists reveal their sources. The journalists demurred claiming the need to protect their sources. The court accepted this line of reasoning.

A debate ensued (see Appendix 7.2) about the right of journalists to conceal the identity of their sources. There are several interesting points that were made in this debate.

- Journalists do not have the sacrosanct right to withhold information under any and every circumstance, says Rebecca-Mammem John, a Supreme Court lawyer, in reference to a 2003 case which challenged certain aspects of the Prevention of Terrorism Act of 2002.
- A journalist is obliged only to reveal the identity of her/his sources to a judge, who can be entrusted to maintain confidentiality, and is not obliged to disclose the same information to the police or anyone else, observes Anirban Mazumdar of the National University of Judicial Sciences in Kolkata.
- To access confidential information is a crime but it is not a crime to receive and be in possession of it 'passively', Mazumdar further states. It is a crime, however, to publish confidential information even if it was gained passively. This is presumably because the publication of confidential information plays an active role in its distribution, he adds.

FIRs

An FIR, or a first information report, is the documentation of an alleged wrongdoing, or a complaint lodged with the police. Anyone can access FIRs and they are often used as sources of information by media reporters. The press is permitted by law to publish the content of an FIR. However, there is some contention over the use of FIRs by the press. The main point of concern is that an FIR is merely an allegation or a complaint: anybody can lodge an FIR against anyone levelling any kind of allegation. The fact that a complaint has been lodged and documented is not the same thing as proving the occurrence of a wrongdoing. It is plausible that an FIR can be lodged out of personal vengeance and is unfounded. The content of such an FIR, if used by the media, might end up falsely accusing a person. Even if the alleged wrongdoer is guilty, it is still erroneous for the media to accuse her/him merely on the strength of an FIR because the law holds that a person is innocent until proven guilty.

Journalists who wish to publish the contents of an FIR should use the correct language. The fact that a wrongdoing is only alleged must be emphasized and the fact that the source of information is an FIR should also be specifically mentioned. Some argue that it is best not to use FIRs as sources of information; others feel that if used, reporters should ascertain the circumstances and context and also present the 'other side' of the story if required. If an FIR, which has been reported in the media, is proven to be unfounded, there is a danger of the information being considered libellous in tort.

Sub-judicial Reporting

The issue of reporting cases that are sub judice is a rather awkward area for journalists. The major problem is accuracy—or rather lack of accuracy—which sometimes permeates reports on court proceedings. There are several reasons why this happens:

- reporters seldom attend court and receive their information second-hand or third-hand resulting in the information getting distorted as it is passed on from one person to another
- legal jargon is often difficult for the layperson and journalists to understand
- reporters are often untrained in legal matters and therefore lack the necessary knowledge and understanding of judicial processes

Journalists are advised to be aware of the fact that a judge might make statements in court which are not necessarily her/his actual opinion or final judgement: they may be intended to elicit particular information or may only be a tentative judgement.

Legal experts have proposed that an office be established by the Supreme Court of India to give mediapersons comprehensive information on court proceedings. The information would be technically accurate and readily understandable to the layperson. They have also suggested that extensive training be offered to media students on law and judicial issues. Practical steps which could be taken immediately include pairing a new, inexperienced journalist with one who is well acquainted with legal matters to report on sub-judicial matters as a form of on-the-job training (see Appendix 7.2).

RIGHT TO INFORMATION

The Right to Information Act, 2005 is a revision of the Freedom of Information Act, 2002. It was formulated to facilitate smooth access to information for all citizens. The Right to Information act is based on the premise that democracy must involve an informed citizenry and that a government must be accountable to those governed. However, the act recognizes several circumstances in which information can be reasonably withheld. Several aspects of the act are pertinent to the media in two areas: in the sourcing of information; and the exposure of failures to adhere to the provisions of the act.

Under Section 4 of the act, all public bodies are required to disclose information pertaining to their functioning; their employees, officials and representatives; and a comprehensive audit of their accounts. The act encourages that such information be made public through the media like newspapers, the internet, hoardings and broadcasts. The act also encourages regular dissemination of such information to minimize the occasions that members of the public need to resort to the procedures of the act to obtain information. This is because it takes time and money to obtain information through the act. In this capacity, the media plays an important role in disseminating public information.

Circumstances for Withholding Information

Some of the circumstances for withholding information are as follows:

- Its disclosure would undermine the sovereignty and integrity of the Indian nation; the security, scientific or economic interests of the state; the state's friendly relationship with foreign states; or would incite offence.

- Its publication has been forbidden by the courts and would amount to contempt of court.
- Its disclosure would breach the privilege of Parliament.
- It pertains to trade secrets or intellectual property and its disclosure would harm the financial interests of those to whom it relates.
- Its disclosure would endanger a person's life or safety or is a breach of confidentiality rights.
- Its disclosure would impede judicial procedures.
- Its disclosure would infringe a person's copyrights.

If an application for information is rejected due to one of the above reasons, the applicant would be informed of the reason. If it is possible to abstract or edit the unauthorized information on a requested area, the abstracted/edited information would be disclosed. This provision is called 'severability' and the act requires that the severed information be acknowledged as such and that information regarding the applicant's right to appeal the decision of non-disclosure be provided.

Any activity undertaken in good faith in adherence to this act or the intended adherence to it, shall be protected from prosecution or penalty. Media practitioners may take this provision in the law to indicate that they might engage in activities which promote the right to information and guard against corruption. It must be remembered, however, that good faith—which could perhaps be understood as public interest—could be difficult to prove. Furthermore, before exposing an authority or official for non-compliance with the provisions of the act, it should be remembered that the accused is afforded the right to prove diligent execution of duty before a penalty is issued.

SUMMARY

In this chapter we have considered libel, privacy, copyright, obscenity, contempt of court and the right to information. We have looked at those aspects of the law that have special relevance to media professionals. We have seen how basic human rights and democratic principles form the basis for the formulation of media laws. This chapter has considered laws in the international and the Indian context. It is important to realize that laws are constantly changing and revisions are often based on previous cases from around the world. Throughout the chapter, there are several complex and probing questions to which there are no simple 'rightz' or 'wrong' answers. Answering these questions will provide an understanding of the nuances and subtleties of the law. By considering different angles as objectively as possible, one would become familiar with the law as well as with the principles covered in the earlier chapters.

REVIEW QUESTIONS

1. What are the key provisions of the First Amendment to the American Constitution's Bill of Rights?
2. Why is it argued that the right to freedom of expression underpins all other rights?
3. In what respects should the right to freedom of expression be considered relative and context-sensitive?
4. What is libel and why is it more serious than slander?
5. What are the criteria for libel?
6. Why are there different libel criteria for public/private complainants?
7. What are the problems with the 'actual malice' rule?
8. What are the defences against libel?
9. What is qualified privilege?
10. What are the two key features of libel cases?
11. What is invasion of privacy and what are the forms of intrusion?
12. What is understood as private facts?
13. What is appropriation?
14. What are the key features of copyright?
15. What circumstances determine fair use?
16. What media activities might constitute contempt of court?

REFERENCES

Campbell, Richard 2002, *Media and Culture*, Bedford/St Martin's, Boston, US.

Grayling, A.C. 2007, 'Freedom of Speech' at http://commentisfree.guardian. co.uk/ac_grayling/2007/12/freedom of speech.html (accessed on 15 August 2008).

Lessig, Lawrence 2004, *Free Culture*, Penguin, New York, US.

Retief, Johan 2002, *Media Ethics: An Introduction to Responsible Journalism,* Oxford University Press, Cape Town, South Africa.

Rodman, George 2001, *Making Sense of Media*, Addison Wesley Longman, Boston, US.

Seetha 2007, 'Caught in the Net' at http://www.telegraphindia.com/1070321/asp/atleisure/story_7542223.asp (accessed on 15 August 2008).

APPENDIX 7.1

Contempt of Court and 'Trial by Media'

What follow are extracts from the 200th report of the Law Commission of India on 'Trial by Media: Free Speech and Fair Trial under the Criminal Procedure Code, 1973 (Amendments to the Contempt of Courts Act, 1971)'. The report of the commission, headed by Justice M. Jagannadha Rao, was submitted to the Union Minister for Law and Justice H.R. Bharadwaj in August 2006.

The subject was taken up *suo motu* having regard to the extensive prejudicial coverage of crime and information about suspects and accused, both in the print and electronic media. There is today a feeling that in view of the extensive use of television and cable services, the whole pattern of publication of news has changed and several such publications are likely to have prejudicial impact on the suspects, accused, witnesses and even judges and in general, on the administration of justice. According to our law, a suspect/accused is entitled to a fair procedure and is presumed to be innocent till proved guilty in a court of law. None can be allowed to prejudge or prejudice his case by the time it goes to trial.

Article 19(1)(a) of the Constitution of India guarantees freedom of speech and expression and Article 19(2) permits reasonable restrictions to be imposed by statute for the purposes of various matters including 'Contempt of Court'. Article 19(2) does not refer to 'administration of justice' but interference in ... the administration of justice is clearly referred to in the definition of 'criminal contempt" in Section 2 of the Contempt of Courts Act, 1971 and in Section 3 thereof as amounting to contempt. Therefore, publications which interfere or tend to interfere with the administration of justice amount to criminal contempt under that Act and if in order to preclude such interference, the provisions of that Act impose reasonable restrictions on freedom of speech, such restrictions would be valid.

At present, under Sec. 3(2) of the Contempt of Courts Act, 1971 read with the explanation below it, full immunity is granted to publications even if they prejudicially interfere with the course of justice in a criminal case, if by the date of publication, a chargesheet or challan is not filed or if summons or warrant are not issued. Such publications would be acting in contempt of court only if a criminal proceeding is actually pending, that is, if a chargesheet or challan is filed or summons or warrant are issued by the court by the date of publication. The question is whether this can be allowed to remain so under our Constitution or whether (publication of information) relating to suspects or accused persons from the date of their arrest should be regulated?

The Supreme Court of India and the House of Lords in the UK have...observed that publications which are prejudicial to a suspect or accused may affect judges also subconsciously. This can be at the stage of granting or refusing bail or at the trial. The Supreme Court holds prejudicial publication after 'arrest' can be criminal contempt. Under the Contempt of Courts Acts of 1926 and 1952, unlike the Act of 1971, there was no specific definition of 'civil' or 'criminal' contempt. Further, before 1971, the common law principles were applied to treat prejudicial publications made even before the 'arrest' of a person as contempt. In fact, some courts were treating as 'criminal contempt', prejudicial publications even if they were made after the filing of a First Information Report (FIR). But the Supreme Court, in *Surendra Mohanty* versus *State of Orissa* (1961), however, held that filing of an FIR could not be the starting point of pendency of a criminal case. Because of that judgement, a prejudicial publication made after the filing of the FIR gained immunity from law of contempt. But in 1969, the Supreme Court held in *A.K. Gopalan* versus *Noordeen* (1969) that a publication made after 'arrest' of a person could be contempt if it was prejudicial to the suspect or accused. This continues to be the law as of today so far as Art. 19(1)(a), 19(2) and Art. 21 are concerned.

In the meantime, from 1963, efforts were made to make a new law of contempt. The Sanyal Committee (1963) which was appointed for this purpose, while observing that our country is very vast and publications made at one place do not reach other places, however, recommended that so far as criminal matters are concerned, the date of 'arrest' is crucial, and that should be treated as the starting point of 'pendency' of a criminal proceeding. It conceded that filing of an FIR could not be the starting point. The Sanyal Committee prepared a Bill ...stating that prejudicial publications could be criminal contempt if criminal proceedings were 'imminent'. But thereafter, nothing happened for six years.

The Bill of 1963 prepared by the Sanyal Committee was reviewed by a Joint Committee of Parliament (1969–70) (Bhargava Committee) and after a brief discussion, the Joint Committee decided to drop reference to 'imminent' proceedings. This was done for two reasons (1) that the word 'imminent' was vague and (2) such a vague expression may unduly restrict the freedom of speech if the law applied to 'imminent' criminal proceedings. The recommendations of the Joint Committee resulted in the 1971 Act which omitted all references to 'imminent' proceedings or to 'arrest' as the starting point of pendency of a criminal proceeding.

The attention of the Joint Committee was not drawn to the decision of the Supreme Court in *A.K. Gopalan* versus *Noordeen* (1969) when it gave its report on 23 February 1970. Once the Supreme Court judgement fixed the date of 'arrest' as the starting point for treating a criminal proceeding as pending, there remained no vagueness in the law. In that case, the Supreme Court has also balanced the rights of the suspect and accused on the one hand and the rights of the media for publication. In fact, in A.K. Gopalan's case, the editor of the newspaper and others who made (the) prejudicial publication after arrest was convicted for contempt, while... A.K. Gopalan who made the statement after the FIR had been filed but before his arrest had been made was exonerated by the Supreme Court.

Apart from the declaration of law and fair balancing of the competing rights as above by the Supreme Court in *A.K. Gopalan* versus *Noordeen* (1969), the date of arrest is the starting point under the UK Contempt of Court Act, 1981 and the Bill of 2003 prepared by the New South Wales Law Commission. The case law in Scotland, Ireland, Australia or the Law Commission Reports of those countries have also declared that if a person is arrested or if criminal proceedings are imminent, prejudicial publications will be (liable to be held guilty of) criminal contempt. The leading judgment in *Hall* versus *Associated Newspaper* (1978, Scotland) has been followed in other jurisdictions and is the basis of the provision in the UK Act of 1981 for fixing 'arrest' as the starting point of pendency of a criminal case.

According to Hall, once a person is arrested, he comes within the 'care' and protection of the court as he has to be produced in court in 24 hours. In India, this is a guarantee under Art. 22(2) of the Constitution. The reason for fixing (the) arrest as the starting point is that, if a publication is made after arrest referring to the person's character, previous conviction or confessions, etc., the person's case will be prejudiced even in bail proceedings when issues arise as to whether bail is to be granted or refused, or as to what conditions are to be imposed and whether there should be police remand or judicial remand. Such publications may also affect the trial when it takes place later. (Based) on this, in England and other countries, 'arrest' and 'imminent' proceedings are treated as sufficient and are not treated as vague. In this context, we have referred to the comparative law in several countries where the

Constitution guarantees protection to freedom of speech as also the liberty of suspects or accused.

Another important point here is that, in ...1978, the Supreme Court of India in the *Maneka Gandhi* versus *Union of India* case, AIR (All India Reporter) 1978 SC Supreme Court 597 has altered the law as it stood before 1978 to say that so far as liberty referred to in Art. 21 is concerned, 'procedure established by law' in Art. 21 must be a fair, just and reasonable procedure. This was not the law in 1970 when the Joint Committee gave its report nor when the 1971 Act was enacted. Hence, the Joint Committee's observations and its omitting the word 'imminent' and its not treating 'arrest' as starting point, do not appear to be constitutionally valid. The starting point of pendency should be 'arrest' and not filing of chargesheet.

In view of the changes in the constitutional law of our country as declared by the Supreme Court in the *A.K. Gopalan* versus *Noordeen* (1969 (2) SCC 734) case insofar as Art. 19(1)(a) and Art. 21 are concerned and the Maneka Gandhi case (AIR 1978 SC 597) insofar as Art. 21 is concerned, the two reasons given by the Joint Committee in 1970 for omitting the word 'imminent' and for not treating 'arrest' as the starting point, are no longer tenable. Sec. 3(2) of the Act and the explanation below sec. 3 as of now, treat a criminal proceeding as pending only if a chargesheet or challan is filed or if summons or warrant is issued at the time of 'arrest'. This has to be rectified by adding a clause 'arrest' in the explanation below sec. 3 as being the starting point to reckon 'pendency' of a criminal proceeding as in the UK Act of 1981 and as proposed by other Law Reforms Commission proposals in other countries.

Further, when such an amendment is made, it is not as if no publications are permitted after arrest. Only those which are prejudicial publications are not permitted. In addition, publications made without knowledge of arrest, or filing challan or without knowledge of summons or warrant, remain protected. In this report, we have also exhaustively discussed the *Sunday Times* judgement of the European Court 1979 (2) EHRR 245 which related to prior restraint of publications relating to a 'civil' case and there the restraint was absolute and not temporary. That case is not a precedent in the present context. The above amendment as to 'arrest' as being starting point is proposed by using the word 'active' criminal proceeding in sec. 3, rather than 'pending criminal proceeding' and inserting the word 'arrest' in the explanation below sec. 3.

Again, as at present, if there is criminal contempt of subordinate courts, the subordinate courts have to make a reference to the high court. This procedure applies to scandalizing the judges under sec. 2c (i) as also to publications interfering with administration of justice under sec. 2c (ii) and (iii). So far as contempt of prejudicial publications is concerned, a procedure of reference by the subordinate court to the high court is cumbersome and time consuming. We have, therefore, proposed sec. 10A that so far as criminal contempt of subordinate courts under sec. 2c (ii) and (iii) by way of publication is concerned, there is no need for a reference by the subordinate courts, but that the high court could be approached directly without the consent of the Advocate General. This is provided in sec. 10A of the bill.

In addition, there is need to empower the courts to pass 'postponement' orders as to publication. While courts have held that conditions for passing orders of prior restraint should be permitted only under stringent conditions, it is, however, accepted that temporary postponement of publication can be passed. This is accepted in several jurisdictions across the world. For passing of 'postponement orders', the UK Act of 1981 requires special proof of 'serious risk of prejudice' to be shown. We have proposed clearer words, that 'real risk of serious prejudice' has to be proved before any 'postponement' orders are issued. We have proposed this in sec. 14A. Any breach of a postponement order will be contempt under sec. 14B. Such a procedure exists in the UK too.

The report also mentions ... what publications can be prejudicial if made after a person is arrested. It is recognized in several countries and also in India that publications which refer to character, previous convictions, confessions could be criminal contempt. Publishing photographs may hinder proper identification in an identification parade. There are various other aspects such as judging the guilt or innocence of the accused or discrediting witnesses, etc. which could be contempt. We have referred to these aspects as a matter of information to the media. We have also discussed the recent phenomenon of media interviewing potential witnesses and about publicity that is given by police and about investigative journalism. We have also annexed a draft bill.

We have also recommended that journalists need to be trained in certain aspects of law relating to freedom of speech in Art. 9(1)(a) and the restrictions which are permissible under Art. 19(2) of the Constitution, human rights, law of defamation and contempt. We have also suggested that these subjects be included in the syllabus for journalism and special diploma or degree courses on journalism and law be started. The report is important and is also exhaustive on the issues which today are crucial in our country so far as criminal justice is concerned and we are of the view that, as at present, there is considerable interference with the due administration of criminal justice and this will have to be remedied by Parliament.

The subject of 'trial by media' is discussed by civil rights activists, constitutional lawyers, judges and academics almost every day in recent times. With the coming into being of the television and cable channels, the amount of publicity which any crime or suspect or accused gets in the media has reached alarming proportions. Innocents may be condemned for no reason or those who are guilty may not get a fair trial or may get a higher sentence after trial than they deserved. There appears to be very little restraint in the media in so far as the administration of criminal justice is concerned.

We are aware that in a democratic country like ours, freedom of expression is an important right but such a right is not absolute in as much as the Constitution itself, while it grants the freedom under Article 19(1)(a), permitted the legislature to impose reasonable restriction on the right, in the interests of various matters, one of which is the fair administration of justice as protected by the Contempt of Courts Act, 1971.

If media exercises an unrestricted or rather unregulated freedom in publishing information about a criminal case and prejudices the mind of the public and those who are to adjudicate on the guilt of the accused and if it projects a suspect or an accused as if he has already been adjudged guilty well before the trial in court, there can be serious prejudice to the accused. In fact, even if ultimately the person is acquitted after the due process in courts, such an acquittal may not help the accused to rebuild his lost image in society.

If excessive publicity in the media about a suspect or an accused before trial prejudices a fair trial or results in characterizing him as a person who had indeed committed the crime, it amounts to undue interference with the 'administration of justice', calling for proceedings for contempt of court against the media. Other issues about the privacy rights of individuals or defendants may also arise. Public figures, with slender rights against defamation, are more in danger and more vulnerable in the hands of the media after the judgement in *R. Rajagopal* versus *State of Tamil Nadu* (AIR 1995 SC 264).

The *UN Special Rapporteur* on Freedom of Expression and Opinion received a submission from British Irish Watch against a very sustained attack by the press on Bernadette and Michael McKevitt who had been advocating national sovereignty for Ireland and who were claiming the Irish people's right to self-determination through a committee. It was the media which started linking these two persons to the Omagh bombing of 15 August 1998 which killed 29 people. The media attack started even before the police questioned these two persons. The contents of the representation to the UN Rapporteur by British Irish Watch quoted below, fits well into what is happening with the media in our own country.

The representation stated: 'Guilt by association is an invidious device. In the case of Bernadette and Michael McKevitt, the media (has) created a situation where almost no one in Ireland is prepared to countenance the possibility that they may be innocent, notwithstanding the fact that neither of them has even been questioned by the police in connection with the Omagh bombing. They have (been) demonized...such media campaigns are self-defeating. If the media repeatedly accuses people of crimes without producing any evidence against them, (it) creates such certainty of their guilt in the minds of the public that, if these persons are even actually charged and tried, they have no hope of obtaining a fair trial. When such trials collapse, the victims of the crime are left without redress. Equally, defendants may be acquitted but they have lost their good name....'

The observations of Andrew Belsey in his article 'Journalism and Ethics, Can they Co-exist?' (published in *Media Ethics: A Philosophical Approach*, edited by Mathew Kieran) quoted by the Delhi High Court in *Mother Dairy Foods & Processing Ltd* versus *Zee Telefilms* (IA 8185/2003 in Suit No. 1543/2003 dated 24.1.2005) aptly describe the state of affairs of today's media. He says that journalism and ethics stand apart. While journalists are distinctive facilitators for the democratic process, to function without hindrance the media has to follow the virtues of 'accuracy, honesty, truth, objectivity, fairness, balanced reporting, respect or autonomy of ordinary people'. These are all part of the democratic process. But practical considerations, namely, pursuit of (a) successful career, promotion to be obtained, compulsion of meeting deadlines and satisfying media managers by meeting growth targets, are recognized as factors for the 'temptation to print trivial stories salaciously presented'. In the temptation to sell stories, what is presented is what 'public is interested in' rather than 'what is in public interest'.

Suspects and accused apart, even victims and witnesses suffer from excessive publicity and invasion of their privacy rights. Police are presented in poor light by the media and their morale too suffers. The day after the report of crime is published, (the) media says 'police have no clue'. Then, whatever gossip the media gathers about the line of investigation by the official agencies, it gives such publicity...that the person who has indeed committed the crime, can move away to safer places. The pressure on the police from (the) media day by day builds up and reaches a stage where police feel compelled to say something or the other in public to protect their reputation. Sometimes when, under such pressure, (the) police come forward with a story that they have nabbed a suspect and that he has confessed, the 'Breaking News' items start and few in the media appear to know that under the law, confession to police is not admissible in a criminal trial. Once the confession is published by both the police and the media, the suspect's future is finished. When he retracts from the confession before the magistrate, the public imagine that the person is a liar. The whole procedure of due process is thus getting distorted and confused.

The media also creates other problems for witnesses. If the identity of witnesses is published, there is danger of the witnesses coming under pressure both from the accused or his associates as well as from the police. At the earliest stage, the witnesses want to retract and get out of the muddle. Witness protection is then a serious casualty. This leads to the question about the admissibility of hostile witness evidence and whether the law should be amended to prevent witnesses changing their statements.

Again, if the suspect's pictures are shown in the media, problems can arise during 'identification parades' conducted under the Code of Criminal Procedure for identifying the accused. Sometimes, the media conducts parallel investigations and points its finger at persons who may indeed be innocent. It tries to find fault with the investigation process even before it is completed and this raises suspicions in the minds of the public about the efficiency of the official investigation machinery.

The print and electronic media have gone into fierce competition, that a multitude of cameras are flashed at the suspects or the accused and the police are not even allowed to take the suspects or accused from their transport vehicles into the courts or vice versa. The Press Council of India issues guidelines from time to time and in some cases, it does take action. But, even if apologies are directed to be published, they are published in such a way that either they are not apologies or the apologies are published in the newspapers at places which are not very prominent.

Apart from these circumstances, basically there is greater need to strike a right balance between freedom of speech and expression of the media on the one hand and the due process rights of the suspect and accused. Art. 19(1)(a), 19(2), Art. 21 and Art. 14 of the Constitution play a very important role in striking an even balance. As we shall be showing in the ensuing chapters, the present Contempt of Court Act, 1971 requires some changes in view of the law that has been declared by the Supreme Court at least in two leading cases, one is *A.K. Gopalan* versus *Noordeen* 1969 (2) SCC 734 and the other is *Maneka Gandhi* versus *Union of India* AIR 1978 SC 597. These judgements have struck a balance between competing fundamental rights which were not noticed or available at the time when the Joint Parliament Committee (1969) made some drastic changes in the bill prepared by the Sanyal Committee (1963). These issues fall for consideration.

In addition, we have the judgement in the *Sunday Times* case decided by the European Court on prior restraint on press publications, the (UK) Contempt of Court Act, 1981 and the reports of Law Commissions in Canada, Australia, New Zealand and other countries which have tried to strike an even balance between competing fundamental rights. It is in the light of the problems mentioned, the drastic changes in the interpretation of Arts. 14, 19, 21 of the Constitution of India that have come about on account of judgements of the Supreme Court and the reforms brought in or proposed in other jurisdictions, that we have taken up the subject *suo motu*....

In our country, lack of knowledge of the law of contempt currently shows that there is extensive coverage of interviews with witnesses. This is highly objectionable even under current law, if made after the chargesheet is filed. This chapter is, in fact, intended to educate the media and the public that what is going on at present in the media may indeed be highly objectionable. Merely because it is tolerated by the courts, it may not cease to be contempt.

APPENDIX 7.2

Guidelines for Reporting Criminal Cases

A workshop on legal reporting organized by the Legal Services Committee of the Supreme Court of India, the Editors Guild, the Press Council of India and others in March 2008, raised a number of issues on media coverage of criminal cases and trials, some of which are given below.

If a person who has been accused of having committed a crime confesses before a journalist (including a television journalist with a camera), this confession is not admissible as evidence in a court of law nor is a confession made to the police. Only a confession made before a judicial magistrate is admissible as evidence. During the workshop a judge of the Supreme Court pointed out that the media often brands a person as a criminal, but in the absence of evidence such a person may not be convicted. The public then blames the judiciary for not taking action against an accused person. Journalists were urged not to brand anyone as an accused in a way that could obstruct the working of the judiciary. Thus confessions should be reported with a disclaimer that these are not admissible as evidence in a court of law.

The judges at the workshop were of the view that there was no harm in reporting mistakes made in the process of prosecution by investigators. On the issue of whether the media should report the contents of FIRs filed in police stations, it was felt that the media had the right to report FIRs but should nevertheless seek the views of individuals who are named in the reports. This was because the contents of an FIR are strictly not evidence even if the information contained in it can be used in legal proceedings.

On the issue of reporting observations made in a court, the judges were of the view that reporting such observations could pose a peculiar set of problems for the judiciary. For instance, in January 2008, a bench of the Supreme Court had made certain observations on a *bandh* that had taken place in Tamil Nadu and a judge had observed that the court 'may' ask the central government to impose President's rule in the state. This observation was reported in certain newspapers as the Supreme Court 'wanting' President's rule in Tamil Nadu.

An observation made by a judge is not an order and hence, not legally binding or enforceable. Observations cannot be quoted to argue a case unless these observations find place in a judgement. Observations do not carry any weight in law and are unlikely to influence subsequent judgements in similar cases. To ascertain information, a judge may ask questions to lawyers and during such a conversation, certain observations could be made that could be considered newsworthy. The judges said that there was nothing wrong in reporting such observations provided these were reported in the correct context and there was also nothing wrong in journalists identifying the judge who made a particular observation.

APPENDIX 7.3

Why Narayanan had to Resign in Ignominy for Plagiarism

One of the most controversial cases of plagiarism in the Indian media is that of V.N. Narayanan, editor of the *Hindustan Times*. He was forced to resign from his post in 1999 after another newspaper, *The Pioneer*, exposed the fact that his column entitled 'Forever in Transit' had been plagiarised from another column by Bryan Appleyard in *The Sunday Times* of London. In the preface to his publication, *I Muse, Therefore I Am*, a compilation of his columns in the *Hindustan Times*, Narayanan ridiculed those who accuse authors of plagiarism and made a case for taking the ideas and words of others 'to innovate something of your own'. B.N. Uniyal, the author of *The Pioneer* expose, retorted: 'You have not only lifted entire paragraphs and sentences from Appleyard's article, but have actually stolen all his experiences, his ideas, his reflections, even his person and personality.'

In an article published in *The Sunday Times* on 3 October 1999, Appleyard wrote: 'Of its 1,263 words, 1,020 were identical to those in an article of mine published in *The Sunday Times Magazine* in February under the headline "No time like the present". Of its 83 sentences, 72 were mine. Mr Narayanan even spoke of a sign he had seen while walking through Newark airport in the United States. I did the walking; I saw the sign. Apart from a touch of local Indian spin in theme, detail and tone, Narayanan had ripped me off.'

Appleyard recounted that 'investigating what had actually happened on the phone and the internet turned out to be a startling experience…Indian journalism seems to be modelled on Fleet Street *circa* 1965. The switchboards are surly and lunch is serious.

'"He's just gone out to lunch, call back in 3-5 hours," I was told when I tried to contact one executive. But finally a picture of sorts emerged. Narayanan is a somewhat grand figure, given to insisting that he is more than "a mere journalist". In addition, elderly editors in Delhi are in the habit of bemoaning the low standards of their younger colleagues. As a result, old hacks in general and Narayanan in particular were, to use an Australianism, cruising for a bruising.

'Furthermore, Narayanan had been in trouble before. A 1992 column was referred to the Indian Press Council on a charge of plagiarism. He then said he had a photographic memory, causing him unconsciously to repeat the words of others. That case was dismissed as "pure harassment". Now, since his resignation, rumours have been circulating at the *Hindustan Times* that he has lifted four other articles of mine.'

Narayanan, when contacted by Appleyard, confessed his interest in the Hindu concept of 'eternal transit'. He had purportedly lectured students on the subject and had somehow 'internalized' Appleyard's writing! 'My article was about the contemporary sensation of constantly being on the move without knowing where one was going. Had he "internalized" my walk through Newark airport?' wondered Appleyard.

He pointed out that Narayanan did not say 'sorry' to him during their phone conversation but was evidently upset and that he sympathized with him. The following day, Narayanan sent Appleyard a long e-mail apologizing profusely.

What evidently surprised Appleyard about this episode was Narayanan's behaviour given how easy it is to detect plagiarism—conscious or unconscious—in this day and age. A question that Uniyal too asked in his *Pioneer* story was: 'How could you do such a thing in the age of the internet, Mr Narayanan?' Appleyard concedes that he shrugs off similar incidents on most occasions, exasperated by the endless internet piracy people are subjected to these days, but, in this instance, makes a telling point:

'There are crazed internet sites and there are respectable publications—of which the *Hindustan Times* is one. Furthermore, there are columns and columns. This article was one over which I had sweated blood. It was the last in a four-part series, 12,000 words in all, in which I had outlined a personal view of the contemporary human condition. It was an article that depended as much on the texture of the writing as it did on any facts it contained. Ideas may be a form of public property but the way they are expressed is not. The article was, in short, mine and mine alone. By putting about a third of it in a personal column called "Musings", Narayanan was, in effect, saying: "It's mine, all mine." So, desperately trying to avoid the pomposity to which Indian journalism seems to be prone, I will say that what we have here is at least a bad case of humbug. Narayanan would have lost nothing by rewriting my article in his own words and giving me credit.'

Appleyard wondered why Narayanan did not give him credit. He wrote that a similar query had been raised by Nilanjana S. Roy writing in the *Business Standard*. She had said that a simple step of acknowledging the column that had inspired him to write 'would . . . have allowed a man in the twilight of his career to leave, halo intact'. Appleyard ended his article in *The Sunday Times* with a sentence dripping with sarcasm: 'I hope Mr Narayanan's enforced early retirement is long and happy. But next time—well, it's Bryan with a "y". Okay?'

APPENDIX 7.4

Kaavya Viswanathan: A Classic Case in Plagiarism

A case of plagiarism that received unprecedented media attention in 2006, concerned Kaavya Viswanathan, an Indian-American woman studying in the prestigious Harvard University in the US. She got herself into trouble when portions of her debut novel, *How Opal Mehta Got Kissed, Got Wild and Got a Life*, were found to have been lifted straight out of several books. Viswanathan had reportedly received an advance of $500,000 from Little, Brown and Company for a two-book deal. She had also sold the movie rights of the book to DreamWorks SKG. The novel, which deals with the social aspirations of an academically oriented Indian-American girl, was reported by *The Harvard Crimson* to have been plagiarised from the novels *Sloppy Firsts* and *Second Helpings* written by Megan McCafferty.

Far from acknowledging what had been written by the author of the original books, Viswanathan first claimed that 'nothing' she had read gave her the inspiration to write her book. However, days later, Little, Brown issued a statement in which Viswanathan 'admitted' to have 'accidentally' borrowed some passages from Megan McCafferty's novels. She later apologized to Megan McCafferty. Meanwhile, Random House, the publisher of the two novels written by McCafferty, issued a statement: 'We have documented more than forty passages from Kaavya Viswanathan's recent publication ... that contain identical language and/or common scene or dialogue structure from Megan McCafferty's first two books... This extensive taking from Ms. McCafferty's books is nothing less than an act of literary identity theft'.

On 1 May 2006, Viswanathan landed herself into fresh trouble when *The New York Times* reported that parts of her novel may have been plagiarised from Salman Rushdie's 1990 novel *Haroun and the Sea of Stories*. On 2 May 2006, *The New York Times* again alleged that Viswanathan's novel had been plagiarised from *Can You Keep a Secret*? by Sophie Kinsella.

This case re-opened old debates and discussions on what could be considered original writing and what constituted plagiarised writing.

CHAPTER

8

STING JOURNALISM

This chapter explores a specific aspect of investigative journalism, that is, sting operations, which is a particularly contentious area of journalism. A case study of a sting operation that went wrong serves as a good example of what not to do. Thereafter, the chapter considers the processes involved in conceiving, conducting and publicizing a sting operation using guidelines from media codes around the world. Some notable sting operations that have been successful in upholding public interest are then considered. The chapter ends by considering some of the legal implications that might result from a sting operation.

INVESTIGATIVE JOURNALISM

Investigative journalism is the branch of journalism which aims at uncovering complex and often little-known facts of interest and relevance to the public through thorough research. Investigative journalism in societies with a free and independent mass media often exposes corruption and abuse of power by those in positions of influence and authority. The subject of investigative journalism is often crime or other misdemeanours, whose exposure would benefit society as a whole. The PCI notes that investigative journalism is warranted when there has been an attempt to hide the truth.

From the time India became politically independent, journalists have unearthed facts about those in positions of power to expose corruption in high places. Such instances include the jeeps' purchase scandal involving

V. Krishna Menon (who was then India's envoy to the UK); the financial scandal relating to Kolkata-based stockbroker Haridas Mundhra (both in the 1950s); the import licence scandal involving Member of Parliament (MP) Tulmohan Ram; the working of trusts associated with former Maharashtra Chief Minister A.R. Antulay; the oil import controversy relating to a firm called Kuo; the favours given to the Reliance group by the government; the blinding of prisoners in a jail in Bhagalpur, Bihar, the way a poor woman Kamala was 'bought'; the Bofors and HDW deals when Rajiv Gandhi was prime minister, the financial scandals involving stockbrokers Harshad Mehta and Ketan Parekh; and many others.

Write a few paragraphs on each of the investigative stories listed above that were broken by journalists and mention five more instances of media exposes of corruption in India.

STING JOURNALISM

One form of investigative journalism that involves deception and/or the use of hidden cameras and/or sound recording equipment is often described as sting journalism. The word 'sting' literally means to pierce or painfully wound with a sharp-pointed structure or organ (by some insects) but in this context it signifies an illegal operation by journalists and undercover government agents to collect or unearth evidence of wrongdoing including criminal activities.

Before examining sting operations in greater detail, let us look at one of the world's best-known investigative reports, namely, the Watergate scandal.

The Watergate Scandal

A significant example of investigative journalism occurred in the US in the 1970s. In the aftermath of the 'Pentagon Papers' case, when detailed confidential documents on the Vietnam war were leaked to journalists of *The New York Times,* the White House was keen to prevent any other leak of confidential information. Richard Nixon, the then President of the US, set up a team called the 'plumbers', whose job was to prevent the leak of any confidential information from the White House. The team was authorized, among other things, to illegally tap journalists' phone calls. The 'plumbers' were, however, caught in the act by the police when they tried to break into the headquarters of the national committee of the opposition Democratic Party which was located in a building complex called Watergate in Washington DC—hence the term 'Watergate scandal' to describe the episode.

Two journalists, Bob Woodward and Carl Bernstein, who worked with *The Washington Post*, were assigned to cover the story. Woodward and Bernstein regularly received information from a confidential source who worked with the Nixon administration and was referred to as 'Deep Throat'. The source told them that the 'plumbers' had been commissioned to break into the Watergate headquarters by the Committee to re-elect the President (Nixon). The journalists discovered that those responsible for the break-in were connected with the Nixon administration and the CIA. Through their tenacity and determination, the reports by Woodward and Bernstein managed to attract the attention of other newspapers in the US who also picked up the story. Due to the wide media coverage and the public outrage over the scandal, Nixon resigned as President in 1974.

More than thirty years later, in May 2005, Mark Felt, a former agent of the Federal Bureau of Investigation (FBI), who was 91 years old at that time, admitted that he was 'Deep Throat'.

Can the US Media do Another Watergate?

Three decades after Woodward and Bernstein wrote a series of articles based on Felt's revelations, what are the chances of the US media 'breaking' another scandal? This is a question that Liza Porteus attempts to explore in an article released by Associated Press (AP) on 27 June 2005. Many media analysts she interviewed felt that a story like Watergate, where Woodward and Bernstein relied on a single anonymous 'essential' source, may be difficult to replicate in the wake of a series of recent controversies relating to media ethics in the US. Porteus points out that a number of news outlets in the US use more than one secret source.

'What is likely to happen now, when an anonymous source is used is that they'll have to use more than one anonymous source before they're comfortable. Obviously, the more controversial it is, the more important it is to get it accurate', Eric Burns, the host of Fox News Watch tells Porteus.

The article refers to Mark Felt who admitted to *Vanity Fair* that he was indeed 'Deep Throat', the man Woodward would meet in a parking garage late at night to gather information as well as confirm or deny information obtained by him and Bernstein.

Due to the story's huge impact, writes Porteus, Watergate came to glorify the use of anonymous sources. Woodward's secret source, Felt, personified the ultimate insider who not only could verify or nullify information a reporter had on a hot story, but could point the finger at other high-level officials within a conspiracy. 'There was a surge in anonymous sourcing right after Watergate as there was a sort of "anonymity chic" in journalism, where every reporter fashioned himself a Woodward and every source fancied himself a 'Deep Throat,' Matthew Felling, media director for the Center for Media and Public Affairs, tells Porteus.

But, says the article, 'the Jayson Blairs and Jack Kellys of the world, as well as the recent brouhaha surrounding *Newsweek*'s retracted story built on one unnamed official who claimed interrogators at Guantanamo Bay, Cuba, flushed a copy of the Koran down the toilet have helped change all that'. 'Those scandals took a toll on the media far more than they took a toll on individual journalists' credibility and the media's image has taken some serious hits in recent years but their credibility is still on par with politicians in America,' says Felling.

Some news outlets have voluntarily revised their policies regarding the use of anonymous sources since publications like *The New York Times* and *Newsweek* blackened their own eyes in the wake of journalistic scandals, some involving the use of secret sources. In fact, Al Neuharth, founder of *USA Today*, and others (including White House officials) have gone to the extent of arguing that the use of anonymous sources is the 'evil of journalism'. 'These policies are an attempt to tighten, to eliminate a looseness that's developed in the last 20 years, not to make it difficult to do investigative reporting,' Tom Rosenstiel, director of the Project for Excellence in Journalism and the Committee of Concerned Journalists, tells Porteus. 'I haven't seen anything in these rules that would chill investigating,' he adds.

Woodward and Bernstein frequently used anonymous sources when reporting on Watergate. The then *Post* editor Ben Bradlee confessed that he did not know the identity of Woodward's secret source until after Nixon had resigned. He also admitted that *Post* publisher Katharine Graham never asked him who Deep Throat was. 'The important thing about Deep Throat from Day 1 was that he was telling the truth. Everything he told us was true and in that sense, that was all I needed,' the AP article quotes Bradlee from a www.washingtonpost.com online chat. 'I didn't know exactly who the information was coming from but I gained confidence week by week when his information proved to be accurate. There were almost 400 Watergate stories and I think we gained confidence as these stories proved to be on the button.'

There were few rules governing the use of such sources at that time, and 'not only was there more trust of journalists by the public, there was more trust by journalists of fellow journalists', Burns of Fox News tells Porteus. In Woodward's book, *All the President's Men*, the Pulitzer Prize-winning journalist wrote that 'gradually, an unwritten rule was evolving: unless two sources confirmed a charge involving activity likely to be considered criminal, the specific allegation was not used in the paper.

In Woodward and Bernstein's 29 September 1972 page one article in the *Post* entitled 'Mitchell Controlled Secret GOP Fund', the two reporters unveiled that while serving as attorney general, John N. Mitchell ran a secret Republican fund that was used to gather information about Democrats. The story is mostly attributed to 'sources involved in the Watergate investigation' and 'several reliable sources'. Other information is attributed to 'one federal source' and 'the *Post*'s sources'. The only people quoted in this particular story is Mitchell himself, who called the story 'crap', and a spokesman for Nixon's re-election committee.

In another story, 'Dean Alleges Nixon Knew of Cover-up Plan', which ran on 3 June 1973, also on the front page, the opening paragraph which explained how former presidential counsel John W. Dean told prosecutors that he discussed aspects of the Watergate cover-up with Nixon or in his presence at least 35 times, was attributed to 'reliable sources'. This news was explosive at that juncture, given the fact that it was a senior Nixon adviser admitting that the former president knew of the cover-up efforts going on. Other information in the story is sourced to unnamed Justice Department and Senate sources, 'investigators', 'one source with first-hand knowledge of Dean's statements' and 'four White House sources'.

According to Porteus, the lack of guidelines governing the use of such sources at that time is in sharp contrast to the policies governing journalists that are in place in the US at present. *USA Today*, for example, has mandated that the identity of an unnamed source must be shared with and approved by a managing editor prior to publication. It also requires that anonymous sources must be cited only as a last resort, not only in direct quotes but also the use of anonymous sources generally. 'An editor must be confident that there is no better way to present the information and that the information is important enough to justify the broader cost in reader trust. This is not to be taken lightly,' the policy states.

Many local newspapers in the US ban the use of such sources outright, according to a survey conducted by AP and the Associated Press Managing Editors' Association. A study by the Center for Media and Public Affairs found that the use of anonymous sources has declined by 33 per cent, from nearly one in four sources during President Reagan's first year in office to one out of six in President George W. Bush's first year. The AP article contends that today's fast-paced, 24 × 7 news cycle, slashed newsroom budgets and too few reporters to cover all the news fit to print, often lead journalists to resort to using unnamed sources. On top of that, television reporters traditionally don't work sources as thoroughly as their print counterparts do.

However, tight budgets need not mean big stories cannot be broken, observers point out to Porteus. 'This kind of reporting can still be done. It will have to be more time consuming and that's the problem more news organizations will have to face,' says Burns. 'Which is to say, "might somebody else beat us?" and that's going to be the real struggle in journalism. How do they balance their desire to be first, which is understandable and maybe admirable in some cases, with their need to be accurate,' he adds.

During Watergate, Woodward and Bernstein frequently went directly to the sources of information such as secretaries of the officials involved. Rosenstiel tells Porteus that unlike the media, which are doing more 'investigations into investigations,... they were not getting a lot of leaks from special prosecutors or anyone else'. He adds: 'Today, a large percentage—a growing percentage of watchdog reporting is actual investigations of investigations being done by prosecutors' offices or police agencies. Those agencies are leaking to reporters—that's very different from what I call original investigative reporting.'

Talking to analysts, Porteus found that Watergate's influence may have made government officials more wary about sharing information, even with colleagues. 'It caused government officials to perhaps talk less to one another because they would wonder, "Is this person I'm talking to here Deep Throat or some other leaker?" Burns says. 'I don't think it affected tremendously the relationship between government and press but it did affect the need for secrecy between people in government. People on that "need-to-know" list shrank greatly.'

Some analysts even point out that government officials like Congressional aides and agency spokesmen are taking advantage of the lax, unnamed sources rules of the past few decades. 'What happened with anonymous sourcing between Watergate and now is they used anonymity as a tool to coax reluctant sources to come forward. Today, particularly in big cities like New York and Washington DC, anonymity is a condition the source imposes on journalists, often before the conversation begins,' says Rosenstiel.

Rosenstiel surmises that with the tighter restrictions, some officials may be wary to talk to national reporters if they are not sure their names can be kept out of stories. But in local publications, vital to elected representatives' political livelihoods, reporters generally have an easier job getting sources on the record. 'It's too important to demonstrate to people back home that they're actually doing something,' Rosenstiel says, adding that this '...would be great, if the power shift can go back to, "you're only anonymous if you've got something we can't get any other way".'

According to Porteus, while experts agree that stories of the magnitude of Watergate can still be uncovered, Felling doubts that the unravelling of scandals could play out the same way. 'Could a Watergate investigation pass the public sniff test in America? I believe so,' he says. 'The question isn't whether Watergate-style media leaks could occur in 2005 but how the identity could be kept secret in the current media environment. I don't think the journalists would loosen their lips, I just think other entrepreneurial reporters would dig through enough trash cans and file through enough credit card reports to make a name for him or herself.'

STING JOURNALISM IN INDIA

In India, the intrepid investigative reporting of *Tehelka* journalists brought sting operations into the limelight.

Fallen Heroes

In 1997, former Indian test cricketer Manoj Prabhakar had stated in an interview to *Outlook* that he had been offered a bribe of Rs 25,00,000 by a 'senior cricketer' to underperform in a match against Sri Lanka in 1994. The interview was part of the magazine's cover story by Krishna Prasad and Aniruddha Bahal on how cricket matches were rigged. Subsequently, the CBI started conducting an investigation into the allegations that were codenamed Operation Gentleman. In 2000, the website www.tehelka.com decided to investigate allegations of match-fixing in Indian cricket (*India Today*, 5 June 2000).

Tehelka's journalists managed to get nearly 50 hours of footage over three months, which was then edited into a 90-minute film called *Fallen Heroes.* Hidden cameras were used to record conversations with several important figures from the world of cricket who all confirmed that they believed match-fixing took place in collusion with bookies who ran illegal betting operations. The film implicated former captains of the Indian cricket team Kapil Dev and Mohammed Azharuddin, and former manager Ajit Wadekar, who were all later summoned for questioning by the CBI. The sting operation caused a huge stir among the general public revealing the fallibility of those whom the nation had elevated on pedestals. Kapil Dev staunchly denied the implication and even broke down during a television interview protesting his innocence. He was later exonerated.

Not everyone applauded *Tehelka*'s sting. Mukund Padmanabhan of *The Hindu* (2000) described *Fallen Heroes* as 'a long and inconclusive sting of surmise'. He contended that the sting revealed no hard evidence and did not provide answers to the most important questions: Who took bribes and from whom? And, when and where were the bribes taken? Padmanabhan wondered whether the deception, betrayal and invasion of privacy which the sting entailed were ethically justifiable. Furthermore, he queried whether the inclusion of gossipy personal opinions was really integral to a story on corruption in a game. Subsequently, it was found that cricket players from other countries were also involved in corrupt and unethical practices.

Operation West End

Tehelka's next sting operation had an even more wide-ranging consequence. Less than a year after the *Fallen Heroes* film was broadcast, *Tehelka* journalist Aniruddha Bahal conceived the idea of investigating murky defence deals. Tehelka's editor-in-chief Tarun Tejpal said that there were three factors which prompted their desire to investigate this area. First, there had been an unusual fire at an ammunition depot in Bharatpur, Rajasthan. Second, questions had been raised about the quality of leadership of India's defence services during the Kargil war in 1999. Third, the Bofors scandal of the 1980s had revealed that there was high-level corruption in the Indian government and defence services relating to large contracts for purchase of equipment.

Bahal and fellow journalist Samuel Matthew found that hand-held thermal cameras were in the queue for purchase by the Ministry of Defence. After researching the product, the *Tehelka* team designed a brochure of a fictitious UK-based company called West End. Bahal and Matthew posed as employees of West End and attempted to secure a contract for non-existent equipment. Tejpal said that the pair started discussions with the lower-level officials of the defence hierarchy but were gradually 'sucked up into a web of graft and deal-makers'. The reporters managed to film 90 hours of footage using spy cameras and, while doing so, also captured important politicians and army officers accepting bribes or arranging bribes. Bangaru Laxman, the then president of the Bharatiya Janata Party (BJP), which was leading the ruling coalition at that time, was caught on camera accepting an advance of Rs 1,00,000 ahead of an anticipated bribe equivalent to $30,000. Around this juncture, the sting operation was forced to conclude as *Tehelka* could not proceed further without the product and the money.

Tehelka edited the tapes and the final four-hour-long version of the film was screened in a New Delhi hotel on 13 March 2001 before a large invited audience that comprised a wide cross-section of the public.

Tehelka represents a peculiar case in Indian journalism: it is an organization which arouses strong feelings of both admiration and disapproval. It has been criticized for using the services of commercial sex workers during Operation West End. Tejpal himself has acknowledged this criticism but nevertheless has defended the action claiming that it was important for the reporters to keep up the guise of defence agents for whom the use of sex workers as bribes is apparently a common practice.

More than *Fallen Heroes*, Operation West End (www.tehelka.com, 13 March 2001) demonstrated the huge impact that sting journalism could have on Indian society. These initiatives earned the journalists concerned and *Tehelka* a reputation for unparalleled, innovative and intrepid journalism besides awards and citations. Sting journalism was even perceived as a springboard for career development for young journalists. In this chapter, we note, however, that not all sting journalism is glamorous, nor should decisions on this kind of journalism be made lightly. John Sweeney, an award-winning British investigative journalist, dispels the false image of glamour when he says 'investigative journalism is less banana daiquiris in Miami and more a cup of tea in (a) bus station in an undistinguished town in England'. Sweeney highlights that much of investigative journalism is a long-drawn-out process, involving hard, painstaking, boring and repetitive work. Such work often entails travel and expenditure and could lead to frustration.

Investigation of surreptitious activities sometimes requires the use of covert technology and deceptive tactics to ascertain hard evidence of suspected wrongdoing. Sting journalism can be risky business as well. Sweeney describes sting operations as an attempt '...to find the largest crocodile in the pond and give it a poke in the eye with a sharp stick and see what happens'. Sting operations, based as these are on suspicions, involve provocation and an uncertain outcome. These two key characteristics of sting journalism are the basis of many ethical concerns. Before discussing the ethical and legal implications of conducting sting operations, it is important to realize that sting journalism is a deeply contentious area of media practice.

Hirst and Patching (2007) argue that there is only a 'fine line between legitimate investigative reporting and using illegitimate methods to get a story'. Illegitimate methods include disguising one's identity and using concealed microphones or cameras. We have already seen the implications of the use of such methods in Chapter 7 on Media Laws. Such techniques run a serious risk of infringing privacy rights. The use of hidden cameras or microphones is a form of deception and, therefore, can be construed as an inadmissible form of gathering information.

Investigative journalism is traditionally associated with newspapers and television news programmes. However, the internet is rapidly becoming another medium for sting journalism, pioneered in India by www.tehelka.com and also by www.cobrapost.com (headed by former *Tehelka* journalist Bahal).

What are the advantages and/or disadvantages of using (a) newspapers, (b) television and (c) the internet to highlight a sting operation?

There are at least two important reasons for the popularity of sting journalism in a country like India. The first is the high level of corruption in government and police establishments. Soutik Biswas of BBC Online has commented that sting journalism is popular with the public because 'Confidence in the bureaucracy, police and judiciary is possibly at an all-time low'. The media is an essential tool for ensuring that the rights and principles of a democracy are upheld. The corruption extant in India, the world's largest democracy, threatens to undermine these core principles and creates situations in which the use of sting operations is determined to be the only way to ascertain the truth. As Tejpal commented with reference to the match-fixing expose, 'nobody was going to admit they were taking money. This was the only way.'

The second reason for the popularity of sting journalism in India relates to the sheer volume of competing news media: television, newspapers, magazines and internet portals. The proliferation of media organizations in India has created an environment of intense competition to secure readership or viewership figures. Despite *Tehelka*'s successes and the compliments it has received from large sections of the public for its 'fearlessness', it has often been criticized for being overzealous while conducting sting operations. However, there is no doubting the fact that the exposure of clandestine dealings of public figures and officials increases readership or viewership (See Box 8.1: The Sting and the Confidence Vote).

A thorough understanding of the process of a sting operation is crucial if it is to be performed legitimately and as ethically as possible. However, before examining the stages of a sting operation, we shall first consider a sting operation that was ill-conceived and went terribly wrong.

Box 8.1

The Sting and the Confidence Vote

On 22 July 2008, the UPA government won the confidence vote in the Lok Sabha with a comfortable margin of 19 votes after Left parties withdrew their support. However, a couple of hours before the voting, three Opposition members displayed bundles of currency notes in the House alleging that the leader of another party had tried to bribe them to abstain from the trust vote. They claimed that the incident had been caught on camera by a TV channel. However, the channel that conducted the sting handed over the tapes to the Speaker of the House, instead of televising it. The editor-in-chief of the channel said that it did not want to be part of a bitter political battle. A statement from the channel stated: 'While trying to investigate deeper into this trail, we realized that the issue needed further probing and we could not, at this stage, telecast it without further verification'.

The Editors Guild of India supported the editor's decision. 'The freedom of an editor to publish or telecast any news item cannot be subject to the approval or disapproval of a political party... In this case, the editor of the channel has made it public that the investigation into the bribery case is incomplete and only if all the facts are authenticated, the channel would telecast the tapes', the Guild said. The Code of Practice of the Editors Guild of India also exhorts editors to check and verify facts before publication or telecast.

Source: Adapted from 'Cash-for-vote sting tapes doctored: BJP MPs,' *The TOI* (7 August 2008)

Was it the job of a TV channel to provide proof to any constitutional authority, in this case the Speaker, before it telecasted the news to its viewers? By doing so, did the channel invite criticism that it had been silenced?

Schoolteacher, Sex Scandal and the Fabricated Sting

Uma Khurana was a mathematics teacher at a government school in Delhi. She purportedly owed money to a man named Virender Arora whom she had partnered in a business venture. When she failed to pay her debts, Arora sought the help of his journalist friend Prakash Singh to get back at Khurana. The two men devised a scheme through which Khurana would be framed as a person who was enticing her students for commercial sex work. Besides helping Arora, Singh stood to gain a reputation as a hard-hitting investigative journalist.

Singh asked an aspiring journalist Rashmi Singh to aid him in the sting operation. She posed as one of Khurana's students. Singh set up a meeting between him, Rashmi and Khurana which he secretly filmed. The footage showed Khurana accepting money from Singh in exchange for one of her students. It was later revealed that Khurana and Rashmi had never met or spoken before and that the money that was exchanged in the film was an innocuous transaction. Singh attempted to insinuate that Khurana had filmed her students in compromising positions as part of the sex racket.

The television organization where Singh had been working as an intern did not want to use his footage. A senior editor of the channel reportedly wanted to meet Rashmi to ascertain the truthfulness of the allegations against Khurana. Singh did not arrange for this meeting and subsequently, quit the organization. But before that, he stole the tapes featuring Khurana. He then joined another television channel, Live India, that decided to broadcast the so-called 'sting' on 30 August 2007.

Khurana was teaching at her school when the footage was aired on television. Shortly thereafter, a mob gathered outside the school and tried to assault her. The mob was dispersed by the police. Khurana was arrested and suspended from her post. As investigations got under way, it began to emerge that there was lack of evidence of the criminal activity that had been insinuated. Khurana denied all the allegations against her. None of her pupils claimed to have been enticed into commercial sex work by her. No pornographic films or magazines were found in her apartment. Eventually, Khurana was cleared of all charges.

Prakash Singh and Rashmi Singh were both arrested and interrogated. Trial proceedings against Prakash Singh were started on seven counts, including criminal conspiracy. Khurana's lawyers stated that they would bring a case of libel against Prakash Singh and Live India for intentionally maligning her reputation. They argued that the damage to her character and reputation merited that damages of over Rs 1 crore be awarded to her. Subsequently, however, Khurana decided not to file a case of libel against Prakash Singh and Live India, stating that no amount of money could restore what had been taken from her—her reputation and her mental peace.

The Khurana incident highlighted the weaknesses of sting operations. The question as to why Live India aired the sting without prior editorial scrutiny and gate-keeping was raised by media watchers. Another question that became a subject of debate in media circles was whether sting journalism should be banned on the ground that its abuse could cause extensive damage.

Enumerate all the elements of the Uma Khurana sting operation that were unethical. What do you think are the broader implications of the sting for Khurana and her family, Prakash Singh and Rashmi Singh?

THE THREE STAGES OF A STING OPERATION

A sting operation is composed of three separate stages.

Before Deciding to conduct a sting operation.

During Conducting the sting operation.

After Editing and using the material gathered from the sting.

Each stage involves careful planning and execution and must factor in several ethical dimensions. There is a fourth stage as well and this pertains to what happens after the discoveries of the sting have been made public. This stage is different from the preceding three stages, as it is beyond the control of the journalists concerned. Therefore, it is important to try and anticipate all possible outcomes before the sting is made public.

Deciding to Use Sting

Sting operations should only be undertaken as a last resort after careful consideration. It is important to clearly conceive the intention of the investigation. The following questions should be considered:

- Is there substantial reason to believe that underhand or criminal activity has occurred?
- Have reasonable steps been taken to obtain the desired information through open and straightforward means?
- What is the motivation for undertaking a sting operation?
- Is it certain that public welfare is a motivating factor?
- Are there any personal motives for conducting a sting and if so, are these likely to compromise objectivity and fairness?
- What are the risks involved?
- What are the possible outcomes of making the findings of the sting operation public?

The National Union of Journalists of the UK advises that information should only be obtained through straightforward means, unless there is overriding public concern at stake. The Society of Professional Journalists' Sigma Delta Chi's code of 1973 states that surreptitious means of obtaining information should be avoided, except when traditional methods do not yeild information vital to the public. The PCI states that members of the press should not record conversations without the involved parties' acknowledgement and consent, unless there is a compelling good reason to act otherwise. However, the phrases 'public concern' and 'compelling good reason' are vague and open to interpretations. Generally, however, these exceptions are understood as information which the readers deserve to, have access to on the grounds that it is necessary to protect their safety or well-being (see Box 2: The Corrupt Quack) or that the citizenry is entitled to information about those by whom they are governed (see Box 3: Operation Duryodhan).

Box 8.2

The Corrupt Quack

In 2004, *Tehelka* magazine published a story based on a sting operation which revealed the corruption of an Agra-based psychiatrist, Dr S.K. Gupta, who was caught on camera accepting money for signing false documents certifying a person's mental illness. He reportedly boasted that he had helped ten men 'dump sane wives' with such documents. In 2000, a woman called Meera Singh died under mysterious circumstances. In the three years since her marriage, her husband had harassed her demanding dowry from her family. In December 2000, Meera's family members were told by her parents-in-law that she had committed suicide by hanging herself. Her family went to the police; a criminal case was registered and Meera's husband was arrested. However, he was released without charges when Dr Gupta presented a certificate which stated that Meera had been mentally unstable. The doctor claimed that she had been his patient and provided evidence of prescriptions for medicines he had given her. Meera's family was not satisfied and decided to check the authenticity of Dr Gupta's certificate with the director of the hospital where he worked. The director said that the certificate was false. It was believed that Dr Gupta received Rs 40,000 to help conceal a case of murder. *Tehelka*'s report supported the claims of the victim's family that Dr Gupta was, in fact, an accomplice to a murderer. The magazine posed these rhetorical questions: '...what else do you call a man who declares in court that a woman—whose relations, say, her in-laws murdered her—was insane and that she was prone to suicide. What else do you call a man who colludes with the accused in a dowry murder case and helps them get away?'('Dr Gupta's Laboratory of Madness', *Tehelka,* 17 July 2004).

The rendering of a service for public good is encompassed in the ethical system of utilitarianism. Utilitarianism holds that 'the greatest good for the greatest number' of people is the most satisfactory and realistic ethical basis for all actions. In the context of the present discussion, what utilitariansim would imply is that sting operations are justifiable and legitimate if more people stand to benefit from its results than the number of people who are caused suffering, harm or inconvenience.

Utilitarianism is a consequentialist system as it factors in the end result of an action as a way of justifying the means. There are many practical advantages to this approach, one of which is that it ensures that an action will be undertaken after careful consideration and awareness of possible consequences. On the other hand, it can be argued that it is impossible to know with absolute certainty what the outcome of an action will be. We can, of course, estimate an outcome based on previous similiar experiences. This leaves open the scope for damaging errors of judgement. If a sting is conducted on someone who turns out to be innocent of the suspected misdemeanour, she/he would have suffered from invasion of privacy, humiliation and possible defamation without any good having been achieved. It is perhaps because of this inherent danger that the Council of Europe's Parliamentary Assembly stated in its resolution in 1993 on ethical journalism (see Appendix 8.1) that the ends do not justify the means in journalism, and that, therefore, all information must be gathered legally and ethically.

?

Do you think the utilitarian argument justifies the use of deceptive means in sting operations? Can you identify any other shortcomings in the utilitarian argument?

Sting operations present ethical dilemmas to journalists. Consider what some of these dilemmas might be.

Box 8.3

Operation Duryodhan

Operation Duryodhan 2005 was another sting operation conducted by a team led by Aniruddha Bahal. The operation caught MPs accepting cash for raising questions in Parliament. The journalists who had conducted the sting operation pretended to be lobbying on behalf of an association of small-scale manufacturers. The sting operation conducted by www.cobrapost.com caught eleven MPs accepting bribes on camera, which was aired by *Aaj Tak* channel. Each MP took between Rs 15,000 and Rs 40,000. The eleven MPs were forced to resign after the ethics committees of both Houses of Parliament found them guilty: this was the first time since 1951 that MPs were expelled for corruption.

Source: Operation Duryodhan was well-named,' *The Indian Express*, New Delhi (15 December 2005).

It is important to be as objective as possible while deciding to undertake a sting operation. The Council of Europe's Parliamentary Assembly 1993 resolution warns that investigative journalism cannot be deemed legitimate if campaigns are executed on the strength of previous positions or vested interests. This means that it is important to judge each situation on its own peculiar merits. It would be wrong to subject a person to sting investigation based solely on that person's previous record. All factors in determining a case of sting operation should pertain specifically to the situation at hand. A sting operation should not be undertaken in the spirit of retribution for personal grievances, as was done in the case of Uma Khurana. The PCI cautions that all evidence should be fact based and not merely based on hearsay.

The PCI identifies three factors that must be present to justify a sting operation.

- The work must be that of the journalist and not of those reported. It means that all work undertaken as part of a sting operation must be objective; it must not involve proselytizing or mala fide framing.
- The subject of a sting operation should be of public interest and importance. A sting operation should not be flippant; both the decision to conduct a sting operation and the subject should be well considered.
- No attempt should be made to hide the truth. That the truth has been hidden can only be ascertained after attempts to obtain it honestly have been fruitless. Alternatively, there must be reasonable cause to doubt the veracity of information obtained by straightforward means.

?

The Uma Khurana episode is an example of mala fide framing. Provide examples of bona fide framing during sting operations that can be deemed to be in the public interest. In what ways can a journalist determine that the truth is being hidden?

It is advisable for journalists to seek permissions and get authorizations for a sting operation from their seniors or employers. This will ensure that its planning will be subjected to more thorough scrutiny. Senior media professionals might be able to give advice on possible legal implications and how the sting might be received by the public and how it may be criticized. The trend of media organizations outsourcing their sting operations is fraught with uncertainty and danger—the organization that disseminates the material obtained through a sting operation may not be able to ensure proper scrutiny of the operation that, in turn, could raise doubts about its relevance to the public at large.

The Sting

If, after having considered all the preliminary aspects highlighted above, a journalist and a media organization decide that a sting operation is necessitated by overriding public interest, the operation needs to be carefully planned and conducted. Sting operations can become lengthy affairs, spanning months. A legitimate sting operation could require this investment of time to ensure that the material collated is substantial and conclusive. All those involved should be properly briefed and fully informed about the sting operation, including the reasons for conducting it and the methods to be deployed. The lack of this aspect is evident in the Uma Khurana incident. Although the accomplice in the case, Rashmi, had no malicious intent, her ignorance cannot justify her actions. It was her responsibility to be better acquainted with the facts, given the gravity of the allegation. In other words, journalists must ensure that they are not liable for negligence.

As with all forms of sourcing, it is important to uphold the ethical principles of fairness, accuracy and objectivity when conducting a sting operation. In sting investigations, there is pressure to capture unequivocal evidence of incriminating behaviour on film or tape. Herein lies a danger that the journalist concerned may attempt to influence the course of the criminal activity. The Broadcasting Standards Commission of the UK states in its guidelines that no attempt should be made to promote further dubious behaviour of those investigated. This may be difficult to achieve when trying to prove wrongdoing. Hence, all sting operations should be considered objectively: that is, without having preconceived notions of guilt. It is highly unethical to attempt to manipulate a person's behaviour. At best, it is entrapment and at its worst, it is no better than the behaviour of those being investigated.

Aniruddha Bahal faced accusations that his team had trapped MPs in Operation Duryodhan. Bahal maintains that the journalists did not 'go fishing' but that the MPs had contacted them. He adds that the sting operation would not have been possible if they had identified themselves as journalists. Tarun Tejpal claims that the *Tehelka* team had not intended Operation West End to be a witch-hunt against particular individuals.

In deciding the means to conduct a sting operation, the Broadcasting Standards Commission of the UK advises that the level of deception used in an operation should be proportionate to the alleged wrongdoing. As a broad rule of thumb, this is practical advice. However, there is no scientific equation which equates wrongdoing to the level of deception its exposure merits. Furthermore, it assumes that an allegedly serious crime is, as it stands, far graver than an allegedly petty crime. In fact, as both crimes are only alleged and unsubstantiated, one crime cannot be said to be worse than the other as neither of them necessarily exist. Pursuant to the Broadcasting Standards Commission's logic, it would mean that a person wrongly suspected of a serious crime deserves to be subjected to greater deception and therefore a greater intrusion of privacy.

?

Do you think it was appropriate for *Tehelka* to have used the services of commercial sex workers in Operation West End? What are the reasons for and against their use?

The PCI warns that all sting operations should be seen through to their logical conclusion. For example, if before a sting operation a wrongdoing is alleged, by the end of the operation the wrongdoing should be known to be either true or unsubstantiated. The PCI's suggestion is that a sting operation is of no journalistic value if it remains speculative forever. The very point of investigative journalism is to get to the bottom of an issue by unearthing facts. Anything less than a firm conclusion is, thus, 'half-baked', the PCI points out.

What might be the motivation to leave a story 'half-baked' and what are the problems therein? Why do you think Padmanabhan of *The Hindu* described the *Fallen Heroes* sting as an 'inconclusive surmise'? Do you think as per the PCI's guidelines, *Fallen Heroes* would be considered to be lacking in journalistic merit?

Editing and Airing

After the completion of a sting operation, it is very likely that a lot of editing will need to be done. In the case of Operation West End, which lasted eight months, the reporters had recorded 90 hours of footage that were edited down to four hours. Before the footage from a sting operation is broadcast or printed, it needs to be summarized. It is important to use footage which demonstrates most conclusively the purported wrongdoing. It is equally important to demonstrate the context of the footage to remcve possible doubts that the final clips were staged or manipulated. Voiceover commentaries should provide background information about what is not apparent from the visual material. The report should be accurate and eschew sensationalism by avoiding exaggerated language or gratuitous gossip. Padmanabhan, who criticized *Tehelka* for including gratuitous celebrity gossip in *Fallen Heroes*, suggests that during the editing process, all material which is not directly relevant to the central focus of the sting should be removed.

Several journalistic codes which permit investigative journalism in mitigating circumstances warn that care should be taken to mask the identity of innocent bystanders who might have been filmed during the operation. It is important to ensure that no association of innocent people with criminal activity can be inferred. Negligence in this respect would constitute an invasion of privacy, could be potentially libellous and might even endanger the safety of an innocent bystander.

It is best to obtain a large consensus before airing or printing a sting story. Before airing a sting, the possible immediate and long-term outcomes of the operation should be considered. Is there likely to be a big public outcry? Is violence likely? If yes, why and where? Should the police or other authorities be informed of the potential public disturbance? Is the footage offensive? Does it contain scenes of violence, sex, nudity or extreme suffering? Have expletives been used? If yes, then what would be an appropriate time to broadcast such material and what medium should be used? Finally, and most importantly, the question that needs to be asked: has the outcome of the sting operation yielded material that should be publicized in the overriding public interest and the people's right to information; in other words, is public welfare at stake?

CONSEQUENCES

If a sting operation goes awry and gets out of hand (like the Uma Khurana episode), its consequences can be very serious. A reputation once blackened may never be salvaged, a career once jeopardized might be lost forever.

Legal

It is plausible that people whose reputations have been tarnished will file a case of libel. In such circumstances, the media organization and the journalists concerned have to establish overriding public interest and prove that their actions were bona fide and guided by professional and not personal considerations. Care should be taken to ensure that sting operations and their consequences do not amount to contempt of court. Sting operations involving members of the judiciary run a risk of being contemptuous of the judiciary (see Box 4: The Unforthcoming Apologies).

Box 8.4

The Unforthcoming Apologies

In 2004, Zee News journalist Vijay Shekhar sought to expose corruption in the judiciary in the Ahmedabad High Court. He paid three lawyers Rs 40,000 to secure the arrest warrants of former President of India A.P.J. Abdul Kalam and the then Chief Justice of India V.N. Khare. The intention of the sting was to highlight the negligence and unprofessional conduct of sections of the lower echelons of the judiciary. Shekhar even sought permission from the Supreme Court to broadcast the sting operation on television. The apex court, however, felt that Shekhar's sting was a criminal act for which he must apologize. Shekhar stood his ground, defended the intention and 'legitimacy' of his sting operation and refused to apologize. Three times, the court asked him to apologize, but he refused. A bench of the Supreme Court maintained that the sting operation was 'nothing less than a calculated bid to lower the image of the judiciary and scandalize it in no uncertain terms'. As of August 2008, the case is still pending.

Source: Adapted from 'Fake warrants struck at the root of the system: SC,' www.rediff.com (6 February 2006).

An example of a sting operation that assisted considerably in the administration of justice is the one conducted by New Delhi Television on lawyers in the Sanjeev Nanda case.

BMW Hit-and-Run Case: The NDTV Expose

In the early hours of 10 January, 1999, a BMW car driving at high speed crashed through a police check-point in Lodhi Road in New Delhi killing six people and injuring one. It was believed that Sanjeev Nanda, grandson of S.M. Nanda who was once the Chief of Naval Staff of India, was at the wheels of the BMW car that night. The accident led to a high-profile, long-running court case in which Sanjeev Nanda and five others were tried but later let off on bail because key witnesses turned hostile. The case hogged the media headlines on and off with news of witnesses backtracking on their views or witnesses being bought off.

In a sting opreation carried out by the television news channel NDTV 24×7, the criminal lawyers involved in the case, R.K. Anand who was the counsel for Sanjeev Nanda, and I.U. Khan, who was the public prosecutor, were caught on camera offering money to Sunil Kulkarni, a key witness to the gory accident on the fateful night. The expose brought to light the startling fact that the public prosecutor and the defense counsel had colluded in order to try and save the accused from prosecution. The Delhi High Court later barred the lawyers from practising for four months, fined them a token amount and also dismissed the evidence of Sunil Kulkarni considering his statements to have been made after inducements were given to him. In September 2008, a court in Delhi sentenced Sanjeev Nanda to five years in prison for culpable homicide.

SUMMARY

By the end of this chapter you should be familiar with what sting operations entail and under what circumstances such operations may be deemed to be in the overriding interest of the public. Sting operations can yield information of great public interest but these can also go terribly wrong. The three stages of sting operations offer a detailed approach to the ethical and legal implications of sting investigations.

REVIEW QUESTIONS

1. Why is sting journalism contentious?
2. What are the two main reasons which account for the popularity of sting journalism in India?

3. Prakash Singh framed an innocent schoolteacher. What are the ethical principles which he transgressed?
4. What are the factors that should be considered before deciding to undertake a sting operation?
5. Which is the most cited ethical argument favouring sting journalism? What, if any, are the problems with this argument?
6. What, according to the PCI, are the considerations or factors that should be present in any sting operation?
7. How can you promote objectivity in sting operations?
8. What is the problem with determining the level of deception used in a sting operation with the level of the alleged wrongdoing?
9. What should be considered while editing footage from a sting operation?
10. What questions should be considered before deciding to broadcast or publish a sting story?

DEBATE

To deceive in order to uncover the truth is sheer hypocrisy. There are no circumstances in journalism in which the use of deceptive measures is an ethically admissible practice.

REFERENCES

Hirst, Martin and Roger Patching 2007, *Journalism Ethics: Arguments and Cases*, Oxford University Press, South Melbourne, Australia.

http://www.hinduonnet.com/2000/11/05/stories/1305017m.htm

http://www.india-today.com/itoday/20010326/c-tehelka.shtml

'Pitch Hunt,' India Today (5 June 2000).

Rodman, George 2001, *Making Sense of Media*, Allyn & Bacon, US.

Shrivastava, K.M. 2005, *Media Ethics: Veda to Gandhi and Beyond*, Ministry of Information and Broadcasting, Government of India, New Delhi, India.

'Sleaze, senseless greed and dirty heroes,' www.tehelka.com (13 March 2001).

Soutik Biswas at http://news.bbc.co.uk/2/hi/south_asia/6076040.stm

Sweeney at http://news.bbc.co.uk/1/hi/programmes/4770498.stm

www.dnaindia.com

www.hinduonnet.com

www.india-today.com

www.news.bbc.co.uk

www.tehelka.org

www.thehoot.org

APPENDIX 8.1

Resolution 1003 (1993) of the Council of Europe's Parliamentary Assembly on the Ethics of Journalism

The Assembly affirms the following ethical principles for journalism and believes that they should be applied by the profession throughout Europe.

News and Opinions

1. In addition to the legal rights and obligations set forth in the relevant legal norms, the media have an ethical responsibility towards citizens and society which must be underlined at the present time, when information and communication play a very important role in the formation of citizens' personal attitudes and the development of society and democratic life.
2. The journalist's profession comprises rights and obligations, freedoms and responsibilities.
3. The basic principle of any ethical consideration of journalism is that a clear distinction must be drawn between news and opinions, making it impossible to confuse them. News is information about facts and data, while opinions convey thoughts, ideas, beliefs or value judgements on the part of media companies, publishers or journalists.
4. News broadcasting should be based on truthfulness, ensured by the appropriate means of verification and proof, and impartiality in presentation, description and narration. Rumour must not be confused with news. News headlines and summaries must reflect as closely as possible the substance of the facts and data presented.
5. Expression of opinions may entail thoughts or comments on general ideas or remarks on news relating to actual events. Although opinions are necessarily subjective and therefore cannot and should not be made subject to the criterion of truthfulness, we must ensure that opinions are expressed honestly and ethically.
6. Opinions taking the form of comments on events or actions relating to individuals or institutions should not attempt to deny or conceal the reality of the facts or data.

The Right to Information as a Fundamental Human Right – Publishers, Proprietors and Journalists

7. The media's work is one of 'mediation', providing an information service, and the rights which they own in connection with freedom of information depends on its addressees, that is the citizens.
8. Information is a fundamental right which has been highlighted by the case-law of the European Commission and Court of Human Rights relating to Article 10 of the European Convention on Human Rights and recognized under Article 9 of the European Convention on Transfrontier Television, as well as in all democratic constitutions. The owner of the right is the citizen, who also has the related right to demand that the information supplied by journalists be conveyed truthfully, in the case of news, and honestly, in the case of opinions, without outside interference by either the public authorities or the private sector.
9. The public authorities must not consider that they own information. The representativeness of such authorities provides the legal basis for efforts to guarantee and extend pluralism in the media and to ensure that the necessary conditions are created for exercising freedom of expression and the right to information and precluding censorship.

Moreover, the Committee of Ministers is aware of this fact, as demonstrated by its Declaration on the Freedom of Expression and Information adopted on 29 April 1982.

10. When dealing with journalism it must be borne in mind that it relies on the media, which are part of a corporate structure within which a distinction must be made between publishers, proprietors and journalists. To that end, in addition to safeguarding the freedom of the media, freedom within the media must also be protected and internal pressures guarded against.
11. News organizations must consider themselves as special socio-economic agencies whose entrepreneurial objectives have to be limited by the conditions for providing access to a fundamental right.
12. News organizations must show transparency in matters of media ownership and management, enabling citizens to ascertain clearly the identity of proprietors and the extent of their economic interest in the media.
13. Inside the news organization, publishers and journalists must coexist, bearing in mind that the legitimate respect for publishers' and owners' ideological orientations is limited by the absolute requirements on truthful news reporting and ethical opinions. This is essential if we are to respect the citizens' fundamental right to information.
14. These requirements are such that we must reinforce the safeguards of the journalist's freedom of expression, for they must in the last instance operate as the ultimate sources of information. In this connection we must legally expand and clarify the nature of the conscience clause and professional secrecy vis-à-vis confidential sources, harmonizing national provisions on this matter so that they can be implemented in the wider context of democratic Europe.
15. Neither publishers and proprietors nor journalists should consider that they own the news. News organizations must treat information not as a commodity but as a fundamental right of the citizen. To that end, the media should exploit neither the quality nor the substance of the news or opinions for purposes of boosting readership or audience figures in order to increase advertising revenue.
16. If we are to ensure that information is treated ethically, its target audience must be considered as individuals and not as a mass.

The Function of Journalism and its Ethical Activity

17. Information and communication as conveyed by journalism through the media, with powerful support from the new technologies, has decisive importance for the development of the individual and society. It is indispensable for democratic life, since if democracy is to develop fully it must guarantee citizens participation in public affairs. Suffice it to say that such participation would be impossible if the citizens were not in receipt of the information on public affairs which they need and which must be provided by the media.
18. The importance of information, especially radio and television news, for culture and education was highlighted in Assembly Recommendation 1067. Its effects on public opinion are obvious.
19. It would be wrong to infer from the importance of this role that the media actually represent public opinion or that they should replace the specific functions of the public authorities or institutions of an educational or cultural character such as schools.
20. This would amount to transforming the media and journalism into authorities or

counter-authorities ('mediocracy'), even though they would not be representative of the citizens or subject to the same democratic controls as the public authorities, and would not possess the specialist knowledge of the corresponding cultural or educational institutions.

21. Therefore journalism should not alter truthful, impartial information or honest opinions, or exploit them for media purposes, in an attempt to create or shape public opinion, since its legitimacy rests on effective respect for the citizen's fundamental right to information as part of respect for democratic values. To that end, legitimate investigative journalism is limited by the veracity and honesty of information and opinions and is incompatible with journalistic campaigns conducted on the basis of previously adopted positions and special interests.
22. In journalism, information and opinions must respect the presumption of innocence, in particular in cases which are still sub judice, and must refrain from making judgements.
23. The right of individuals to privacy must be respected. Persons holding office in public life are entitled to protection for their privacy except in those cases where their private life may have an effect on their public life. The fact that a person holds a public post does not deprive him (sic) of the right to respect for his (sic) privacy.
24. The attempt to strike a balance between the right to respect for private life, enshrined in Article 8 of the European Convention on Human Rights, and the freedom of expression set forth in Article 10, is well documented in the recent case-law of the European Commission and Court of Human Rights.
25. In the journalist's profession the end does not justify the means; therefore information must be obtained by legal and ethical means.
26. At the request of the persons concerned, the news media must correct, automatically and speedily, and with all relevant information provided, any news item or opinion conveyed by them which is false or erroneous. National legislation should provide for appropriate sanctions and, where applicable, compensation.
27. In order to harmonize the application and exercise of this right in the member states of the Council of Europe, we must implement Resolution (74) 26 on the right of reply—position of the individual in relation to the press, adopted by the Committee of Ministers on 2 July 1974, and also the relevant provisions of the European Convention on Transfrontier Television.
28. In order to ensure high-quality work and independence on the part of journalists, they must be guaranteed decent pay and proper working conditions and facilities.
29. In the relations which the journalist must maintain in the course of his (sic) duties with the public authorities or the various economic sectors, care should be taken to avoid any kind of connivance liable to affect the independence and impartiality of journalism.
30. In journalism, controversial or sensational items must not be confused with subjects on which it is important to provide information. The journalist must not exploit his (sic) duties for the principal purpose of acquiring prestige or personal influence.
31. In view of the complexity of the process of providing information, which is increasingly based on the use of new technologies, speed and conciseness, journalists must be required to have appropriate professional training.

Rules Governing Editorial Staff

32. Within the newspaper business, publishers, proprietors and journalists must live side by

side. To that end, rules must be drawn up for editorial staff in order to regulate professional relations between the journalists and the publishers and proprietors within the media, separately from the normal requirements of labour relations. Such rules might provide for the setting up of editorial boards.

Situations of Conflict and Cases of Special Protection

33. In society, situations of tension and conflict sometimes arise under the pressure of factors such as terrorism, discrimination against minorities, xenophobia or war. In such circumstances the media have a moral obligation to defend democratic values: respect for human dignity, solving problems by peaceful, tolerant means, and consequently to oppose violence and the language of hatred and confrontation and to reject all discrimination based on culture, sex or religion.
34. No one should remain neutral vis-à-vis the defence of democratic values. To that end the media must play a major role in preventing tension and must encourage mutual understanding, tolerance and trust between the various communities in regions where conflict prevails, as the Secretary General of the Council of Europe has set out to do with her confidence-building measures in the former Yugoslavia.
35. Having regard to the very specific influence of the media, notably television, on the attitudes of children and young people, care must be taken not to broadcast programmes, messages or images glorifying violence, exploiting sex and consumerism or using deliberately unsuitable language.

Ethics and Self-regulation in Journalism

36. Having regard to the requisite conditions and basic principles enumerated above, the media must undertake to submit to firm ethical principles guaranteeing freedom of expression and the fundamental right of citizens to receive truthful information and honest opinions.
37. In order to supervise the implementation of these principles, self-regulatory bodies or mechanisms must be set up comprising publishers, journalists, media users' associations, experts from the academic world and judges; they will be responsible for issuing resolutions on respect for ethical precepts in journalism, with prior commitment on the part of the media to publish the relevant resolutions. This will help the citizen, who has the right to information, to pass either positive or negative judgement on the journalist's work and credibility.
38. The self-regulatory bodies or mechanisms, the media users' associations and the relevant university departments could publish each year the research done a posteriori on the truthfulness of the information broadcast by the media, comparing the news with the actual facts. This would serve as a barometer of credibility which citizens could use as a guide to the ethical standard achieved by each medium or each section of the media, or even each individual journalist. The relevant corrective mechanisms might simultaneously help improve the manner in which the profession of media journalism is pursued.

CHAPTER

9

NEW MEDIA: THE INTERNET

This chapter elaborates on the ethical issues that have arisen on account of the phenomenal growth of the 'newest' of the mass media, namely, the internet. As a medium that is used for mass communication and personalized communication, it offers 'unlimited information' on a variety of subjects. However, it has also raised fresh ethical concerns relating to plagiarism, misinformation, disinformation, obscenity, indecency, violation of privacy and the impact on children. This chapter highlights the impact of social networking, blogging and new forms of journalism like citizen journalism.

THE INTERNET AND ITS USES

The internet is often described as the 'information superhighway'. While books, newspapers, television and radio can be compared to a road where the flow of traffic is well organized, access being provided at major intersections, the internet offers thousands of capillary junctions and sprawling, unchartered access to obscure nether regions of the mass media, much of it still under construction (Campbell 2002). This analogy serves to indicate the sheer enormity and scope afforded by the internet, which is the most important aspect of the world wide web (www) or an international network of computers connected with one another.

The other salient feature of the internet, as Steve Stecklow of the *Wall Street Journal* commented, is that it has no single owner and is akin to a non-profit food cooperative (Campbell 2002). In other words, the internet is decentralized, which means it does not carry the hierarchical structure of typical corporate businesses and is, therefore, largely unmanaged and unregulated. Indeed, it is this characteristic of the internet that led Burnstein and Kline to conclude that the internet is not policed, and is 'ungovernable' (Campbell 2002). Thus, the internet makes the implementation of sound media ethics very difficult. Another factor which contributes to the internet's so-called ungovernability is the exponential growth rate of its usership.

Compared to other media, the growth of the internet has been remarkably rapid. While the proportion of American households with cable television connections increased from 13 per cent of the total in 1975 to 60 per cent twenty years later, it took just four years for half the households in the US to be connected to the world wide web from just a few in 1991. In 1993, the number of internet users was doubling every three months. At the end of 2007, according to Internet World Stats, the total number of internet users all over the world was 1.3 billion. The growth has been tremendous and fast but seen from the wrong side of the digital divide there are at least 4.3 billion people on the planet who still have no access to the internet. The digital divide is as real as the fact that the internet has changed—and continues to change—human society in ways few would have imagined in the early 1990s. The influence of the internet has undoubtedly created the need for some kind of regulation but the rapidity of its growth renders it difficult. Some of the problems posed by the internet are discussed in the following sections.

The decentralized nature of the internet makes it the most effective tool to uphold democratic values. Do you agree? Does the internet represent the 'social responsibility' model of the media or the 'libertarian' model?

PLAGIARISM

Plagiarism involves presenting another person's work or ideas as one's own, either with the intention to gain credit for it or by merely neglecting to cite the source of the work (see Box 9.1: A History of Plagiarism). As the internet offers ready access to a vast library on countless subjects, it is increasingly easy and tempting to plagiarize. Furthermore, because the internet is decentralized, plagiarism is not easily detectable. However, irrespective of whether or not a person is penalized, plagiarism is an unethical practice and is an example of 'lazy journalism' in mass media (Hirst and Patching 2007).

Lori Robertson, former managing editor of the *American Journalism Review*, believes that the reason for recurring plagiarism is not so much the unregulated nature of the internet but the newsroom culture which rewards journalists for unique stories (Hirst and Patching 2007).

Box 9.1

A History of Plagiarism

What is plagiarism? In an article entitled 'The history of plagiarism' and published in *The Guardian* of the UK in November 2005, Stephen Moss wrote: 'Plagiarism (is) the attempt to pass off the ideas, research, theories or words of others as one's own...... The word plagiarism derives from Latin roots: plagiarius, an abductor, and plagiare, to steal. An example of plagiarism would be copying this definition and pasting straight into a report.'

In the article, Moss argues that plagiarism is a serious academic offence. A recent study by the Qualifications and Curriculum Authority of the UK, he pointed out, warned that examination boards appear to be failing to spot cheating, even though the number of cases of fraud are increasing. In 2004, for instance, 3,600 teenagers (in the UK) were caught breaching the rules, a 9 per cent rise over the previous year.

Plagiarism, however, is not a modern art! Shakespeare, says Moss, stole the majority of his historical plots directly from Holinshed. Laurence Sterne and Samuel Taylor Coleridge were both accused of plagiarism. Just how much Coleridge appropriated has been debated by scholars ever since Thomas de Quincey, himself an accomplished borrower, published an exposé in *Tait's Magazine* shortly after the poet's death. Oscar Wilde was repeatedly accused of plagiarism: hence the celebrated exchange with Whistler: 'I wish I'd said that, James.'

'Don't worry, Oscar, you will.'

In more recent times, contends Moss, plagiarism has not been limited to lazy and dishonest students. Martin Luther King pirated part of a chapter of his doctoral thesis. Alex Haley copied large passages of his novel *Roots* from *The African* by Harold Courlander and Princess Michael was accused of plagiarism over her book on royal brides.

In his article, Moss cites more examples of plagiarism. In 1997, less than six months after winning the Booker prize, Graham Swift's *Last Orders* was accused of having crossed the line between inspiration and plagiarism by 'directly imitating' an earlier work, the 1930 novel *As I Lay Dying* by William Faulkner. Confronted with the accusations, Swift said his book was an 'echo' of Faulkner's novel. To read T.S. Eliot's *The Waste Land* is also to read Shakespeare, Chaucer, Webster and many others. According to one critic, Eliot practised a kind of 'verbal kleptomania'.

Originality may have mattered a great deal over the last two centuries, writes Moss, but the importance attached to it may be declining. In that sense, he argues, all culture is plagiarism. 'I can sum up my thoughts on this in two lines,' he quotes novelist Julian Barnes on the Swift–Faulkner affair, adding: 'When Brahms wrote his first symphony, he was accused of having used a big theme from Beethoven's Ninth. His reply was that any fool could see that—much like what Eliot said, "Immature poets imitate; mature poets steal!"'

Moss concludes his article with a quip: 'We apologize for the fact that three words of the above piece are the author's own.'

A website called www.plagiarism.org has been established because of the growing concern about the prevalence of internet plagiarism. It outlines the following practices which can be considered plagiarism:

- turning in someone else's work as your own
- copying words or ideas from someone else's work without giving credit
- failing to put quotation marks while quoting from someone else's work
- giving incorrect information about the source of a quotation
- changing words but copying the sentence structure of a source without giving credit
- copying many words or ideas from a source that it makes up the majority of your work, whether you give credit or not

The practice of plagiarism is unethical in a journalistic context because it transgresses the basic tenets of accuracy and truthfulness. Plagiarism is taken seriously among media professionals and is incorporated into many professional codes of conduct for journalists. The Philippines code of ethics (Clause 6) simply states: 'I will not commit any act of plagiarism.' This might be understood as the Eleventh Commandment today, if we are to follow a model of self-regulation of the media. Given the ease with which plagiarism is possible on the internet compared to other media, self-regulation is most important for ensuring ethical standards. To self-regulate, it is important to be clear about what constitutes plagiarism and the ways in which to avoid it.

Black et al. (Retief 2002) have compiled a checklist to consider when using sources.

- Have you carefully attributed any material that is not your own?
- Are you working from notes, or from your head? If you are working from your head, are you certain that you are not taking out of your memory someone else's phrases or sentences?
- Will reasonable people recognize the difference between your writing and that of others?
- Are you informed well enough about the topic to be able to recognize potential problems with your work?
- Have you encouraged others to read your work to see if it triggers any memories that might indicate plagiarism?

The website www.plagiarism.org also suggests that due to the decentralized nature of the internet, it is often perceived as a public tool or service whose contents are also public property. This makes the act or intention of plagiarism harder to identify.

Can you think of ways to regulate the internet? Can a regulated internet be as powerful and inclusive as a freewheeling, unregulated world wide web?

Rules of Thumb

The charge of plagiarism is a serious one. The best way to avoid it is to cite all the sources.

Although plagiarism is often difficult to trace, it is more likely that lifted material would be recognized when it is circulated in the media because of its wide dissemination. If detected, plagiarism does not go unpunished. In some incidents, plagiarism cases can be brought to court. In other cases, the revelation of plagiarism results in the deep embarrassment of the journalist or media organization concerned, as well as seriously undermining their professional credibility (see Box 9.2: Napster and YouTube).

What should you do if you have reason to believe your source has plagiarized?

Why, in your opinion, has plagiarism been called 'lazy journalism'?

Box 9.2

Napster and YouTube

Plagiarism can also take the form of unlawfully copying and distributing material. A high-profile example of this form of plagiarism was the case of Napster, an internet website that allowed its users to share music on their hard drives via the internet. In 2000, Napster was sued by A&M Records and several other record companies for infringement of the laws of the US Digital Millennium Copyright Act. Napster was found guilty on three counts of infringement of copyright.

Microsoft has accused Google, which owns the video sharing website YouTube, of having a 'cavalier attitude' towards copyright and this is not the first time such a charge has been made. In 2007, Viacom, which owns MTV (Music Television), launched a $1 billion lawsuit against Google for infringing copyright. Viacom claims that 160,000 clips available on YouTube have breached copyright regulations. Some of the videos in the centre of the controversy include the satirical comedy *South Park*, and the children's programme *SpongeBob Square Pants* (Johnson 2007).

MISINFORMATION

The expanse of information and ideas available on the internet makes it an appealing source for journalistic material. The internet provides not only supplementary facts about a chosen story but also offers ideas for whole new stories from around the world. This can be a time-saving and cost-efficient method of gathering facts. The danger of this method of collation or gathering information is, aside from plagiarizing, that of being misinformed by erroneous sources.

Just as it is easy to make advertisements look like editorial content, it is possible to present opinion or unverified information as hard fact. The presentation of opinion as fact has never been as easy as it is on the internet, where material can pass unmonitored. Sir Harold Evans, former editor of *The Times*, London, has observed that opinion, rather than fact, is the commonest traffic in cyberspace. He cites the example of the rumour which circulated on the internet shortly after 9/11 which held that the attacks were the work of a Jewish secret service which had tipped off 4,000 Jews not to go to work in the targeted buildings that day. Evans tracked the source of this rumour and found that it originated from AI Manor television in Beirut and a Syrian newspaper. A Washington-based web service called Information News put it on the internet from where the rumour spread rapidly. The most alarming part of such stories is that they have the capacity not only to misinform the public, but also to falsely incriminate.

It is not fair to impart bogus information as this is contrary to the idea that knowledge is empowering. As responsible media professionals, the lack of intention to deceive through false information is not an acceptable reason for the practice and it does not excuse the offence. Richards (2006) expresses concern that the unregulated nature of the internet, and the challenges presented by new technologies, means that technology—by virtue of its complications—will become a 'scapegoat for the misdemeanours' of media professionals.

Where should one draw the line between 'unconscious plagiarism' and 'intended plagiarism'? Is there danger that intended plagiarism could be disguised as unintended copying?

Guarding Against Misinformation

Anton Vedder, an academic at Tilberg University, the Netherlands, identifies primary and secondary criteria by which we can judge the veracity and the merit of a piece of information. The primary criteria pertain to assessing the material itself. It involves considering consistency, coherence, accuracy and concordance with observations. However, this kind of assessment is dependent on at least a rudimentary understanding of the material and a frame of reference.

The secondary 'epistemic' criteria pertain to assessing the source of information or the content provider. The criteria include authenticity, trustworthiness and credibility. For example, a seeker might consider whether the information has been provided by an academic in a university, and if so, which university. These standards are informed by entrenched social conventions and as such are not cross-culturally transferable (Vedder 2001).

Rules of Thumb

- It is good practice to always verify information. This can be done by using a variety of different sources to ensure that facts about a particular story are the same across sources.
- It is advisable to use only reputable news websites as sources.
- Check up on your sources' sources: has your source used reliable sources such as international news agencies? Can you identify authoritative sources—people with specialist knowledge and experts? How near is your source to first-hand experience?

The lack of internet censorship places a greater onus on the individual media professionals to ensure the veracity of their material. For journalists, it is imperative to ensure that the standards of accuracy and fairness are protected from dangers inherent in internet usage. Hence, journalists must be extra careful and cautious in guarding against misinformation.

OBSCENITY AND INDECENCY

The absence of a regulatory body for the internet means that censorship has to be exercised by the content provider. This has resulted in an inordinate amount of online material which might commonly be considered obscene, indecent, pornographic or violent (see Box 9.3: Children). The ready availability of online material coupled with the freedom and choice exercised by the user has resulted in a situation where indecent material is considered almost acceptable on the internet. Indeed, one of the most salient features of the internet is that it is entirely free from regulation and is, therefore, an unparalleled means of free expression and speech. While responsible adults should be free to access information privately without restriction, the internet indiscriminately awards this privilege to not just adults but also to children and to people who can cause harm to society. To formulate a code of governance for the internet, notions of acceptability need to be defined. The social standards of 'real life' can be applied to 'cyberspace'. However, the nature of the virtual 'community' is different from physical communities and hence, it would be erroneous to assume that the same set of social values can be transposed on both communities.

This was argued in the case of *United States* versus *Thomas* (1996), which saw Robert and Carleen Thomas convicted for knowingly transporting (through the internet) material of obscene content between states for commercial purposes. The nub of this case lay in the fact that different US states had different laws pertaining to obscene material. The Sixth Circuit Court of Appeals used the notion from the *Miller* versus *California* (1973) obscenity test which determined that obscenity rules of the place to which the material was transported, would apply. The couple argued, however, that computer technologies warranted a new definition of communities and community standards. They posited that standards of obscenity should be those of a cyber community, and not those of a physical, geographical community. The *United States* versus *Thomas* case highlighted an inherent problem of internet regulation. In a world where communities separated by culture and geography may have different social standards, how far would it be possible to devise a uniform code of ethics for the internet to reflect all social standards without encroaching on the freedom of speech and intellectual rights?

Websites offering pornographic content have often chosen domain names which contain popular search words entirely unrelated to pornography. The intention is to lure more viewers to a website by default. This practice has offended the sensibilities of some internet users who feel that such a tactic is duplicitous and underhand. In April 2003, a law called the PROTECT Act (Prosecutorial Remedies and Other Tools to End the Exploitation of Children Today) was passed in the US. Under this act, for the first time, the law made it illegal to use misleading domain names to lure unsuspecting users.

Can you think of any examples of subjects that were once considered indecent but are now acceptable? Can you think of examples of practices or customs prevalent in one culture or community which would be considered indecent elsewhere?

Box 9.3

Children

One of the most pressing issues concerning the proliferation of obscene information on the internet is the circulation of child pornography. This is perhaps the most serious example of the dangers of the lack of internet regulation.

Another related issue arising from unrestricted access to the internet is the use of chatrooms to groom underage children for sex. Internet chatrooms make it possible for a person to conceal her/his identity and assume a false identity. Some paedophiles use these chatrooms to befriend children and establish a relationship of trust and then arrange to meet them alone. In the UK, there are advertising campaigns aimed at exposing the dangers of unsupervised internet use by children. The British Home Office has developed a website to offer support to victims and investigate reported incidents of paedophilia.

Do you think the internet can survive as a credible, socially friendly medium only if it is supported and supplemented by alternative media?

PRIVACY

The internet poses a potential threat to the right to privacy as users sometimes have to share information to acquire information. Leslie (2004) points out that the internet has the capacity to violate a person's right to privacy actively and passively.

Active violation might involve, for example, putting defamatory and/or personal information concerning a private individual on the internet with unrestricted accessibility. Leslie (2004) cites the example of an undergraduate of the University of Maryland who heard about a girl being mistreated by her parents. Keen to take the matter into his own hands, the student 'posted' the allegations on the internet with the family's home telephone number and suggested that users call the girl's mother and tell her that they were 'disgusted' with her behaviour. The family was inundated with threatening phone calls from vigilante citizens which caused the girl's mother to suffer a nervous breakdown. This example serves to highlight the many dangers of an unregulated internet and demonstrates how easily the private lives of ordinary citizens can be affected.

How far can it be argued that inciting other people to make abusive phone calls is not the same thing as actually making the phone calls and hence perfectly innocuous and acceptable?

In 2003, a Canadian high school student Ghyslain Raza filmed himself playing with a golf ball retriever in the manner of a fictional *Star Wars* character called Jedi for the amusement of his family. Ghyslain's classmates got hold of the video and posted it on the internet and made him a laughing stock. Ghyslain later told a Canadian newspaper, *National Post*, that he was desperate to get his 'life back'.

Do you think that the case of Ghyslain involved an invasion of privacy? How far could it be argued that since Ghyslain played a consenting and knowing part in the making of the film his claims of invasion of privacy are undermined?

An example of passive intrusion is the data-collection practices that websites use to gain information about consumers. Electronic commerce or e-commerce, the phenomenon of trade via the internet, has grown rapidly and is highly profitable but has also led to concerns about the safety and privacy of consumer data. Internet fraud is well recognized but despite this, e-commerce continues to grow. Where there is a market, however, there will always be marketing, and the internet is extensively used not just as a way to expose consumers to commodities (advertising), but also to measure spending patterns (market surveys). Cookies, which provide information about an internet user and their internet behavioural patterns, are often accepted by web browsers and perform the function of 'spies' by tracking a user's previous use of a website. The information gathered by cookies is valuable for market research and can be sold to advertisers.

To prevent invasion of privacy on the internet, the US Federal Trade Commission (FTC), in 1998, drew up four fair information practice principles: notice, choice, access and security. In accordance with these principles, websites are required to:

- disclose methods of data collection
- allow website users to control the quantity and nature of the information collected
- grant access to databases to individuals for data verification
- ensure data security

However, these guidelines have faced problems in implementation. The FTC lacks the power to enforce adherence to the guidelines. According to an FTC survey, in 2000, only 20 per cent of the websites which collect data follow, at least in part, the above guidelines. The results of this survey highlight the problems of depending on self-regulation for the maintenance of ethical practices on the internet.

SOCIAL NETWORKING

The recent phenomenon of social networking websites such as Orkut, Facebook and Bebo, which allow users to create a personal profile that can be viewed by other users, is an example of the popularity and demand for online communities. It is also demonstrative of changing social attitudes, particularly among younger generations, towards privacy. Many users exhibit their personal and private information on these sites. This information can be used by marketers, employers, journalists or, for that matter, just about anybody. As the information is provided by the user, it is difficult to argue an ethical case against the use of this information. There is a view that the phenomenon of social networking sites is indicative of the exhibitionistic and voyeuristic tendencies inculcated by our postmodern 'Big Brother' society. (George Orwell's novel *1984*, about life in a dictatorship, frequently refers to the phrase 'Big Brother is watching you' to signify the loss of personal privacy to national security.) Others, however, argue that the growing popularity of networking sites, such as Facebook, indicate that this phenomenon would not only become more acceptable among substantial sections of internet users but would acquire new forms and dimensions in the years ahead.

EVERYONE'S A JOURNALIST

The internet has given rise to a new form of journalism, web logging or blogging. Blogs are pieces of writing that can be posted on the internet by anybody, anywhere. Unlike in conventional print journalism, blogs

- can be of any length: less care needs to be employed in choosing appropriate and accurate expressions to avoid misleading the readers.
- are not subjected to editorial scrutiny: sometimes there are no distinctions between fact and opinion and there is a strong possibility of misinformation being presented.
- their authorship can be withheld or distorted: it is extremely difficult to check the veracity of the content and to trace a blog's sources.

Baghdad Blogger

In 2003, a diarist, using the pseudonym Salam Pax, maintained a web log documenting life in Iraq in the time of war. His entries were considered uniquely insightful and entertaining, which, coupled with their 'reality' appeal, rendered them a sought-after source of news by both individuals and established media organizations.

The example of the Baghdad Blogger shows the positive side of web logging. The man's ordinariness, his anonymity and the personal nature of his entries distinguished his journals from impersonal journalism, while at the same time indicating that he was not interested in commercial gains. However, not all blogging has been as well received. Paul Andrews, a US columnist, argues that blogging is a potentially harmful form of journalism as bloggers do not possess the skills in fact-checking or in-depth research (Richards 2006). The ordinary blogger is not bound by established and accepted ethical codes that apply to conventional journalism. Andrews concludes by saying that 'calling a typical blogger a journalist is like calling anyone who takes a snapshot a photographer'.

What defines a journalist? If an ordinary citizen practices blogging in accordance with the ethical norms prescribed for media personnel would he/she be considered a bona fide journalist?

Is blogging a threat to mainstream media? Is there a danger that this form of writing could become more popular than conventional journalism?

Even before blogging became popular, online journalism had become fairly well established. One prominent example is that of controversial journalist Matt Drudge—born Mathew Nathan Drudge—proprietor and editor of the Drudge Report website. The report began as an e-mail newsletter service providing news and gossip. Its subscribers grew from 1,000 in March 1995 to 85,000 two years later and by 2002, the site had crossed the 1 billion mark for page views. In 1998, Drudge became well known after he broke the news about Monica Lewinsky's relationship with the then US President Bill Clinton. (When videotapes of the Lewinsky affair became public, television networks decided not to air the tapes on the ground that their content would be inappropriate. But, after one channel broke the informal embargo others followed suit.)

Drudge moved from the internet to television and received a mixed response. Between June 1998 and November 1999, he hosted a Saturday night television programme on the Fox News channel that was terminated abruptly after Drudge refused to go on air charging Fox News with censorship. *Fox* did not want him to show visuals of a surgery on a foetus to support his opposition to abortion. Drudge reportedly wanted to use a picture of a tiny hand reaching out from a womb. However, a senior editor at Fox rejected the photograph as it was not taken during an abortion but during an emergency operation on a woman's foetus. Fox News subsequently claimed Drudge had breached his contract and after he issued an apology, the news channel described the parting of ways as 'amicable'. In 2006, *Time* magazine described Drudge as one of the hundred most influential individuals in the world while disparaging the Drudge Report as a 'ludicrous combination of gossip, political intrigue and extreme weather reports... still put together mostly by the guy who started out as a convenience store clerk'. Drudge is, of course, a wealthy man earning over $1 million a year.

It is not just blogging that has made the ordinary citizen help shape the circulation of information. The development of cameraphones has made the ordinary bystander a key witness and news source. Hirst and Patching (2007) cite the example of ABC Online which encouraged its viewers, after the second terrorist blasts in Bali, to contact them with eyewitness accounts and photographs. Saddam Hussein's last minutes were captured on a mobile phone equipped with a camera. The wide circulation of a video depicting the gruesome decapitation of American journalist Daniel Pearl in February 2002 also raised questions relating to the ease with which audio-visual information could be disseminated through the internet. Pearl, who was kidnapped and murdered in Karachi, Pakistan, was serving as the South Asia Bureau Chief of the *Wall Street Journal* in Mumbai, and had been investigating the case of 'shoe bomber' Richard Reid's alleged links with the Al Qaeda terrorist group and Pakistan's Inter-Services Intelligence.

The era of the citizen journalist has evolved because of the instantaneous mobility afforded to most people by the internet. This phenomenon of 'user-led content' prompted *Time* to name 'you' (the reader, the public) its 'person of the year' for 2006. The magazine enumerated the merits of the public, 'seizing the reins of the global media,...founding and framing the new digital democracy for working for nothing and beating the pros at their own game...' (Grossman, *Time*, December 2006).

However, citizen journalism is not without its negative consequences as well. The phenomenon has led to an increased rise in the use of hidden cameras by ordinary, untrained citizens and the rise of amateur paparazzi. Citizen journalism can be valuable if it is routed through a reputed news organization. Newspapers, magazines and television channels can encourage citizen journalism by dedicating space to it in their news bulletins or newspapers. This way, citizen journalists can also get expert editorial assessment. In India, CNN-IBN was among the first news channels to initiate this form of journalism through a half-hour programme called *Citizen Journalist*.

The Intrusive Photographer

Paparazzi is the plural form of paparazzo and means photographers who take photographs of famous people, usually against their wishes and often by following relentlessly them. Celebrities who claim they have been hounded by photographers use 'stalkarazzi' as a derogatory word. The word paparazzi became popular after the 1960 film *La Dolce Vita* (The Good Life), directed by Italian director Federico Fellini, in which one of the characters is a news photographer named Paparazzo. In his book *Word and Phrase Origins*, Robert Hendrickson writes that Fellini took the name paparazzi from an Italian dialect word for a particularly noisy, buzzing mosquito. In his school days, Fellini remembered a boy who was nicknamed Paparazzo because of his fast talking and constant movements.

The use of hidden cameras to expose supposedly questionable behaviour and the intrusive practices of the paparazzi has long been accepted. Hirst and Patching (2007) suggest that by offering cash for amateur footage, media organizations are encouraging unethical behaviour. However, this problem could also be because of a modern 'Big Brother' society which encourages and glorifies social vigilantism and voyeurism.

In 2006, Lane Hudson, a political insider in the US, decided to take a stand against the 'worst-kept secret in Washington'. Hudson decided to expose the 'sleazy behaviour' of Mark Foley, a member of the US Congress, who purportedly made repeated amorous advances on his colleagues. Apparently, Foley had made unsuccessful advances on Hudson. Hudson posted examples of sleazy e-mail messages written by Foley on his weblog 'Stop Sex Predators'. His blog aroused the interest of other bloggers and the story was promptly covered by mainstream news networks. As a result of the exposé, Foley resigned from Congress and discontinued his re-election campaign while Hudson was fired for using company resources in his exposé. He, however, feels that 'whistle-blogging' holds a magnifying glass over public citizens and will encourage public accountability.

Was Lane Hudson right in exposing the behaviour of Foley? Could the matter have been settled in a more private and less damaging way?

THE NEW FACE OF JOURNALISM

The phenomenon of community-centric, citizen journalism has become known as Web 2.0. *Time* calls it a 'revolution' and a 'social experiment' (Grossman, *Time*, December 2006). But Web 2.0 has led to confusion about what defines a journalist because everyone is free to write and publish material. In the same vein, it has become increasingly difficult to distinguish between valuable and credible news and 'mere regurgitations of public relations handouts' (Richards 2006). This is where the journalist's role as interpreter of information becomes especially pertinent. It has been observed that the role of the journalist is shifting from that of collator and disseminator of information to that of interpreter in the era of the internet. Jane Singer has noted that the duty of journalists to interpret credibly the 'unprecedented volume' of information available on the internet is of fundamental importance and is even integral to the survival of journalists (Richards 2006).

Separating the wheat from the chaff is an indispensable job and one that provides journalists with a new identity. To discern information of value, journalists must have:

- the capacity for in-depth and pertinent research
- the ability to digest a wide range of information
- the aptitude to identify relevant information
- the ability to present digested information succinctly and clearly

Journalist Tom Carver has suggested that alongside a new role for the journalist in the era of mobile and internet technology, a new interactive relationship with the medium's audience was also created. Carver followed the 2000 US elections campaigns for the BBC, seeking to answer questions on themes suggested by the public. People from all over Europe and Asia e-mailed Carver their questions which he was able to check regularly 'on the ground' from his mobile phone. The questions received from the public helped shape the reportage and sourcing he conducted. Carver argued that this was an unparalleled way of a journalist maintaining a relationship with the audience, and a means to get to understand the audience better. This kind of journalism has been labelled 'user-controlled journalism' as the wishes of the audience dictate to a certain degree what a journalist covers. Carver, however, is wary of the scope of this phenomenon of user-dictated or user-controlled content. He feels that journalists must still retain control over content and must use their editorial prowess to discern interesting audience suggestions.

New Delhi Television (NDTV) has a half-hour programme every weeknight called Newsnet that explores different facets of the internet and the 'ripple effect' of major news stories on message boards, social networking communities, blogs and video sharing websites. The programme showcases opinions and satirical responses and amateur videos of breaking news stories that on occasions blur conventional boundaries of reportage in the 'traditional' mass media. For instance, the May 2008 earthquake in China's Sichuan province was put on the internet on a social networking site before the country's largest news agency Xinhua reported it.

However, what cannot be denied is that the advent of the internet has made traditional media—print, radio and television—more personalized and participative.

REVIEW QUESTIONS

1. Identify some of the key characteristics of the internet.
2. What are the implications of the decentralized structure of the internet?
3. What do you understand by plagiarism?
4. What should you consider to help guard against plagiarism when using sources?
5. What are some of the major problems of misinformation? How can you guard against misinformation?
6. What are the primary and secondary criteria for verifying information?
7. In what ways does the internet challenge notions of 'community'?
8. Give some examples of active and passive violation of privacy.
9. In what ways does blogging differ from traditional journalism?
10. What is meant by 'citizen journalism'?
11. What is 'user-controlled journalism'?

DEBATE

1. The popularity of social networking sites is an indication that people are becoming less concerned with matters of privacy and more inclined towards voyeurism.
2. Journalists should be cautious in using sources from unregulated institutions (such as the internet) as it encourages the practice of careless distribution of incorrect information.

REFERENCES

Campbell, Richard 2002, *Media and Culture*, Bedford/St Martin's Boston, US.

Carver, Tom 2000, Internet Shaping Journalism at http://news.bbc.co.uk/2/hi/in_depth/americas/2000/us_elections/election_challenge/996852.stm (accessed on 10 August 2008).

Grossman, Lev 2006, 'Time Person of the Year You', *Time*.

Hirst, Martin and Roger Patching 2007, *Journalism Ethics: Arguments and Cases*, Oxford University Press, South Melbourne, Australia.

Johnson, Bobby 2007, YouTube Faces $1 Billion Lawsuit for Alleged Breach of Copyright at www.theguardian.co.uk (accessed on 10 August 2008).

Learning Center at http://www.plagiarism.org/ (accessed on 10 August 2008).

Leslie, Z. Larry 2004, *Mass Communication Ethics: Decision Making in Postmodern Culture*, Houghton Mifflin Company, Boston, US.

Retief, Johan 2002, *Media Ethics: An Introduction to Responsible Journalism*, Oxford University Press, Cape Town, South Africa.

Richards, Ian 2006, *Exploring Journalism Ethics: Quagmires and Quandaries*, Anmol Publications Pvt. Ltd, New Delhi, India.

Vedder, Anton 2001, Misinformation through the Internet at http://www.ccsr.cse.dmu.ac.uk/conferences/ccsrconf/ ethicomp2001/abstracts/vedder.html (accessed on 10 August 2008).

APPENDIX 9.1

Wikipedia: Liberating Human Knowledge?

The free online encyclopaedia, Wikipedia, is arguably one of the most unique contributions of the internet. The site, www.wikipedia.org, allows anyone to edit its articles through the simple click of a button. An article entitled 'The Wiki principle: Are many minds better than a few?' published in the London-based *Economist* (20 April 2006) as part of a series of stories on the internet, highlighted the case of a peculiar prank by one Brian Chase, a prank that earned Wikipedia many sceptics. Chase, an 'unremarkable' middle-level executive in a Tennessee (US) courier firm, decided 'for some reason known only to himself' to post a hoax entry on Wikipedia. Chase's subject was John Seigenthaler, a distinguished journalist and former editor of the *Tennessean* who was, for a while, assistant to the then US Attorney-General, Robert Kennedy. Chase, however, 'fabricated an entirely different life for Seigenthaler, one that had him living in the Soviet Union, founding a public-relations firm and, most perniciously, suggested that he was implicated in the assassinations of both John and Robert Kennedy.'

According to *The Economist* article, normally such vandalism 'is corrected within minutes on Wikipedia because other people see it, remove it and improve the entry with their own genuine insight—which, in a nutshell, is the philosophy and power of collaborative intelligence'. 'This particular item, however, fell through the cracks. For 132 days, the libellous lies went unnoticed and remained on the site. Eventually, some volunteer sleuths traced the vandalism to Chase, who finally came clean. . . and apologized profusely to an impressively gracious Seigenthaler. With that, the episode became a scholarly footnote in media history.'

Seigenthaler subsequently summarized the promise and peril of the latest media revolution in the *USA Today:* 'And so we live in a universe of new media with phenomenal opportunities for worldwide communications and research—but populated by volunteer vandals with poison-pen intellects.'

Poison pens or phenomenal opportunities: what ought to be the frame of reference for new media? According to *The Economist*, 'Wikipedia's promise is nothing less than the liberation of human knowledge—both by incorporating all of it through the collaborative process, and by freely sharing it with everybody who has access to the internet. This is a radically popular idea. Wikipedia's English-language version doubled in size last year and now has over one million articles. By this measure, it is almost 12 times larger than the print version of the *Encyclopaedia Britannica*. Taking in the other 200-odd languages in which it is published, Wikipedia has more than three million articles. Over 100,000 people all over the world have contributed, with a total of almost four million "edits" between them. Wikipedia already has more "visitors" than the online *New York Times*, CNN and other mainstream sites. It has become a vital research tool for huge numbers of people. And Wikipedia is only five years old.'

The Economist argued that its success has made Wikipedia the most famous example of a wider 'wiki' (derived from the Hawaiian word meaning 'quick' but also 'what I know is') phenomenon. 'Wikis' are web pages on the internet that allow anybody who logs on, to change them, making them the 'purest form of participatory creativity and intellectual sharing'. According to David Weinberger who is writing a book on collaborative intelligence, Wikipedia represents 'a socialization of expertise'. All these make wikis perfect complements to blogs. 'Whereas blogs contain the unedited, opinionated voice of one person, wikis explicitly and literally allow groups of people to get on the proverbial "same page" rendering them good at summarizing debates, but ill-suited for biased opinion,' *The Economist* article stated.

Curiously, the article added: 'Wikipedia's numbers makes it an anomaly among wikis. Joe Kraus, co-founder of wiki software-provider JotSpot, feels that wikis are designed for small, well-defined groups of people who might, for instance, use them to collaborate on presentations or project calendars. Wikis are communities, and "communities require trust," says Kraus, and since trust is highest when people know one another and are consequent for their contributions, the optimal group size would be under 150 members.'

Does that make Wikipedia too large for its contributors to trust each other? A common assumption, expressed most cuttingly by Robert McHenry, a former editor-in-chief of the *Encyclopaedia Britannica*, is that Wikipedians trust in 'some unspecified quasi-Darwinian' process, whereby accuracy 'evolves' as more and more 'eyeballs' examine an item: a 'faith-based encyclopaedia' premised on 'the moist and modish notion of community and some vague notions about information wanting to be free'.

Jimmy Wales, who founded the (not for profit) Wikimedia Foundation that operates Wikipedia, as well as lesser-known sites such as Wiktionary, Wikinews and Wikibooks, says that such quasi-Darwinian logic is 'not the way we talk about ourselves within the community'. Instead, says Wales, the process 'is much more traditional than people realize'. Fewer than 1 per cent of all users do half the total edits, adding up to a few hundred committed volunteers like himself, 'a real community of people who know each other' and value their reputations. Besides fostering 'democracy' on the site, he says, there is occasional 'aristocracy' (when editors with superior reputations get more say than others) and even occasional 'monarchy' ('that's my role') in cases such as the Seigenthaler biography, when quick intervention is needed.

To put this process to the test, says *The Economist* article, the journal *Nature* recently commissioned a study to compare the accuracy of a sample of articles drawn from Wikipedia and the *Encyclopaedia Britannica* respectively. *Nature's* experts found 162 errors in Wikipedia's articles and 123 errors in *Britannica*'s. Jorge Cauz, *Britannica*'s president, immediately claimed victory because Wikipedia had 'a third more errors'.

'Privately, however, *Britannica*'s editors were shocked to have to concede that their creation contained any errors at all. Total accuracy, after all, is the main selling point for the old media. So Dale Hoiberg, *Britannica*'s editor-in-chief, commissioned his own review of the study and found that "*Nature* did everything wrong that they could possibly have done wrong". Then *Nature* issued a rebuttal. But if it did get it wrong, it is not clear why it would have erred more for *Britannica* than for Wikipedia. Hoiberg put up a brave face claiming that 'our model, although not perfect, is the best'.

The Economist added: 'For a lot of new-media watchers, the most interesting thing about the episode was something entirely different: that *Britannica*, somewhat representative of old media in general, instinctively regards Wikipedia as a threat, whereas Wikipedians are not the least bit tempted to reciprocate. "I'm a big fan of *Britannica*'s work," says Wales, adding that he is not motivated by "disrupting" anybody, and is glad that *Brockhaus*, the biggest encyclopaedia in Germany (where Wikipedia is very popular), appears to be doing better than ever. But why not have a free alternative as well? And why not test the limits of what social collaboration can do? Wales is the first to admit that "there are some inherent limitations", and says they are busy trying to discover what they are.'

'Contrast that with the joyful reaction of Wikipedia's detractors to Brian Chase, the dodgy biographer (whose article was literally one in a million),' *The Economist* article pointed out.

'Somebody who reads Wikipedia is 'rather in the position of a visitor to a public restroom,' it quotes McHenry, *Britannica*'s former editor. 'It may be obviously dirty, so that he knows to exercise great care, or it may seem fairly clean, so that he may be lulled into a false sense of security. What he certainly does not know is who has used the facilities before him.'

In conclusion, *The Economist* wonders whether an individual like McHenry would prefer there to be no public lavatories at all.

APPENDIX 9.2
What Went Wrong with Mediaah!

Pradyuman Maheshwari, who wrote the following first-person account especially for this book, is a Mumbai-based journalist who used to run a blog on the Indian media called Mediaah! that is now defunct.

At the outset, I must confess that Mediaah! happened quite by chance. I was looking at converting my fortnightly media column in a Sunday paper to a media website that I would update daily. I used the blog format more because of the rush to set up the site and the ease of use of the content management tool that weblogs afford, than the intent to set up a blog. However, once on it, I enjoyed the conversational style that the medium affords.

I started Mediaah! in July 2003, upset with a daily (part of a major media group) for taking on a popular TV network over foreign equity of its news channel. The TV channel was growing in prosperity and power and I thought the daily had misused its editorial columns to stifle the channel's rise. More importantly, no one in my business was willing to take on the daily in public on this issue.

Commenting and reporting on events daily on Mediaah! was quite different from the fortnightly column I would do for a weekend newspaper. I started out with five readers and stray commentary on news and the trade. This number peaked to over 9,500 readers with extensive reportage and views on the news media. It was a near-full-time job, though in my second stint (January – March 2005), I also had a day job. [Aside: of my 9,500 subscribers, some 600 were from the media group alone.]

It's unfortunate that despite a country which boasts of an exceedingly independent press, hardly any major mainline national dailies have columns tracking the media. Quite, unlike the West. In fact, even the Indian avatar of a business daily, which boasts of one of the best media columns amongst international newspapers, has shied away from a commentary and restricts itself to just extensive reportage.

In my first stint, I got one legal notice from a leading national daily, which has recently been amicably resolved. It was in the second running that people began taking serious note of the site. Blogs had started gaining in popularity and people were a lot more vocal in their views on the mainstream media.

At first I received a notice from this large media group to purge a report that had some insider information. I complied, and expressed my regret (on the site). Then I received another notice asking me to knock out 19 posts. My sources at the conglomerate told me that if I did not shut up, the legal eagles were set to slap innumerable cases against me from across the land.

I could've dismissed these attempts to muzzle my blog. I could've of course also deleted the 19 posts and stopped writing about the biggie in question, but that would be unfair to myself. I could've also written under an assumed name or twisted the name of the media entity but that would be unfair to readers. There were several people who came out in my support; however, I did not have the financial muscle to fight a biggie. So: my decision was to shut the site, and start it some day with adequate support.

Some mediapersons have said that I singled out the media group. That's not true. I commented on other big players, too, significantly. I don't think it's fair to say that I singled out the group.

What does the Mediaah! episode mean for blogging in India? I think it brought about an awareness that bloggers are taken very seriously, and if they are popular, then they can be subjected to all the legal provisions of publishing as with other media entities.

The basic requirement of a journalist is a lot of personal integrity and a resolve to conduct oneself ethically. I am a firm believer in that. Mediaah! did not accept any advertising from media companies because being a one-person operation, I thought that would influence me. I believe that you must practice what you preach. Given my opposition to paid-for content, I have resolved never to work for this media organization until it stops what I consider this pernicious practice.

The views expressed here are my own and not those of the organization I work for at present or have worked for in the past.

APPENDIX 9.3

How Goa Bloggers Exposed Gullible Journalists

In June–July 2008, a group of bloggers based in Goa called 'Penpricks' successfully pulled off an elaborate hoax on mainstream journalists belonging to a number of reputed Indian newspapers like *The Indian Express, The Telegraph, The Asian Age* and *Deccan Herald* (a detailed account of this hoax is available on penpricks.blogspot.com). The group of bloggers concocted an account of a so-called Nazi German war criminal named Johann Bach who was supposed to be hiding in Goa and had in his possession a valuable grand piano that was built in the eighteenth century. With the help of images and logos obtained from the internet, Penpricks prepared a media release that was followed up by telephone calls to newspaper offices by a person who mimicked a German accent.

In April 1983, the prestigious German news magazine *Stern* had published what were allegedly extracts from diaries maintained by deceased Nazi dictator Adolf Hitler that later turned out to be forged. The so-called diaries had been purchased by the magazine for 10 million German marks. On that occasion, the episode had raised a slew of questions relating to journalistic ethics and had become an international controversy. However, the hoax perpetrated by the group of Goa bloggers generated more mirth than serious discussion even if the episode highlighted how disarmingly simple it is to fool journalists from established publications.

Using anagrams and absurd clues, the bloggers' group cooked up the story of the arrest of the 88-year-old German 'war criminal'. It took on the mass media for highlighting 'every rumour, every sliver of gossip' while reporting the unusual deaths of British teenager Scarlet Keeling in Goa and Aarushi Talwar in Noida. The story was first published in local newspapers from Goa and thereafter picked up by national newspapers. Some newspapers not only published the account without verifying the facts, but even embellished their reports by concocting more 'facts' about an already concocted story. Some reports stated that the German had been 'nabbed after a 36-hour hot chase' and had 'been airlifted to Berlin' although these details did not figure in the original media release.

Writing in the weekly *Outlook* (14 July 2008), Anjali Puri said the national newspapers 'were apparently in no mood for introspection—at least not publicly' even after the report had been exposed as a hoax. In her report, Puri has quoted media critic Sevanti Ninan saying: 'Hats off to Penpricks…They have sometimes been criticized for being biased in their attacks on the media, but this one is delicious and audacious, and does show up the media. Did no one even run a Google check on the names in the press release? How were reporters given bylines for a story they didn't check out?'

CHAPTER

10

ETHICS OF ADVERTISING

Advertising has been, and continues to be, the biggest source of revenue for most media organizations and is thus, an important area of examination in this book. In this chapter, we first identify what advertising is and then consider some of the important processes involved in advertising practices, with special attention on research techniques and media selection. Subsequently, we consider the social implications of advertising. It is observed that advertising both reflects and influences social trends, demonstrating the potency of advertising. This leads us to look at how the audience becomes akin to a commodity and how the media becomes the instrument of advertising. We examine some ethical aspects stipulated in the regulatory codes on advertising and note that there are certain aspects of advertising which cannot be readily regulated. The chapter finally considers the main social issues which pervade the advertising industry and the ethical dilemmas involved therein.

WHAT IS ADVERTISING?

Advertising, like PR, is a commercially motivated persuasion industry that seeks to inculcate positive images of a commodity and promote its consumption. Advertisements are defined by the Advertising Standards Council of India (ASCI) as a 'paid-for communication, addressed to the public... to influence (their) opinions or behaviour'. Advertising, therefore, is different from PR, as its communication must be purchased and the advertiser's identity is overt. Advertisements are not a medium unto themselves but are communicated through a wide range of mass media. So although the media and advertising are separate fields, they are inextricably linked.

Advertising is not a modern phenomenon. There is evidence of commercial engravings on stone walls in ancient Egypt and Rome. Ancient Grecian society used town criers to spread advertising messages, besides social and political ones. Excavation of the remains of the Indus Valley Civilization has revealed seals which were used to mark traded products. This could plausibly have been a method for traders to brand and distinguish their wares from those of their competitors. In England during the fifteenth century handbills were the first form of advertising, although it was not until 1622 that the first printed advertisement appeared in newspapers.

Advertising has often come under the scrutiny of social and political leaders and commentators because of worries that its practices are not always socially responsible or ethical. Gandhi, in his autobiography, *The Story of My Experiments with Truth*, spoke of his disillusionment with advertising and even called it 'undesirable' (Shrivastava 2005). Gandhi disapproved of advertising in news media, understanding its implications on editorial independence.

ADVERTISING PROCESSES

Advertising basically falls into four areas.

1. **Research** This involves surveying and reviewing the desires, behaviour and patterns of consumption of the general public.
2. **Media selection** After research, advertisers have to decide which medium or media should be utilized to communicate their message and the specific form of the advertisement in a particular medium.
3. **Creation** This involves conceptualizing the message into a design format, which includes visuals and/or copy.
4. **Account management** This involves maintaining existing client accounts and expanding the number of clients.

Let us examine some aspects of research and media selection as they are of relevance to the media.

Research

Research is conducted to assess the demographics and the psychographics of heterogeneous social groups. The findings of this research determine the message of an advertisement campaign and the medium/media that can be used to communicate it. Demographics involve the study of society in terms of age, sex, ethnicity, occupation, income and location. Psychographics is the study of behavioural traits, including beliefs, goals, motivations and interests.

The acronym VALS, which stands for 'Values, Attitudes and Lifestyles', is a popular psychographic segmentation that was developed in the US in the 1970s and has thereafter been changed on a number of occasions to explain and predict consumer behaviour. (As of now, research based on VALS is a proprietary product of SRI Consulting Business Intelligence.) As per this methodology, people are grouped according to various criteria such as the extent to which they are innovative and self-confident, besides their levels of income, education and intelligence. Individuals are slotted in categories depending on whether they are driven by knowledge, principles and ideals, whether they are primarily motivated by a desire to achieve or a desire for social or physical activity and so on.

The VALS framework divides consumers into the following eight categories.

Innovators These are the consumers with the highest incomes, high self-esteem and many resources. Hence, they are considered as the leaders of change. Their idea of image revolves around taste, independence and character. They are the consumers of the 'finer things in life'.

Thinkers This category has educated professionals who are mature and responsible. They are a high-resource group motivated by ideals. Their leisure activities are centred on their homes, but they are aware of the happenings in the world. Though they have high incomes, they are practical consumers who are open to new ideas and social change.

Believers The consumers of this category are a low-resource group with modest incomes. They are motivated by ideals and are conservative and predictable. They favour American products and established brands and their lives are centred on family, church, community and the nation.

Achievers This is a high-resource group that is motivated by achievement. They are successful, work-oriented people who are politically conservative and respect authority and the status quo. They favour established products and services.

Strivers This is a low-resource group that is also motivated by achievement. However, they have fewer economic, social and psychological resources. Style is extremely important to this group and they try to emulate people they admire.

Experiencers The youngest of all segments, the consumers of this category are a high-resource group. The median age of this group is 25 and they are motivated by self-expression. They spend more on clothing, fast foods, music and particularly on new products and services. They indulge in physical exercise and social activities.

Makers This is a low-resource group motivated by self-expression. They are practical people focused on family, work and physical recreation. They have very little interest in the happenings of the world. They favour practical and functional products.

Survivors The oldest of all segments, this category has the lowest incomes. The median age of this segment is 61 and their resources are few. Hence, they are generally not considered as a target segment. They are consumers who are brand-loyal.

In-depth research provides advertisers with valuable targeting devices, which aim at maximizing an advertisement's efficiency. However, some advertisers focus more on appealing to the subtler motivations and attitudes of consumers and in the process do not provide information about a product like its prices, varieties, material/ingredients, and addresses and phone numbers of sellers and stockists.

Media Selection

This section looks at the advantages and disadvantages of different mass media as vehicles of advertising.

Press

The earliest advertising agencies in the nineteenth century in the US established themselves as a point of contact for both newspapers and their prospective advertisers. This allowed the editor to concentrate on sourcing stories, rather than chasing clients and ensured that a product would be advertised in a variety of newspapers. Palmer Volney is considered to be the first advertisement broker; in 1841, he took on the task of relieving newspapers of their burden of locating and servicing advertisers. In 1869, the first modern advertising agency, N.W. Ayer & Son, was founded; the agency was the first of its kind dedicated to servicing advertisers or clients rather than the publisher.

Newspapers and magazines are still a popular medium for advertising. As a means of communicating advertisements, the print media offers the following qualities.

Durability Print advertisements can be stored and referred to when required. It is also a preferable medium for issuing coupons to attract potential customers.

Tangibility Printed paper can be felt, which means readers experience advertising through the sense of touch as well as sight.

Activity Reading magazines or newspapers involves a more active engagement with the medium than listening to the radio or watching television. This suggests a more dynamic and active frame of mind and mood.

Intimacy Reading newspapers or magazines is a solitary exercise and therefore entails a direct and more personal relationship with the reader and the medium (see Box 10.1: Haagen-Dazs Campaign).

Low cost Advertising in print tends to be less expensive than advertising on radio or television, both in terms of purchase from the medium and production.

Niche target reach Many magazines and newspapers are specialized and thus, appeal directly to certain interest groups. There are, for example, magazines for women and magazines for gardening. This means that a specific audience is clearly predefined and minimizes wastage when it comes to targeting segments.

Mobility A newspaper or magazine can be conveniently carried and since publications are inexpensive, they are left behind in public places, on trains, for example, to be read by other passengers thereby enhancing circulation.

The print medium activates a person's imagination more than other forms of mass media. For example, when we are reading about a character or a description of a place in printed black text on white paper, in our mind's eye we conjure bright, colourful and fantastic images. This is one reason why we sometimes react indifferently or negatively to a film version of a novel.

The print medium is heavily dependent on advertising both for content and for revenue. According to one estimate quoted in Campbell (2002), approximately 65 per cent of newspaper content and half the content of magazines in the US comprised advertisements and constituted three-fourths and half, respectively, of revenue. These figures illustrate just how integral advertising is to the press. Given the centrality of advertising to the media industry, Campbell states: 'without consumer advertising, mass communication industries would cease to function in their present form'. In many large media organizations in India, advertising revenue accounts for 80–90 per cent of the total revenues of the organization. Many publications are distributed free or are priced very low. Hence, a newspaper is different from other products as its cost of production and its consumer price is hardly linked since its advertising income determines its viability and profitability. In other words, it can be contended that advertising is the dynamism that allows for the very functioning of the mass media.

Box 10.1

Haagen-Dazs Campaign

Haagen-Dazs, a brand of ice cream, decided to develop its brand identity in the UK by promoting an image of luxury, seeking to establish itself as a world leader of the finest ice cream. Through market research, the advertising agency in charge of the campaign, Bartle Bogle Hegarty (BBH), found that traditionally, ice cream advertising centred on family life and shared enjoyment. To differentiate Haagen-Dazs as a new brand, BBH's campaign centred on the enjoyment of Haagen-Dazs in sensual terms; something to be savoured in private without interruption. The print media was considered to be the most effective for the campaign, because it offered tangibility, intimacy and durability. These qualities were identified as complementary to the message of sensuality, prolonged and leisurely indulgence and an intimate and private experience. The advertisement that was released in magazines and weekend newspapers showed a man and a woman enjoying privacy and intimacy with a tub of Haagen-Dazs. The campaign was hugely successful and Haagen-Dazs was pronounced the 'New Product of the Year' by the Marketing Society.

Radio

With radio, a new form of advertising was introduced. Radio, like the town crier, 'spoke' to its audience and therefore utilized the sense of hearing. Radio programmes run in a linear, scheduled fashion, which means that, unlike the print media, the time at which the content is received is determined by the media, not by the audience. This characteristic of the radio was perceived as a way to guarantee audience attention to advertisements, which could be wilfully overlooked in newspapers. Thus, in 1926 in the US, commercial radio became the operational norm for that medium. Radio offers the following qualities as a means of advertising communication:

Mobility Radios are portable devices and can be used around the world in all kinds of situations; radio is associated with travel and is particularly effective for advertisers during commute times.

Captivity Radio captures the listener's attention particularly during active travel.

Vocal The vocal or aural nature of radio lends itself to jingles and music which is often considered an effective way to appeal to an audience.

Most privately owned radio stations are heavily dependent on advertisements for their revenue. In the US as well as in other countries, commercial radio stations typically obtain all their revenues from advertising. Advertising content comprises a quarter of total radio content in the US.

Television

The popularity of television and the volume and breadth of its audiences creates the impression that it is the most widely used advertising tool. In fact, in the US, only 22 per cent of every dollar of advertising budget is spent on television advertisements. According to surveys, in 2000, every hour of prime time television in the US contained 16 minutes and 43 seconds of advertising.

Television operates on a linear schedule like radio. Television utilizes two key senses of its audience simultaneously: sight and hearing. This means that watching television is an exclusive activity unlike listening to the radio as it is difficult to do other things while watching television. Radio and television are generally not considered to be in competition with each other, as their consumption levels are optimum at different times of any given day. For example, we can listen to the radio in a car on the way to or from work. Unlike television and newspapers, the audience does not have to give their undivided attention while listening to the radio. Television viewing is considered preferential because its exclusivity makes it a passive activity. As far as news coverage is concerned, the advantage television has over other mass media (especially print and to a lesser extent radio and the internet) is that it is able to provide audio-visual live coverage of news as it is happening. The exclusivity of television and the fact that it is amenable to passive consumption means that it is essentially a captive medium. However, hand-held remote controls have made 'channel-surfing' a convenient way to opt out of viewing advertisements. This can be countered to a certain extent by running commercial breaks at the same time as other channels.

Television as a medium of advertising offers the following qualities:

Captivity Audiences are in a passive frame of mind and are easily captivated.

Exclusivity The use of two senses which means that audiences are not distracted.

Dual-sensory impacted As more senses are utilized, the impact of the sensory data is higher.

Wide reach Television tends to draw high audience levels and can be broadcast nationally and across international borders.

Motion Television is not static and the motion that it affords is utilized to make advertisements into mini stories which could lead to greater audience interest.

Niche targets Television programmes cater to a variety of different interests, both mainstream and specialist. Given the plethora of television channels, niche programmes are directed at specific audiences and it is easy to tune in to the interests of these groups—for example, programmes on sports, news, animation, hobbies, history and drama all appeal to different groups of people.

Choose two advertising campaigns on television and print and analyse these by answering the following questions. Which section/ sections of the population comprise the main target audience for each advertisement? Do you think the advertisements have been well placed? What are some of the techniques used to gain attention? Do the advertisements manage to convey their messages?

ADVERTISING REFLECTING SOCIETY

Advertising developed with the rise of industry and social mobility. As more products were manufactured, the need to advertise a particular brand or commodity increased. With mass production and the achievement of economies of scale, production costs came down, which allowed for greater expenditure on advertising. Mobility, or the capacity to travel, meant that commodities could reach consumers across a wider geographical area. The mobility of society is ever increasing, perhaps more so with the advent of the internet, which has led to the phenomenon of what Toronto-based communications theorist Marshal McLuhan first called the 'global village'. As early as 1964, McLuhan had written: 'Today, after more than a century of electric technology, we have extended our central nervous system itself in a global embrace, abolishing both space and time as far as our planet is concerned' (McLuhan and Lapham 1964).

The 'global village' is at present a technical reality. An e-mail message takes seconds to travel from one corner of the world to another. McLuhan, who was considered by many to be the 'oracle of the electronic age', titled one of his best-known books *The Medium is the Massage* (McLuhan and Fiore 1967). McLuhan probably believed that the media massages us or was punning on the construction of the word 'mass-age'.

Globalization has led to significant social changes. Commercialism has played an important role in the globalization process. The generation of disposable income has given rise to an increased propensity to spend money and the consumption of luxury products. In India, the growth of the economy has made the country's upper classes and a section of the 'upwardly mobile' middle classes voracious consumers whom advertisers are exploiting.

Advertising, seeking to communicate a commercial message, has had to address various social issues like gender, race equality, health and the environment. The ways in which advertising has changed its approach to some of these issues over the years is testimony to the changing social values. In this sense, advertising has had to be careful and sensitive to social values and behavioural patterns which differ not only through generations, but also across cultures.

Advertising codes regulating content have throughout the world reflected the culture of the particular place in which the commodity is sold or service provided. There are certain common features of such codes that have transcended time and space. It is worth going back to the first code of ethics that was devised by the American Association of Advertising Agencies in 1924. Member agencies pledged not to knowingly produce advertising that contained

- false or misleading statements or exaggerations, visual or verbal
- testimonials that do not reflect the real choice of a competent witness
- price claims that were misleading
- comparisons that unfairly disparaged a competing product or service
- unsupported claim/claims that distorted the true meaning of statements made by professional and scientific authorities
- statements, suggestions or pictures offensive to public decency

While notions of 'public decency' vary across countries and regions and also change over time, the substance of the ethical code outlined continues to remain relevant. It is not uncommon at present to find advertisements where actors convey the impression that they are professionals.

Which of the points in the code of the American Association of Advertising Agencies would a toothpaste advertisement today violate and why?

Advertisers recognize that what will be successful and appropriate in one country may not necessarily be the same in another. A one-size-fits-all approach to campaigning does not reflect the multiplicity and heterogeneity of different societies and cultures. Thus, a multinational brand will advertise the same product through different campaigns in different countries. However, cross-cultural media like the internet means that advertising can reach all over the world, regardless of varying social values. This poses a potential problem for regulation, as regulations are country specific.

Stereotyping is a regular feature of advertisements. We shall consider social issues in advertising later in the chapter where we observe that people belonging to different ethnic and religious groups are sometimes subject to stereotyping. Although, humanity is heterogeneous, it is frequently homogenized in advertising. This occurs due to logistical factors such as cost, time and reach. Multitudinous social attitudes have to be pared down to a few general trends; it is simply not feasible to appeal to every variant or combination of attitudes. Stereotyping presents an awkward stumbling block in advertising: on the one hand it is almost unavoidable, and on the other hand, it is easily detectable and often considered patronizing and offensive by those at the receiving end. This dilemma is sometimes remedied to a certain degree by the principle of reverse stereotyping. In India, some characters in advertisements now are depicted as free-thinking, independent individuals. These advertisements seek to highlight the value of individualism in a society that has traditionally emphasized the virtues of loyalty to a family and an organization.

SOCIETY REFLECTING ADVERTISING

Today, extensive and sophisticated market research techniques are employed to gauge the moods and motivations of a consumerist society. On the strength of this research, advertisements are designed to reflect social trends in order to appeal to consumers. If the imitation or representation of life is the cause of advertising, the effect is life imitating advertising. This scenario is an extension of the perennial debate over whether art imitates life, or life imitates art. In the case of advertising, however, the two are not mutually exclusive predicaments. Advertisements are representations of real life, which tend to beautify or simplify rather than present real life with its 'warts and all'. One of the reasons for this is the limited space and time advertisements enjoy to arrest '...the human intelligence just long enough to get money from it' (Bagdikian 2000). Hence, in advertising, temporal and spatial restrictions inevitably result in the simplification and beautification of life to create an immediate impact. The representation of life in advertising through distortion of reality can be understood as a facet of the postmodernist concepts of hyper-reality and fictitiousness.

Italian philosopher and novelist Umberto Eco coined the notion of 'absolute fakes' in his book *Travels in Hyper-reality*. Eco notes that in consumerist 'Disney' America, representations of life proliferate. These 'fakes', be it Disneyland or Las Vegas, are not merely representations of reality but are 'improved' and transformed versions of reality. These versions of reality are 'absolute' because these are no longer imitations of life but are entirely fake to the point where these are only representations of falseness. The effects of hyper-reality are summed up by Eco's anecdote: in Disneyland we can take a boat down a fake river and be diverted by fake alligators. A boat trip down the Mississippi, however, did not result in encounters with alligators and Eco caught himself feeling nostalgic for the pseudo-reality of Disneyland.

Advertising, in beautifying reality, possesses the potency to evoke in consumers disappointment in ordinary life and the desire for something better than what is real. The slogans of advertising campaigns in India reinforce this model: Coca-Cola's '*Life Ho To Aisi*' (life should be like this), and Pepsi's '*Yeh Dil Maange More*' (the heart wants more) are two such examples. This effect of advertising has brought about formulaic trends in advertising.

A myth analysis of advertisements reveals the pattern of using 'narratives with stories to tell and social conflicts to resolve' (Campbell 2002). Typically, an advertisement will involve conflicts—of social values, domestic chores, work duties—which are invariably resolved by access to the commodity/product advertised. Advertising intends to create in consumers the desire and capacity to resolve life's problems, perhaps even those we never knew we had. Leslie (2004) comments that sex and fear are the two potent aspects of advertising that are frequently employed to motivate consumers. Sex and fear are universal emotions and advertisements use these elements to widen the gulf between advertisements and real life.

Media as Instruments

Given the power of advertising to influence consumer behaviour, exposure to audiences (or potential consumers) becomes an integral part of marketing strategies. The media is thus a vital tool for communicating the messages (advertisements) to an audience. Thus, the audience is often understood as the commodity that the media sells to advertisers. This has important ethical implications. In order to make a product attractive to the audience, the media will strive to deliver content that is likely to enhance a sense of need or indulgence. For example, advertisements for fine foods will not be juxtaposed with programmes on poverty and famine.

As advertisers are a vital source of revenue, there is a fear that the media will become the instrument of advertisers. Some media barons in India and elsewhere, who are heads of organizations that disseminate information, also lead corporate conglomerates that bring consumers to advertisers. Thus, the mission of journalism that is meant to be in the public interest becomes subservient to commercial considerations of profit maximization. Inevitably, therefore, some content editors play second fiddle to the marketing bosses of media organizations.

Advertising Ethics: General Codes

Most countries have strict laws and guidelines about what can or cannot be advertised. In many countries, the content of advertisements is not generally governed by a statute but by self-regulatory bodies. The ASCI has a motto: 'Regulate yourself, or somebody else will.' Many agencies prefer self-regulation to external regulations because it allows for autonomy and carries greater credibility. The ASCI code was formulated to 'achieve the acceptance of fair advertising practices in the best interests of the ultimate consumer'. The body, which issues the codes, is also responsible for handling complaints, endorsing the code and ensuring that advertising practices are compatible with public interest.

The ASCI regulates in the following four majors areas:

Honesty All factually ascertainable statements like graphs, statistics, scientific explanations and comparisons must have substantiating proof; it is not permissible to undermine the reputation or damage the business endeavours of rival companies by unfair and unjust comparisons; advertisements are not permitted to distort facts, to mislead consumers intentionally through implication or omissions; advertisements must not abuse the consumer's trust through exploiting ignorance or inexperience.

Decency It is impermissible to use material which is deemed vulgar, indecent or repulsive in light of generally accepted principles and is likely to cause widespread and grave offence.

Social safeguarding Advertisements will not be permitted if they are likely to incite violence, hatred or intolerance; deride race, caste or religion; present criminality as desirable; adversely affect relations with foreign states; exploit the vulnerability of minors; promote brazen disregard for safety; breach the law; promote the use of products which are illegal.

Fairness of competition Comparisons to other products must make clear the particular feature which is being compared; be factual, accurate and capable of substantiation; not mislead the consumer; not unfairly undermine or discredit other products. Advertisements shall not appropriate the name or logo of another firm without consent; they must not be similar to previous campaigns of other advertisers.

Caveat Emptor

Caveat emptor, or 'let the buyer beware', is a concept which implies that the consumer is ultimately responsible for safeguarding her/his own rights. According to the caveat emptor concept, advertisers are not bound by ethical practices—particularly those pertaining to honesty and social responsibility. Professor Gunnar Trumbull of the Harvard Business School says that this term has now become redundant in Western countries due to stricter consumer protection rules. He suggests that no other economic player—the worker, investor, PR manager—is as well protected as the consumer. Journalist and consumer rights activist Sucheta Dalal, however, feels that the caveat emptor imperative is 'still alive and kicking in India' and that greater consumer protection is achieved through the activities of consumer rights activists, who, in India, lack resources to conduct compelling comparative product research.

Caveat emptor, though not generally credited as a wholesome principle of commerce, might yet be applicable to certain areas of advertising which cannot be regulated by codes of conduct or law. Stereotyping that does not cause 'grave and widespread offence' but still offends individual sensibilities, might fall under this principle. Stereotyping and forms of mockery might appeal to certain sections of society but could aggrieve others. The Advertising Standards Authority (ASA), the independent regulator for advertisements, sales promotion and direct marketing in the UK, states that the grievances of a few are not necessarily grounds for censorship or withdrawal.

Another area which cannot be regulated is the pseudo-reality or 'absolute fakes' in advertising. Although advertisements are sometimes accused of bearing no resemblance to reality, such complaints are so general and unspecific that they are unlikely to cause grave offence, and cannot plausibly be said to transgress the principle of honesty prescribed in the codes. In such cases, caveat emptor might generally be applicable.

Freedom of Speech

As already explained in Chapter 7 on Media Laws, freedom of speech is not an absolute right but is subject to conditioning factors. The same conditions and restrictions apply to advertising, both in the law and the regulatory codes. However, freedom of speech is still a pertinent and accepted argument in certain controversial advertisements. Audacious humour is often the subject of contention. However, all expression is permitted as long as it does not deride or defame particular social interests—religion, ethnicity, state—or is likely to cause violence or intolerance. Freedom of speech in advertising is necessary to communicate diverse opinions, which is arguably a fundamental aspect of democracy and is therefore an exercise in social responsibility.

On 27 July 2007, the I&B Ministry banned advertisements of two underwear brands (Lux Cozy and Amul Macho) on the ground that these were 'indecent, vulgar and suggestive'. In its order, the ministry said that the advertisements violated Rule 7 (8) of the government's Advertising Code. The Amul Macho advertisement showed a newly-wed woman suggestively washing her husband's innerwear. Earlier that year, in April, the ministry had advised television channels to be 'more careful' in the selection of advertisements and strictly adhere to the code. The ministry stated that the ban had been imposed because the advertisements were broadcast in spite of the code. The self-regulatory ASCI had not placed restrictions on these advertisements although many complaints had been made against these advertisements, the ministry pointed out.

ADVERTISING AND SOCIAL ISSUES

The causes and effects of advertising show that they are inextricably linked to key social issues. The issues which often contain important ethical dimensions are gender, ethnicity, health and environment.

Women

Across the globe, many advertisements in the past frequently depicted women as home-bound, helpless and brainless. Commodities like cleaning products, domestic appliances and food products were aimed at housewives and shown as capable of providing satisfaction and delight to consumers. Feminists objected to the stereotypical portrayal of women as happy home-makers who were less competent than men. The activities of feminist groups created awareness among the public and gender equality became a significant social issue.

Advertising, in seeking to reflect social trends, had to adapt to the changing environment. Feminists tried to demonstrate that women were independent, capable, intelligent and free-thinking individuals. However, despite these changes in social attitudes, there is still considerable evidence of gender stereotyping in advertising. Writer John Camm feels that being subjected to stereotyping is tiresome, as the stereotypes characteristically bear little resemblance to real life people and laments 'the absolute reliance of advertising on its own regurgitated cliches'. He comments that there are several cliches which have become advertising norms. For example, 'women are locked in a constant battle with their weight/body shape/hairstyle....have jobs they never do in real life (like dock work)... chocolate will cause women to immediately fall into the languor of the opium eater'.

These cliches are all too familiar. However, some would identify a more sinister motive that underlies these cliches: to create problematic scenarios which pertain to all aspects of life, in order to present the advertised commodity as the solution. Leslie (2004) comments that advertisements in women's magazines help 'perpetuate readers' sense of themselves as defective and in need of improvement'.

In Indian advertising today, strands of gender prejudices are still apparent. Dowry, fairness and beauty, for example, are still the subject of some advertising campaigns. For instance, the advertisements of the Fair & Lovely cosmetic cream, manufactured by Hindustan Unilever, have attracted criticism from social activists for indirectly promoting racism as they seem to encourage users to believe in the desirability of fair skin. The manufacturer, of course, argues that the cream is nothing but an 'aspirational product'.

There are fears that exploiting these sensitive subject matters will only help compound them and propagate their prevalence in society. Such advertisements can be revoked if they are deemed to be offensive (socially prejudiced) or deride certain social groups. However, while stereotyping can be offensive to individual sensibilities, it is a difficult thing to regulate. The ASA of the UK and the ASCI contend that advertisements transgress norms of decency only if they cause 'serious and widespread offence'. The example given in Box 10.2 (The ING Vysya Ad) highlights the fact that both the media and the advertising industries are responsible for delivering socially responsible and acceptable messages. While the advertising industry must adhere to its own code in producing its messages, the media must be responsible for approving the content.

Box 10.2

The ING Vysya Ad

In March 2008, the Government of India ordered an advertisement for ING Vysya Life Insurance to be withdrawn and asked the ASCI to take action against the company for producing the advertisement. The advertisement showed a girl with the caption '*hai to pyaari lekin bojh hai bhari*' (although she is lovable, she is still a burden) and then demonstrated that insuring the 'burdensome' daughter would help alleviate the problem. The National Commission for Protection of Child Rights (NCPCR) claimed that the advertisement was 'totally unethical' and fears were expressed that the advertisement would encourage oppression of women and might even contribute to female foeticide. The advertisement had to be withdrawn by all television channels as they are not permitted to air advertisements that do not conform to the standards of the prescribed advertising code (Cable Network Regulation Act, II. 6). The NCPCR also pointed out that the television channels have a duty to censor the content of advertisements before they are aired.

The advertising industry has continuously demonstrated that it is enamoured of the notion that sex sells. Sex has been linked to all commodities including household appliances, soft drinks and food. Most commonly, sexual imagery is used in advertisements for alcohol, cars, perfumes and clothing. Sex in advertising includes nudity (partial or full) that is obvious as well as sexual innuendoes. One explanation for this is that the acquisition of assets—money, power, property and prestige—has, throughout the history of mankind, been a method of flaunting male virility. The capacity to acquire many assets is intended to imply this quality. Therefore, associating a certain product with sex, appeals to one of the most basic principles that govern the behaviour of humanity, namely, survival.

Opinions about sexually explicit advertisements are divided. There are some who believe that nudity and other gratuitous allusions to sex are obscene. There are others who feel that sex sells and, sometimes, sells rather well. The ASA warns that a sensitive issue like sex should be handled carefully to avoid causing offence. Media codes also warn against obscene content, but as we have seen, the precise nature of obscenity is often difficult to define.

Men

Stereotypical male characters and male-dominated ideologies are also present in advertising. Although male stereotypes are not generally oppressive towards men, they can still have a serious and tangible impact on society as a whole. Stereotyping portrays men as being impressed by macho behaviour, inclined to emulate strong hero types, and often, lazy. Men's interests are stereotypically women, beer, gadgets and sports. In India, there is a tendency to glamorize commodities aimed at men—cars, motorcycles, soft drinks, mobile phones, music and liquor—by associating the product with sporting activities, stunts and sexual innuendoes. An advertisement for Thums Up depicted a man bungee-jumping off a bridge into a river to catch a bottle of the fizzy drink. It was reported that a person was killed while emulating the stunt though it is not confirmed if the person had been influenced by the advertisement. In a Pepsi advertisement, a popular actor drives recklessly through narrow streets, trying to save a bottle of the soft drink but ends up in a hospital after crashing into a wall.

The ASCI deems it inappropriate for advertisements to show dangerous, cavalier driving in a gratuitous manner. Advertisements which feature dangerous sports or professional stunts are required to carry clear warnings. When such advertisements are broadcast on television or on the large screen, a disclaimer is usually placed at the end stating that professional actors and stuntmen feature in the advertisements and that their actions should not be copied. These words are, however, flashed across the screen rather quickly, barely giving the viewer time to read what has been written.

While in the past, women were sexually objectified in advertising, in recent times, men are also being increasingly depicted as sex objects. According to a survey conducted in 2002 by the University of Wisconsin, men felt insecure and suffered low self-esteem about their appearance as a consequence of such advertising campaigns.

Race and Ethnicity

Racial groups have been subjected to stereotyping in two ways in advertising: visibly and invisibly. In countries with strong ethnic diversity like India and the US, there has been an unfortunate tendency to associate ethnic groups with certain behavioural patterns. The ASCI does not allow material which derides race, caste, religion, language, ethnic or regional affiliation and nationality. Although not all racial stereotyping is derogatory, race is still a very sensitive issue and the fact that ethnic groups should at all be stereotyped is seen as a bar to full social integration. Social segregation can lead, in extreme cases, to communal hatred and/or violence. Any material that is likely to result in hatred and/or violence, or promotes intolerance is not permitted by the ASCI.

In invisible stereotyping, certain ethnic groups are underrepresented in advertising and this indirectly results in social segregation. Invisible stereotyping in advertising in ethnically diverse societies might be tantamount to false representation. Invisible stereotyping can perhaps be explained by the fact that ethnic or caste minority groups are often the underprivileged sections of society. Ethnic minorities are often undereducated, low-income groups. These demographic characteristics mean that the ethnic minorities are less likely to be targeted by consumerist advertisements which want to attract people who have high disposable incomes. Invisible stereotyping is an awkward area for advertising codes. It is possible to restrict and regulate the content of advertisements to guard against prejudice, offence and social segregation, but it is very difficult, and impracticable, to regulate non-content.

Health

Some of the earliest advertisements which appeared in newspapers were for medicines and remedies which made unlikely claims about relieving any manner of symptoms or complaints. The nature of these early 'quack' advertisements caused a certain cynicism among consumers and led to the passing of the Food and Drug Act, 1906 in the US to regulate the claims of producers of medicines. In 1924, the American Association of Advertising Agencies formulated a code of ethics, the first principle of which eschewed the use of false or misleading statements or exaggerations, either verbal or visual. In India, a special law was enacted to control advertisements of medicines—the Drugs and Magic Remedies (Objectionable Advertisements) Act, 1954. Advertising codes today place great emphasis on the need for honesty in advertising, which is also reflected in the provisions of the ASCI.

The need for truthfulness in the media has been considered and explained in some depth. It should be remembered that less-than-truthful advertisements not only damage the credibility of the brand, but also that of the medium through which it is communicated. The media has a responsibility to ensure the honesty of its content and this extends to advertisements as well.

Health issues are a major concern of consumer rights groups. There are several aspects of advertising which have come under scrutiny for health reasons. The health implications of the commodity advertised, such as alcohol, cigarettes and junk food, and also the content or message of the advertisements have been criticized from time to time.

Drinking

Campbell (2002) notes that the compelling statistics which demonstrate unequivocally the dangers of alcohol and tobacco consumption have made health campaigners more vocal. As many as 100,000 Americans die each year from alcohol-related causes and a further 15,000 die from drunk-driving incidents. The figures for India and China—the two most populous countries accounting for roughly 40 per cent of the world's population—are higher and could be proportionately comparable to those for the US (which accounts for less than 5 per cent of the planet's population).

There is a debate about whether alcohol advertising actually promotes and increases consumption of alcohol. There are concerns that young people are particularly influenced by advertising and are often the target of alcohol advertisements. Countries, such as the UK, which have high rates of alcohol-related deaths and alcohol consumption among young people, have codes which regulate the content of alcohol advertisements. Advertisements showing drinking as the ladder to sexual/social success are deemed highly inappropriate. Some feel that these restrictions are insufficient and restrictions on advertising alcohol at particular times should be imposed. Advertisers, however, claim that advertising is an essential function of a competitive market and that its purpose is to aid the battle between rival brands and not to increase overall consumption.

Even as alcohol advertising continues, one of the ways in which its influence can be tempered is through counter-advertisements. An advertising campaign for the prevention of drunk-driving can demonstrate the potentially fatal consequences of irresponsible drinking. It is plausible that such advertisements might have equal influence as alcohol advertisements if they were equal in volume. However, research conducted by the University of Bath, UK, suggests that counter-advertisements might be 'catastrophically misconceived' and may actually encourage consumption because alcohol-related exploits are seen as a mark of the social identity of young people.

In India, liquor advertisements are banned. However, advertisers have got around this restriction by 'surrogate' advertisements. Surrogate liquor advertising typically involves displaying a brand which is most associated with alcohol in a party/night-time environment. At the end of the advertisement, usually in small text, products like 'packaged drinking water' or 'cassettes and CDs' or even 'playing cards' are mentioned. This thinly veiled brand-building for liquor has recently been questioned by the Indian government. In March 2008, the I&B Ministry warned that surrogate advertisements would soon be banned and stricter monitoring of such advertisements would be implemented.

Tobacco

The dangers of smoking are well known. In India, it is estimated that 700,000 people die of smoking-related diseases every year. Tobacco advertisements have faced tighter restrictions over the last thirty years and in several countries all forms of tobacco advertising have been banned. The European Union banned tobacco advertising on television in the 1990s and in 2003, a ban was placed on tobacco advertising via all print media, radio and the internet. In the UK, the Tobacco Advertising and Promotion Act, 2002 put an end to all forms of public marketing, including advertising, promotions and sponsoring by cigarette and tobacco companies. The act makes it an offence to produce or publish public advertisements for British citizens. However, it is not an offence for a business that is not operational in the UK to advertise tobacco products on websites which can be accessed from the UK. The internet is a means to overcome bans in specific countries: a country's law only extends to its citizenry and activities which take place within its bounds. In an ironical tragedy, the actor who played the iconographic Marlboro Man—a rugged cowboy used in advertisements for Marlboro cigarettes—David McLean, died from lung cancer (see Box 10.3: Marlboro Man).

Box 10.3

Marlboro Man

In August 1996, Lilo McLean, widow of actor David McLean—known as the 'Marlboro Man'—and their son, Mark Huth, filed a legal suit in a Texas court against cigarette manufacturer Philip Morris, Inc. seeking 'punitive and exemplary damages for wrongful death and personal injuries'. They claimed that on account of David's addiction to smoking, he died at the age of 73 from lung cancer. He had been hired in the early 1960s by Philip Morris and was regularly gifted boxes of cigarettes. David had started smoking when he was only 12 years old and remained addicted to nicotine almost till he died on 12 October 1995. It was not until 1964 that warning labels about the adverse health effects of tobacco were placed on cigarette packages sold in the US as well as on tobacco advertisements. However, these warnings did not mention nicotine addiction. In 1985, David McLean began to suffer from emphysema due to smoking and in 1993, he underwent a surgery to remove a cancerous tumour in his right lung. In 1995, doctors discovered that the cancer had not disappeared and in fact, had spread to his brain and spine. Chemotherapy and other treatments were unsuccessful on him.

Lawyers who represented McLean's family highlighted the way cigarette companies enticed smokers at a young age through macho advertising and then relied on the addictive qualities of nicotine to keep them hooked for life.

In 2004, tobacco advertising and sponsorship was banned in India. However, after the ban was implemented, cigarette branding in Indian films increased threefold. The Burning Brain Society, an anti-smoking non-government organization, conducted a study which found that branded tobacco products occurred in 40 per cent of the films made in India since 2004. The head of the Burning Brain Society commented that 'Indian films are being turned into blatant cigarette commercials'. In 2005, the government considered implementing a blanket ban on all 'placement' strategies, which would preclude showing any branded or generic tobacco products and smoking in films and television serials.

Health Minister Anbumani Ramadoss sought to ban on-screen smoking by popular film stars but was not successful. He also faced considerable resistance to his proposal to make it mandatory for cigarettes, bidis and gutka manufacturers to print ghastly pictures of diseased lungs on the packets of their products. The tobacco lobby in India (and elsewhere) is powerful and influential. Tobacco cultivation provides a livelihood to thousands of farmers (mostly in Andhra Pradesh and Karnataka) and sales of tobacco products generate substantial revenues for the union and state governments.

Eating Disorders

Advertising has been criticized at both ends of the scale: for encouraging anorexia on the one hand, and obesity on the other hand. The charge of increasing anorexia among young women and girls in particular is levelled across the entire spectrum of advertising. Most advertisements use women who are slimmer, taller and prettier than the average woman. One survey found that women used in advertising typically weigh less than average women.

Normal women are significantly underrepresented and this trend has been blamed for fostering low self-esteem and image consciousness among women. In particular, the glamorization of ultra-thin models, who are often used in advertising campaigns, has led to the conception that thinness is synonymous with beauty and anything less is ugly. Research on advertisements of toys for girls indicated that half the advertisements made references to physical attractiveness, while none of the advertisements of toys for boys did. Furthermore, it has been suggested that the pressure to be thin has prompted both men and women to smoke to curb appetite.

Feeding off the desire to be thinner and aiding the process are an array of diet foods and drinks, as well as dieting schemes. Weight loss programmes depict individuals in 'before' and 'after' shots portraying the thinner version as being happier.

Some advertising experts feel that junk food and 'convenience' food advertisements have led to increased obesity levels. The increase in the number of double-income families has led to the growing demand for commodities of 'convenience'. Ready-made meals and 'instant' food products proliferate in time-stretched societies. Advertisements for snack foods, such as potato chips, chocolates, fast foods like pizzas and carbonated soft drinks aimed at children have come under the scanner. In the UK, Ofcom pronounced that the effect of advertising on child obesity was only modest and rejected calls for a total ban on fast food advertisements. It felt that there were other contributing factors to childhood obesity like lack of exercise, school policies and parental demographics. In March 2006, Ofcom noted that a ban on snack food advertisements during prime time television would cost channels advertising revenue worth nearly £141 million.

Obesity is becoming a serious health concern in India too, especially among the affluent sections as well as the upwardlymobile middles classes. A survey conducted by the All India Institute of Medical Sciences (AIIMS) found that three-quarters of women residing in Delhi were suffering from abdominal obesity. Obesity-related illnesses such as diabetes and heart disease are rapidly increasing in India and AIIMS is predicting 'disastrous' consequences. The spread of obesity in India has been directly linked to the increasing prosperity of the middle classes, who can afford snack foods. While in Western countries obesity is linked to poverty, in India, it is associated with prosperity. The fact that obesity exists among the affluent in India means that advertising has a greater impact on dietary habits given that it primarily targets people with disposable incomes.

Environment

Many people are today worried about environmental degradation and want ecologically sustainable economic development. As climate change threatens the future of the planet and evidence points towards human responsibility for much of global warming, there is a call for responsible consumption. Several products used every day have, over recent years, been found to be harmful for the environment: plastics, car, airplanes, petroleum products and refrigerators are a few such products. Leo Hickman, writing for *The Guardian* (24 January 2008), laments the absence of environmental responsibility as a provision in advertising standards codes. He considers examples of environmentally irresponsible advertising that have been collated on the website, www.climatedenial.org, which typify the consumerist culture of denial.

In India, an advertisement for Ford Endeavour shows the large vehicle gliding over icecaps leaving in its wake track marks on melting ice and two polar bears. Ironically, icecaps melting due to climate change and their inhabitants, polar bears, have become potent symbols of global warming. Hickman queries: 'Could Ford have chosen a more inappropriate setting to sell their wares?' The advertisement seem particularly crude considering how uneconomical the vehicle is: its mileage is 7.5 km per litre in traffic conditions compared to the 22 km per litre that will be achieved by the Tata Nano car. Even more insensitive was an advertisement for Ford Zetec in the UK, which stated: 'Most people would prefer a hot climate.'

In India, concern has been expressed over the veracity of claims of eco-friendly products in advertising. Investigations into such claims by Jaipur-based civil society organization Consumer Unity and Trust Society (CUTS) revealed that several claims made by leading manufacturers were misleading or baseless. CUTS concluded that advertising contributed to unsustainable development and recommended that the ASCI should be more finely tuned to the requirements of the International Standards Organization (ISO) norms stipulated in the ISO 14000 series.

SUMMARY

This chapter has looked at the ways in which the advertising industry functions. We have considered the research techniques that motivate this industry. We have looked at the mass media as a means of communicating advertising messages. We have also seen how social trends are both the cause and effect of advertising. After perusing the main advertising codes, you should be able to discern the ways in which advertising standards are compatible with media norms. Lastly, the chapter gives a firm understanding of the circumstances in which the ethical dimensions of advertising become important in influencing consumption patterns and social norms.

REVIEW QUESTIONS

1. What is advertising?
2. What are the principal processes involved in advertising?
3. What are the problems with depending on research data to formulate advertising campaigns?
4. What are the major 'pull' factors of the press, radio and television for the purposes of advertising?
5. In what ways, and why, does advertising create a pseudo-reality?
6. What are the dangers of making media audiences commodities?
7. What are the key provisions for ethical conduct specified by the ASCI?
8. Do you feel that caveat emptor is an appropriate principle?
9. In what ways is gender stereotyping used and under what circumstances might it be inappropriate?
10. What are the dangers of visible stereotyping of ethnic groups?
11. What accounts for invisible stereotyping of ethnic minorities?
12. What are the arguments for and against alcohol advertising?
13. What are the potential problems with counter-advertising?
14. How would advertising contribute to anorexia?
15. How would snack food advertising contribute to obesity levels in India?
16. What are the provisions that the ASCI can adopt for environmentally responsible advertising?

DEBATE

1. The marketplace is for healthy competition and individuals are responsible for their own well-being. Therefore, caveat emptor!
2. Advertising is a 'wholly undesirable' practice that is a blatant manipulation of an audience's trust and shows total disregard for the good of society.
3. Advertising must be denied by the media to claim editorial independence and earn the trust of society.

REFERENCES

Bagdikian, H. Ben 2000, *The Media Monopoly*, Beacon Press, Uckfield, UK.

Camm John, 'The modern rules of advertising?' at http://news.bbc.co.uk/1/hi/magazine/4204412.stm (accessed on 20 August 2008).

Campbell, Richard 2002, *Media and Culture*, Bedford/St Martin's, Boston, US.

Dalal, Sucheta 2006, Caveat Emptor is Still the Norm in India at http://www.indianexpress.com/story/10528.html (accessed on 20 August 2008).

Hickman, Leo 2008, 'Driven by Mischief' at http://www.guardian.co.uk/environment/2008/jan/ 24/ethicalliving.climatechange (accessed on 20 August 2008).

Leslie, Z. Larry 2004, *Mass Communication Ethics: Decision Making in Postmodern Culture,* Houghton Mifflin Company, Boston, US.

McLuhan, Marshall and Lewis H. Lapham 1964, *Understanding Media: The Extensions of Man,* Mit Press, US.

McLuhan, Marshall and Quentin Fiore 1967, *The Medium is the Massage: An Inventory of Effects,* Bantam Books, US.

McLuhan, Marshall and Bruce R. Powers 1986, *The Global Village: Transformations in World Life and Media in the 21st Century,* Oxford University Press, New York, US.

'The Modern Rules of Advertising' at http://news.bbc.co.uk/1/hi/magazine/4204412.stm (accessed on 20 August 2008).

Rodman, George 2001, *Making Sense of Media,* Allyn & Bacon, USA.

Shrivastava, K.M. 2005, *Media Ethics*: *Veda to Gandhi and Beyond*, Ministry of Information and Broadcasting, Government of India, New Delhi, India.

Smith, P.R. 1996, *Marketing Communications*, Kogan Page, London, UK.

Surmanek, Jim 1993, *Introduction to Advertising Media*, NTC Business Books, Chicago, US.

APPENDIX 10.1

Examples of Objectionable Advertisements

In its report for the period January–March 2008, the ASCI highlighted instances of advertisements that were either modified or withdrawn. The report stated that out of a total of thirty-five advertisements against which the self-regulatory organization received complaints, eight were withdrawn, seven modified, one was a special case, seven were upheld by the Consumer Complaints' Council (CCC) citing 'due assurance against the complaint', while twelve complaints were not upheld by the CCC. Details of the four print advertisements that were withdrawn follow:

Axis Bank Limited—'Quick and Easy Personal Loans' This advertisement was printed on the bank's 'national bill mail service envelope' that depicted a parakeet picking up a fortune card with the tagline, 'Your wishes are now fulfilled within 48 hours'. According to the CCC, parakeets are protected under the Wildlife (Protection) Act, 1972, as well as under the Performing Animals (Registration) Rules, 2001, and the visual violated both these acts. The bank thereafter gave an assurance that the visual would not be used again.

Alapatt Jewellers—'916 Gold and Certified Diamonds' The copy of this advertisement, first published in a Malayalam-language publication, read (in English translation): '916 purity should be there not only in the advertisement but also in the gold ornament. Without hallmarking there is no purity and (the gold) will not get a good price when exchanged. At a wholesale rate, the jewellery that you get at one per cent or two per cent discount will have a lower value when exchanged.' The CCC decided that this advertisement was misleading and it was withdrawn.

Dabur India Limited—'SaniFresh Thick Toilet Cleaner' This advertisement produced by O&M had been printed in *Good Housekeeping* magazine's January 2008 issue) with a caption that read: 'SaniFresh Thick. The secret of my shiny, silky hair.' The CCC agreed with the complaint that the caption was misleading as the product could be construed to be a shampoo instead of a toilet cleaner. The advertisement was withdrawn.

Kent RO Systems Private Limited—'Kent Water Softener' This product had been advertised in the *Hindustan Times* (10 January 2008) with the claim: 'Not only it smoothened skin and prevented hair loss, but it also enhanced the lather formation...' The CCC was of the view that the company had not substantiated its claim with supporting technical information and test/trial reports. The advertisement was withdrawn.

Two advertisements in the 'digital category' were withdrawn. Hyundai Motors India Limited had advertised its Verna car on the company's website and claimed: 'Hyundai Verna diesel variant "CRDI VGT" has a fuel economy of 32.8 kmpl.' The complaint was that the vehicle could travel for just over 1 km per litre of diesel consumed. The CCC ruled that the company's claim had not been substantiated and the advertisement was discontinued. An e-mail advertisement for Sisley Fall Winter Collection 07 manufactured by Trent Limited carried the caption: 'You'll melt once inside' with a visual depicting a woman in a seductive pose. The CCC was of the opinion that the manner in which the woman had been visually depicted could 'cause grave or widespread offence' and the advertisement was withdrawn.

The ASCI report mentions the following two television commercials that were withdrawn:

Godrej Sara Lee Limited—'Good Knight Maha Jumbo Mosquito Coil' This commercial was broadcast on the Zee Marathi television channel (14 January 2008) wherein it was claimed: '*Jitki sugandhi, titkich prabhavi*' ('As fragrant as it is effective'). A model was shown inhaling the so-called fragrant vapours. The CCC agreed with a complainant that what had been visually depicted in the advertisement could be a 'dangerous practice' and the advertiser agreed to withdraw it.

Parle Agro Private Limited—'Mintrox Mint' This television advertisement aired on the Star Cricket channel on 25 January 2008 showed a convict in a mental hospital where the jailor teases him. A mental hospital was shown in the background of the advertisement with some of its inmates. The CCC was of the view that the advertisement portrayed mentally challenged people in an 'insensitive' and 'offensive' manner and it was withdrawn.

The ASCI report provided details of the following six advertisements in the print category that were modified:

Haier Appliances (India) Private Limited—'Haier Air Conditioners' This advertisement that was printed in *The TOI* (27 April 2007) claimed that Haier air conditioners saved power up to 51 per cent, offered 'future comfort technology, superior air conditioning, refresh function, intelligent air flow, four-stage air filter, revolutionary digital DC inverter technology, super ioniser and healthy UV ray generator'. As the claims in the advertisement had not been substantiated, the CCC directed the company to modify it.

'NaiDunia is No. 1 again in Indore city' This advertisement for a newspaper was apparently based on data obtained from a 'private survey' and not on either the Indian Readership Survey or the National Readership Survey—both of which are considered reputed. After the CCC upheld a complaint against the claim in the advertisement, it was modified.

Kinetic Engineering Limited—'Kinetic SYM Flyte' Publicis Ambience, the advertising agency for Kinetic Engineering, devised an advertisement that made the following claim: 'It's made by the two companies that know scooters best—Kinetic and SYM, Europe's fastest growing two-wheeler company. Largest two level storage, our confidence, three years warranty for the first 10,000 customers only, and four-in-one magnetic key for initial customers only.' The CCC ruled that the claims as well as the 'initial customer offer' had both not been substantiated, were misleading and ambiguous. The advertiser thereafter modified the advertisement.

Garware Polyester Limited—'Garware Suncontrol Window Film' This advertisement was published in *Auto India* (January 2008) and made the following claims: 'A non-fading dyed film, unlike imported coated film, which fades in three months, clear distorted free view, no peeling or bubbling of film, best film for Indian conditions, exported to more than 50 countries, including USA, UK, Australia and Japan, No. 1 brand in India and up to five years' warranty.' The CCC was of the view that the warranty claim was misleading and ambiguous and the advertiser gave an assurance that the advertisement would be modified.

Belle Aarogya Biotech Private Limited—'Elevation-Remedy for Breast Care' This advertisement appeared in *Hindustan Times City* (15 January 2008) and claimed that extensive research by qualified and eminent medical experts made 'elevation' a 'path-breaking' remedy for breast care, and that 'extensive trials" indicated '92 per cent satisfaction' for those in the 20–50 age group. The CCC ruled that this advertisement contravened the provisions of the Drugs and Magic Remedies (Objectionable Advertisements) Act, 1954, and it was modified.

An advertisement issued by **Trinity Health Clinic** that appeared in *Mumbai Mirror* (6 February 2008) claimed 'natural and permanent hair growth within 30–40 days'. The CCC decided that the advertiser should provide proof of the claim made with supporting technical information and details of tests/trials conducted. This advertisement, too, was modified.

A television commercial that was modified had been issued by **Reckitt Benckiser (India)**

Limited for **Dettol Soap**. Broadcast on the Zee Marathi television channel on 28 August 2007 and on 20 December 2007, the advertisement implied that the product should be used for eliminating organisms that caused cough and cold, as it 'eliminates organisms ten times faster than other soaps'. The advertisement also claimed that the Indian Medical Association had 'approved Dettol and elimination of organisms that cause gastrointestinal diseases'. The CCC found that these claims had not been substantiated and the advertiser gave an assurance that the advertisement would be modified in an appropriate manner.

APPENDIX 10.2

Code for Commercial Advertising on Doordarshan

Definitions: In this Code, unless the context otherwise requires:

(i) 'Government' means, Government of India.
(ii) 'Director General' means, the Director General, Doordarshan or any officer duly authorized by him on his behalf and includes the Director, Doordarshan Kendra.
(iii) 'Advertiser' means any individual or organization including a commercial concern which has offered any advertisement to telecast over television.
(iv) 'Advertising Agency' means any organization which is accredited to, or registered with Doordarshan as such.
(v) 'Advertisement' includes any item of publicity for goods or services inserted in the programme telecast by Doordarshan with a view to increase sales.
(vi) 'Spot Advertisement' means any direct advertisement mentioning products/services, their merits and other related details.
(vii) Advertising Association' means an Association or Society or any other body of whose constituent members are Advertising Agencies registered or accredited to Doordarshan.

Scope:

(a) The Director General, Doordarshan shall be the sole judge of the suitability or otherwise of an advertisement for telecast and his decision in this regard shall be final.
(b) Doordarshan time shall be sold to the Advertisers/Advertising Agencies at the sole discretion of the Director General, Doordarshan according to the prescribed rates.
(c) The advertisement should be clearly distinguishable from the programme by using suitable wipes/blank, in order to avoid the message of the programme getting mixed up with the content and images of the advertisement.

I. Introduction

Advertising is an important and legitimate means for the seller to awaken interest in his goods and services. The success of advertising depends on public confidence. Hence no practice should be permitted which tends to impair this confidence. The standards laid down here should be taken as minimum standards of acceptability which would be liable to be reviewed from time to time in relation to the prevailing norms of viewer's susceptibilities.

The following standards of conduct are laid down in order to develop and promote healthy advertising practices in Doordarshan. Responsibility for the observance of these rules rests equally upon the Advertiser and the Advertising Agency.

All those engaged in advertising are strongly recommended to familiarize themselves with the legislation affecting advertising in this country, particularly the following Acts and the Rules framed under them:

1. Drugs and Cosmetics Act, 1940.
2. Drugs Control Act, 1950.
3. Drugs and Magic Remedies (Objectionable Advertisements) Act, 1954.
4. Copyright Act, 1957.
5. Trade and Merchandise Marks Act, 1958.
6. Prevention of Food Adulteration Act, 1954.
7. Pharmacy Act, 1948.
8. Prize Competition Act, 1955.
9. Emblems and Names (Prevention of Improper Use) Act, 1950.
10. Consumer Protection Act, 1986.
11. Indecent Representation of Women (Prohibition) Act, 1986.
12. AIR/Doordarshan Code.
13. Code of Ethics for advertising in India issued by the Advertising Standard Council of India (see Annexure I).
14. Code of Standards in relation to the advertising of medicine and treatments (see Annexure II).
15. Standards of practice for Advertising Agencies (see Annexure III).

(The list is illustrative and not exhaustive.)

II. The Code

General Rules of Conduct in Advertising:

1. Advertising shall be so designed as to conform to the laws of the country and should not offend morality, decency and religious susceptibilities of the people.
2. No advertisement shall be permitted which—
   (i) derides any race, caste, colour, creed and nationality;
   (ii) is against any of the directive principles, or any other provision of the Constitution of India;
   (iii) tends to incite people to crime, cause disorder or violence, or breach of law or glorifies violence or obscenity in any way;
   (iv) presents criminality as desirable;
   (v) adversely affects friendly relations with foreign States;
   (vi) exploits the national emblem, or any part of the Constitution or the person or personality of a national leader or State Dignitary;
   (vii) relates to or promotes cigarettes and tobacco products, liquor, wines and other intoxicants;
   (viii) in its depiction of women violates the constitutional guarantees to all citizens such as equality of status and opportunity and dignity of the individual. In particular, no advertisement shall be permitted which projects a derogatory image of women. Women must not be portrayed in a manner that emphasizes passive, submissive qualities and encourages them to play a subordinate, secondary role in the family and society. The portrayal of men and women should not encourage mutual disrespect. Advertiser shall ensure that the portrayal of the female form is tasteful and aesthetic, and is within the well established norms of good taste and decency.
3. No advertisement message shall in any way be presented as News.
4. No advertisement shall be permitted the objects whereof are wholly or mainly of a religious or political nature; advertisements must not be directed towards any religious or political end or have any relation to any industrial dispute.
5. Advertisement for services concerned with the following shall not be accepted:

(i) Unlicensed employment services;

(ii) Sooth-sayers etc., and those with claims of hypnotism;

(iii) Betting tips and guide books etc., relating to horse racing or other games of chance.

6. Doordarshan accepts the advertisements of educational institutions/colleges. However, it must be ensured that the institutions/colleges are genuine so as to ensure that students do not get misled.

   Doordarshan will also accept advertisements relating to holiday resorts and hotels.

   Doordarshan also accepts the advertisements relating to real estate including sale of flats/land, flats for rent both commercial and residential. However, to ensure that viewers do not get misled by false claims, it has been decided that all such advertisements must carry a statutory message at the end in the form of super imposition or caption as follows:

   'Viewers Are Advised To Check The Genuineness Of The Claims Made' Doordarshan has also allowed the telecast of:

   (i) Foreign products and foreign banks including financial services;

   (ii) Jewellery and precious stones;

   (iii) Mutual funds approved by SEBI (Securities and Exchange Board of India);

   (iv) Hair dyes;

   (v) Matrimonial agencies;

7. The items advertised shall not suffer from any defect or deficiency as mentioned in Consumer Protection Act, 1986.

8. No advertisement shall contain references which are likely to lead the public to infer that the product advertised or any of its ingredients has some special or miraculous or supernatural property or quality, which is difficult of being proved, e.g. cure for baldness, skin whitener, etc.

9. No advertisement shall contain the words 'Guarantee' or Guaranteed', etc. unless the full terms of the guarantee are available for inspection by the Director General, Doordarshan, and are clearly set out in the advertisement and are made available to the purchaser in writing at the point of sale or with the goods. In all cases terms must include details of the remedial action available to the purchaser. No advertisement shall contain a direct or implied reference to any guarantee which purports to take away or diminish the legal rights of a purchaser.

10. Scientific or statistical excerpts from technical literature etc., may be used only with a proper sense of responsibility to the ordinary viewer. Irrelevant data and scientific jargon shall not be used to make claims appear to have a scientific basis they do not possess. Statistics of limited validity should not be presented in a way as to make it appear that they are universally true.

11. Advertisers or their agents must be prepared to produce evidence to substantiate any claims or illustrations. The Director General reserves the right to ask for such proofs and get them examined to his full satisfaction. In case of goods covered by mandatory quality control orders, the advertiser shall produce quality certificate from the institutions recognized by the Government for this purpose.

12. Advertisements shall not contain disparaging or derogatory references to another product or service.

13. Imitation likely to mislead viewers shall be avoided.

14. Visual and verbal representation of actual and comparative prices and costs shall be accurate and shall not mislead on account of undue emphasis or distortion.

15. Testimonials must be genuine and used in a manner not to mislead the viewers. Advertisers or Advertising Agencies must be prepared to produce evidence in support of their claims.
16. The picture and the audible matter of the advertisement shall not be excessively 'loud'. This is to ensure that between the programme and the advertisement there is a smooth change-over avoiding jerkiness or shock to the viewers.
17. Information to consumer in matters of weight, quality or prices of products where given shall be accurate.
18. Advertisements indicating price comparisons or reductions must comply with relevant laws.
19. No advertisement shall be accepted which violates AIR (All India Radio) and TV Broadcast Code which is reproduced below:

General AIR/TV Code

(i) Criticism of friendly countries;
(ii) attack on religions or communities;
(iii) anything obscene or defamatory;
(iv) incitement to violence or anything against maintenance of law and order;
(v) anything amounting to contempt of court;
(vi) aspersions against the integrity of the President and Judiciary;
(vii) anything affecting the integrity of the Nation; and
(viii) criticism by name of any person.

20. Any such effects which might startle the viewing public must not be incorporated in advertisements. For example, and without limiting the scope, the use of the following sound effects will not be permitted:

    Rapid gunfire or rifle shots

    Sirens

    Bombardments

    Screams

    Raucous laughter and the like.
21. Any pretence in advertising copy must be avoided and such copy shall not be accepted by Doordarshan Kendras. The 'simulation' of appearance or voice of a personality in connection with advertisements for commercial products is also prohibited unless bona fide evidence is available that such personality has given permission for the simulation and it is clearly understood that stations telecasting such announcements are indemnified by the advertiser or advertising agency against any possible legal action.

Advertising and Children

22. No advertising for a product or service shall be accepted if it suggests in any way that unless the children themselves buy or encourage other people to buy the products or services, they will be failing in their duty or lacking in loyalty to any person or organization.
23. No advertisement shall be accepted which leads children to believe that if they do not own or use the product advertised they will be inferior in some way to other children or that they are liable to the condemned or ridiculed for not owning or using it.
24. No advertisement likely to bring advertising into contempt or disrepute shall be permitted. Advertising shall not take advantage of the superstition or ignorance of the general public.
25. No advertising of talismans, charms and character-reading from photographs or such other matter as well as those which trade on superstition of general public shall be permitted.
26. Advertising shall be truthful, avoid distorting facts and misleading the public by means of implications by false statements, as to:

(i) the character of the merchandise, i.e. its utility, materials, ingredients, origin etc.

(ii) the price of the merchandise, its value, its suitability or terms of purchase.

(iii) the services accompanying purchase, including delivery, exchange, return, repair, upkeep etc.

(iv) personal recommendations of the article or service.

(v) the quality or the value of competing goods or trustworthiness of statement made by others.

27. Testimonials of any kind from experts etc. other than Government recognized standardization agencies shall not be permitted.

28. No advertisement shall be permitted to contain any claim so exaggerated as to lead inevitably to disappointment in the minds of the public.

29. Methods of advertising designated to create confusion in the mind of the consumer as between goods by one maker and another maker are unfair and shall not be used. Such methods may consist in:

(i) the imitation of the trademark of the name of competition or packaging or labelling of goods; or

(ii) the imitation of advertising devices, copy, layout or slogans.

30. Indecent, vulgar, suggestive, repulsive or offensive themes or treatment shall be avoided in all advertisements. This also applies to such advertisements which themselves are not objectionable as defined above, but which advertise objectionable books, photographs or other matter and thereby lead to their sale and circulation.

31. No advertisement in respect of medicines and treatments shall be accepted which is in contravention of the code relating to standards of advertising medicines and treatments as per Annexure II.

Note I: In all other respects, the Director General will be guided for purposes of commercial broadcasting in All India Radio by Code of Ethics for Advertising in India as modified from time to time (relevant excerpts appended at Annexure I).

Note II: Notwithstanding anything contained herein, this code is subject to such modification/directions as may be made/issued by the Director General from time to time.

Note III: All advertising agencies shall adhere to the standards of practice as prescribed by Advertising Agencies Association of India, Bombay, as given in Annexure III.

Procedure for the Enforcement of the Code

1. Complaints or reports on contraventions of the Code, received by All India Radio may in the first instant be referred by Director General to Advertisers' Association concerned with request for suitable action.
2. If complaints under the Code cannot be satisfactorily resolved at Association(s)' level, they shall be reported to Director General who will then consider suitable action.
3. For any complaints under the Code received by All India Radio concerning a party outside the purview of various member Association(s), the Director General will draw attention of such party to the complaint and where necessary, take suitable action on his own.

ANNEXURE I

Excerpts from the Code of Ethics for Advertising in India Issued by the Advertising Council of India

Introduction

Along with the development of a very complex distribution system, the requirements of a market economy, faced with the need for ensuring a regular flow of mass production, have given rise to the development of new techniques of sales promotion.

Of these, advertising has proved itself to be of inestimable value for producers and distributors as well as for consumers. It enables the former to maintain contact with customers who are widely scattered and often unknown, and it assists the latter in choosing those goods and services that are the best suited to their particular requirements.

Advertising has become an important social and economic force in the world today. It is therefore, essential that any unfair advertising practice likely to alienate public confidence would be eliminated. Hence the need for rules of conduct drawn up for the purpose of preventing possible abuse and of promoting and increasing sense of responsibility towards the consumer on the part of the advertisers, advertising agencies and media owners and suppliers.

Recognizing that the legitimate function of advertising is the advocacy of the merits of particular products or services, this code is intended to be applied in the spirits as well as in the letter and should be taken to set out the minimum standards to be observed by the parties concerned. This code does override all ethical standards in advertising laid down by individual organizations, but it does not supersede the standards of practice laid down by individual organizations as incumbent upon their own members and appealing to their own particular trade or industry.

ANNEXURE II

Code of Standards in Relation to the Advertising of Medicines and Treatment

This code has been drafted for the guidance of advertisers, manufacturers, distributors, advertising agents, publishers and suppliers or various advertising media. The harm to the individual that may result from exaggerated, misleading or unguaranteed claims justified the adoption of a very high standard and the inclusion of considerable detail in a Code to guide those who are concerned with this form of advertising.

Newspaper and other advertising media are urged not to accept advertisements in respect of any other product or treatment from any advertiser or advertising or publicity relating to that product or treatment. The provisions of this Code do not apply to an advertisement published by or under the authority of a Government, Ministry or Department, nor to an advertisement published in journals circulated to Registered Medical Practitioners, Registered Dentists, Registered Pharmacists or Registered Nurses.

Section 1

General principles

1. **Cure:** No advertisement should contain a claim to cure any ailment or symptoms of ill-health, nor should any advertisement contain a word or expression used in such a form or context as to mean in the positive sense the extirpation of any ailment, illness or disease.
2. **Illness etc., properly requiring medical attention:** No advertisement should contain any matter which can be regarded as offer of medicine or product for, or advise relating to, treatment of serious diseases, complaints, conditions, indications or symptoms which should rightly receive the attention of a Registered medical practitioner (see Sec.2).

3. **Misleading or exaggerated claim:** No advertisement should contain any matter which directly or by implication misleads or departs from the truth as to the composition, character or action of the medicine or treatment advertised or as to its suitability for the purpose for which it is recommended.
4. **Appeals to fear:** No advertisement should be calculated to induce fear on the part of the reader that he is suffering, or may without treatment suffer from an ailment, illness or disease.
5. **Diagnosis or treatment by correspondence:** No advertisement should offer to diagnose by correspondence diseases, conditions or any symptoms of ill-health in a human being or request from any person or a statement of his (sic) or any other person's symptoms of ill-health with a view to advertising as to or providing for treatment of such conditions of ill-health by correspondence. Nor should any advertisement offer to treat by correspondence any ailment, illness, disease or symptoms thereof in a human being.
6. **Disparaging references:** No advertisement should directly or by implication disparage the products, medicines or treatments of another advertiser or manufacturer or registered medical practitioner or the medical profession.
7. **College, clinic, institute, laboratory:** No advertisement should contain these or similar terms unless an establishment corresponding with the description used does in fact exist.
8. **Doctors, hospitals etc.:** No advertisement should contain any reference to doctors or hospitals, whether Indian or foreign, unless such reference can be sustained by independent evidence and can properly be used in the manner proposed.
9. **Products offered particularly to women:** No advertisement of products, medicines or treatments of disorders or irregularities peculiar to women should contain expression which may imply that the product, medicine or treatment advertised can be effective in inducing miscarriage.
10. **Family planning:** Advertisements for measures or apparatus concerning family planning would be permissible in so far as they conform to the generally accepted national policy in this behalf.
11. **Illustrations:** No advertisement should contain any illustration which by itself or in combination with words used in connection therewith is likely to convey a misleading impression, or if the reasonable reference to be drawn from such advertisement infringes any of the provisions of the Code.
12. **Exaggerated copy:** No advertisement should contain copy which is exaggerated by reason of improper use of words, phrases or methods of presentation e.g., the use of word's magic, magical, miracle, miraculous.
13. **Natural remedies:** No advertisement should claim or suggest contrary to the fact, that the article advertised is in the form in which it occurs in nature or that its value lies in its being a natural product.
14. **Special claim:** No advertisement should contain any reference which is calculated to lead the public to assume that the article, product, medicine or treatment advertised has some special property or quality which is in fact unknown or unrecognized.
15. **Sexual weakness, premature aging, loss of virility:** No advertisement should claim that the product, medicine or treatment advertised will promote sexual virility or be effective in treating sexual weakness or habits associated with sexual excess or

indulgence or any ailment, illness or disease associated with those habits. In particular such terms as 'premature aging', 'loss of virility' will be regarded as conditions for which medicines, products, appliances or treatment may not be advertised.

16. **Slimming, weight reduction or limitation or figure control:** No advertisement should offer any medical product for the purpose of slimming, weight reduction or limitation or figure control. Medical products intended to reduce appetite will usually be regarded as being for slimming purposes.
17. **Tonics:** The use of this expression in advertisements should not imply that the product or medicine can be used in the treatment of sexual weakness.
18. **Hypnosis:** No advertisement should contain any offer to diagnose or treat complaints or conditions by hypnosis.
19. **Materials to students:** Materials meant for distribution in educational institutions must not carry advertisement of anything other than those of value to students.

Section 2

Restrictions imposed by statute on advertising on Medicines and Treatments:

1. Rule 106 of the Drug Rules, 1945, provides that, no drug may convey to the intending user thereof any idea that it may prevent or cure one or more of the diseases or ailments specified in schedule 'J'.

   Schedule 'J'.

   Blindness, Bright's disease, Cancer, Cataract, Deafness, Delayed Menstruation, Diabetes, Epilepsy, Hydrocele, Infantile Paralysis, Leprosy, Leucoderma, Lockjaw, Locomotor Ataxia, Insanity, Tuberculosis, Tumours, Venereal Diseases (in general), Female Diseases (in general), Fevers (in general), Fits, Glaucoma, Goitre, Gonorrhoea, Soft Cancer, Heart Disease, High Blood Pressure, Lupus, Obesity, Paralysis, Plague, Rupture, Sexual Impotence, Small Pox.

2. No drug may purport or claim to procure or assist to procure or may convey to the intending user thereof any idea that it may procure or assist to procure miscarriage in women.

   Definition

   'Drug' includes for internal or external use for human being or animals all substances intended to be used for or in the treatment, mitigation, or prevention of disease in human being or animals, other than medicines and substances exclusively used or prepared for use in accordance with the Ayurvedic or Unani system of medicines.

ANNEXURE III

Standards of Practice for Advertising Agencies

(As approved by the Advertising Agencies Association of India, Bombay);

1. Every member of the Association shall carry on his profession and business in such a manner as to uphold the dignity and interests of the Association.
2. Every member shall refrain from canvassing Advertisers or prospective Advertisers in such a way as to reflect detrimentally upon Advertising Agents as a whole or this Association or any Advertising Agent in particular.
3. Canvassing is permitted to the condition that a member may make known to the client of another member its own capabilities as an Advertising Agency but may not submit a specific report or detailed recommendation concerning the clients' advertising unless so requested by him in writing.

4. No members shall pay or undertake to pay or allow to an advertiser or his agent or representative the whole or any portion of the standard rate of commission resulting or to result to such member from any advertising medium nor promise or procedure or undertake to procure advertising space of facilities free of charge, to any advertising, or at a reduced rate nor supply free or party free to any advertiser, any advertising material, including finished drawings, or other art work, photographs, blocks stereos matrices or the like, typesetting or printing nor defray in whole or in part the salary of any employee of an advertise nor grant any allowances, discount or the like nor render any service having the effect of rebating the commission allowed by an advertising medium. The sharing of commission with member or overseas agency or with agent by this Association shall, however, be permitted.
5. The practice of submitting speculative campaigns is unhealthy to the growth of the advertising services and no speculative campaign shall be submitted by any member of the Advertising Agencies Association of India.

   By speculative campaign, it is meant, producing a campaign unsolicited by an advertiser and equally producing a campaign where the advertiser had requested one or more advertising agencies to do so, unaccompanied by a firm offer of business. That members shall notify the Secretary of the Association if any such queries were made by prospective advertiser, and that such information shall be circulated by the Secretary to all members.
6. Any member relinquishing an Account on the ground of slow payment, doubtful credit or incurring a bad debt, shall immediately notify the Secretary of the Association and such information shall be circulated in strictest confidence for information and protection of the members.
7. No business shall be accepted which is conditional upon the payment of commission free or reward to a third party not a full time employee of the members either for introducing the business or for services in connection with the account thereafter. This rule, however, shall not preclude a member from employing copywriters or production men at fees commensurate with the value of their work.

Obligation to Client

1. Member Agencies must continue to render full Agency Service in reasonable conformity to the Association Agency Service Standards.
2. Member shall retain either commission granted by media owners or charge the clients a service fee which shall never be less then 15% of the Client's gross expenditure.
3. Nor shall they supply material for advertising an any basis that can be considered as direct or indirect or secret, rebating. Where no commission is allowed by the Media Owner, the member will charge his clients minimum of 15% on the gross cost.
4. Members will not accept discount or commission, other than the regular agency commission allowed by the publishers without the client's knowledge and consent.
5. Members shall at all time use their best efforts to obtain for their clients the lowest rates to which such clients are entitled.

Obligation to Suppliers

Member shall take all steps to assure themselves as to the financial soundness of their clients.

Obligations to Fellow Agencies:

1. Members are required to use fair methods of competition; not to offer the services

enumerated above or services in addition to them without adequate remuneration or extension of credit facilities or banking services.

2. Members shall neither prepare nor place any advertisement in any medium, which
   (a) is knowingly a copy or a plagiarism of any other advertisement of any kind whatsoever;
   (b) makes attacks of a personal character, or makes uncalled for reflections on competitors or competitive goods;
   (c) is indecent, vulgar, suggestive, repulsive or offensive either in theme or treatment;
   (d) is objectionable medical advertising and an offer of free medical treatment, advertising that makes remedial or curative claims, either directly or by interference not justified by the facts of common experience;
   (e) concerns a product known to the member to contain habit forming or danger drugs; or any advertisement which may cause money loss to the reader, or injury in health or morals or loss of confidence in reputable advertising and honourable business or which is regarded by the Executive Committee of the Advertising Agencies Association of India, as unworthy.

In the event of a member providing to the satisfaction of the Executive Committee that a client has withdrawn his Account on the grounds of the member's refusal to undertake unethical Advertising (as described above) no other member shall accept any business whatever from the said clients.

CHAPTER

11

ETHICS OF PUBLIC RELATIONS

This chapter considers what the phrase 'public relations' (PR) means since it denotes a very broad area of operations and encompasses many techniques. The chapter attempts to focus on the ways in which PR practices influence the media and concentrates on the relationship between the media and PR, specifically on the ethical issues involved in this relationship. PR depends heavily on the media for its communications strategies and some of the more popular methods of harnessing it to communicate PR messages are discussed here. While delineating the processes involved in PR practices, it will be observed that these bear certain similarities to the processes of media practices. It is seen that the relationship between the media and PR is symbiotic, and that the media is also dependent on PR and uses PR practices. The ethics and codes of PR and their similarity to journalistic ethics are discussed. Finally, three of the most important aspects of media ethics—accuracy, fairness and objectivity—are examined in the context of PR practices that are incompatible with upholding these ethical values.

WHAT IS PR?

Edward Bernays, considered the forefather of modern PR, described PR as 'the attempt, by information, persuasion and adjustment, to engineer public support for an activity, cause, movement, or institute' (Campbell 2002). PR is concerned with creating and sustaining a beneficial image of a particular entity with its various publics. The plural of public is used to convey the fact that there are many different kinds of public, distinguished through certain characteristics. Publics can be divided into two categories: internal and external (Rodman 2001). Internal publics are those which have a direct link with a particular establishment. For example, a corporate establishment's publics include employees and shareholders. External publics have an indirect link with an establishment: consumers, supporters, media, general public and legislators for example. PR is a wide ranging field, with very divergent practices. Thus PR is practised across many fields, groups and entities including multinational corporations, NGOs, MPs, besides specific interest groups and people in general.

Background

While the definition of PR that is given here is contemporary, the concept of communicating with the public in order to enhance relations is a very ancient practice indeed. In the third century BC in India, Emperor Ashoka, noted for his conversion to Buddhism and commitment to non-violence after the bloody conquest of Kalinga, used principles of PR to promote his message of peace. To convey an intention of violence, one only has to wage war. To convey the message of peace, however, subtler methods must be found. Ashoka inscribed edicts which expounded Buddhist principles across his territory. These edicts were strategically placed along major roads, where they were likely to be read by large numbers of people. The edicts served a dual function: to inform the public of the nature of their emperor and his intentions; and also to imbue Buddhist values in them.

More recently, propaganda was a technique used in America and Britain during the two world wars to elicit public support for the wars, boost public morale and to encourage enrolment in the services. Propaganda is considered by many as an unethical means of public relations, but its effectiveness in manipulation served to demonstrate to the earliest PR practitioners the degree to which public opinion could be influenced. Bernays called the practice of eliciting public goodwill and support through persuasion the 'engineering of consent'. Born in 1892 and a nephew of reputed psychologist Sigmund Freud, Bernays pioneered modern PR as a specialist industry by putting into practice concepts and methods of the social sciences. Bernays and Ivy Lee, the other key figure of the 1920s, American PR scene, realized that public approval could be engineered and manipulated, and that it was the responsibility of those at the top end of society—intellectuals, elite and the 'cultured'—to guide and motivate the moral sensibilities of the public at large. This notion contains an important ethical dilemma. On the one hand, PR is ideally concerned with the betterment of society through communicating information and values. On the other hand, the communication of these values is understood as a means of 'engineering', manipulating or moulding public opinion. Critics argue that it is arrogant—and potentially dangerous—to believe that public good should be but a reflection of the interests (which might be commercial, political or religious, for example) of elitist power groups. PR is therefore in danger of being one-sided and could promote the interests of a particular group at the expense (or to the detriment) of large sections of society.

Research and trace propaganda that was used by the Allies as well as by the Nazis during the second World War and explain in what ways war PR has changed over the years? What are the similarities between war PR and propaganda? Do you believe war PR and 'spin' is ethically appropriate?

The PR Process

PR, in its simplest form, involves a three-step process:

1. **Getting the message** In order to be able to present oneself or one's cause in a favourable light, it is important to understand what the motivations, interests, concerns and desires of one's publics are. Therefore, PR often involves research of societies and markets and utilizes techniques used by social scientists.
2. **Creating the message** Having researched and established the feelings of the particular publics, work begins on how best to convey one's message in a way that will appeal to these feelings.
3. **Spreading the message** The formulated message then has to be reached to the concerned publics or target groups. An effective way to achieve this purpose is through the media, which conveniently serves as a firmly established communications conduit.

In this respect, one can see how the process of PR is not much different from the processes followed by the mass media in general. Both involve understanding the needs, interests and feelings of publics in order to determine and shape the message one wants to communicate and, in order to be effective, both require optimum levels of dissemination and circulation.

Can you think of any examples from history or current affairs where you can identify PR practices at work?

You cannot hope to bribe or twist,
thank God! the British journalist.
But, seeing what the man will do
unbribed, there's no occasion to.
From *The Uncelestial City*, Humbert Wolfe, 1930

WHY PR NEEDS THE MEDIA

In order to communicate messages, PR frequently involves using the media for broad dissemination. Parsons (2004) notes that from a PR perspective, 'media relations is...one of the most important, and certainly the most high-profile' communication strategies.

It is important that the message one wishes to convey is newsworthy, to ensure that it will be taken up by the media. This can be achieved in a variety of ways. A news 'hook' or a news 'peg' is the technique of presenting a message in a certain light to quickly catch the attention of the media. For example, if a company is organizing a charity event and wishes to publicize the fact in order to create an image of social responsibility, a celebrity might be invited to participate. The presence of the celebrity will help the event stand out and will appeal to public interest. It may also be noted that the celebrity involved might consider her or his participation beneficial for her/his own public image. The other carrot that PR professionals may at times dangle before the media to get an event covered is an interview—preferably an exclusive interview—with a top official of a company who is otherwise elusive. Another way to create a news hook might be to draw special attention to the way in which an activity or message addresses popular issues or fads. For example, an oil company might stress its commitment to finding renewable energy sources or an auto company to clean fuel technologies, appealing to the topicality of environmental concern.

Ready-made News

In order to make a PR endeavour media friendly, PR professionals will attempt to make its message as accessible as possible. The most common exercise in this regard is a press release which involves preparing a message or statement of news or activities of a particular group in the form of a news report. It is then distributed to journalists in the print and other media. A similar practice, intended specifically for radio broadcast, is audio news releases that contain a condensed message using pithy sound bites—or short statements, comments or speeches intended for convenient insertion into news bulletins. Video news releases (VNRs) are videos of interviews or special events, produced by PR professionals that are intended to be broadcast on television news programmes.

Some PR media releases are more comprehensive. Generally referred to as press 'kits', these are packages designed for use by the media, and include a range of information in different forms. A press kit might include photographs of a product, person or event; slides and short films; detailed background information; survey results and samples. These kits are intended to provide a reporter with the necessary information to put together a story. Press kits can be elaborate and sometimes very expensive, but if they are utilized by the media, they prove to be a cheaper and more credible form of brand promotion than advertising. PR professionals correctly point out that the more the effort and creativity involved in putting together a press/media kit and in creating 'ready-made' news, the more the likelihood of the information and audio-visual material contained in the kit being used by journalists.

Another common tool used by the PR to attract the media nowadays is 'pseudo-events' or events engineered for the sole purpose of gaining the attention of the media. Daniel Boorstin coined the term in 1961 in his book *The Image*, in which he demonstrated how pseudo-events had become more important than 'real' events, and that a 'pseudo-event' would have no value if the media were not present to cover it. Pseudo-events include press conferences, community events, interviews or demonstrations. These events, designed especially for the media, are orchestrated to fit the needs of journalists; for example, an event intended for live broadcast on television will be staged during prime time. Many travel and tourism programmes, for instance, are sponsored by interested organizations such as tourism authorities, airlines or hotel chains. Entertainment shows too are sponsored by advertisers and no clear guidelines exist about how journalists should be reporting on such 'pseudo-events'.

In order to ensure the efficacy of their communication endeavours, PR professionals try to nurture positive relationships with media personnel. Maintaining a strong network of contacts in the media will help to gain and encourage favourable coverage, and increase the possibility of press releases, information in media kits and other news threads being picked up and disseminated in newspapers, magazines, radio and television broadcasts and websites.

'When a pseudo-event takes place, it becomes a real event. There is no difference in the outcome of a pseudo- or a real-event, and therefore, pseudo-events are ethically sound.' What ethical theories are at work in the above notion? In what ways is a pseudo-event ethically sound or unsound?

'A pseudo-event is a play that journalists go and watch. Thus, the media and PR agencies are equally responsible for engineering and perpetuating fake news. Do you agree?

Do editors and reporters in media organizations deliberately let themselves fall into the pseudo-event trap set by PR companies? Do you think the viewer/reader in India is equipped to understand the difference between 'real' and 'pseudo' news?

WHY THE MEDIA NEEDS PR

The endeavours of PR professionals to produce media friendly material do not go unnoticed by the media. Many newspapers depend quite heavily on news releases for their stories. Surveys have revealed that as much as half of all news reported could be sourced from PR material (Parsons 2004). PR handouts, as we have seen, are designed to be media friendly and accessible. It presents a very convenient and regular source of news stories which involves little effort or expense on the part of the media. In the pressured environment of sourcing and reporting stories to short and tight deadlines, PR handouts present a welcome solution for many journalists. Media professionals benefit from maintaining positive and cordial relationships with PR personnel: it helps ensure that information can be acquired easily when necessary and may, on occasions, also encourage early and 'exclusive' acquisition of news.

In spite of the symbiotic relationship between journalists and PR practitioners, unethical practices such as exchange of bribes or expensive gifts have crept into interactions between the media and PR professionals. For a brief period during the 1980s, two Indian newspapers (*The Indian Express* and *The Financial Express*) made it a matter of editorial policy to mention at the end of a news report of a media conference what was given to journalists attending the event—even if the 'gift' given was a fancy folder, a pen, a calculator, or even a sample of a product being sought to be publicized.

Certain media organizations have made it a practice to inform their readers, listeners or viewers if a journalist visited a particular venue or location on a 'junket' that was paid for by someone other than the media organization the journalist represented. This, it is believed, is a fair way of informing the constituents of a media product or service the truth behind 'sponsored coverage'. For instance, the report of a journalist whose visit to a holiday resort has been funded by a hotel chain or a tourism authority interested in promoting the particular destination, would be expected to be different from the coverage of the reporter who visited the same location at his own expense or at the expense of the media organization to which she or he is assigned. Similarly, a writer on the attributes of a new car would be expected to be biased in favour of the car manufacturer that has paid for his expenses. That a sponsorship or a 'junket' is a form of 'bribery' to ensure favourable media coverage has been acknowledged by all independent journalists and media organizations—unfortunately, however, many media organizations deliberately fail to disclose such facts to the public.

MEDIA PR

PR concerns are also present in media organizations. Like any business, media organizations need to ensure that revenue is maximized through, among other things, maintaining high circulation figures. Media's PR publics, for example, include audiences, journalists, sources, shareholders and advertisers. Media's PR involves maintaining a strong and favourable image amongst its various publics. The media's audiences require high levels of honesty, accuracy and objectivity, and they impose trust in the media to ensure that all relevant news will reach them. The media must thus demonstrate all these qualities to uphold its audience's confidence. In March 2008, four British newspapers ran front-page apologies to Madeleine McCann's parents, who the newspapers had repeatedly suggested had murdered their missing daughter (see chapter on Media Law). The apologies followed a libel case which was won by the McCanns. The libel case would have seriously damaged the newspapers' credibility and it was extremely necessary for them to take initiatives to prove their remorse. The front-page apologies were as much intended for their readership in general as they were for the McCanns.

Journalists commonly employ PR strategies to maintain a large network of sources among public officials, members of the corporate world, policemen, lawyers, academics and experts in various fields. Journalists must be friendly, respectful and trustworthy in order to encourage these potential sources to cooperate with their future endeavours and, perhaps, provide newsworthy information first and, sometimes, on condition of anonymity. All PR endeavours of the media should be ethically sound, and should not put a question mark on their professionalism and integrity. In conducting PR activities, codes of ethics for PR practices should be observed within the broader framework of media ethics. Here are some of the key ethics of PR and the ethical concerns that arise when the media and PR meet.

ETHICS OF PR

The dual needs of disseminating news on the part of PR agencies and of sourcing news on the part of the media, would seem to present a harmonized, symbiotic relationship between PR and the media. However, the relationship between the two professions is an 'uneasy' one (Hirst and Patching 2007), mainly because of the ethical issues that arise in these practices. Traditionally, PR practices have been stereotyped as dishonest and manipulative. In order to rid the profession of ethically questionable practices, codes of ethics have been devised in many countries.

The Public Relations Society of America (PRSA) is a body of PR professionals which was established in 1947 to formalize and advance the profession. It is the largest PR society in the world, boasting a 32,000-strong membership. The PRSA has two notable characteristics: accreditation and code of ethics. Its code states that 'the level of public trust PRSA members seek, as we serve the public good, means that we have taken on a special obligation to operate ethically' (www.prsa.org). A glance at the PRSA's ethics reveals striking similarities to media codes of ethics. Emphasis is placed on honesty and accuracy; on promoting informed public debate and decision-making; on fairness and the importance of the right to free expression. Formal accreditation can be earned from the PRSA after extensive examination and proven adherence to its code of ethics. The Institute of Public Relations, a UK-based body, is the largest of its kind in Europe. It advocates the importance of integrity, honesty, accuracy, respect and confidentiality. The Public Relations Society of India adopted the International Code of Ethics for Public Relations in 1968. The ethics of the code are founded on the basic human rights of all individuals, recognized and upheld in democratic societies. It expounds the requirements of PR professionals to act with integrity, loyalty, honesty and accuracy, and to promote the free flow of information and ideas of human rights.

The requirements of these codes should be very familiar to students and professionals of the media. What, then, and wherein lie the ethical dilemmas? It should be noted that, as the PRSA mentions, ethics have precedents and might be subject to change due to unforeseen and new situations. What are now considered key ethical principles of media and PR practices, have evolved over a period of time and involve the media that could compromise adherence to these principles.

Accuracy

The efforts of PR communication have often been described as 'spin'. Spin is the attempt to present events or circumstances for an intended audience. Spin can be achieved either by using euphemisms or by highlighting only certain aspects of a situation to the exclusion of other facts that may be deemed less 'comfortable' for particular interests. Spin is often used in a pejorative sense and assumes that attempts are being made to conceal the whole truth. According to the results of a survey of 2,000 PR personnel, '25 per cent admitted to lying on the job, 39 per cent said they had exaggerated the truth, and 44 per cent were uncertain of the ethics of the job they were required to perform' (Campbell 2002). However, the concept of spin is very ancient. Upaya, or skilful means, involves presenting a message in such a way that it will be easily understood by a specific audience. Parables, or allegorical stories, are a popular form of delivering a message using situations, imagery and language which the ordinary or common person can relate to. The Buddhist Jataka tales could be regarded as a form of spin used by the Buddha for disseminating the truth (dhamma).

'Spin is a part of everyday life. To believe that spin does not or should not happen is to believe in absolute truth.' How far do you agree with this statement? Think about absolute/relative truths and consider how far, and in what ways, spin is used in the media.

News hooks, sound bites, press releases, and pseudo-events are communication methods which could all contain spins. PR professionals are susceptible to spinning information because they have a responsibility to protect the image and reputation of those they represent. Ivy Lee claimed that spin, in the sense of interpreting a situation, is all that is humanly possible: we can only understand a situation in so far as we perceive it, and therefore we can only relate our interpretation of an event (Campbell 2002). There is some truth to his argument, as we saw in Chapter 2 on Truth, Fairness and Objectivity. However, the subjective nature of humanity cannot be allowed to be an excuse for propagation of falsehood. The biggest ethical dilemma about PR and truthfulness arises out of the circumstances under which most PR agencies and PR professionals operate. PR operates behind the scenes and works through the media. PR material is, therefore, more often than not, presented as media material. This leaves the audience unaware of the origin as also the intention of the information they receive, and without that knowledge they cannot be expected to discern for themselves what kinds of information contained in media stories are truly impartial, and what constitute part of image-building efforts orchestrated by professional PR practitioners.

The ethics of accuracy in the media requires that information should be correct, should present the whole truth, and should be placed in its proper context. There is a danger in relying too heavily on PR handouts for news reporting. Press releases which have been especially formulated for media use are sometimes used verbatim, especially in smaller media establishments that lack resources of time and money to use the material only as a basic source of background information. Although accuracy and honesty are values expounded in all PR codes of ethics, media professionals have a duty to follow their own codes. The media should not depend only on PR principles, but should treat all material originating from PR agencies/agents as they treat all other sources of information. That is to say that the onus of the responsibility of fact checking, research and verification falls on the shoulders of the journalist. Verification of information from press releases, for example, is advisable to ensure that fact is fact and not just opinion. Research into a story suggested by PR handouts should be conducted to ensure that the ensuing report presents the information in its full and proper context.

Special care should be taken while using quotes. There has been a tradition of quote-manufacturing in PR, whereby PR practitioners quote the person they represent as having said something which she or he actually did not. It is very usual for politicians to have their speeches written by PR professionals and sometimes the content of a speech will be made known to the media before the speech has been made. In such circumstances it would be prudent to wait until the speech has been made, before quoting from it for it could prove highly embarrassing to all concerned if a reporter quoted from a speech that never happened! To safeguard against falsehood, and to present an accurate and complete picture of a situation, one might employ the verification techniques suggested by Anton Vedder, which have already been detailed in Chapter 9 on New Media: The Internet. Material can be judged on its own merit to ascertain whether it is characterized by consistency, coherence, accuracy and concordance with observations. Alternatively, and more effectively, one can consider authenticity, trustworthiness and credibility as attributes to judge the quality of the information provided.

In today's world of instant communication and easy access to most subjects via the internet, there can be little excuse for compromising accuracy by neglecting to verify information and, in turn, running the risk of compromising credibility and the trust of the public.

It should also be noted that to publish information which has not been verified, and is later established to be false, might run the risk of being libelous. Another requirement of ethical journalism is to attribute sources. Critics find fault in media professionals for often failing to credit PR material. PR devices such as sound bites and VNRs are specifically designed to be inserted directly into a report without requiring editing. VNRs, for example, are often sought to be passed off as the work of a particular media organization. This is sometimes deemed a less than honest practice: to pass off someone else's work as your own is not just 'lazy reporting'—it could be tantamount to plagiarism or copyright infringement.

Even though the actual producer or writer of PR material would not generally be concerned about copyright infringement—after all, they aim at creating and spreading a particular message—the indulgence of such a practice could be considered inappropriate. Furthermore, given the right of the public to information, audiences (readers, listeners and viewers) deserve to be properly and fully informed about the source of information. If a news channel accredited a VNR to its PR parenthood, viewers would become aware of the possibility that a certain message is being conveyed. Although this would help to promote an informed society—the democratic ideal venerated by both the media and PR industries—it could well simultaneously undermine the efficacy of such PR endeavours. In this respect, the media faces a conflict of interest: should journalists serve their sources and/or PR practitioners by protecting their respective vested interests? Or is not the media's first and foremost responsibility to serve the public by delivering accurate and objective news reports that, if required, should contain a variety of viewpoints on a particular topic or issue?

Fairness

Two of the key characteristics of fairness, as far as the media is concerned, are balance and equal opportunities. Balance means to ensure that undue coverage is not given to one side of a story, and that a story should be presented with equal weight to all sides. Equal opportunities involve affording each party the right to respond. An important thing to note about fairness is that efforts must be made on the part of the media to ensure fairness through balance and equal opportunities. Does this mean, therefore, that if a newspaper decides to run a piece on fox-hunting issued by the government which outlines arguments of animal cruelty as a reason why the practice should be banned, then the newspaper should, soon after, seek a press release from a farmers' organization which supports fox-hunting? Should articles about the dire conditions of Asian sweatshops appear to balance reports about a multinational fashion label's new product? On the one hand, it can be argued that if too much coverage is given to certain interest groups, the medium which conveys these interests runs the risk of appearing partisan, and could compromise the ethic of objectivity. Furthermore, to give editorial space to only one side of an argument is to mislead—albeit indirectly—the public and this too could compromise the ethic of accuracy. The answers to the questions raised are not simple and could vary from situation to situation, issue to issue.

If the media uses PR handouts to source its reports, there is a very real danger of creating an environment in which he who shouts the loudest will be heard. Multinational corporations, governments and other prestigious, elitist and affluent organizations are groups which have the largest PR budgets. The larger the budget, the more savvy the PR techniques can afford to be: press releases and VNRs will be high quality and media-ready and can be produced regularly; their news hooks will be catchy and slickly produced since expenses will not be a constraint. It is these groups that inevitably catch an editor's eye, through quantity, quality and readiness. John C. Merril, in his book *Media Debates*, suggested that PR is important because it 'expands the public discourse, helps provide a wide assortment of news, and is essential in explaining the pluralism of our total communication system'. (Campbell 2002). Such a position may, however, be questioned in today's world of market monopolies and where money influences communication systems, notably the mass media. The question, therefore, arises as to the extent to which PR really highlights pluralism and provides audiences the widest possible range of news and views.

What practices of PR are in conflict with the ethics of the media? What measures can be taken to prevent or curb such practices ?

How can editors put in place a system of checks and balances within a media organization to ensure fair reporting of PR-promoted stories?

Objectivity

Objectivity is a fundamental ideal of journalism. Objective journalism requires refraining from bias, and maintaining editorial independence. What has been observed, however, in the earlier chapters on Truth, Fairness and Objectivity and the Media Market, is that objectivity is difficult to achieve and easily compromised. In the media, objectivity can be preserved by refraining from accepting gifts, by fair and balanced reporting and limiting the influence of 'journalistic horizons'. Without objectivity, accuracy and fairness might also be compromised. Objectivity is the most significant point on which media and PR differ: it is a central ethic in media codes, but is almost entirely absent in PR codes. PR codes, on the other hand, expound the importance of loyalty. The PRSA states, 'We are faithful to those we represent, while honoring our obligation to serve the public interest.' This is closely echoed by the Protocol of the Global Alliance of Public Relations Institutes, but adds the need to 'support the right of free expression'.

India's Public Relations Society's Code of Ethics differs a little, underlining the need 'to act in all circumstances in such a manner as to take account of the respective interests of the organization which he (the PR professional) serves and the interests of the publics concerned'. All of the above guidelines recognize the dual loyalties of a PR practitioner. To serve an interested party's goals loyally is to foresake objectivity. In recognizing dual loyalties, the codes go part of the way in redressing this problem. However, none of the codes of ethics for PR professionals address the fact that in serving the interests of many different groups simultaneously, conflicts of interest will invariably arise. Consider the following scenario: a PR firm is employed by a company which produces and sells medicines. New scientific research shows, however, that a particular drug manufactured by the represented company might cause serious and harmful side-effects. The PR firm is then caught between serving the interests of the drug company that wishes to promote this contentious drug and the general public whose health might be at stake. Such conflicting loyalties are common occurrences. The codes, however, do not state which PR loyalty takes precedence. It is perhaps this seemingly insoluble dilemma that is responsible for the absence of loyalty ethics in various codes of conduct for PR professionals.

Media professionals also experience their share of conflicts of interest. This can be seen most pertinently in market-based dilemmas. Media organizations have an interest in protecting the interests of those who advertise with them; their business is a crucial source of revenue. On the other hand, serving the needs of corporate enterprises compromises objectivity and editorial independence, and might influence what news is reported and how. In this eventuality, the media can no longer be said to be serving the public interest. This is a very sticky area of debate, as we have already seen. Nonetheless, in media codes, objectivity is stressed as fundamental for upholding the duty to serve the public interest. The media will inevitably shoulder the conflicts of interest dilemma faced by PR practitioners when it is so heavily dependent on PR material for its content.

The 'private treaties' scheme, which is detailed in the Media Market chapter, involves a swap or trade of favourable and notable media coverage for company shares between media organizations and corporations that are advertisers. In return for shares, companies enjoy favourable coverage. This coverage is not confined to advertising but reportage as well and, in this sense, is a form of PR. PR is preferable to advertising because it carries more credibility. The concern, however, is that is by going ahead with private treaties, the media forsakes its objectivity; coverage is awarded out of obligation to an involved company and not out of editorial judgement. Furthermore, when the media organization has stakes in an involved company, it is working in its own interest to offer favourable editorial coverage as a form of PR. In this sense, the media organization in effect becomes a PR organization.

Such business transactions have been likened to bribery of journalists, who are obliged to support the interests of their employers. Bennett, Coleman & Company Limited (BCCL), the company which is said to have pioneered the private treaties scheme, had argued that the transaction was no different from PR strategies and therefore, sought to make the intermediaries or middlemen—in this case, PR agents—dispensable. But the situation is more complex than that: the PR 'middlemen' practise their profession in accordance with their own objectives and ethics. What applies to PR does not necessarily apply to journalists in the media, as we have seen in the dichotomy between ethics of loyalty and objectivity. If PR is dispensed with, and the money earned by media organizations instead, such practices necessarily alter interests and loyalties of media organizations that are meant to purvey news and views in an objective and unbiased manner. The phenomenon of private treaties is a good example of how the ethical dilemmas inherent in PR are experienced by the media and how, in taking on the role of PR practitioners, the media loses sight of the ethic of objectivity. An article, entitled 'Don't "pay" for media coverage' by the author of this book is reproduced in Box 11.1.

Box 11.1

Don't Pay for Media Coverage

At a time when the distance between large sections of the Indian media and the people of the country has perhaps become wider than ever before, journalists as well as their employers have to introspect yet again on the principles and norms that should govern their work.

There was a huge hue and cry after one of India's largest publishing groups devised a rather disingenuous strategy of accepting money for assuring editorial space.

By this scheme PR firms or individuals would shell out funds to ensure that complimentary articles and/or photographs about the persons or organizations concerned were published in the group's publications.

When competing newspapers pointed out the blatant violation of journalistic ethics and norms implicit in following such a practice, the group's managers put up a weak (if unconvincing) defence of their actions. They argued that such 'advertorials' were not appearing in the main broadsheet but only in the city-specific supplements that highlight society trivia rather than hard news.

There was another, even more blatant, justification of this pernicious practice. It was argued that if PR firms are, in any case, 'bribing' journalists to ensure that stories/pictures of their clients are carried, what was wrong if the intermediary—in this instance, the PR agency— was eliminated from the process?

These specious arguments convinced few and angered many. At a seminar, this correspondent had jocularly asked a senior executive of the group if he would publish my photograph with a caption saying I'm the most handsome man on earth if I paid his company Rs 100,000. He predictably laughed away my remarks. But I was trying to make a point.

From what one learns, the practice of accepting money for assured editorial coverage has been discontinued (at least, overtly) by the group.

However, the phenomenon of bribing journalists to make them do their work (diligently or otherwise) is not new, nor is it peculiar to the Indian media—media that is supposed to be upholding freedom of expression in a country that calls itself the world's largest democracy.

The problems associated with bribing for media coverage were obviously considered an important enough issue for six global organizations to come together recently to formulate a set of principles designed to foster greater transparency in the dealings between those in the media and those in PR.

These six organisations—the International Press Institute (IPI), IFJ, Transparency International, the Global Alliance for Public Relations and Communications Management, the Institute for Public Relations Research and Education, and the International Public Relations Association—announced their support for a set of principles aimed at curbing bribery for media coverage.

The International PR Association is an organization of over 1,000 senior PR professionals. The IPI, with members in 115 countries, is dedicated to the promotion of press freedom, protection of journalists and improving journalistic practices.

The IFJ contends that it is the world's largest association of journalists—it has some 500,000 members in over 100 countries—promoting press freedom and social justice through independent trade unions. Founded in Berlin, Transparency International is a non-profit organization that aims at fighting corruption in every form all over the world.

The Global Alliance for PR and Communications Management comprises 50 member organizations representing over 150,000 PR professionals, while the Institute for PR Research and Education (located at the University of Florida) seeks to improve PR practices through research, education, measurement and evaluation.

The principles embodied in the 'charter for media transparency' are as follows:

- News material should appear as a result of the news judgement of journalists and editors and not as a result of any payment in cash or in kind or any other inducements.
- Material involving payment should be clearly identified as advertising, sponsorship or promotion.
- No journalist or media representative should ever suggest that news coverage will appear for any reason other than its merit.
- When samples or loans of products or services are necessary for a journalist to render an objective opinion, the length of time should be agreed in advance and loaned products should be returned afterwards.
- The media should institute written policies regarding the receipt of gifts or discounted products or services, and journalists should be required to sign the policy.

Dr Donald K. Wright, president of the International PR Association, said: 'In too many countries, bribery of the news media robs citizens of truthful information that they need to make individual and community decisions.'

He added that this campaign was started with the goal of eliminating unethical practices in dealings between news sources and the media. Johann P. Fritz, director, IPI, said that 'all attempts to corrupt the media compromise the freedom of expression that protects all other rights'.

Peter Eigen, chairman, Transparency International, observed: 'The media has an important watchdog role to hold to account those in positions of power. To be credible in this role, it is essential that journalists refuse bribes and the corporate sector desists from offering bribes. It is also crucial that editors, publishers and media owners give journalists all the support they need to implement the media transparency principles announced... '

'Courageous reporters risk life and limb everyday to defend press freedom and human rights,' said Aidan White, secretary of the Brussels-based IFJ. 'We cannot stand by while bribery mocks those sacrifices...' Jean Valin of the Global Alliance for PR and Communications Management, said the attempt to bring 'grassroots strength to this coalition for media transparency... is closely linked to ethics in organizations, which is a cornerstone for effective and credible communication with the public' .

The Institute for PR Research and Education with the International PR Association had released an index ranking 66 nations on the basis of the likelihood that print journalists will seek or accept cash for news coverage, said Frank Ovaitt, president and CEO-elect of the Institute. He believes that 'this is a critical issue that serious journalists and public relations people must address together'. This study can be accessed at: *www.instituteforpr.com/international. phtml? article_id=bribery_index*.

Bribe-givers and bribe-takers have to be both penalized if media operations are to become more transparent and responsive to what society expects of journalists. It used to be said that it is easy to bribe Indian journalists because most of them were rather poorly remunerated.

This logic would hold good for people in other professions as well, be they in the bureaucracy, the police force or in education. At a time when the distance between large sections of the Indian media and the people of the country has perhaps become wider than ever before—witness the inability of large sections of the media to anticipate the outcome of the 14th general elections—journalists as well as their employers have to introspect yet again on the principles and norms that should govern their work.

It is not as if a code of conduct will dramatically alter the ethical environment—nevertheless, the charter on media transparency is a step in the right direction.

Source: Adapted from Paranjoy Guha Thakurta, *Business Line*, 10 August 2004.

In another veiled disapproval of what has come to be known in media circles as 'paid-content' service, a new rival newspaper, *DNA* published the following advertisement (reproduced in Box 11.2) in early 2008 to stress upon its own credibility.

Box 11.2

For Sale, Headlines, Editorials and Your Trust

Journalism isn't what it used to be. News is fabricated, not reported.

Newspapers aren't what they used to be. They aren't reams of paper crammed with truth. Instead they are crammed with advertisements.

And what's frightful is, not all these advertisements stand up and admit they are advertisements. They disguise themselves as headlines. As news reports. At times even editorials. Because each of them come with a price tag.

A price tag that is, regrettably, set by some newspapers and, more regrettably, one that has takers by the dozens. In fact, there are rate cards for buying space. And no, we are not talking about advertising space.

There's a fee for interviews. Another for news articles. With any luck, the only space they can probably not sell is the section on the weather. They even have a fancy term for such news—a Public Relations exercise.

You have always believed news was the truth. Some may term that old-fashioned. But so is truth.

And unlike others, truth is in our DNA.

The PR dilemma is just another facet of the decline in editorial quality, driven by market forces. PR is usually driven by money and if it is not, its expenses assume the possession of it. Veteran journalist Khushwant Singh, in a hard-hitting comment on today's media scene in India, wrote in *Outlook* weekly: 'The hard truth about Indian journalism is that proprietors matter, editors don't.'

Leslie believes that a solution to the conflict of interests dilemma can be found in Aristotle's 'golden mean'—that is to say that there is a middle ground to be trod. Leslie suggests that this will involve self-restraint on the part of practitioners from both fields, journalism and PR (Leslie 2004).

As mentioned earlier, it is in the interest of both PR and media professionals to nurture positive relationships. From the media perspective, a strong network of PR contacts will help ensure the continued flow of substantial and comprehensive handouts which can ease the mediaperson's workload to an extent. Furthermore, PR people are often at the front of significant events, or activities which the media would benefit from covering—so healthy relationships might ensure that news and tips are received promptly by the media. PR also benefits from this relationship, but even then, the media is required to bolster good relations. If a journalist were to write a report using PR material as a starting point but included in his report, information which contradicted, or opinions which undermined, the PR standpoint, there is a chance that the 'cordial' relationship could be damaged—and the flow of PR handouts might be curtailed. To resolve the ethical problems that arise between PR and the media, the two should strive to find an area of mutual trust. Journalists might attempt to nurture relations with those PR practitioners they know to be professional, whose work upholds ethics of honesty, accuracy and public welfare.

SUMMARY

This chapter has provided an understanding of the general objectives and practices of PR. In particular, of the ways in which the PR industry uses the media, and why the relationship between the media and PR is symbiotic. Despite this complementary relationship, however, there are several complex and sticky ethical dilemmas inherent in this relationship. Although the media and PR share some important professional ethics, the fundamental objectives of the two industries inevitably lead to ethical complications from the point of view of the media.

REVIEW QUESTIONS

1. Think of a definition of public relations. What are the main objectives of PR?
2. What do you understand by the term 'engineering of content'?
3. What are the three steps of the PR process and how is it similar to media processes?
4. What are the characteristics of the major forms of ready-made news?
5. What is a 'pseudo-event'?
6. Why does the media need to maintain good relations with the PR industry?
7. What are the key aspects of PR ethics?
8. On which points do PR and media ethics differ?

9. What is spin?
10. How can the media ensure the accuracy of reports based on PR material?
11. Why should PR media releases be attributed?
12. What are the challenges to fairness while using PR material?
13. In what ways can objectivity be compromised while using PR material?

DEBATE

1. PR is incompatible with the media's duty to disseminate disinterestedly, information for the public good. The media should, therefore, refuse all PR material and source material themselves.
2. It is the prerogative of the educated and cultured members of society to guide, educate and govern the social, emotional and material needs of the rest of that society.

REFERENCES

Campbell, Richard 2002, *Media and Culture*, Bedford/St Martin's, Boston.

Hirst, Martin and Roger Patching 2007, *Journalism Ethics*, Oxford University Press, Melbourne.

Leslie, Larry Z. 2004, *Mass Communication Ethics*, Houghton Mifflin Company, Boston.

Parsons, Patricia, J. 2004, *Ethics in Public Relations*, Kogan Page New Delhi, India.

Rodman, George 2001, *Making Sense of the Media*, Allyn and Bacon, Boston.

Sahay, Uday (ed.) 2006, *Making News*, Oxford University Press, New Delhi.

Shrivastava, K.M. 2005, *Media Ethics*, Ministry of Information and Broadcasting, Govt. of India, Publications Division, New Delhi.

Thakurta, Paranjoy Guha 2004, 'Don't Bribe for Media Coverage', *Hindu Businessline*. 10 August.

www.outlookindia.com

www.prsa.org

CHAPTER

12

MEDIA FREEDOM

Media freedom is a multi-faceted and complex issue that includes aspects of ethics. In this chapter, the views of three senior journalists are provided to highlight issues relating to media freedom as well as media ethics. The chapter opens with an interview with P. Sainath, Rural Affairs Editor of *The Hindu* newspaper and winner of the 2007 Ramon Magsaysay Award; an interview with Aidan White, General Secretary, International Federation of Journalists and the text of the K.C. Mammen Mapillai lecture that was delivered in New Delhi on 15 November 2007 by Sir Harold Evans, and former editor of *The Times* and *The Sunday Times* of London.

'MEDIA...THE MOST EXCLUSIONIST INSTITUTION IN INDIAN SOCIETY': P. SAINATH

This is the transcript of an interview with Palagummi Sainath, Rural Affairs Editor of The Hindu *newspaper and winner of the 2007 Ramon Magsaysay Award, that was broadcast on the Lok Sabha Television channel on 10 August 2007. The interviewer was the author of this book. The transcript is being reproduced with permission from Lok Sabha Television.*

Q: I understand you are the 11th Indian and the 6th journalist to have been given the Magsaysay award in the JLCCA (Journalism, Literature and Creative Communication Arts) category. You have been a journalist for the last 26 years and I would like you to describe the current state of journalism in India. Unlike many journalists who have been spending most of their time behind desks and in cities, you travel to different parts of rural India for nearly 300 days in a year. How have you seen journalism evolve in India over the last 30 years or so?

A: If you are asking me about the present state of the media, I think it is defined by one feature: the growing disconnect between mass media on the one hand and mass reality on the other. That, for me, sums up the status of the media as of today. The last 20 or 30 years have been really a process of growing concentration of media ownership. Normally we look back at how media has changed in technological terms, its spread and reach, but what you are also seeing is the rising clout of a very few owners that really diminishes diversity and it marginalizes the smaller voices in the media. The game has become far more expensive. You want to start a little afternoon tabloid in a city or you are talking about tens of crores of (rupees worth of) investment and the ability to absorb losses for some years. So, the richness or diversity is dying even though the numbers are proliferating. The statistics show all sorts of growth.

Q: Let us look at the numbers. Right now, there are close to 60,000 publications registered with the Registrar of Newspapers in India. If you look at television channels, India is the only country in the world with forty 24-hour news and current affairs channels. There are an equal number of channels waiting to enter the market. But as you rightly pointed out, quantity does not mean quality! What you do see is the domination of this market by a few but at the same time you see an intensification of competition. Has this resulted in a lowering of standards?

A: Certainly in many respects. I am not saying that everything is bleak. In fact, I think there is an incredible amount of young journalistic talent in the country. But I am saying that much of the competition is about a race to the bottom, (about) how much you can lower the bar. If you look at it in terms of journalists available or the quality of journalists coming into the profession, there are excellent people. The real issue I think is about the bankruptcy of media leadership. It is a fact that you have 40 channels or 50 channels. Let me recall the title of the Bruce Springsteen song, *57 channels and nothing on.* You keep flipping your channels. On one screen, Prabhu Deva is dancing and going out one way. On another screen, Prabhu Deva is going out in another direction. That is diversity. That is the dance and choreography stuff. There is hardly any variety, any diversity because everyone is trying to do the same thing. Many of your programmes are licenced formats of other programmes shown in the West. The originality factor is minimal.

Q: What has this meant for ethical standards? You say that a journalist should be truthful, he or she should be fair and objective. Reporting should be balanced and should provide the full story, different points of view, the proper perspective, the historical, social and economic perspectives. Why are these basic norms or principles of good journalism being virtually given the go-by in much of what you read in the newspapers and what you see on the idiot box?

A: Again, what I am saying is that the culture and the mindset that monopoly creates, the homogenization it creates, creates this situation. If you look at what is happening, when you talk about fairness or balance or whatever, I want to clarify that I do not divide the world into 'television is bad and print is good'. That is a bogus division. You have equally rotten stuff served on both (media). It is just that the impact of television might be more spectacularly evident. It's not as if print is run by boy scouts or Mother Teresa. One of the things I am noticing is that any distinction between rumour, allegation, charge, FIR (first information report), filing of a case, framing of charges, arguments...has been obliterated. If I say Paranjoy is corrupt, the next questions are: When will his head roll? Why has his head not yet rolled and who is protecting him? It is (an) impossible situation.

Can you identify reports that have appeared in newspapers or broadcast on television in which the differences between rumour, allegation and filing of criminal charges have been blurred? Have these distinctions been deliberately blurred or are these instances of inefficient journalism? How would you have preferred such articles or television stories to have been written or broadcast?

Q: In the name of being first with the news, you publish 'facts' which may not be verified, allegations which may not be substantiated, and not even do the basic duty of trying to get the other side of the story. If an allegation is made against an individual 'A', at least an attempt should be made to contact 'A'. Are you saying that this is a problem?

A: Well, it is a bigger problem. This is the low end of what people are fond of calling the 'rat race' in the media. As far as I am concerned, the rat race in the media is over. The rats have won. These are the fringe battles, these are the peripheral battles, but they still (result in) a lot of damage to the credibility of the profession, to the craft and the practice of the profession. You can make a charge against anyone and from that day on, the person is guilty until proven innocent and then you turn around and make that person a hero. It's just incredible, the kind of low-end competition that is there. If there is an earthquake and if the rival says 20,000 have died, nothing less than 40,000 would do for me. You have to pitch it higher than the other person. Otherwise, you are missing out on exclusivity. All these kinds of problems are there. That is also a strategy. Another way the debate is posed (is) 'serious journalism versus non-serious journalism'. I maintain that non-serious journalism is a very serious business proposition. It is a well thought-out business strategy.

What makes money for you and what does not. What you are left with is what you call 'the news'. So, the non-serious stuff is actually very serious. That is why what we used to call as 'Page 3' culture (is) now on page one.

Q: In one of your articles, you wrote about the wide coverage given to the Lakme Fashion Week.

A: Five hundred and twelve journalists covered that.

Q: At that time, there were large numbers of farmers committing suicide in different parts of the country. For the owners of the media, the newspapers, the magazines and the television channels, what makes news is different. It was the wardrobe malfunction of the model on the ramp and not the plight of the farmer who is committing suicide or what happens to his family thereafter. For the proprietor, the first event is eminently newsworthy. It sells very well and the other (does) not. For them, journalism is no longer a mission. Journalism is about how, as you rightly pointed out, one makes money. Therefore, you do not have readers and viewers but you have consumers. The idea is to bring the advertiser closer to the consumer. Is it not this mindset which is dominating the major media organisations in our country?

A: Yes, you are right, except that I question the idea—they are not carrying what they see as news; they are carrying what they see as revenue. It is not news – the wardrobe malfunctioning is not news, it is revenue. They are calculating on that basis. There are many proprietors who have said so. It is correct on their part that they were at least explicit about that. They said so quite frankly. Journalism is a business, like any other business. Now, I do not think so. Newspapers might be a business or a part of a business. Channels might be a business or a part of a business. Journalism is not a business but it is a profession. I have a very different take on what journalism is. Bringing out a newspaper is a business, journalism is not.

Q: Is your view not excessively idealistic? It is like going back to the old times.

A: Guilty as charged.

Using the Indian Premier League (IPL) cricket matches as a backdrop, comment on how 'Page 3' society and lifestyle information has been converted into 'Page 1' news.

When India was not independent, when the country was under British colonial rule, all the important political leaders of the country were journalists of sorts...

A: All were journalists in some capacity or the other.

Q: They used the mass media to propagate their ideas, messages and ideologies. But today, as you say, it's a business. How did it all change?

A: Yes. There are two things. One is that I have been teaching journalism for more than 20 years. I still find that compared to any other profession, people come to it out of idealism, because of your entire history of journalism in this country, a country where journalism is the child of the freedom struggle. You made a very good comparison. You were talking about the leaders of the national movement. Gandhi*ji*'s opinions were printed in the *Harijan.* How many copies were printed? Is it 1,500 or 1,800? Look at the moral authority he had. He said something and that influenced everybody, they had to respond to it. The imperialist press had to attack it. The government had to attack it. The other newspapers supported it and other newspapers reproduced it. That was the moral authority that kept journalism aside from commerce. Now, you should not try to look at journalism as commerce. It is not. I am not asking you to run a journal at a loss; I am not asking you to run a newspaper at a loss; I am asking you to run it with some sense of decency and proportion because people are entitled to information. It is not just a question of what your marketing manager wants or what your advertising department wants.

Q: This issue that you have raised is not a new one. If you recall, India's first Prime Minister, Jawaharlal Nehru, talked about the jute press and the steel press. I presume he was referring to the fact that New Central Jute Mills were at that time owned by the Jain family which was also in the newspaper business. The Tatas were in the steel business. Ramnath Goenka tried to buy a steel company but he was not successful. The owners had various businesses, one of which was the media and, therefore, they would use the media to lobby for their other business interests. So this aspect of the working of the media is not new. It is almost as old as the country. Have things changed?

A: It has got much worse. Nehru was very prescient and (yet) he was mistaken. He was prescient, in the sense that he saw the jute press and that he saw the business interests operating in the press on a totally idealistic note. When he thought of setting that right by trying to make the press independent and to make it independent, he gave huge subsidies in terms of free land or land at throwaway rates at Nariman Point and in Bahadur Shah Zafar Marg. The idea was that the newspaper industry should flourish in isolation from the external pressures of corporate India. Instead of that, what happened was that they built a 24-storey building in Nariman Point, ran all their enterprises out of one storey and hired out the remaining 23 storeys to banks, airlines and others. It has got to a point where you cannot tell the difference between 'real estate' and the 'fourth estate'.

Q: That is perhaps why Delhi is the only city in the world with more than a dozen English daily newspapers...

A: With more to come.

Q: So what has changed?

A: It is much worse. A quantitative change has also become a qualitative change. It was not just Nehru. We have had Press Commissions in this country, the first one in 1954. Another worked between 1977 and 1980– it got split because of the post-Emergency turmoil. Both the Press Commissions had very old conservative Supreme Court judges, no flaming radicals. You look at the proceedings of both the Press Commissions. Both of them provided you evidence that the biggest threat to freedom of the press in this country came from business houses. In fact, they even spoke of de-linking newspapers from business houses. That was quite a popular idea at that time.

Q: Now the idea is not at all fashionable, now it is derided.

A: It is derided because the business houses now own the newspapers.

Q: If you look at what is happening, for many of these business houses, media is their main business. You are a part of a publication owned by the Kasturi family; we have the Ananda Bazar group of the Sarkar family, the Goenka family has *The Indian Express*; we have Aroon Purie, the Purie family and the Jain family. For them, media is their main business and everything else is subsidiary...

A: They are subsidiary, fair enough. But I do not think that the situation remains the same. If you look at the global level and if you see which way you are going, that will not remain the picture at all. In fact, in India, you can speak of media monopolies. At a global level, you have monopolies in the media because media is one component, a very vital component, of much larger transnational empires. You have five or six such conglomerates in the world. You have News Corp and you have Time Warner. Some of these corporations are into the armaments businesss; they are into multinational banks; they are into airlines; they are making rockets. One of them is actually a part of the US mint. It mints coins. So, the media is one component of what Ben Dickens describes as not just transnational corporations but planetary corporations. They are integrated in various ways.

Q: Let us discuss what is happening in India. Let us discuss issues pertaining to cross-media ownership. Let us discuss the breaking down of the Chinese Wall that is supposed to exist between advertising content and editorial content. Consider the example of Bennett Coleman Company

Limited, certainly one of the largest media organizations of its kind. Not very long ago, it decided that there should not be a Chinese Wall between advertising content and editorial content. So, they floated an arm called 'Medianet' and you could pay to get your picture published or a particular kind of a write-up published. When you are throwing a party for your friends, they could report on the party and print pictures of that party. Though this practice was widely criticized by other sections of the media, what you found was that sooner rather than later, everybody was following suit. After having criticized *The Times of India*, they are doing exactly the same thing. The media organizations are eliminating the intermediary and going straight to the guy who wants publicity. You pay Rs 2 lakh to have your picture published and to say that you are the most handsome man on the earth.

A: You are absolutely right. After bitterly criticizing *The Times of India*, most of the others fell rapidly in line—not all, but most of them did. Again, it comes back to what your vision of journalism is. Is journalism a business or is it something more than a business? One of the famous proprietors has gone on record saying that it is not in any way different from producing soap or toothpaste or whatever. Actually it is, because you cannot sell yesterday's newspaper today. But you can sell yesterday's packed toothpaste for the next six months at least.

Q: I will give you another difference. What costs Rs 2 actually takes Rs 20 to produce. So, there is no direct link between the price of a newspaper to the consumer and the cost of production because 90 per cent of your revenue is coming from advertisements.

A: A lot of it then (is) about creating the news content, the surrounding territory has to create the buying mood. So, you see your brilliant documentary on (the) Bhopal (gas tragedy) may not sell my toothpaste. In fact, it may make me think of industrial waste before I put the cream on the brush, whereas a sunny-side-up, upbeat story like the one you had fifteen days ago on the front page of *The TOI* about a guy paying Rs 15 lakh for a privileged mobile phone number…

Q: The last seven digits were all zero.

A: Let me also honestly say that it would not be objective and it would be grossly unfair for me not to admit that the same *Times of India* has carried the largest series on poverty ever run in the Indian press that I wrote – 84 pieces – and they carried it very prominently without censoring it. Personally I owe a lot to (the newspaper for publishing) that particular series… So, let me put that on the record. However, you have got this guy who spends Rs 15 lakh and then the next day, you have got another guy propping up to say that he spends Rs 1.5 crore. And the item reads like an editorial where it states that this is the result of the new confidence of the Indian public in the period of liberalization.

Q: This is the resurgent India, the shining India...

A: Then TV has to go one up on that. So you have the scene of the parents of that guy distributing *pedas* celebrating the achievement of their son in borrowing money to spend lakhs on a mobile phone number. In the same period when we were talking about what makes news and what does not make news, let me tell you what makes news, but did not make it either to the masthead nor to page 3 nor even to page 33. In the same country, the National Sample Survey Organization says that the monthly per capita expenditure of a farm household in this country, that is the average between a giant landlord with a farm bigger than Luxembourg and tiny guys with three-quarters of a hectare, is Rs 503. Out of that Rs 503, sixty per cent is spent on food, eighteen per cent on fuel, clothing and footwear. That means he is left with twenty per cent for every other necessity of life, including health-care and education.

Q: One definition of the poverty line is those spending less than one US dollar a day...

A: This is just the average. Take Jharkhand, Bihar, Orissa and Madhya Pradesh out of the average and see the difference. The average goes up because of Kerala and Punjab where the most affluent farmers live. In Kerala, the average farmer spends Rs 950 a month.

Q: Returning to media monopolies, whenever there is talk about restrictions on cross-media ownership, namely that one particular newspaper group or one particular media organization should not dominate all media in a particular area, be in print, radio or television, there is a big hue and cry. When you say that there are restrictions in America or Australia, they say there is an attempt to curb freedom of expression, a right enshrined in the Constitution of India.

A: This is the point. This is where fraud and hypocrisy stands out at its worst. On the one hand, in dealing with the journalist, dealing with content and dealing with the readers, you assert that journalism is a business like any other business. The moment your financial interests are threatened, you talk about freedom of the press. You cannot have it both ways. You cannot have your cake and eat it too. If it is a business like any other business, then it has to be regulated like any other business. If it is a business like any other business, you have to have the rights and responsibilities of any other business and you do not have a special dispensation.

Q: An organization like the Bennett Coleman Company is today purchasing shares in dozens of other companies that are either its current advertisers or potential advertisers. I am not privy to the exact kinds of terms and conditions of the agreements that have been drawn up...

A: The buzzword is 'private treaty clients'. The aim is that almost everyone in a given sector should be your private treaty client by a particular period. Therefore, the chance of reporting objectively shrinks. Every day the space that the journalist gets to report on shrinks. It is not just that. That practice, as you said, is much more widespread. *TOI* is the pioneer, the path-breaker...most of the others fall in line pretty quickly.

Q: Do you not find it ironical that the largest organization of its kind, the most profitable organization of its kind, should be in a sense leading the way, acting as the pioneer to go ahead with what you might consider unethical practices which are not conducive to good journalism?

A: I find it perfectly logical. They are the biggest guys and the most successful ones, and, therefore, their example will be emulated by those who lack imagination and the idea that it can be done differently. I think it is a very stupid thing...If you are fighting with number two or number three, your best bet is to do something totally different. If you are going to give me *The Times of India* diet, then 'no thank you, I will not buy it'. I want the original product. By imitating, you are not persuading me to buy your product.

Q: Let us talk about radio. Do you not find it ironical and paradoxical that in the world's largest democracy, news on radio is still controlled by the government, it is monopolized by the All India Radio? Even today, if you are a private radio broadcaster, you are not technically allowed to put out news and current affairs programmes....

A: It is ironical but it is also paradoxical and complex. Radio is still the most important medium in this country. Its reach and spread is still very wide. It bypasses the problem of literacy like TV does, without the problem of cost. You can run it on batteries. It has got all sorts of features to it which makes it very special and very powerful. You will find the staid portion of it being whittled away and new generations are being made to understand that the kind of stuff that is coming out of FM is journalism. I really need to say this. While I agree with you that those spaces should open up, I think it is extremely important for a democratic society to have a strong public broadcaster, in radio and TV.

Q: Let's talk about the new medium; the internet. There may be 120 million television sets in India but there are barely 20 million personal computers. There is a big digital divide. The world wide web is in a sense not just a medium of mass communication it is also a medium of personalized communication. Do you see its potential to democratize society being realized in a country like ours? Or is it early days?

A: As in the case of every new medium, the internet is very powerful. It is also a trillion (US) dollar direct revenue business in advertising now. Sometimes, we tend to romanticize a new technology. If you look at the evolution of communication over the years, it all happened in the last 75 years. Your human speech evolved 50,000 years ago. Five hundred years ago, the first printing press came; 75 years ago, mass radio came; 50 years ago, mass television began; 25 years ago, satellite broadcasting began; 15 years ago, the internet began. Actually the new media is not that new. That is one side. The second side is that inequalities in society get reflected in this new medium as well—mostly white, mostly male, mostly those with money access the internet.

We tend to exaggerate the potential of everything. I am not for a moment denigrating the internet. If you go back to the history of radio, when radio was launched, you will find all the great minds of that period pronouncing that radio would liberate humankind. Raymond Williams said: 'Radio will liberate mankind'. Ten years later, Hitler was using Radio Berlin to attack Poland and Czechoslovakia. As Philip Adams put it once: 'Gutenberg promised us enlightenment, we got *Penthouse.*' Radio promised us mass education, we got Hitler. Television promised us mass education, we got Jerry Springer. (Jerry Springer's television shows in the US often feature discussion topics such as infidelity, adultery, homosexuality, prostitution, and transvestism, and use of profane language to attract viewers—this explanation has been added by the author since many potential readers may not know who Jerry Springer is.) I think we should take a hard-headed look at who calls the shots on the internet. If you look at news services on the internet, the same giants are there and still control a lot of what is called news.

Q: What can be done to uphold journalistic traditions in India, traditions that say a journalist plays an adversarial role to those in positions of power and authority? A journalist should not just educate and inform ordinary citizens but empower them?

A: Absolutely. There are two kinds of things that we call journalism. There is journalism and there is stenography. Much of what we call journalism today is stenography to the powerful. That's exactly what it is, nothing more and nothing less. If you look at the media during the freedom struggle and now, there is a giant paradox. A tiny media, a tiny press during the freedom struggle with print orders of 1,000, 1,200 or 1,500 copies served a gigantic social function. Today, a gigantic media serves the most elitist and narrow social spectrum. That is the paradox. The size has grown; the relevance has fallen. This is what I maintain having trained over 1,000 mediapersons, many of whom I am still in personal contact with. Apart from the teaching I do in schools, I have worked with dozens and dozens of stringers and district-level correspondents. I have done it for fourteen years. If I go to Kalahandi, there are going to be fifteen journalists with me wherever I go. Their energy, idealism and drive is simply amazing. They are all people who could have done something else and earned more money. In the journalism classes I teach, many kids could be earning a fortune in some other profession but they have chosen journalism. Their idealism, their desire to do things is there in the public as well. The Indian people have always created spaces for our freedom.

Q: We see a change in the kind of people who are today becoming civil servants. People from the underprivileged sections are becoming civil servants. Hopefully not all journalists in India will dumb down their audiences and there will be some good guys...

A: I would be a little nastier than this. I would say that the media (has become) the most exclusionist institution in this country. In the worst government, you have the representation of Dalits, Adivasis in very important positions. Show me one Dalit, one Adivasi in the mainstream leadership of the media who counts for something. That is why it shows in our content. There is an absolutely hysterical, abusive attitude towards reservation (of seats in educational institutions) issues and quota battles. It is as elitist as you can get and it is getting worse.

Q: I understand the Prime Minister called you and asked you for your opinion about the entire package which was given to the Vidharba region where there has been a high incidence of farmers committing suicides. What did you say? Is the government really trying to do something for farmers? Is it just lip service?

A: Actually I was called before the package. He wanted to go to Vidharba and I spoke to hime about the region. But I would not make too much of that. Maybe, he consulted many others. As I said then and I say it now, you cannot have packages going one way and policy going another way. The policy will win over the package. The problems of the Vidharbha farmers or those of any other farmer cannot be solved by such a package. The problem basically is that for the last fifteen years farmers have been encouraged to give up cultivating food crops and go into cash crops. This is the old World Bank policy of exporting agricultural produce. They (the West) want you to grow what they do not grow in their own climate. What they cannot grow in their own climate is pepper or coffee or cotton or vanilla or whatever. That is what they need. They need to export their food crops to you and therefore they are not interested in your expanding food cultivation. So you have pushed millions of small guys into taking big risks. Paddy cultivated over an acre in Kerala costs, say, Rs 8,000; an acre of vanilla cultivated in Kerala costs between Rs 1 lakh and

Rs 1.5 lakh. The risks are incredible; and that's why suicides are taking place. There is huge volatility in the global prices of commodities that are controlled by a handful of corporations.

Q: What can the media do to highlight the problems of farmers. You are seen as a bit of a 'lone ranger'. *The Hindu* is said to be pampering one Sainath whose heart is bleeding for ordinary people. When will the mainstream media start looking at Bharat? I do not believe that everybody who lives in the city is totally oblivious and unconcerned about what is happening in the villages.

A: You have hit upon a fundamental issue. One of the biggest lies propagated by journalism managers and owners is that readers are not interested. You know the ultimate cowardly slogan of every bankrupt media leader is that this is not what the readers want. I will say two things about *The Hindu* and about *TOI.* Many years ago when I tried starting the project which ended up in a book called *Everybody Loves A Good Drought*, the project was rejected by one editor after another with the same words: this is not what the readers want. The book is still in print, it is in its 18th print. Maybe some readers did want it. When *The Times of India* ran that series, it had a phenomenal response which they placed on record, in terms of how many letters they got, how many people contributed, how many people reacted to it.

Well, if you like to think that spending 150 to 200 days in a year without electricity is being pampered, I am pampered. I am pampered by *The Hindu* in terms of the space and the consistency with which they have stayed with an issue, which I think is very important to good journalism. However, I do not consider myself a 'lone ranger'. I am not working alone in any of these areas. Whether I like it or not, all the district stringers, young journalists gather around me and ask: can we go with you, can we travel with you? There is enormous need and curiosity. Let me also say that on two counts, you are right. One, an enormous number of people in the cities, four generations or five generations ago, were villagers. People have ties and people also have hearts, not just purses. They are not just consumers. A lot of my mail comes precisely from urban readers because the urban middle class reads what I write. I am unable to cope with the kind of mail I get. Many people want to help other people in the countryside. There is phenomenal idealism in the public. Your reading public and your viewing public are far ahead of your editors, owners and channel proprietors.

Q: On 31 August 2007 in Manila, when you get the Ramon Magsaysay Award, you are going to receive US$ 50,000. The current exchange rate is about Rs 40 to a dollar and it works out to …

A: I hope it stays at that level before I collect it, looking at the US dollar's downward slide.

Q: What exactly are you going to do with this money?

A: There are some families to whom my friends and I feel a commitment in these areas. We do not want to be a relief agency; we are not an NGO; and we are not a charity organization. But we have actually created problems for these families by writing about them because the laziness of the urban media is such that once we write about the family 'X' in Yavatmal, 300 journalists are going to land up at the doorsteps of the family 'X' asking them to retell the story of their father's suicide which is not a nice thing. It puts too much pressure on that family. We are committed to sort of regenerating their farms, but that is a very tiny amount which we are spending anyway.

The amount of Rs 20 lakh is going to be the seed money to set up an archive of rural India. A lot of professions and occupations are dying. The *kumbhar*, the pot maker, is dying; plastic buckets have taken away his business. He will not be there in a few years. The *lohar* is dying. We want to record, for posterity, the lives of street-side vendors, the small *vyapari*, the landless agricultural labourers, the women farmers. Hundreds of years from now people should be able to see what the Indian countryside used to be (like).

I also hope to set a much smaller archive of the last living freedom fighters in this country. That is why I am so pleased that the award came to me on the sixtieth anniversary of Independence. I am not talking about those freedom fighters who went on to become the President of India or the Prime Minister of India. They are nice, but I am looking at the 'everyday Joe'—the schoolteacher in Chhattisgarh who spent fourteen years in jail because Gandhiji said so and comes out and goes back and teaches in the same school for the rest of his career, who does not think he did anything special. He is proud of the fact that he did his duty. These are the people who have inspired me the most in my life... They are very ordinary people who rose to do extraordinary things in a period of great flux and change.

Q: I hope this award will not go to your head. Are you going to continue to do the work that you have been doing over the last 26 years?

A: I have got friends who will take care of any pomposity. They are extremely rude and will ensure that, that does not happen. I do not see myself as any different after the award. I will do the same work I have been doing. I want to say one thing about covering rural India. A lot of people look at me with awe and admiration and say, 'you are going out there, you are doing this'. I do not suffer. I love it. I am doing what I like, what I enjoy. I am not doing it for greater glory or for the good of my soul. I might have been a sports journalist because, by the way, I'm a cricket fanatic.

Q: You are also a singer. You strum the guitar.

A: I retired a very long time ago.

Q: You did not have an ambition of cutting a disc of your own?

A: I came close. But I would say one thing about my racket, if you like, is that the job that I do gets me to see my country in a way very few people get. I am not going to exchange that very easily.

Q: People like you are sometimes derogatorily referred to as poverty pimps...

A: The same people who say it should know that luxury pimps take up about 96 per cent of your media time and leave very little space for the poverty pimps...If you look at my work, you will not find pictures of kids with distended bellies—the kind of pictures of famine and hunger in Ethiopia that TV often shows. Poverty is not a disease, it is not an affliction. It is rooted in structural inequalities and it is the result of what human beings do to other human beings in terms of a word that no longer exists in the media—it is called 'social exploitation'.

Q: When you talk of the process of exploitation, you invariably find that the media is not interested. If you are gradually denuding a hillside of its forest cover, it is not news. But the day there is landslide, it becomes news. You might be clogging the sewers of Mumbai with plastic bags but when the city is suddenly paralysed and all the film stars have to wade home....

A: This is pretty much rooted in the Indian media's preferences. You see, (what) we are excellent at is in covering events, though even that seems to be declining. We cover events. We have no patience to cover the processes. That is also because of a serious lack of imagination. Events are covered because these events are dramatic. I find the drama in processes infinitely more compelling, but then it requires work. Covering the process is half the battle of journalism.

THE DIFFERENCE BETWEEN FREEDOM OF PRESS AND FREEDOM OF EXPRESSION

These are excerpts from the transcript of an interview with Aidan White, General Secretary, International Federation of Journalists, that was broadcast on the Lok Sabha Television channel on 1 August 2008. The interviewer was the author of this book. The transcript is being reproduced with permission from Lok Sabha Television.

Q: (You are) currently in India to help promote the ethical journalism initiative, which is a campaign and programme of activity developed by journalists and media professionals to restore values to the profession and a certain sense of a mission. This initiative aims to strengthen press freedom, reinforce quality journalism and consolidate editorial independence.... You say that journalism today is more powerful than ever before, perhaps since the days of Gutenberg, and it's not just the way the media influences the way people dress, the way they talk, but...the way the people think... their attitudes and opinions. Yet, at the same time, you also believe there is a crisis of confidence and...a crisis of quality in journalism all over the world and also in India. Would you like to elaborate on... what appears as a paradox to many?

A: Well...it is certainly a paradox, Gutenberg revolutionized the form of human communication with the printing press and right now we are in another communication revolution. The internet is changing very much the whole way that we communicate with one another... we are seeing massive changes in the world of communication which means, as you rightly say, media is more powerful than it has ever been. It's possible to circulate information, images and word around the world (with)in seconds. Satellite television technology has really revolutionized the way we receive and get information. But at the same time, we are seeing great changes in the media market which are putting great pressure on the quality of journalism and content...There is a lot of competition taking place between media companies and very often that commercial competition is leading to challenges, if not downright betrayal (of) some of the aspirations for quality and mission in journalism.

Q: Journalism can't be a philanthropic activity, journalism cannot just be only a mission. I am playing contrarian. Therefore, if media organizations are driven by commercial motives to maximize profits, more importantly, because (be it a) newspaper, television channel, or a radio station, or a website, the bulk of its income and revenues come from advertisers, isn't this bound to happen?

A: Well, it is bound to happen. It is one of the consequences of the market. But I do want to challenge you on one basic idea, because, look journalism is about values. You are wrong to say (that) it is not about values. Freedom of expression is about the right of anyone to say whatever they want, it doesn't have to be true, it doesn't have to be fair, it doesn't have to be decent – because that is what freedom of expression is (about). Freedom of the Press is different, because Freedom of the Press (operates in) a different framework...and that is, a framework of values. It should be accurate, it should be fair, it should be balanced, it should be truthful, and it should, as far as possible, do no harm to people.

So journalism is about values. And the problem we are seeing these days is that there is a tremendous amount of pressure on journalism of values. That pressure comes from governments (that) are trying to manipulate (the) media in terms of controlling information; that pressure comes from advertisers, sponsors and corporations (that) are trying to use the media to sell their products and so on. Pressure (also) comes from (the) owners of media who are trying to get the largest audience (and) wide(st) circulation of their material and all of that pressure means that those simple values of journalism—truth, independence, balance and fairness—are really compromised to the extent that you wonder these days (whether) people can trust what they read in the newspapers.

Q: I want you to elaborate on one thing. You said freedom of expression, which is an integral aspect of democracy, means I can say what I like but it does not have to be true… I don't have the right to criminally defame you. Then you can sue me and …a court could prosecute me. But why do you think that in the media today, this commercial competitiveness… (has) not resulted in (an) improvement in standards, improvement in quality. Normally you would argue that when there is competition (among) a number of players to provide a certain service to an audience, then an attempt would be made to improve the quality of that service…

A: I think we have to be careful about saying these things…Look, today if people are looking for quality, they know where to look. Let me give you an example. If you go to the internet and see what people going to the internet look at and see, you'll see that there are following quality brands if they want quality information. Which (are the) websites they would go to? If you are in Britain, do you go to the mass circulation website of the Sun or the News of the World tabloids? No. You find most of the internet users in the UK go to *The Guardian*, *The Telegraph* and *The Times*, or the BBC. They go to the quality brands. So it's wrong to say that quality doesn't matter. In fact when people are looking for the truth, they are … attracted by the brands that give them quality, that they can rely upon. They know that mass circulation tabloid newspapers are not going to deliver the truth. They may deliver fun, they may deliver a little bit of information, they certainly do deliver an awful lot of celebrity news, they deliver a lot of gossip and that has its place in the freedom of press….

But (what) I am (also) worried about is investigative journalism, (the) scrutiny of people who exercise power in society, independent evaluation and opinion of what is the right thing to do. These are the important contributions that media make to democracy and which have, in my view, been severely put under pressure by competitiveness and changes that are taking place in the media worldwide.

The traditional markets are changing. There is no doubt about it. And there is a great deal of panic in many parts of the developed world like in North America, Europe and elsewhere, media analysts are very worried about the future, because advertisers are leaving prime time television, they are leaving mass circulation newspapers, because circulations are going down, because people are going to the internet. So what's happening is that the media market is thinning and the advertising market is thinning as well. As a result of that, the old reliable television or printed publication markets for media is broken and we don't know what's going to replace it. In fact many of us cannot predict safely what is going to be the media scene in Europe, or in the developed world, in 15–20 years time.

....We can see that the whole news business is in a flux and is changing; now that is a good thing. I am not against change, I am very much in favour of it, what worries me is that in the process of change, we do not lose the extraordinary importance of good quality of information for democracy. Why is information important to democracy is a question you have to ask. We need it. We need good information because people need to be informed about the society (that) they are living in to make the right choices, about the people who are running their country. The right choices about the schools their children are going to, and make the right choices about the local authorities who are providing support to them, the companies that are working in their area... they need to have good quality information.

Q: I am going to return to this theme about quality of information, about reliability of information, about authenticity of information, but let's go back to this issue of online journalism; if you are getting your news for free through your Google, or Yahoo, or through 1001 websites that are available, why then would you buy a newspaper. What would you tell a young woman or a young man in his or her teens or early twenties today?

A: Well...if you look at the Yahoos and Googles of the world, what do you find? You find traditional media because if you look at the aggregators provided by Google news, for the internet – and this is the most popular in the world—90 per cent of the information that is being thrown up comes from traditional media brands. You've only got to look up at Google news, whether it is Google news India, Google news Belgium, Google news Ireland, Google news Argentina, you look at what's on that front page, it's the traditional information brands. So although we have the internet providing information, (what) actually it is mainly doing is repackaging traditional media information and putting it out there.

Now that is undermining absolutely the traditional media market and creating great instability; so there is a big problem, because in the past we had a balance between public information services, (and) private information services, and on the whole, they had managed to survive. Today the private information business is in crisis, there is no doubt about that. (In) some parts of the world, India and China for example, it's expanding, but I am wondering whether that expansion is for the long-term. That's a big question mark, but it's expanding. But in the rest of the world, the traditional market organization is no longer working, so there is a big question about where do you make money in the media business for the future. Now my view about it, and I think it's beginning to be borne out ...even Mr. Rupert Murdoch, himself, who perhaps represents mass media market on a global level, is saying that if there is (a) future for journalism, there is a future for quality, it has got to be in investigative journalism—good quality journalism packaged and going to the people who need it. And now if Murdoch is saying that, I think we should listen. If you look at the way he has taken on *The Wall Street Journal*, he has begun to change *The Wall Street Journal* from a stuffy business paper to a quite different popular paper, but with very serious and very high quality information inside.

Q: Mr. White, (a) lot of people find this whole issue of user generated content, fairly nightmarish. Why, because you are not sure there are gatekeepers, we are not (sure) that the quality of information provided is of a certain standard, the authenticity, whether the facts have been doubly checked, triple checked, or what has been put out, is just innuendo, gossip, rumour or worse, downright lies, misinformation, disinformation. But (what) we are also seeing today, is ordinary citizens getting empowered using technology, the tsunami in December 2004, the pictures that were shown on television, were taken by individuals with their handy-cams, with their mobile phones... More importantly, Saddam Hussein's last moments in 2006 were shot (read captured on) by a mobile phone camera. Also, how do you deal with today's citizens, having the power and means to do what earlier used to be the preserve of technically equipped journalists or media professionals.

A: The first question here is what we are saying is an expansion in freedom of expression, that people are now able to express in different ways that they never had (been able to) before. That they can use their telephone, their video camera, and that's marvelous, and I think that's great for freedom of expression. But it's not Freedom of the Press or Freedom of the Media, because it's quite different, as I said earlier, from that framework in which information needs to be packaged in order to call it journalism. And that ethical framework is one that distinguishes what journalists produce from what local citizen journalists produce—what the people in the street would produce. It's very important to make that distinction and that's why journalism is an important filter, because we live in a world where there is so much information before us, (that) we are overwhelmed with information. We lead busy lives. How do we find out what is going on unless we have access to well-packaged, buy-size pieces of information that are reliable, accurate and trustworthy? That's exactly what journalism is and what journalism has to be. Now user-generated content in my view is a great thing, so-called citizen journalists well I don't know what they are…

Q: The point is what we are seeing is (that) internet at one level is personalized form of communication, you can send your email, but it is also a medium of mass communication…

A: So it is not a threat to journalism at all. It seems to me rather like the introduction of telephone itself, (which) absolutely revolutionized the capacity for mass communication person to person. We are seeing a massive change in the way we communicate with one another, but it is not journalism. Let's not (make the) mistake of confusing the increased capacity that people have to express themselves with the need for journalism, which is shaped by certain moral values, the ethical notions.

Q: We are going to come to that , but what about blogging; you know we are actually seeing bloggers which you know once again, no gatekeepers, but the persons writing a personal diary, or whatever. We see bloggers moving or encroaching into the space that was (once) occupied by journalists, are you worried?

A: Not at all. Not in the slightest. If you look at the internet, the internet is full of information, and (it) is wonderful. It is a wonderful kaleidoscope of pictures, ideas, thoughts and words, and actually 95 per cent of it is irrelevant. It's trivial, it's uninteresting, it's dull, and is personal, and that is great. I have no problem with it at all and (it) is not encroaching upon journalism as long as it does not pretend to be journalism. The only way that we can make sure that there is a distinction, is by protecting the notion of what journalism is in the modern world. What it is—it is actually the preparation, the gathering together, the dissemination of information in a framework of ethical and moral values—that's what distinguishes journalism from a blogger at home.

Q: Let me ask you to comment on one particular incident which took place which is very very controversial. Here we had a Danish newspaper, publishing cartoons of the Prophet Muhammad, which antagonized large sections of people, literally thousands of miles away from Denmark, and it was not just the fact that it was one newspaper that printed these cartoons, thereafter thanks to the internet, these pictures got circulated all over the world and it threw up a slue of ethical issues, would you like to comment what are these ethical issues, what does it mean, what does this particular episode signify, in terms of challenges to freedom of expression in a world that is characterized by religious extremism, by fanaticism of all kinds.

A: Well I think, the cartoon example is a very good example, this was not actually a challenge to journalism, it was a challenge to politics…

....Now, what's important about the cartoon's issue, which is actually rarely admitted but is important, is that the cartoons were published by journalists who weighed up in the balance, should we publish these cartoons or should we not publish these cartoons. I can't think of a single story in the last 20 years, in which almost every news outlet around the world, has sat around a small table like this with the Chief Executive of the newspaper and debated the issue. And, you know, what is the most interesting fact which is rarely referred to in this whole debate (is that) more than 95 per cent of the world's media decided not to publish the cartoon. That the reality of it is, given the opportunity, the vast majority of journalists, senior journalists around the world, (were) able to debate the issue, able to decide what was the right thing to do, (and) decided not to publish the cartoons. Now it seems to (me) that it is a much more important fact, than the extremists reactions which were generated by politicians to satisfy their own political needs. So, if we say whether the cartoons were a test of quality journalism, yes I think they were, and I think that they demonstrated, that left to their own devices, majority (of the) journalists can take the right decisions.

Q: Let's talk a little about the politics and the media. Most journalists have a kind of a love and hate relationship with politicians and (people in) positions of power and authority, and so do politicians at one level. You have to report what they say because that makes news, and as much as they (politicians) hate journalists, they are dependent on journalists to disseminate whatever they have to say. At the same time the government (or) the state has an important role to play, in ensuring that there is freedom of expression, that you have an environment where there is media freedom. Yet at the same time what you see the world over, politicians and governments becoming increasingly intolerant of independent journalism, especially journalism that is critical of the policies and programmes of those who are in power.

A: Absolutely. Right now, it's in the nature of politics that you need a good press and you need good media. You don't get elected unless you are popular and you don't get elected unless your media image is strong. All politicians know this, and that's why they have a vested interest in good press. Now that's naturally why the instinctive political reaction to an opportunity to influence or manipulate the media will be to do it in their own interest. In a democracy we have to have (a) political philosophy based on an absolute clear understanding that there is a need to keep government at arm's length from the administration of media. That it is extremely important doesn't mean that government and politics don't have an important role to play. They do. One of the most important things they can do first of all, as you rightly say, (is that) they need to guarantee conditions for freedom of expression. Political leaders and government officials should ensure freedom of expression within the law. Journalists should not be accused of criminal defamation or sent to jail if they are purveying information that is factually correct and is carrying out their work in an ethical manner. At the same time, there should be recognition of the need to have proper accountability and self regulation on the part of the media. So Press Councils in this light should be supported and so on. There should be (a) public service broadcasting because private media can't deliver what everyone in society needs; because there are marginalized groups in society that don't actually respond to advertisements. Therefore, the state has a responsibility to make sure that all of its citizens whether rich or poor, its people in the regions, people in the metropolitan centres, all of them get access to quality information.

Q: Would you like to elaborate on a statement you made that we are going through difficult and challenging times for journalists because what we see the world over is an unprecedented increase in journalists being attacked, being killed and media personnel being silenced, for doing their duty?

A: Well I think there are two aspects to this – the first is we are seeing (a) terrible rise in violent attacks against journalists in recent years, and I think (this is) largely due to the Iraq war. We (have) seen record levels in terms of killing of journalists in the last three or four years, but the fact of the matter is that there has been an increase in the amount of violence against journalists simply because of the power of media (that) has increased and that led us to create a global institution called the International News Safety Institute, which has brought together employers such as CNN, BBC, Reuters and major media as well as journalists' organizations like our own to work together to lobby for change. The second issue, which is very important, is that we are now seeing more intrusive government(s) globally, and they are using the war on terror, as an excuse....

Q: ...and the phenomena of embedding journalist with defence forces.

A: We are certainly seeing that. On that issue we have seen in the Iraq war where the American army had been involved in killing around 20 journalists who were not embedded journalists and there was a great suspicion that may be those media were targeted. But they (the US army personnel involved) have not been subjected to proper investigation in those cases—that's really a worrying thing—so you are right about the question of embedded journalism. Embedded journalism is not independent journalism and in all wars these days, simply because of the change (in) technology, it's now possible to have a more free reporting of what is going on, and it is important to protect those who are trying to carry that out. But the second thing that is most worrying, I think, is (that), we are (increasingly) seeing this question (read issue) of the war on terror and the use of terrorism as an excuse to limit civic liberties, and also to follow (read track) journalists. We've had very significant cases, even in the most democratic countries of the world—Sweden, France, the Netherlands, Germany, US—countries that had been tapping the telephones of journalists, putting spies in the newsrooms to find out who journalists are talking to, what are journalists up to... There has been more pressure on journalists to reveal their sources of information, and all of this has been part of governmental pressure to find out what journalists are doing... and the problem about that is that it means there will be less investigative journalism, less democratic scrutiny of what those in power are doing, and dangerously, there would be less democracy as a result of that.

Q: Mr. White, before we move on to this issue of sensationalism and trivializing, you talked about journalists acting as moles for security agencies, and you very cynically remarked that security agencies think that they have done something wrong or they've been less than efficient in their work if they don't have a mole in virtually every major media organization. Is this true for most parts of the world?

A: Well....it's to be expected, the security agencies, in order to do their job, are going to want to keep an eye on what the mainstream media are doing and who they are talking to. That wouldn't be a surprise and that's why I would expect particularly in these days of heightened security concern and particularly when there is evidence of widespread telephone tapping in the media that there would be people in the media who are planted there by the security agencies.

Q: ...You are saying that media organizations are not investing enough on editorial quality and often commercial competitiveness is resulting in a betrayal of ethical norms. What happens is journalists end up doing all the wrong things, so they end up stoking fires of intolerance, racism, providing very simplistic one-sided views, say of the minorities, and sensationalist kind of reporting and trivializing, (which) creates all set of problems, creates social tensions—would like to elaborate on this?

A: Absolutely right, this is one of the areas where there is problem about competition, (and) there is problem about political pressure, (which) comes together in a terrible way when you live in a world where there is a great deal of concern about security, about terrorism, and when you live in a world where there is inter-communal violence that we've seen for a very long time. There are many politicians who are ready to be extremist, as you referred to earlier, around the cartoons issue; for example, many politicians were ready to be critical and inflammatory in their commentary to serve their political interests and use media for their purpose. We have seen how media-savvy terrorists use the video as a way of getting information across. So there has never been a time, in my view, in which there shouldn't be greater responsibility on media to hold back, to be measured in their judgement.

Q: Take the issue of Daniel Pearl, here we see a journalist not just decapitated in a ghastly manner, but we actually see videos of that being widely circulated

A: Well...they weren't circulated on the television, they were circulated on the internet, this again is a reflection...it's very important to get the difference of what I'm talking about, difference between freedom of expression and media freedom. That awful killing of Daniel Pearl by extremists in Pakistan was shown by some extremist internet site, mainstream television did not show it, there is no question at that. We have to be very very careful about mixing what's happening on the internet with what's happening on the media, we have to protect standards, and quality and that means, when it comes to questions of reporting terrorism, reporting community relations, we have to (be) measured. We, in media, have to be aware of the consequences of the images, words that we use, so we don't use inflammatory language, we don't use images which are going to store resentment and lead to further conflict, lead to demonstrations... one of the big problems of the history of India, is that (there) is a history of terrible conflict between various communities. You still see it today and when it breaks out.

Q: ...and you do still see the media not only taking sides, (but) come up with unverified information (and) actually end up making the situation worse.

A: And I think there are two problems here...one is the tendency of the media to lose their head; not to have an ethical sense of responsibility, that's one thing. The other thing which is really difficult and this where the public authorities have responsibilities – where do media get their information from: they get their information from politicians, they get their information from the police, and they get their information from the security services.

Q: ...and that's an easy way out because then, if they were really better journalists, they would go out and speak to more people and try and get different points of view, and authenticate that.

A: Now sometime ago here in India, there was this terrible terrible case, of the killing of a school girl, which led to a terrible controversy

Q: You are talking about the Aarushi Talwar case?

A: Absolutely, terrible terrible case. Everyone knows about it. And there was absolutely legitimate criticism, of the way the media reported that, and I absolutely condemned the way the media lost their ethical sense, in dealing with that story. But it must also be said, a lot of those crazy things that were being said in the media, actually came from the mouths of official source—senior police officers—and it seems to me therefore, that we, you are right. The sources of information are extremely important, journalists must use reliable sources. There is a big question to be asked of the authorities. If you can't rely on the information being given to you by senior police officers, who can you rely on? So therefore the authorities themselves also got to teach their people, how to use information, how to make sure it's verified, before you release it to the press. It's also important that the media themselves have to corroborate information, they have to look for alternative sources, one source is not enough, they have to look for a second source.

Q: As I say...give up lazy journalism, I read (of) a teacher of journalism talking (to his students) about his time when journalists would burn leather (read work hard and walk around). These days journalists are burning CDs, you prefer to sit in the comfort of your office, instead of going out.

A: That's exactly the case, the fact of the matter is today, journalists don't have enough time to leave the office. They are told to come in. They are told to sit down. They turn on their computer, they start 'googling' and the story starts appearing, and goodness knows, they don't have any contacts with the real people in the real world. And so therefore, we have to get back to journalism in which journalism takes more time.

I think, one of the most unhelpful developments in recent years, is the concept of breaking news, it's the notion that we have to get that information onto the screen as quickly as possible and to beat the competition. Even the BBC has a little set of rules now, about how quickly they must get information up on the BBC website –within 5 minutes, but there must be something up running about. Now it seems to me that this tyranny of breaking news, the tyranny of time, and being forced to deliver information as quickly as possible, because of competition is leading to an erosion of standards, and, that seems to me, is very very worrying. Anyone who is in journalism will tell you that they don't have enough time to do good journalism.

Q: To double check, to triple check, instead of speaking to two people, speak to 20 people.

A: Absolutely, it's not just to check the information, that you've gotten, it means that investigative journalists, journalists who needs to spend a day, two days, a week, investigating a story, is becoming an extinct species.

...and more importantly such a person is not being encouraged by his or her employers. Which brings me to a point, which I know is a subject close to your heart because you too believe, that in many parts of the world the conditions of employment – the social and economics conditions of employment for media personnel – have actually declined. You too believe that this has actually contributed to the lowering of morale of media professionals, and therefore their attachment to ethical values.

Q: The working conditions for journalists has also had an impact on media freedom. Would you like to elaborate on it?

A: It seems to me, it is absolute nonsense to believe that you can have professional journalism and freedom of the press if the people who are working in the media are subject to poverty wages and insecure conditions of employment. If you have conditions where people are not secure about their job, where they are paid poverty wages, it is inevitable that corrupt financial relations are going to emerge between those individuals and the people they meet. That we are going to have bribery, we are going to have inducements to journalists to suppress information or to publish information, and that is a criminal attack on the central ethics of journalism. The working conditions of journalists are absolutely fundamental to the creation of an atmosphere for good quality journalism. I think it has been recognized more and more and I would really like to acknowledge the decision by the Press Council of India, which has made it clear and taken the view, that actual working conditions of journalists do have an impact on (the) quality and independence of the media. I think this is a welcome recognition.

Q: I want to ask you a few questions on how to react to the editorial content or advertising content masquerading as editorial content – what we call advertorials and we've seen this trend happening more and more, and we actually see newspaper organizations, accepting money to give (information). You know, eliminating the public relations firm. You pay money and you get your picture.

A: I think this is one of the saddest developments in recent years, where some of the great newspapers of the world have been exposed for doing precisely this… sacrificing their editorial independence in order to make a bit of money out of an advertiser or a corporation by guaranteeing them editorial coverage, and, it seems to me, this is a terrible betrayal of the fundamental principles of journalism. Many of the people who run the business in the media have lost all sense of decency when it comes to standards and ethics, and that's why this ethical journalism initiative that we are talking about is not (just) a theoretical debate among academics, it's really about how do we restore public confidence in good quality media.

Q: … Mr. White let me ask you one question on this. Newspaper organizations have struck financial arrangements with existing advertisers or potential advertisers, they call it a private treaties programme, where you have a media organization, with shareholding and cross holdings in large number of companies which are either existing advertisers or potential advertisers, with financial arrangements which are opaque (and) which are not shown to the public at large, because they are between two individuals or two individual entities. To what extent do you think these kinds of financial arrangements compromise journalism ethics.

A: I think they compromise them terribly. We need ethics in journalism, but we need ethics in the journalism industry as a whole. Therefore, when I talk about ethical journalism, I am talking about what you and I as reporters who are working in the industry have a duty, an obligation and a responsibility to follow. But I also want ethical management of the media. We need more openness and we need transparency. If companies are reaching agreements like this, there needs to be a full disclosure. Readers, viewers, listeners, need to know (about) the relationships that are being established between companies that are providing media services and advertisers and sponsors and politicians and so on. Disclosure is absolutely fundamental to the process.

Q: Mr White, in India in recent times, we found this phenomenon of sting journalism, basically using hidden cameras to record politicians and other important persons, and we saw the head of a national political party being stung, and thereafter we have seen a series of these sting operations being carried on, and at the end of the day I want you to comment on the ethics of sting operations, because at one level we have something called the off-the-records statement, then you have here a group of journalists who are committing some crime or the other, they are impersonating somebody else, they are masquerading as somebody else, they are entrapping somebody, they are invading somebody's privacy, but in the process they justify all these relatively minor violations of the law for what they call a greater public interest that is you are exposing, somebody in a position of power and authority of corruption, you are exposing a misdeed, a social evil. What are your views on sting journalism?

A: Well....this whole sting journalism has actually got an honourable tradition in journalism. I think it's fair to say that sometimes it is necessary for journalists to use deceptive methods in order to obtain information and very often that has been very important. I recall during the years of Apartheid, that media bugged for instance a meeting of military leaders in the apartheid (racist South Africa) regime in which they were planning against the ANC (African National Congress of Nelson Mandela) at the time, and I remember as a result of that, the apartheid government was forced to act against those army people. I think lives were saved as a result of that, and that couldn't have happened unless the journalists involved had good information and a good belief that something was going on which was very dangerous and therefore took the risk. It is always a risk that you have to break the law in order to get this (kind of) information. So there are cases where it is necessary for journalists to be deceptive in the public interest. But it is very important that when they do so, to give full disclosure about the way they have carried out their work and so on, and it is also very important to choose your stories very very carefully, and to make sure that when you are invading someone's privacy you are not doing it for sensational reasons. You are not doing it for merely reasons of voyeurism and sexual interest, and titillation and so on. So it has to be very very carefully adjudged, and I think we have to be aware that there are times when we have to step back.

Q: Who decides that, is it the government?

A: No.

Q: For instance, in India there is this huge debate going on about a broadcasting call. Do you need the government writing the code? Or should it be a self-regulated kind of mechanism?

A: Believe me in all my experience, and it is considerable experience, in this field when governments get involved in deciding the content of what goes into journalism it inevitably leads to censorship or forms of censorship, even if it comes from our friends in politics, or even if it comes from the most well meaning; because the problem is that those who make the good law, is what they think is good law today, (but it) will be administered by people who aren't the same people tomorrow, and that may be used against media. So we have to be very careful. I am in favour of self-regulation in journalism but I am not in favour of irresponsible self-regulation and there is a lot of it around.

Q: But that's a kind of an oxymoron.

A: Of course it is, because what it means is that if you are going to be involved in self-regulation, you have to be serious about it; you have to have codes which are (the) kind to be followed up, you have to report effectively, and also you have to take action, when people are breaking your codes. Now I know for example, that there is a great deal of concern about the quality of private broadcasting in some sectors in India and that the private broadcasting groups have decided to set up their own self-regulating process. Well they had better make it as convincing as possible because it seems to me there is nothing worse than having a self-regulating body which actually is just window dressing, and is not doing the job that it is required to. So you need credibility in self regulation. And self-regulation exists at all levels—it exists in the newsroom, around how we behave, how we treat one another, and it exists in management, and it should exist within the industry as a whole.

We in the industry should be prepared to expose those who are betraying the principles of journalism and betraying the principles of our profession. Very often there is a saying in journalism—dog doesn't eat dog. Well actually in my view, when it comes to exposing the betrayal of principles of journalism, the good dogs should always eat as much as they can. Unless we begin to do that effectively and credibly then politicians are going to be encouraged to do the job, because the journalists themselves are not doing it.

Q: I want you to comment on a recent episode that took place in India on July 22, 2008. Here we had three Members of Parliament in the floor of Parliament displaying hordes of currency notes alleging that they have been bribed for not to vote (in a trust motion), and when they were asked that what evidence do you have they said we had contacted a particular television channel, they've recorded everything. But the TV channel did not put it in on air and said that they were still trying to get their story together, before they put it on air. All this happened literally just before there was a vote of confidence for the government. So it has thrown up a whole set of issues – why did the television channel not broadcast that? Should we believe them (the channel) when they said that they wanted to corroborate, (and) ensure that they had the proper story?, Why did the Members of Parliament not go to the police, (or) not go to the speaker of Parliament and instead go to the journalists? Maybe you can make a few observations.

A: Well….I don't know the story in detail, but immediately I am a bit concerned, that if it is true that the channel gave the material that they have recorded to the authorities, before it was broadcast, then it seems to me rather worrying, because it seems to me that media organizations should be very jealous, of the stories that they have, and the material that they use, and that they should never hand over material unless they have fully satisfied themselves that they have reached that stage where it is to be used or not be used, and they have taken a clear decision. So it is quite worrying that happened. It seems to me that the question of relationship between the authorities and the media organizations, and whether or not information is handed over should be entirely voluntary and I think we have to be very careful when we start handing over information in those circumstances…

Q: Ok. Mr. White, you have been coming frequently to India, for quite a few years now and you have seen how the Indian media had been working. How (has) the Indian media evolved in the world's largest democracy? Maybe you can give us a few suggestions, on what can the Indian media learn from best practices being followed in other parts of the world and perhaps what could the rest of the world learn from the Indian media?

A: Let me tell you one of those things which you said earlier in the programme, which I agree with is, actually the crisis which is engulfing much of the media in the western world, is not here in India. In India media are expanding, you have got a private sector which is expanding all the time, you have rising circulation. I think (a) lot of that is due to improving literacy rates in the country. You have much more vernacular media that are being distributed and so on. So actually this is a golden age for media in India, and I think it is rather sad that during this period, we are seeing more pressure being put on journalists. We find that the right of journalists to form unions, the right of journalists to get decent pay is severely constricted. If you look at the differences (in pay) that exist in India today, between the stars who work in Indian journalism and the people who are at the bottom who are basically in the engine room of the journalism producing information, young people coming in, there is a huge gulf. And I think it narrates one great sadness that we see today in India, which is also enjoying economic prosperity, is that we are seeing a widening gulf, a greater inequality between the very rich and the very poor and we see that in journalism too. I would like to think that (the) media in India would provide models – models of quality, models of standards and models of conditions for journalists to enjoy.

Q: ...and is there anything which the rest of the world can learn from the way the media has been working. Yes we've got to learn from the best practices from other parts of the world, but is there something, you admire, or you think is good about the overall media scene in India?

A: Well I think, as I said earlier, I am impressed the way, the Press Council operates. I believe that it is actually a good system, and I think that's pointing in the right direction in terms of self-regulation. I think that's a good thing. I am also very pleased that the journalists I have talked to in India want to support the ethical journalism initiative. They want to see that as India develops, as prosperity comes to the country, as the country addresses the challenge of change and transition, the possibility of reducing inequalities, and of moving into a new period of democratic development, the media would play its role. Then that media would be a model for others; and part of that should be highest quality journalism, ethical standards in journalism, good pay, decent conditions for those working in the industry, and a good balance between the public interest and the private interests operating in media. And I think as we begin to bring those things together, India could be a world leader in a democratic world in terms of developing media that needs all of these high standards.

FREEDOM OF THE PRESS IN AN AGE OF VIOLENCE

This is the text of the K.C. Mammen Mapillai memorial lecture by Sir Harold Evans, renowned journalist and former editor of The Times *and* The Sunday Times *of*

London, that was delivered in New Delhi on 15 November 2007. The speech is being reprinted with the permission of the Malayala Manorama group.

Truly, I am honoured to give this lecture in memory of Mr K.C. Mammen Mapillai so close to the 60th birthday of Independent India. It is rather daunting before this audience, for, as the British historian E.P. Thompson remarked, 'There is not a thought that is being thought in West or East which is not active in some Indian mind'. So if I stumble somewhere with a thought tonight I look to one of you to, well, kindly complete the sentence for me.

Mammen Mapillai is celebrated for many achievements, but tonight we celebrate him as an editor of the great *Malayala Manorama.*

He was an innovative editor; he started columns for women and children. He was a brave editor. He practised a journalism rooted not in mere rhetoric but in fact, and reason in the face of violence. Freedom of the press existed in colonial India in 1938 only so long as the Press did not exercise it. When Mammen Mapillai did, in documenting police brutality sanctioned by the Travancore Prime Minister, he was imprisoned. When he came out two years later, he found all his property had been confiscated.

In short, he was an editor who stood for something beyond the numbers for circulation and revenue.

The proper role of the free and responsible press in an era of violence can only be understood if we agree what we mean by freedom of the press, and if we understand the nature and origins of violence. Of the level of violence, there is no doubt. Almost every day on this visit, I have read of insurgencies challenging the DNA of the great democratic nation of India, of political parties succumbing to the virus of identity politics, one of the provocations of violence in a democracy. Identity politics reduces sentient beings to one identity opposed to other single identities, when we in fact have multiple identities—nationality, religion, family, class or caste, gender, age, income group, value system. Identity politics are most menacing to a plural multi-ethnic democracy when political parties exploit the emotions of a single identity, forsake reason and peaceful persuasion for street violence. Of the fanaticism inherent in identity politics, Jonathan Swift said it best two centuries ago: 'You cannot reason someone out of something he has not been reasoned into'.

Our age imposes new strains on a free press. It is not the most violent in memory but it is the most perplexing. The last century was soaked in blood across the continents of Europe and Asia in wars between sovereign states and for much of the time editors had little freedom from censorship and much inducement to substitute propaganda for news. The violence did not end with Hiroshima—we had wars in Korea, Cyprus, Vietnam, India-Pakistan, and violence resurged with ethnic cleansing in the Balkans where the gunshot in Sarajevo in 1914 had convulsed the rest of the century and ended the lives of hundreds of millions.

We prayed that (the) Millennium would work some magic, but the 21st century has not opened auspiciously. There are many pages to the catalogue of crimes against humanity by international terrorism, the most hideous form of identity politics with no fixed address, as the police dockets would put it. Not just September 11 in New York and Washington, but December 13 in Delhi, October 12 (in) Bali, March 1 (in) Madrid, 7 July in London. These cowardly outrages are harder for the security forces to stop and harder for the press to report. If you publish the hideous videos of beheadings jihadists circulate, or display the image of a hooded hostage, are you doing exactly as the killers wish – creating terror by becoming a tool of terror? Or are you exposing the jaws of the beast? Are you exercising freedom or are you indulging in the pornography of violence? When and how should you show restraint in the exercise of freedom if restraint helps the security forces detect and protect? Should you go further and cooperate?

And to that dismal list of international terror this century, we have to add what we call conventional wars in Iraq and Afghanistan and Lebanon—and in our diary of death we cannot overlook Godhra and Gujarat, stains on India's reputation and heritage.

As to the freedom of the press, we have to recognize that we will never be free of restraint, never free of harassment legally or physically, still less never free of criticism. The press, if it is doing its job, it is exerting power and the laws of physics, never mind politics. Power always meets resistance. The most piquant definition of news, in fact, comes to us from Lord Northcliffe, owner of *The Times* long before my editorship, who declared that 'news is what somebody somewhere wants to suppress. Everything else is advertising.'

Much truth in that, but (the) government is not the only constraint on (a) free and responsible press. Ownership of media by conglomerates, bundles of different businesses in which the press is but one, has yet to prove a blessing to journalism anywhere. My experience and observation is that conglomerates hate the risk of expense and discord inevitable in investigations of any kind – of which the investigation of corruption and violence are the riskiest – the risk to loss of advertising, disfavour with the authorities or with associated businesses, and of course any businesses in which the conglomerate is itself involved. In the US, the anchor of a once great television news channel, now part of a conglomerate, told me the other day that their news leads are now not decided by editorial significance, but what market research has shown plays well with the sections of viewers that advertisers most want to attract. Most of the best newspapers in the world, in fact, have not been owned and managed by conglomerates but by families who regard them as a public trust – like the Grahams of *The Washington Post*, the Sulzbergers of *The New York Times*, the Chandlers of *The Los Angeles Times*, the Thomson and Astor families who developed *The Times* and *Sunday Times* as trusts, the Pearsons at *The Financial Times* and *The Economist*, the Scotts at *The Guardian*, and I have to note, the Mathews, our hosts tonight.

But worst of all is for a national press to be dominated in any sector by foreign ownership. I do not want to sound xenophobic; there should be no custom barrier for ideas and information, no thought police at the portals to the web as in China. But I'd suggest newspapers and broadcasting media in complex, sensitive societies like India, would not be well served by foreign ownership that is blind to the traditions and subtleties, sees a culture only as a marketplace and inevitably becomes a focus of resentment.

Freedom of the press is a moral concept, or it is nothing. When you hear talk of the overweening power of the press, remember Joe Stalin. During World War II, when he was reminded that His Holiness, the Pope, disapproved of the Red Army's annexation of Eastern Europe, he asked: 'How many divisions has the Pope?' We are rather in that position. The press has no guns, editors may marshal facts but do not command soldiers. In the act of seeking information, disclosing and criticizing, we must respect the rule of law on which all our freedoms depend. The right we exercise to ask and argue is a derived right, for we are claiming no greater civil liberties than those of the ordinary citizen, and the freedom of the press ultimately depends on the appreciation and support of that citizenry. Ultimately...since day in or day out we will be offending someone.

This nation that won its freedom by Gandhi's creation of non-violence as a political force has had full experience of the evils of violence. But mark this, too, that what Indian journalists have achieved in establishing a flourishing free press in 60 years of difficulty has won the admiration of journalists worldwide.

When I first came to India in the early sixties for the International Press Institute, the Indian was not tiger or elephant, but distinctly a mouse. You had a population then of 465 million, 40 million able to read, but the total circulation of all the newspapers, vernacular and English, was less than three million. When we met Prime Minister Nehru, he was frustrated that the Indian press was still stuck in the Victorian mode bequeathed by British imperialism, in touch with officialdom but out of touch with the millions of newly literate masses. 'I can't reach the people through the newspapers,' Nehru told Jim Rose, the visionary first director of the International Press Institute who promptly got the Rockefeller Foundation to fund a programme of technical training at the shirt-sleeves level (training for relatively junior and unskilled workers in media organizations). It is fair to say that these IPI workshops on everything from the wording of headlines to code for ethnic reporting started a revolution in Indian newspapers, broadening their appeal, reinforcing their viability and their capacity to monitor government and business. We had some misunderstandings. I remember suggesting that a good headline consisted of simple words in the active voice such as in the old definition of news – 'man bites dog' – and was angrily informed that in India there had been no case of a man biting a dog. By no means was this extraordinary first renaissance all inspired by British and American missionaries and certainly not carried out by them, but by Indian editors who became legends in their own lifetime.

Lightning struck the subcontinent early on in the form of a chubby-cheeked Asian, the sadly late Tarzie Vittachi, a predecessor at this rostrum. Editor of the *Ceylon Observer* at 32, he exposed the role of the government of Mrs Bandaranaike in the incitement of race riots. From my experiences then and since as a reporter and editor, some principles suggest themselves on our topic.

The Primacy of Reporting

The shock of 9/11 was all the greater in America because, both over the years and immediately preceding, the eyes of the American public had been put out. The major television companies and news magazines abandoned sustained foreign reporting, closed bureaus—and people in the US mostly got their news from television. In the immediate months before 9/11, everyone was too bored to cover the very authoritative report from the National Security Commission headed by Gary Hart and Warren Rudman, which laid bare the roots and scale of anti-Americanism and warned that as a consequence, Americans in large numbers would die on American soil. The majors – *The New York Times, The Washington Post* and *The Wall Street Journal* among others – were given special briefings before the report was released in a Senate press conference with heads of the CIA, FBI, you name it. *The NY Times* reporter walked out saying it was a waste of time. The report was ignored and, naturally network television ignored it, too. That grotesque failure was in due course followed by the failure to examine the adminstration's claims of WMD (weapons of mass destruction) in Iraq. Much tragedy from those reporting failures.

It is no use Printing the Truth Once

Running sores in a society require more than a one-time band-aid. The seeds of violence that exploded in 30 incidents (this word was missing – I'll check it again with the original speech) of urban warfare in Ireland and bombings in Britain were sown in years when nobody bothered to follow the escalating grievances of the Catholic minority. It was seen as a boring story. James Reston once said that Americans would do everything for Latin America except read about it. Indian editors, I suspect, believe that applies to coverage of rural India; the challenge is to make it rivetingly interesting.

How close a watch do the elite press in India keep on what is happening in rural India and on the language press? I am sure the intent is there; the challenge is to transform the apparently routine and boring into the rivetingly interesting.

It is no use printing the truth once – the equivalent of what Hollywood calls a 'courtesy read'. From our seminars I remember Serajuddin Hussein, news editor of the Bengali-language daily *Ittefaq* in Dacca, then East Pakistan. He took to heart Amitabha Chowdhury's mantra – that if you stayed with a story your paper would become a magnet for people with information. A missing child was not much of a story in Dacca (now Dhaka). Serajuddin made it one. Every time he heard of a child vanishing in the busy streets and bazaars, he noted it on his front page and reminded everyone that this was the second, third, fourth, fifth, sixth child that month and none of them had returned home. His persistence revealed that not a handful of children were missing, but scores. He asked the authorities to investigate the possibility (that) a kidnapping gang was at work. They laughed at him. A month or so later he went to the authorities with a tip from an informant. Police raided a remote village 80 miles from Dacca and found most of the children, deliberately maimed or blinded so that they would make pitiable beggars on the city streets. The gang leaders were hanged. Within six months, the *Ittefaq* nearly doubled its circulation: he was so proud he wrote to others and me about his plans for investigating other abuses. Alas, when East Pakistan rebelled in 1971, Serajuddin was among the 'intellectuals' sought out and murdered by the Pakistan Army. The deeds of men like Vittachi and Hussein justify the claims we make to justify the freedom of the press.

The Story is Not Dead Until We Know the Why as the What

Why and how did 2,000 die in Gujarat? Who was to blame for Rwanda, Srebrenica? Official commissions are often the answer after disaster. They have the powers of subpoena, but they may not always have the required discipline of detachment, the energy or the imagination or investigative zeal. A classic example of what the free press might do was the investigation by *Tehelka* of the killings in Gujarat and the mob violence at Godhra. I am aware of the criticisms of *Tehelka.* Certainly sting journalism has its perils – entrapment, provocation, impersonation – but with crimes as horrific as Gujarat, to have killers on camera boasting how they killed, why they killed, and with what sense of immunity inescapably dramatized the gravity of the challenge to India. The argument that airing the truth of what happened would provoke more violence was nothing more than moral blackmail. There are things which are bad and false and ugly and no amount of specious casuistry can make them good or true or beautiful.

In the outside world, the shut-down of *Tehelka* was as dismaying as the fact that justice has not yet been visited on the malefactors. Justice delayed is justice denied.

The Snare of a Token Patriotism

At times when emotions run high, the press is all too often tempted to follow the official line out of a mistaken sense of patriotism. True patriotism is in serving the country, not in following either the elite or the mob or the journalistic pack. My predecessor in the thirties as editor of *The Times* wrote in his diary: 'Night after night I'm doing everything I can to ensure publish nothing (sic) that will offend the susceptibilities of Herr Hitler'. He was proud of suppressing news of the violence being done by Hitler in Germany, and the extent of his rearmament, because the policy of the Chamberlain government was not to upset Hitler. The suppression cost Britain dearly in delaying a build-up of its defenses. After 9/11, in the United States, the surge of outrage and patriotism exploited by the Bush administration allowed a reckless and incompetent administration to lead the press and people into the killing fields of Iraq – one of the most stupefying examples of what happens when the press does not use its vaunted freedom – and none is freer in the world than the American press, belatedly vindicated in the exposure of the horrors of Abu Ghraib.

Freedom, Like Justice, is Indivisible

When a newspaper or TV station is under attack for doing its job – as *The Hindu* has been in the Tamil Nadu state – its competitors, once satisfied of the accuracy of the reporting, should not hesitate to cover the case, and, on its merits come to its support. We must not get hung up on competitive jealousies.

Resist, but Recognize Limits

Freedom of the press, exercised in the name of the citizenry, cannot reasonably expose the citizenry to danger. In states facing violent insurgencies, some measure of restraint, whether voluntary or imposed, may be necessary and justifiable. Curtailment of the freedom of expression as in curtailment of the right to incite the killing of innocent people is not a regression. It is a necessary element in a civilized society. The British paid dearly for allowing jihadist incitements to hate and kill in the months before the subway suicide bombings.

What is troubling is the tendency to concentrate a disproportionate amount of attention on security measures. The first casualty of war is not truth. It is the victims. Yes, they require eternal vigilance but priorities are skewed when a 52-page document from the admirable body then called the International Federation of Journalists now the World Newspaper Association – 52 alarm bells – where IFJ describes the response of government to terrorism as 'a devastating challenge to the global culture of human rights established almost 60 years ago. We are sleepwalking into a surveillance society'.

A devastating challenge to the global culture of human rights? What about the devastating challenge to human rights of suicide bombings? Speaking personally of challenges to human rights, I'd rather be photographed by a hidden surveillance camera than travel on a train or bus with men carrying bombs in their backpacks. Speaking personally I'd regard being blowing to bits on the street as less of an intrusion on privacy than having an identity card.

Beware Moral Equivalency

It is too easy to blame both sides. Truth rarely resides in the comfortable middle ground. I was reporting in the deep south of the United States in the fifties when violent crimes against Blacks went virtually unreported in the north, and unpunished in the south. Editorials constantly warned against extremism, on both sides, equating non-violent activists and the White mob. When the Freedom Riders extended the campaign against discrimination, an editorial proclaimed: 'They are challenging not only long held customs but passionately held feelings. No violence that deliberately provokes violence is a logical contradiction'. That was putting on a level of moral equivalency the wielder of the lead pipe and the recipient of the blow.

Monitor the Web

The paradox is that the world is connected as never before in terms of the flow of current, but many of the wires are lethally bare. Opinion, not fact, is the commonest traffic in cyberspace, some of it informative, some provocative, some of it is amusing, but quite a lot without a factual bone in its body. Competition from half-truth masquerades as knowingness, and disinformation and misinformation, travel faster than the speed of light.

How many newspapers, television or radio stations, for instance detected and exposed the stupid canard about the 9/11 attack on the World Trade Center in New York – that it was the work of Jews and the Jewish secret service who had tipped off 4,000 Jews not to go to work that day so Jews were spared? In fact, hundreds of Jews died along with Muslims, Christians, Buddhists, Hindus, agnostics and atheists. I took time to track the source of this lie and found it to have originated with Al Manor television in Beirut and a Syrian newspaper and was picked up by a shadowy web service in Washington ludicrously called *Information Times* and edited by a Mr Sayed Adeeb. It spread on the web as an ineradicable virus with incredible speed. Tom Friedman of *The New York Times* told me that on a visit to Indonesia he was stunned at the dominance of this palpable untruth. What is frightening, he said, is an insidious digital divide. 'Internet users are only 5 per cent of the population – but these 5 per cent spread rumours to everyone else. They say, "He got it from the internet". They think it's the Bible.' Once upon a time Mr Adeeb, and his sly sponsors, would be sending out smudged cyclostyled sheets that would never see the light of day. But now the mysterious Mr Adeeb and others like him have a megaphone to the world, with this spurious authenticity of electronic delivery.

Finally

Should we in the press cooperate in giving information to the security services? No. We should never be identified as an arm of the executive. Never. But we should not impede the security services unless they abuse the law themselves. This, an area where the free individual judgement of the editor of integrity, aware of the complexities, is superior to any official edict. We must maintain our position as an agency independent of the executive. The jihadists will kill and torture come what may, but there are many other situations where the temptation of receiving the official leak, the suspicion of informing, will encourage the deliberate targeting of journalists that might otherwise not occur.

The doctrines of freedom of the press ask much of frontline reporters. In the world, we pay every week with the life of a reporter, a cameraman, a support worker. The world barely notices. The press in each country concentrates on its own. It should not. It is a death in the community of journalism.

The International News Safety Institute calculates that if we include all news media personnel — translators, fixers, office staff, drivers — no fewer than a thousand have died in the last ten years. The second shocking thing is to learn how many of them were murdered. We have a wholly different situation from the sadly familiar fact that war correspondents, who knowingly risk their lives, fall victims to the accidents of combat. But the majority of journalists' deaths now are planned assassinations. They have been targeted, sought out for death at home for a very simple reason: they did their jobs of seeking the truth. Seven out of every ten have died in their own countries at the instigation of government and military authorities, guerrillas, drug traffickers and criminal gangs. Rarely do these crimes attract international attention. Daniel Pearl in Pakistan and the sensational murder in Moscow of Anna Politkovskaya, investigator of abuses by Russian troops in Chechnya, provoked international outrage, but most of the journalists die in obscurity. I think of journalists like Moolchand Yadav who wrote for Hindi dailies, shot dead in Jhansi, Uttar Pradesh, for exposing land deals. I read in *The Week* magazine that of the 250 journalists in the Bundelkhand region, more than half have bodyguards or have to carry guns.

The price of truth has gone up grievously and the price of murder has gone down. Nine out of ten of the killers identified in the world watchdog organizations have never been investigated, let alone prosecuted, convicted and punished. Occasionally, a triggerman is identified and brought to trial, but his paymaster goes free. In only seven per cent of cases examined by the Committee to Protect Journalists has a mastermind been brought to justice. Most go free to kill again; surprisingly, even in war zones, murder is the leading cause of death.

In view of the spotlight the military rightly gets for any violation of the rules of engagement, it has to be noted, that in the wars studied, armed forces, overall, regular and irregular, accounted for less than 10 per cent of fatalities: 85 per cent of the killings were by 'terrorists, insurgents and other unidentified murderers'. The record of government indifference to the killing of journalists is lamentably on display in countries considered more or less stable. Russia, the Philippines, Bangladesh, Mexico and Colombia share the ignominy. India comes sixth in the INSI index.

Every one of the unpunished crimes disgraces the shielding countries and our tolerance of that diminishes us all. This is not a 'press matter'. Without the men and women of a free and plural press willing to risk reporting and investigating and editors and publishers to stand by them, injustice and corruption flourish – within and across national boundaries.

What can be done? It is a waste of time calling on militant insurgents and terrorists to respect the rule of law. But all those states that concede immunity to the wrongdoers live in the real world. They expect to be taken seriously; they ask for aid and protection for their citizens travelling abroad. They are beneficiaries of trade agreements, of support from the World Bank and the International Monetary Fund and UN aid organizations. They value their membership of the United Nations. There is virtue in pressing member states to vote for a Security Council resolution reaffirming that the safety and security of journalists is essential for the free flow of information around the world. The UN should have a central register of unsolved crimes against members of the media, but the UN itself cannot be left to follow through. Its Human Rights Commission is the longest standing joke since Caligula elected his horse. (Roman emperor Caligula had his favourite horse 'elected' as a senator.) A journalist who works for a daily newspaper in Iran testifies that UN organizations 'are too conservative; they don't want to confront the government. They say the government is sensitive'. The very fact that a government is sensitive is, of course, the point. The neuralgic nerve should be pressed hard. The state that consistently fails to investigate and prosecute murder and violence against media personnel should forfeit access, privileges and aid.

By the same token, the immunity states – the iniquity states – should have to face a persistent international campaign of publicity. Not once a year, but every time they acquiesce or sanction the murder of a journalist. There are two purposes here. One is to hold them up to obloquy and shame. The other is to sustain the brave protesters, mark out their lives as significant. I think of my IPI friend Abdi Ipecki, editor-in-chief of *Millyet*, then Turkey's most influential newspaper, telling me in London in 1979 of what the example and support of his international peers meant to him in his ceaseless campaign for national unity and reconciliation against violence and terrorism. He went home to be gunned down by Mehmet Ali Agca, member of the ultranationalist Grey Wolves. Agca soon escaped from prison with assistance from people in the security services and in 1981 tried to assassinate Pope John Paul II. He is now in prison in Turkey agitating for parole. Yet, in recent years, almost every media outlet mentioning the prospect of Mehmet Agca's release in 2006 failed to mention that he was the murderer of Ipecki.

Memo to Every News Editor: Report and Follow up

This brings me to a central closing point: the paramount importance of how we justify the freedom of the press. We cannot justify it by assertion but only by day-by-day demonstration of integrity. It is our principal defence in sustaining public support. On World Press Freedom Day this May, we should remind the critics and ourselves of the sacrifices represented by the 1,665 journalists now named on the Freedom Forum's memorial in Washington. We should remember the common thread among the men and women of such different backgrounds, from such different cultures, who have died for journalism. What was common among the desperate circumstances of their deaths?

Their Aspiration

They believed in the purpose of journalism. Most of them didn't expect to die for it. But nothing in the record diminishes the conviction that they believed theirs was an honourable craft – profession if you like – rooted in reason, dedicated to truth, sustained by a sense of common good, given inspiration by the achievements of others around the world in a universal brotherhood.

Every time a reporter anywhere slants the facts, writes a story to fit his preconception, allows the unclouded face of truth to suffer wrong, he betrays Kurt Schorck, Veronica Guerin, Norbert Zongo, Orlando Sierra Hernandez. Every time a journalist anywhere foments sectional hatred, he shames the memory of Abdi Ipecki, of Thuunaasjari Baradamani Singh, Arun Narayan, Vikram Singh Bhist, Prahlad Goala. Every time a news organization puts excessive profit before excellence — Is 25 per cent not enough? — it betrays all the names on the memorial. Every time a photographer grossly exploits private grief, he betrays the families of all the victims. Every time a journalist in America abuses the First Amendment, he betrays all those around the world who have to struggle for half the freedom. Every time a news organization closes its eyes to the world, it betrays a long line of our journalists – like the man we honour tonight who gave up his liberty and all those who have given their lives in the course of letting us see. We will not deserve freedom of the press if we do not honour them and constantly remember the causes they served.

Index